D1433922

Relationships Within Families: Mutual Influences

Relationships within Families

Mutual Influences

Edited by

Robert A. Hinde

Royal Society Research Professor; Honorary Director, MRC Unit on the Development and Integration of Behaviour; Fellow, St. John's College, Cambridge

and

Joan Stevenson-Hinde

Scientific Officer, MRC Unit on the Development and Integration of Behaviour; Fellow and Tutor, New Hall, Cambridge

CLARENDON PRESS · OXFORD

1988

Oxford University Press, Walton Street, Oxford OX2 6DP
Oxford New York Toronto
Delhi Bombay Calcutta Madras Karachi
Petaling Jaya Singapore Hong Kong Tokyo
Nairobi Dar es Salaam Cape Town
Melbourne Auckland
and associated companies in
Berlin Ibadan

Oxford is a trade mark of Oxford University Press

Published in the United States
by Oxford University Press, New York

British Library Cataloguing in Publication Data
Relationships within families
1. Family 2. Interpersonal relations
I. Hinde, Robert, A. II. Stevenson-Hinde, Joan
306.8'7 HQ734
ISBN 0–19–852170–7
ISBN 0–19–852183–9 Pbk

Library of Congress Cataloging in Publication Data
Relationships within families
edited by Robert A. Hinde and Joan Stevenson-Hinde. p.   cm.
Contributions to a conference sponsored by St. John's College,
Cambridge, held at its School of Pythagoras in January 1987.
Includes index.
1. Parent and Child—Congresses. 2. Family—Psychological
aspects—Congresses. 3. Child development—Congresses.
4. Intergenerational relations—Congresses. I. Hinde, Robert A.
II. Hinde, J. S. (Joan Stevenson) III. St. John's College
(University of Cambridge)
HQ755.85.R447 1988   306.8'7—dc 19   87–31286   CIP
ISBN 0–19–852170–7
ISBN 0–19–852183–9 (pbk.)

Typeset by Cotswold Typesetting Ltd
Printed in Great Britain
at the University Printing House, Oxford
by David Stanford
Printer to the University

Preface

This volume is based on the contributions to a conference sponsored by St. John's College, Cambridge and held in the School of Pythagoras of that college. The conference took place in January 1987, and the contributors had the opportunity to revise their contributions in the light of discussion.

We are grateful to the Master and Fellows of St. John's for their support, and for indirect support from the Medical Research Council and the Royal Society. We are also indebted to a number of colleagues who have contributed to our work over the years, some of whom attended the conference.

We owe a special debt to Mrs Ann Glover, who played a major role in organizing the conference and in preparing the papers for publication.

Cambridge   R.A.H.
1987   J.S.-H.

Contents

List of participants   ix
Introduction *R. A. Hinde*   1

I Coherence within families

1   Relationships within the family: a systems perspective on development
      P. Minuchin   7
2   The coherence of family relationships *L. A. Sroufe and J. Fleeson*   27
3   Child development in a network of relationships *M. Radke-Yarrow,
      J. Richters, and W. E. Wilson*   48
4   Individuals in relationships *J. Stevenson-Hinde*   68

II Marital and parent–child relationships

5   Marital and parent–child relationships: the role of affect in the family
      system *M. A. Easterbrooks and R. N. Emde*   83
6   The interrelatedness of marriage and the mother–child relationship
      A. Engfer   104
7   Marital and mother–child relationships: developmental history, parent
      personality, and child difficultness *H.-J. Meyer*   119

III Parent–first-born–second-born relationships

8   Changes in dyadic relationships within a family after the arrival of a
      second child *K. Kreppner*   143
9   Connections between relationships: implications of research on
      mothers and siblings *J. Dunn*   168
10 Triadic interactions: mother–first-born–second-born *J. Barrett and
      R. A. Hinde*   181

IV Coherence across generations

11 Developmental history, personality, and family relationships: toward
      an emergent family system *J. Belsky and E. Pensky*   193
12 Emergent family patterns: the intergenerational construction of
      problem behaviour and relationships *A. Caspi and
      G. H. Elder, Jr.*   218
13 Maternal attachment representations as related to patterns of
      infant–mother attachment and maternal care during the first year
      *K. Grossmann, E. Fremmer-Bombik, J. Rudolph, and
      K. E. Grossmann*   241

V   Families in distress

14 Conflict and alliance in distressed and non-distressed families
     A. Christensen and G. Margolin   263
15 Multilevel family process models: traits, interactions, and relationships
     G. R. Patterson and T. J. Dishion   283
16 Parents, children, and siblings: six years after divorce
     E. M. Hetherington   311
17 Functions and consequences of relationships: some
     psychopathological considerations *M. Rutter*   332
18 The effect of relationships on relationships: a developmental approach
     to clinical intervention *R. N. Emde*   354

Epilogue *R. A. Hinde and J. Stevenson-Hinde*   365

Index   386

Participants

J. Barrett, MRC Unit on the Development and Integration of Behaviour, Madingley, Cambridge CB3 8AA, U.K.

J. Belsky, College of Human Development, The Pennsylvania State University, University Park, Pennsylvania 16802, USA.

A. Caspi, Department of Psychology, 33 Kirkland Street, Harvard University, Cambridge, Massachusetts 02138, USA.

A. Christensen, Department of Psychology, University of California, Los Angeles, California 90024, USA.

J. Dunn, College of Human Development, The Pennsylvania State University, University Park, Pennsylvania 16802, USA.

A. Easterbrooks, Eliot-Pearson Department of Child Study, Tufts University, Medford, Massachusetts 02155, USA.

G. H. Elder, Jr. Carolina Population Center, University of North Carolina at Chapel Hill, University Square 300A, Chapel Hill, North Carolina 27514–3997, USA.

R. N. Emde, University of Colorado Health Sciences Center, 4200 East Ninth Avenue, Denver, Colorado 80262, USA.

A. Engfer, Institute for Early Education and Family Research, Arabellastr.1. 8000 Munich 81, West Germany.

J. Fleeson, Minneapolis Children's Medical Center, Minneapolis, Minnesota 55455, USA.

Karin Grossmann, Institut für Psychologie, Universität Regensburg, 8400 Regensburg, West Germany.

E. M. Hetherington, Department of Psychology-Gilmer Hall, University of Virginia, Charlottesville, Virginia 22901, USA.

R. A. Hinde, MRC Unit on the Development and Integration of Behaviour, Madingley, Cambridge CB3 8AA, UK.

K. Kreppner, Max Planck Institute for Human Development and Education, Lentzeallee 94, D-1000 Berlin 33, West Germany.

H-J. Meyer, Technische Hochschule Darmstadt, Institut für Psychologie, Steubenplatz 12, 6100 Darmstadt, West Germany.

P. Minuchin, 70 East 10th Street, New York, New York 10003, USA.

G. R. Patterson, Oregon Social Learning Centre, 207 East 5th Street, Suite 202, Eugene, Oregon 97401, USA.

M. Radke-Yarrow, Laboratory of Developmental Psychology, National Institutes of Health, Bethesda, Maryland 20892, USA.

J. Richters, Laboratory of Developmental Psychology, National Institutes of Health, Bethesda, Maryland 20892, USA.

M. Rutter, MRC Child Psychiatry Unit, Institute of Psychiatry, De Crespigny Park, London, SE5 8AF, UK.

L. A. Sroufe, Institute of Child Development, University of Minnesota, 51 E. River Road, Minneapolis, Minnesota 55455, USA.

J. Stevenson-Hinde, MRC Unit on the Development and Integration of Behaviour, Madingley, Cambridge CB3 8AA, UK.

Introduction
ROBERT A. HINDE

From before birth, children form parts of networks of relationships—relationships that are crucial to their development. At a gross level, they are dependent on one or more caregivers for nutrition and protection throughout their early years. More importantly, the course of their emotional and cognitive development is markedly affected by the relationships in which they are involved. As implied by the term 'network', these relationships also mutually influence each other, and such influences may reflect back on the child's relationships and thus on the child's developing personality. And since the effects on personality may persist into adult life, early relationships may affect parenting style, and thus personality development in the next generation too.

That is the theme of this book. Accepting that, at any rate at this time, most children in our culture grow up in a family-like structure, we ask how relationships affect relationships within the family, and what are the consequences for the children.

Before proceeding, what exactly do we mean by a relationship?* At the behavioural level, a relationship involves a series of interactions between two individuals, each interaction being relatively limited in duration but affected by past interactions between the same individuals and affecting future ones. But a relationship can persist in the absence of interactions, and involves also subjective aspects—including especially memories of past interactions and expectations of future ones, which have both cognitive and affective aspects. These memories and expectations, as well as the personality of each participant, will influence the persona that each displays in the interaction, and the nature of the interaction that results will depend on the personae of both participants. Thus not only do the nature of interactions influence the relationship of which they form part, but the nature of that relationship affects its constituent interactions. And in the longer term the interactions and relationships an individual experiences affect the range of personae he/she *can* display. We are thus dealing with two-way influences—of individuals through interactions upon relationships, and of relationships upon interactions and individuals.

---

*Discussion of relations between relationships can lead to verbal confusions. We have tried to reserve the term 'relationships' for what goes on between individuals over time, and to use 'relations' when referring to how one variable affects another.

But that is not all. As we have seen, each relationship is embedded in a network of other relationships, and its nature both affects and is affected by that network. In the present context that network constitutes the family, though both the family as a whole and its constituent members form parts of larger networks. We must thus come to terms with a series of levels of social complexity—individuals, interactions, relationships, families, and groups of higher order, each level being in dialectical relations with the others. Furthermore, each level has properties not relevant to the preceding one—for instance relationships have properties consequent upon the patterning of their constituent interactions that are not relevant to isolated interactions, and families may be 'matrifocal' or 'hierarchical', properties not relevant to the individual relationships.

The behaviour of each participant in an interaction is influenced also by the values and beliefs that he/she has acquired from those around him/her. In adults, these will involve knowledge of the institutions current in the society in which they live, together with their constituent roles, and the rights and duties associated with those roles. In our own society this includes prescriptions for behaviour appropriate to the roles of wife, husband, father, mother, child, sister, and brother. These values, beliefs, and other aspects of social knowledge can be referred to as the socio-cultural structure. Just as relationships have both objective (behavioural) and subjective aspects—the former apparent to an outside observer, the latter to some extent specific to each individual and known in its entirety only to him or her—so also does the socio-cultural structure. The objective aspect may be deduced by an outside observer, and is often partially codified in laws or customs, but subjectively the socio-cultural structure may be subtly different for each individual. Furthermore, each family may have its own accepted practices and values that differ somewhat from those of other families but are embraced within the overall socio-cultural structure. And individuals, interactions, relationships, and groups may both influence and be influenced by the aspects of the socio-cultural structure that they share (Fig. Int. 1; for further discussion of this framework, see Hinde 1979, 1987; Hinde and Stevenson-Hinde 1987).

In describing these complex interrelations, it is all too easy to conceptualize the levels of social complexity as discrete entities. But just because of the dialectical interrelations between them we must see the socio-cultural structure (as least in its subjective aspect), groups, relationships, interactions, and even individuals not as entities but as processes, in continuous creation through the agency of the dialectics.

Because the course of an interaction or relationship depends on both partners, we must beware of ascribing its properties to either one: what goes on between mother and child depends on both mother and child. Furthermore, because there are some continuities in the behavioural propensities of individuals, the properties of relationships (and families) at one point in time

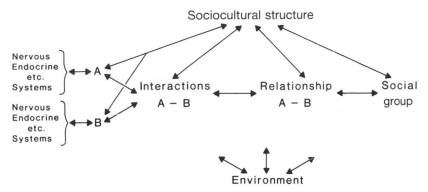

FIG. INT. 1   The dialectics between successive levels of social complexity (from Hinde 1987).

are likely to be related to their earlier properties. Indeed, the new relationships that individuals enter into have properties related to those they have had in the past. This, however, does not necessarily mean *identity* of content or other characteristics between the old and the new. With time and experience individuals grow and develop: their behavioural propensities change and are displayed in new ways. These processes are both consequences of their relationships and affect their relationships. Relationships are thus never static: each interaction, each thought, and of course any change in one or both participants, may affect its future course. And behaviour in a new relationship may well differ from that in earlier ones because the persona displayed by the new partner calls forth a new combination of behavioural propensities, or causes the individual's propensities to be displayed in new ways, creating in fact a new persona in the individual concerned. Indeed, as we shall see, an individual's behaviour in a new relationship may take on the properties of the behaviour of his/her partner in a previous one.

But somewhere behind all this complexity, waiting to be revealed, is orderliness. The processes involved must eventually be susceptible to description and explanation in terms of psychological principles. For that reason, the chapters in this volume aim not only to document the ways in which relationships affect relationships within the family, but to make some progress in specifying the processes involved. These processes may be of very diverse types. There may be direct behavioural effects: the time a mother spends caring for the new baby affects her relationship with an older child. These may lead to sequential effects: the first-born may seek help from her/his father—help that would formerly have come from the mother, and this may lead to long-term changes in family relationships. There may be subjective influences, as when the mother's interactions with one child arouse jealousy in another family member, which then affects the latter's relationships. Or effects may be mediated by the socio-cultural structure—for instance by changes in family rules ('No noise in the evening in case the baby is woken up'). And there may be long-term effects on personality.

Because of this diversity, a major problem is to find the appropriate level of analysis at which to seek for influences between relationships within the family. The early chapters in this volume exemplify a number of different approaches, ranging from conceptualization of the family as a total system with constituent subsystems to the analysis of moment-to-moment interactions between individuals.

Although each of the chapters impinges on many issues, the remaining chapters consider successively the relations between the marital and parent/child relationships, interactions within the mother/first-born/second-born triad, and the way in which effects may be carried across successive generations. Contributions in the last main section concern families some of whose members are in, or have experienced, distress or deprivation. Finally, in an epilogue we have tried to bring together some of the threads that pervade most or all of the contributions.

References

Hinde, R. A. (1979). *Towards understanding relationships*. Academic Press, London.
Hinde, R. A. (1987). *Individuals, relationships and culture: links between ethology and the social sciences*. Cambridge University Press.
Hinde, R. A. and Stevenson-Hinde, J. (1987). Interpersonal relationships and child development. *Developmental Review* 7, 1–21.

I

Coherence within families

1

Relationships within the family: a systems perspective on development

PATRICIA MINUCHIN

Psychologists have long been interested in family relationships. For many decades, that involved a particular focus on the mother's relationship with the child, which was seen as the crucial context for growth, and studies of the mother–child dyad have been the hardiest perennial in the developmental field. In recent years, however, the scope of research has expanded, and studies of father and child, siblings, and so forth, are increasingly common. It seems likely that broad theoretical developments outside the field—systems theory, and the twentieth-century alertness to context—have been influential triggers for expansion. The impact of such ideas is recent, however, and there is still much to be explored about the integration of developmental theory with concepts of the family as a system, and about the implications of systems theory for developmental research.

In this chapter, I will adopt a systems perspective for considering relationships within the family, focusing particularly on the implications for developmental research. The chapter has four sections:

(1) a review of systems concepts relevant to family relationships;

(2) an analysis of selected developmental studies, highlighting compiementary and discrepant elements of their relation to system principles;

(3) a summary of dimensions and methods in family research that may be useful for the expansion of developmental investigations; and

(4) description of an exploratory study of family interactions which attempts to use systems concepts.

In general, I will be suggesting that the current expansion in developmental research is promising but not sufficiently radical to be fully consistent with systems principles, and that there are still difficult issues to be addressed in the formulation of systemic developmental research.

Systems concepts

The basic principles of systems theory are applicable both to the research discussed in this chapter and to the work reported in the remainder of the volume. It seems useful, therefore, to state the principles briefly and to indicate the kinds of questions they generate for developmental research. (See P. Minuchin 1985, for a fuller statement and relevant bibliography.)

Wholeness, organization, and circularity

From a systems perspective, an open system such as the family is a complex, integrated whole, with organized patterns of interaction that are circular rather than linear in form. That conception raises questions about appropriate units of research, effective methodologies for studying process, and assumptions of cause and effect—questions that arise repeatedly in this chapter in the consideration of specific research studies. The requirements of research design have usually limited the investigation of human relationships to the dyad, which is generally a family subsystem rather than a total family unit. Traditional research has also focused on effects rather than processes, and has employed linear rather than circular means of analysis. If we are to study the family as an organized whole with recurrent circular patterns, however, those traditions are challenged; the task implies research tools that encompass multiple family members and document the nature of their interactions. Furthermore, questions about linear and circular processes challenge basic developmental principles. Psychologists have always assumed that socialization has a primary direction, since adults and children are inherently unequal in skill and power. Are the two 'truths' incompatible, or can the principle of circularity and the assumption of unequal parent–child power coexist at different levels?

The interdependence of system elements

This basic principle maintains that elements (people) in a system are necessarily interdependent, contributing to the formation of patterns and organized in their behaviour by their participation in those patterns. The implications of this concept go to the core of the developmental field, which has always been concerned with the growth of the individual. What does it mean to be part of a recurrent pattern, and how does that relate to 'individual functioning'? If the behaviour of the individual has a function in the family system, what is the relevant research unit, and does that vary according to the problem under study? What of the concept of continuity, as the individual moves from one system to another? Such issues are relevant not only to research considered in this chapter but to many of the studies reported elsewhere in the volume.

Homeostasis and change

In systems theory, as in the developmental field, periods of stability and change are considered to be part of the same unified process—a process that characterizes all open systems moving through time. Family systems have homeostatic features that maintain the stability of their patterns, but they are recurrently perturbed by developmental or other less predictable events, which trigger a period of exploration and a necessary reorganization of patterns. Those patterns are then stable as long as they are adaptive, but when the system is challenged again the patterns must again be revised, and so on through the life cycle of the family. Given that conception of human reality, it is important to develop a map of family developmental stages and to pay particular attention to periods of transition. How shall homeostasis and change be documented? What are the core questions and the relevant methodologies? How are individuals involved in family reorganization? And how do developmental realities and established family patterns interact with divorce, illness, economic reverses, and so forth, when these non-developmental crises challenge the family? We have customarily depended on statistical techniques for handling such complex issues and multiple factors. However, the concept that the family is both a changing and a self-regulating system suggests that we must directly study the process of moving from one set of patterns to another, preserving the evolutionary nature of the change and focusing on the systemic reorganization of family relationships. These issues have particular pertinence in this volume, since several chapters are concerned with developmental or traumatic transitions (e.g. Chapters 8, 12, and 16, this volume).

Subsystem boundaries and interactions

Complex systems are composed of subsystems. Subsystems have their own integrity, defined metaphorically by the boundaries between them, and interactions across subsystems are governed by implicit rules and patterns. The nature of subsystem relations is the central concern of this volume, with some authors considering effects across time while others consider the contemporary family. There are difficult questions in this area, particularly in formulating the relation of the parts to the whole. To what extent, and in what ways, are subsystem relations governed by larger family patterns? When is it appropriate to study particular subsystems, and what conclusions can be drawn from the information derived? How can a concept like 'boundaries' be operationalized? And what methods are appropriate for studying the interactions between one subsystem and another, particularly when each unit includes more than one member, as in the relations between the children, as one subsystem, and the parents, as another?

In the following section, these principles will be applied to three developmental studies of relationships in the family. They have been selected both for their high quality as developmental research and for their heuristic value in sharpening the questions raised by a systems perspective.

Developmental studies revisited

The studies discussed in this section have been selected from the special issue of *Child Development* on family development and the child (April 1985). They offer the opportunity to consider a variety of issues, including the definition of the problem, the selection of the relevant research unit, the methods for gathering and analysing data, and the conventions for drawing inferences from research findings.

Belsky and Isabella

The first study is focused on the transitional period before and after the birth of a baby, and it is concerned with connecting past and present in the behaviour of the parents (Belsky and Isabella 1985). From a systems perspective, it raises a theoretical question about assumptions of cause and effect, and a methodological question about the customary process for co-ordinating and interpreting questionnaire data.

The investigators ask whether marital and parent–child relationships in the family of origin, as reported by adults, predict changes in the current marriage after the child is born. They tap the current marital relationship at two points in time, and two subsystems recalled from childhood (parent–child relationships and the marital system of the parents). All data are obtained through questionnaires. Marital and parent–child relationships are scored for positive–negative recall, and the quality of the current marriage is assessed through the summed satisfaction scores of husband and wife and the discrepancy between their two scores (the latter operationalizing the extent of disagreement about satisfaction in the marriage). Findings suggest that those who recall poorer marital and parent–child relationships in childhood are more apt to show increasing discrepancies in their views of the marriage after the birth of the baby.

The use of self-report data raises interesting questions concerning both the recall of the past and the evaluation of the current marriage. From some perspectives, one could argue that all the data of this study are present data, including the report of relationships in the family of origin. Systems theorists assume that current functioning includes what is vital and operative from the past. People bring templates of their past experience into current situations but, as many historians would agree, their recall of history is essentially a construction—selective in content and relevant to present realities, which maintain certain echoes of the past more than others.

It is usually assumed, in a study of this nature, that the effects are linear and their direction known: the past influences the present. When the data are introspective, however, the power of current experience works in the opposite direction and causality is, in fact, unclear. The investigators point out that the current relationship of the spouses may colour their sense of the past, and it seems likely that their experiences as new parents affect the recall of parent–child relationships in childhood. Furthermore, the current relationship between the respondents and their parents (now grandparents) is a major, neglected factor. They are currently in a transitional phase, adapting to the advent of a new baby and reorganizing the established patterns of intrusion and support across generational boundaries. The nature of that experience may well affect the way in which respondents describe family relationships in the past. There is no question that experiences at one stage of life affect functioning at a later stage, or that the connections can be investigated. The problem, rather, is that the questionnaire data is a present construction on the past. It cannot stand in for data gathered in its own time, and it does not indicate a clear cause–effect relation between past and present.

Different questions are raised by the use of questionnaire data to evaluate a couple's interactions, and by the combination of individual scores to form composite statements about a marriage. Can introspective data accurately describe social interactions? And can a family be statistically constructed? Systems theorists would vote 'no' on both questions. They would assume that inner monologues are transformed by social interactions and that interactions are transformed by inner monologues; thus, introspective data do not directly describe the interaction. Nor can the pattern of a couple be accurately recreated by statistically combining their separate perspectives. We are familiar with the methodological problems that stem from combining data (Cairns 1979), but the issue here is conceptual as well. Individual reports and the statistical construction of a system miss the process of feedback and adjustment that characterize people in interaction. To describe the interaction, it would be necessary to observe and/or interview the wife and husband together. At the same time, it is important to note that this critique applies more to some variables than to others. From a systems perspective, conflict and marital stress, like other interactive family processes, should be studied *in vivo*, since self-report and statistical constructions do not capture the process by which a couple handles disagreements. However, satisfaction with the marriage is a subjective experience, and introspective methods appear valid for gathering this kind of information.

Other questions raised from a systems perspective are primarily a matter of orientation and choice. The study might be recast, for instance, in interactive terms. Marital satisfaction, an experiential variable, might be reframed in terms of the couple's demonstrable cohesiveness, and the central problem rephrased as a question of change in their proximity or distance after the birth of the baby. To address certain questions, the two perspectives might fruitfully be combined, e.g. Do some couples demonstrate greater distance after a child is born without feeling less satisfaction in the marriage? And how do changes in satisfaction or cohesiveness relate to effective parenting?

The systems researcher might also direct more attention to process. In the transition to parenthood, a couple moves toward simultaneous membership in two subsystems: as spouses and as parents. Little is known about the specific implications of this change, despite its obvious importance for family relationships and child development, or about the process of working out viable new patterns for relating as spouses, for functioning as a parenting system, and for maintaining boundaries that separate and support the different functions. Since that is so, a systems theorist would be especially interested in the process of adaptation; in documenting the small calibrations, the differences between couples, the management of conflict, the involvement of other people. The methodological problems in this kind of study have often been indicated, but it is not often noted that some familiar problems of traditional research disappear. In the study reviewed here, for instance, the variance is limited, meaning that the 50 couples in this middle-class sample did not change greatly in their reports of marital satisfaction after the birth of the baby. In process research, however, such problems cease to be an issue. Every couple goes through a process of adaptation in this situation, and they are all candidates for intensive study. Research of this kind would probably involve small samples and very detailed description.

Grotevant and Cooper

The second study draws observational data from a four-person family and focuses on the relation between individual development and family patterns (Grotevant and Cooper 1985). As such, it highlights the issues that arise when a complex family group is studied and when the relations between individual and system are examined. We will consider, in particular, the methods for data gathering and analysis, the framework for selecting the relevant research units, and the form of presenting the findings.

The authors ask how identity exploration in late adolescence is related to individuation in the family, defining the latter as a mixture of individuality and connectedness. They deal with four family members—two parents, 17-year-old adolescent, and sibling—focusing on all dyads that include the adolescent, as well as the dyad of husband and wife. Data on adolescent identity are gathered through a structured interview, and interaction in the family is assessed through a Family Interaction Task. Findings highlight the generalization that among male adolescents identity exploration is related only to aspects of father–son interchange, while among females such exploration is related to aspects of individuation in all dyads.

The framework of this study is consistent with a systems approach: it conceptualizes adolescence as a transitional period, when the ongoing interchange between generations moves the family from the unequal authority structure of earlier years toward a more peer-like mutuality, and it uses a family task for gathering observational data. The issues arise around the handling of the data and the generalizations that emerge from data analysis.

From a systems perspective, for instance, the coding and organization of data fragments the process of interaction and limits the representation of family patterns, even though the latter are realistic and visible during the family task. That is, every comment during the task is coded separately, noting speaker and person addressed, so that son-to-mother and mother-to-son become separate entities. Scores for these separate units are correlated with identity exploration, and patterns of interaction in the dyad are then inferred from the findings. The fragmentation and statistical construction involved in this process are obvious. It is possible, of course, to draw some generalizations in this way. For instance, since identity exploration among males is associated with expressions of mutuality from father to son and is also associated with the son's direct expression of opinion to his father, it is plausible to posit a complementary pattern of connectedness and individuality in this dyad, as these authors have done. However, this form of handling the data provides no information on more differentiated questions of process: Is father-son communication directly sequenced? Is there a recurrent order, in which the supportive communication of father precedes the assertions of the son, or vice versa? Does the pattern occur during phases of family disagreement? More important, it is impossible to know whether other people are part of the pattern, and in that sense the inferences may be inaccurate. For instance, if the mother or sister enters consistently in a cycle that includes father and son, that would not appear in the data analysis, even though her participation may be a necessary facilitator in the communication pattern. From a systems perspective, it is important to organize information so that it includes all relevant participants, no matter how many, and reflects the naturally occurring sequences, of whatever length. The modification of existing schema and the development of new methodologies to encompass that complexity is an important direction for the future.

A second problem reflects a clash between the assumptions of systems theory and the customary conventions for summarizing research. Traditional research paradigms trap us in the assertion that what does not show a statistically significant association is not meaningfully related. In what would be a typical statement in the field, the authors state: 'These differences suggest that sources of family influence on identity exploration may be more diverse for female adolescents than for males' (p. 425), and '. . . sons' relationships with their fathers and daughters' relationships with each parent appear to provide the context for experiencing both individuality and connectedness' (p. 425). From a systems perspective, that is not believable. It is a basic assumption of systems theory that members of an intimate system are interdependent. The mother of an adolescent boy is, was, and will be implicated in her son's explorations of identity, as well as her daughters'. There may be various explanations for the findings—the definition of identity, the variables, the methods of analysis, the assumption of linear relationships—but these findings would be considered evidence of what we do not yet understand rather than what we can eliminate as a factor. The point is general, challenging the traditional assumption that a family figure whose assessed behaviour does not co-vary statistically with that of another has no significance for that person's behaviour. We need a different way of summarizing what has and has not been found, and serious consideration of how to fill the empty spaces with information concerning subsystems that do not show systematic correlations.

Perhaps it is an extension of this same point to consider the relation of adolescent identity formation to family structure and to raise the question of who is relevant. It is a strength of this study that it includes a sibling in the family task and analyses the communication between siblings. However, the interactions between parents and sibling are not considered relevant. From a systems perspective, the sibling would necessarily have full status. It would be assumed that the self-image of the target adolescent is partly a matter of what is reflected about the self, in this family, *vis à vis* other family members (e.g. who is considered the responsible, or creative, or difficult child), and that the explorations of a 17-year-old who is the oldest sibling take place in a different context from those of a peer who is the youngest of three.

The relationship between the target adolescent and each parent has been formed in the context of other family relationships. Schachter (1982) has proposed a concept of 'deidentification', suggesting that the second child tends to identify with a different parent from the first child, regardless of gender. Carrying that concept to a systemic level, one would posit that both parents and children have participated in the creation of these different alliances, and have formed complementary subsystems in the family that are especially close. Since family communication and identity exploration depend on the complete family map, data on all parent–child subsystems in the family would be germane, even though the study is focused on a particular child.

It is likely that developmental research will continue to be anchored in a particular family member. To the extent that it takes account of systems formulations, however, it will need to include much of what is currently considered extraneous data, dealing with subsystems that do not directly include the anchor person. The attention to the marital dyad, in this study, is a positive example, and does, in fact, provide useful information.

Dunn and Munn

The third study investigates social development during the second year of life, drawing on observational data in the home setting (Dunn and Munn 1985). It is also a study of family patterns concerning conflict, as the child is inducted into the family's rules and the family adapts to the child's input. The study highlights the potential value of detailed studies of process, and raises, again, the important question of the relevant research unit.

The investigators ask how the child's understanding changes, during the second year, with regard to social rules and the feelings of family members. They focus on conflict in three dyads—siblings, mother and younger (target) child, mother and sibling—and look at the younger child's response to conflict between mother and sibling (a triad). Data are gathered through narrative and pre-coded records. Findings highlight developmental changes, including increased understanding of family rules, more intense anger and distress in conflict situations, and an increase in the social perception required to tease siblings effectively or support family members.

From a systems perspective, other findings are equally interesting, since they point to interactive processes that change over time. For instance, it is noted both that the younger child shows increased understanding of family rules over time and that the mother and sibling each increase their direct reference to rules in conflict situations with the child. That suggests a spiralling pattern, in which communication is continually calibrated: others take account of the child's growing comprehension over time and the child responds with greater understanding to the increased specificity of input. For developmental psychologists, the detailed study of interaction around conflict and control should be just as germane as the assessment of the child's understanding, since these are the basic processes of socialization in early childhood, and more differentiated questions should be pursued: What are the details of the calibrating process? How does the process differ in interactions involving siblings *vis à vis* adult and child? What are the patterns of communication when both mother and father are present? How do patterns differ across families, and what are the markers of interchange that do and do not support growth?

These data also supply information about the permeability of 'boundaries' between subsystems. The concept of boundaries is important in systems thinking, but little is known about developmental changes in the family concerning proximity and distance or the natural conditions for communicating the rules. These data offer two relevant observations. One is that the younger child reacts differently to varied conditions of conflict between mother and sibling, being more apt to enter (cross boundaries) when affect is playful or neutral and more apt to watch (stay out) when affect is negative. The process by which that is learned probably takes place in a triad, and is worth further study.

The other observation concerns the crossing of generational boundaries when the siblings are in conflict. Intervention by adults and the seeking of help by children is a recurrent event in the daily life of young families, and the natural patterns of interaction across generations are certainly understudied. These data indicate that in certain families, where the mother customarily talks to the older child about the younger child's feelings, the younger child comes more readily to invoke the mother's help during sibling quarrels. The finding suggests a process of evolution: sibling–sibling conflict→mother intervenes (crosses the boundary) to talk with the older and support the younger→cessation of hostilities. In time, the pattern changes: sibling–sibling conflict→younger child solicits the mother (crosses the boundary), apparently expecting support. The natural evolution of patterns like these deserve considerably more study, including the detail of next steps in the sequence and reactions of the sibling. The data are germane to a core issue in family development: how do viable families maintain age-appropriate boundaries between adult and sibling subsystems and adjust them as required, honouring the limited capacities of young children to solve their own battles, their need for negotiating experience within the sibling group, their changing competencies over time, and the legitimate demands of each child for fair treatment?

While this study draws attention to the important potential in studying process, it also raises the question, again, of the relevant research unit. In this area of study, and at this developmental stage, the absence of the father is a crucial omission. The evolution of acceptable patterns for expressing and controlling conflict is a primary task for young families. In the experience of family therapists, family viability and healthy child functioning, at this stage, depend significantly on the ability of the parents to negotiate their different expectations concerning control, keep spouse and parenting issues separated, and support each other's communications with the children. The work reported by Christensen and Margolin in this volume bears that out. To understand how family rules are communicated and enforced, therefore, it would be necessary to observe both parents in situations of sibling conflict. It is not only a matter of seeing the father with the children; it is an emphasis on father and mother functioning together as a parenting system. Their interaction has implications both for the internalization of rules and for the child's perception of how disagreements are resolved between adults and across generations.

Of course, the triad of mother and two children has valid boundaries and patterns of its own. How that relates to family patterns as a whole is a theoretical and pragmatic frontier for investigation. What seems clear, however, is that our information is incomplete or distorted if we do not study the patterns of the family as a whole.

From a systems perspective, these studies represent some of the most promising trends in the expansion of developmental research: the study of relationships, inclusion of fathers and siblings, an interest in varied subsystems and in family groups of three or more members, the use of observational data, and the effort to develop refined systems for coding social interactions. At the same time, like much of the developmental research to date, they are not fully consistent with systems principles in procedures or emphasis. There is a prevailing preference for studying effects rather than process and a tendency to construct the family statistically, using the individual or dyad as the unit of analysis even when more complex data are available. It seems difficult for researchers to take on the family as a natural unit, with multiple members and with organized patterns that involve more than two people and sequences of more than two steps. Since that is the realistic context of development and of relationships within the family, however, it must eventually be studied in its own terms. From that point of view, it may be useful to consider some concepts of family organization and some methods for family assessment that have been developed in related fields.

Family-oriented concepts and research tools

From the perspective of therapists who observe the family over time, there is an organismic quality to family functioning.* Families respond to events in characteristic ways that define them as differentiated wholes. Two concepts describe this 'wholeness' of the family: family style, which deals with behavioural interactions, and family world view, which deals with family self-perceptions. Family style was first captured by Minuchin's concept of structure (S. Minuchin 1974). Structure indicates the rules of interaction that organize the family's behaviour. It is essentially the crystallization of process, and is the underpinning of family style. Theorists have described a variety of stylistic dimensions, including enmeshed and disengaged (S. Minuchin 1974); centripetal and centrifugal (Stierlin et al. 1973; Beavers 1982); combinations of flexibility and cohesiveness (Olson et al. 1979); and open, closed, random, and synchronous styles (Kantor and Lehr 1975; Constantine 1986). The concept of style covers both normal variations and dysfunctional extremes.

The concept of world view has been described by Ferreira (1963) as family myth, and by Watzlawick (1984) as invented reality. It refers to the shared set of conceptions by which families define themselves, their members, and the way they fit into the world. This world view contains the family's shared construction of its history, and is akin, in some way, to the individual 'self'. Like the 'self', family myths direct the thinking, affect, and behaviour of family members.

*I am indebted to S. Minuchin for his input into these comments.

Measurement techniques in the family field do not cover all the complexities of structure and world view, but they do approach the family as a unified whole and may be useful to developmental researchers in the search for new tools (see Grotevant and Carlson 1987). Three of the most widely known schemes are charted in Table 1.1: the Beavers–Timberlawn Family Rating Scales (Lewis *et al.* 1976; Beavers 1982; Lewis and Looney 1983); the Family Adaptability and Cohesion Scales, or FACES (Olson *et al.* 1979; Olson *et al.* 1983; Olson 1986); and the card-sorting technique of David Reiss (Reiss 1981; Oliveri and Reiss 1982).

These techniques employ different modes of gathering and analysing data. Reiss' work and the Beavers–Timberlawn scales are based on family tasks, a procedure for gathering observational data that has been used productively elsewhere in the family field and is expanding into developmental research (e.g. Minuchin *et al.* 1978; Blechman and McEnroe 1985; Grotevant and Cooper 1985). FACES is a questionnaire technique and incorporates the usual problems of self-report data, but it brings information about the nature of the family from multiple members. In so doing, it highlights an issue that must eventually be dealt with by all systems-oriented research: how to take account of the perspectives of different members while assessing the family as an organized system (see Barnes and Olson 1985).

All the dimensions used in these schemes imply interactive units (see Table 1.1). Each model has its own language but certain ideas recur, reflecting concepts that have arisen out of clinical experience and that appear in the general family therapy literature. Synthesizing the dimensions, one can see three areas that subsume considerable family functioning and that might profitably be employed by developmental researchers. Family *closeness* or *cohesion* concerns the regulation of proximity and distance, includes affect, and is relevant for questions concerning boundaries and subsystem relations. *Decision making* and *conflict resolution* concerns the family's patterns for negotiating among themselves, implementing power and authority, orchestrating the expression of negative affect, and regulating the input of different members as well as the functioning of alliances and coalitions. *Flexibility* concerns the family's ability to adapt to changing circumstances, and involves openness, communication, feedback, and calibration. Most of these are not unfamiliar ideas for developmental psychologists. In the way they are used here, however, they imply a family style and world view within which subsystems and individuals function, and are therefore part of a systemic paradigm for assessing human behaviour.

Incorporating systems principles in research: a pilot study of family adaptation to illness

In this last section, I will describe a study in progress that attempts to use systems principles and to explore the issues that have been raised. It

Table 1.1 *Family assessment systems*

System	Data gathering and analysis	Family dimensions
Reiss' Problem-Solving Model	Standardized problem solving procedure for the family (card-sorting problem). Discrete indices, based on non-verbal behaviour, yield scores on each of the three dimensions (e.g. indicators include complexity of solution, evolution of solution via new information, time taken, temporal pacing of family members, etc.).	*Configuration*: the family's belief in an ordered comprehensible world, and in their ability to meet and deal with reality. *Coordination*: the family's orientation to consensus, and their tendency to take a unified, collaborative approach to problem solving. *Closure*: degree (or lack of) openness to new information bearing on problem solution
Beavers–Timberlawn Family Rating Scales	Family Interaction Test (five tasks: discussions of family strength, aspects of marriage, family relationships, simulated situation, planning as a family). Videotaped sessions scored on 13 scales.	Five superordinate concepts encompassing 13 dimensions: *family structure* (overt power relationships, parental coalitions, closeness); *family mythology*; *goal-directed negotiation*; *autonomy* (clarity of expressed feelings, responsibility for actions, invasiveness, permeability); *family affect* (range of expressed feeings, feeling tone of interactions, degree of unresolvable conflict, empathy for others' feelings). Families evaluated for *family competence* (based on scales) and *family style* (centripetal–centrifugal). Model identifies *optimal, adequate, mid-range,* and *severely dysfunctional* families.

Table 1.1—*continued*

System	Data gathering and analysis	Family dimensions
Circumplex Model of Family Functioning: Family Adaptability and Cohesion Evaluation Scales (FACES)	Questionnaires about the family filled out separately by each family member (current form is FACES III; Olson 1986). Questionnaires yield scores on cohesion and adaptability. Clinical Rating Scales, recently developed, allow evaluation of family by others, drawing on interviews or observation of task interaction. Combination of scores on cohesion and adaptability allow family placement on the Circumplex Model.	*Cohesion*: the emotional bonding of family members. *Adaptability*: the family's ability to change relationships and power structure in response to developmental and situational stress. *Communication*: a facilitating dimension that includes clarity, empathy, etc. From gradations of cohesion and adaptability, charted on Circumplex Model, 16 types of family system are indicated (e.g. flexibly separated, structurally connected, etc.). Model identifies *balanced*, *mid-range*, and *extreme* family types. The model is curvilinear, in that the middle areas are considered balanced.

approaches the family as an organized whole, albeit with clear subsystems; explores the patterns of interaction around a central anchor person; and looks at homeostasis and change at a point of dramatic transition, considering the interaction of developmental realities with the current trauma and the process by which changing relationships are calibrated.

The project is a study of families faced with the serious illness of an adult member.* All families are at the same developmental stage: the cancer patient and spouse are middle-aged and their offspring are young adults. They are normal families, living under stress but coping out of their own resources without seeking professional help. There are two videotaped interviews, the first with the couple and the second with the extended family. The interviews focus on the process of change, starting with a general query, 'What has changed in your family since (S) developed cancer?' They are open-ended, exploring different subsystems and following the issues that arise. In this study, certain variables are of major interest: family cohesion; instrumental adaptations; decision-making processes; the handling of anxiety; and the management of conflict. The specifics are less important, however, than the effort to consider the family as an organized differentiated whole, and to explore the nature of homeostasis and change in such a situation.

The family as a research unit

In the second interview, the extended family is the research unit. One purpose of the study is to explore the family interview as a source of systematic data, and to describe natural patterns that may involve several people or a sequence of several steps. In family interviews, there are two levels of data, both of which are valuable sources of information: the content of what is said, and the visible interactions of family members.

As an example of patterns involving the whole family, consider Family A: a couple in their late fifties (the husband is ill); daughter and her husband, in their thirties; son in his mid-twenties. At moments of stress, this family has a recurrent pattern: a blocking action—usually humour—followed by a more serious expression of affect and a discussion of realities; at some point of discomfort, humour returns. This is a family pattern involving the management of anxiety, family cohesion, and mutual protection. Though the sequence is recurrent, it is not always carried by the same people—an important point. Different family members provide the joking, for instance, though some individual behaviour is predictable, e.g. the daughter most frequently begins the serious, emotionally charged phase. The family is not

*The project, 'Family adaptation to illness and hospitalization', is conducted by S. and P. Minuchin under the auspices of the New York University Medical Center, Department of Psychiatry (Project No. 4136), and with the co-operation of the Cooperative Care Unit. It is partially supported by a grant from Mr Sol Katz.

aware of this observable sequence, but they do describe the fact that they are protective of each other, joke a lot to hide their feelings, and keep some of their fears to themselves.

In another family, a recurrent pattern appears for dissipating conflict, and it is both visible and described. Here, the wife/mother has sensitive antennae and is the catalyst for conflict resolution. She enters when there is blocked communication between family members, clarifying perspectives and fostering their direct communication. When the husband is rattled by the advice of a concerned son that they explore alternative medicine, she says to him, 'Do you feel confident about the doctors? . . . Then that's that. It's your life'. She tells the son that dad is considering his advice because he loves him, not because he wants to, and father and son then move to a direct discussion in which they resolve their differences. The same sequence occurs when the husband is upset by the infrequent visits of the second son. These patterns seem relevant to the larger question of the individual in the system, since adaptations centre around the cancer patient as anchor, yet they are clearly relational, involving other family members and general family processes. The point seems applicable, by analogy, to developmental studies that focus on the child in the family.

The relation between general family patterns and those of the various subsystems is, as has been indicated, a major question for systems theory and research. It is a goal of the study to document patterns in the various dyads and triads, and to explore ways of describing the relation between the parts and the whole.

Transitions as a point of study

This study focuses on a traumatic transition in the life of a family. It has much in common with research on divorce or economic depression, as reported elsewhere in this volume. In such situations, established patterns are challenged and the family must reorganize relationships and its way of life. Researchers have investigated long-term effects of such crises, suggesting that some individuals are rendered particularly resilient (see Chapters 12 and 16), but the details of family reorganization during the transitional phase have not been as thoroughly studied. From a systems perspective, the following aspects are of special interest.

The balance of homeostasis and change. A core question at points of transition concerns the balance between stability and change. From a theoretical perspective, family patterns must change when the system is challenged. In human terms, however, it is clear from the interviews that the 19 viable families in this project hang on to what they can of the familiar (an antidote to chaos) and change what they must (an antidote to dysfunctional rigidity). The basic issue is not change *per se* but the balance between continuity and change.

In this project, we are trying to document that balance in different families, particularly in terms of cohesion, instrumental behaviour, and decision making. Most of these families have drawn closer under stress, and have made changes in power hierarchies and the management of daily life. The extent and nature of change, however, seems related not only to practical factors, such as the gravity of the illness, but to family style, which may vary considerably within a normal range. 'Embedded' and 'disengaged' families handle changes in proximity and distance differently, and the risk of over- or underprotecting the sick family member varies accordingly. Such issues as family style, and the balance between maintaining and changing family patterns, would apply equally to inquiries about the handling of predictable developmental transitions, such as the child's entrance into school.

The interaction with developmental issues.   The management of transitions is a function not only of family style but of the family's developmental stage. At the stage we have chosen for study, the reorganization of relations between generations, in response to the crisis, is particularly complex. At this stage, a typical middle-class family has overlapping but relatively autonomous subsystems, with comparatively firm boundaries between generations for contact and decision making. Whatever the family style, boundaries would be firmer than at earlier stages, when children were young, or than they may be at later stages, when the elders may be needy. At this point, the older generation is usually still the more powerful and giving, while the young are not yet 'generative' in relation to their own parents. The question is how that situation changes when a parent suddenly becomes vulnerable.

By and large, families in this study show increasing contact between generations and a shift in the direction of concern. The young become more nurturant, helpful, and involved, and the elders may look more to their children for practical help and emotional support. Families vary widely in the degree of adjustment and their comfort with the shift, but the process is active in all families. In Family A, the son and daughter indicate that they did not worry about their father's illnesses when they were young ('I guess because he was my father he was always stronger than everything else that's ever hit him'). As young adults, however, they are worried, involved, and vigilant ('He might try to joke but you can see he's turning blue. You know he's just trying to tell you nothing's wrong ... He really wants the help.') And they take responsibiltiy for decisions, even in the face of resistance.

The shifting relationships between generations do not proceed automatically. They involve a detailed process of calibration, and the adequacy of that process is obviously essential to effective adaptation.

The process of calibration.   The project is focused on the study of process, with particular attention to the calibration of change, as family members seek new patterns of interaction appropriate to their changed circumstances. For families in this situation, that process often centres on the issue of how much help and nurturance to offer the sick person, so that it is neither too much nor too little. In characteristic joking style, the man in Family A describes the process, 'If I don't trip she'll push me so she can pick me up. She's on my shoulder every minute, like a hawk. I'm not used to people grabbing me . . . putting on a sweater. Sometimes I tell her, "I'm your husband, not your son!"'

These cycles, described by many families, include increasing nurturance offered by family members, corrective feedback by the person who is ill, and an adjustment by the helper. Calibration, based on the accurate reading of feedback, is crucial in this situation, since seriously ill patients in loving families may become depressed if they are unable to signal limits to protection or be understood when they do. However, the point is more general. The regulation of family response to developmental changes in its members has not been intensively studied, at least in terms of the details of self-regulation or the functioning of subsystems beyond the dyad. Hopefully, mechanisms worked out for studying the process of calibration in this project will also be useful in developmentally oriented studies of relationships in the family.

Coda

In this chapter, I have adopted a systems perspective for considering relationships within the family. I have reviewed systems concepts; considered the fit between those principles and current developmental research; summarized potentially useful ideas and methods from a related field; and described a study of family relationships conducted from a systems perspective.

An examination of current psychological research on the family suggests that the field is expanding, but it has not yet fully addressed the issues that would make the work consistent with systems principles. The strengths of the field are also the greatest stumbling blocks: it is more familiar and comfortable to construct the family statistically than to face it head on, in the undisciplined complexity of people and patterns that represent the child's reality. And it is apparently more rewarding to employ sophisticated techniques for testing general hypotheses than to accumulate the detailed descriptive data that are necessary for exploring a new scientific paradigm. As developmental psychologists become more involved in systems formulations, however, the reservoir of theory and information should make it possible to do what practitioners in related fields do not, or cannot, do: explore the relation of the individual to the system; apply the understanding of interpersonal relation ships to larger units; and expand the methodology for documenting system patterns. Developmental psychologists are particularly well equipped to study change. It will be the task of systemically oriented researchers to study the impingement of developmental changes on the family system throughout the life cycle, and to document the process of reorganization in the system, as it relates to healthy functioning and growth.

References

Barnes, H. and Olson, D. (1985). Parent–adolescent communication and the Circumplex Model. *Child Development* **56**, 438–47.

Beavers, W. (1982). Healthy, midrange and severely dysfunctional families. In *Normal family processes* (ed. F. Walsh). Guilford, New York.

Belsky, J. and Isabella, R. (1985). Marital and parent–child relationships in family of origin and marital change following the birth of a baby: a retrospective analysis. *Child Development* **56**, 342–9.

Blechman, E. and McEnroe, M. (1985). Effective family problem solving. *Child Development* **56**, 429–37.

Cairns, R. (1979). *The analysis of social interactions: methods, issues, and illustrations.* Erlbaum, Hillsdale, NJ.

Constantine, L. (1986). *Family paradigms: the practice of theory in family therapy.* Guilford, New York.

Dunn J. and Munn, P. (1985). Becoming a family member: family conflict and the development of social understanding in the second year. *Child Development* **56**, 480–92.

Ferreira, A. (1963). Family myths and homeostasis. *Archives of General Psychiatry* **9**, 457–63.

Grotevant, H. and Cooper, C. (1985). Patterns of interaction in family relationships and the development of identity exploration in adolescence. *Child Development* **56**, 415–28.

Grotevant, H. and Carlson, C. (1987). Family interaction coding systems: a descriptive review. *Family Process* **26**, 49 74.

Kantor, D. and Lehr, W. (1975). *Inside the family: toward a theory of family process.* Jossey-Bass, San Francisco.

Lewis, J. and Looney, J. (1983). *The long struggle: well-functioning working-class black families.* Brunner/Mazel, New York.

Lewis, J., Beavers, W., Gossett, J., and Phillips, V. (1976). *No single thread: psychological health in family systems.* Brunner/Mazel, New York.

Minuchin, P. (1985). Families and individual development: provocations from the field of family therapy. *Child Development* **56**, 289–302.

Minuchin, S. (1974). *Families and family therapy.* Harvard, Cambridge, Mass.

Minuchin, S., Rosman, B., and Baker, L. (1978). *Psychosomatic families.* Harvard, Cambridge, Mass.

Oliveri, M. and Reiss, D. (1982). Family styles of construing the social environment: a perspective on variation among nonclinical families. In *Normal family processes* (ed. F. Walsh). Guilford, New York.

Olson, D. (1986). Circumplex Model VII: validation studies and FACES III. *Family Process* **25,** 337–51.

Olson, D., Sprenkle, D. and Russell, C. (1979). Circumplex Model of marital and family systems I: cohesion and adaptability dimensions, family types and clinical applications. *Family Process* **18,** 3–28.

Olson, D., McCubbin, H., Barnes, H., Larsen, A., Muxen, M. and Wilson, M. (1983). *Families: what makes them work.* Sage Publications, Beverly Hills.

Reiss, D. (1981). *The family's construction of reality.* Harvard, Cambridge, Mass.

Schachter, F. (1982). Sibling deidentification and split-parent identification: a family tetrad. In *Sibling relationships: their nature and significance across the life-span* (ed. M. Lamb and B. Sutton-Smith). Erlbaum, Hillsdale. NJ.

Stierlin, H., Levi, L., and Savard, R. (1973). Centrifugal versus centripetal separation in adolescence: two patterns and some of their implications. In *Annals of the American Society for Adolescent Psychiatry*, Vol. 2 (ed. S. Feinstein and P. Giovacchini). Basic Books, New York.

Watzlawick, P. (ed.) (1984). *The invented reality.* W. W. Norton, New York.

2

The coherence of family relationships*
L. ALAN SROUFE and JUNE FLEESON

The coherence of family relationships

Some of the problems in understanding family relationship systems are unique, given the gender and generational features of families, the enduring nature of family relationships, and the special affective bonds that tie family members together. These characteristics have to do with the special functions typically served by families. At the same time, key principles derived from consideration of all relationships also apply to the family, as do general systems concepts. In this paper we will present a view of the family based on an *organizational/relationship* perspective. We will substitute organizational concepts for the idea of reciprocal influences in accounting for interdependencies among relationships in the family. But first we will review our relationship principles and some empirical work which supports them.

Our relationship principles, outlined at a previous conference (Sroufe and Fleeson 1986), are similar to listings presented by others (Cottrell 1969). They also are quite congruent with concepts from family systems theory (S. Minuchin 1974). Moreover, they are similar to principles proposed to govern individual behavioural organization (Sroufe 1979; Epstein 1980). These propositions may be briefly summarized as follows:

1. *Relationships are wholes.* Just as individuals, however diverse their characteristics, are coherent and unified (Sroufe 1979), so relationships may be considered as totalities. As such, they may not be reduced to characteristics of participating members. As Hinde (1979) has suggested, it therefore should be possible for relationships to be the unit of analysis. This proposition is supported by numerous findings, including the fact that infant attachment relationships with one parent may be of distinctly different quality from those with the other (Main and Weston 1981). Other examples will be provided below.

*This paper was supported in part by a research grant from the National Institute of Mental Health (MH-HD40864).

2. *Relationships exhibit coherence and continuity.* Relationships, like individuals, manifest coherence across contexts and stability across transformations (Sroufe and Waters 1977). Behavioural manifestation may change from context to context but it does so in predictable ways; for example, sons who behave with father one way when mother is present may behave in a different but predictable fashion towards father when mother is not present. Moreover, despite changing surface behaviour, qualitative features of relationships may tend to persist. Qualitative aspects of the parent–child relationship at Time 1 may predict qualitative aspects at Time 2, even though in many other ways the relationship is changed. As one example, unusual sensuality in a parent–young child relationship may give way to emotional reliance of parent on child in later years, but the generational boundary issue remains similar. (Sroufe *et al.* 1985; Sroufe and Fleeson 1986). Qualities of relationships are maintained despite changing forms. Caregiver behaviour toward the 6-month-old predicts the infant's attachment behaviour later (Sroufe 1985) which, in turn, predicts the mother's behaviour when the infant is 2 years old (Matas *et al.* 1978) or even with another sibling 3 years later (Ward 1983). This is similarly true on the individual level. Tantruming, explosive behaviour at age 8–10 years may not predict similar behaviour in adulthood, but it does predict later interpersonal and authority issues—lack of success in the military, difficulties in the work place, marital instability, and 'ill-tempered parenting' (Caspi *et al.*, in press).

3. *Individuals internalize (represent) relationships.* The coherence of the internal self system of an individual makes it possible to predict behaviour in novel situations. Similarly, participation in a relationship has implications beyond the particular roles an individual has played. We believe that by participating in a salient relationship, an individual learns and internalizes aspects of the whole. At the simplest level this involves expectations concerning (anticipation of) the other's behaviour, as well as an understanding of reciprocation or one's own expectable response within the system. This is analogous to an actor knowing not only cue lines from the other actors but also enough about the other's roles to know what emotions and attitudes are called for in various scenes. But beyond this, each individual must learn the particular nature of complementary responses and other key aspects of the relationship so that continuity and coherence are guaranteed even with change or development in the relationship. A specific set of particular responses or even a generalized role would be inadequate to this task. In the manner proposed by 'script' theorists (Nelson and Gruendel 1981), an abstraction of the relationship itself is internalized.

4. *Represented relationships are carried forward.* It is now maintained by diverse theorists that previously formed models or expectations concerning the self influence ongoing behaviour (Rotter 1966; Epstein 1973; Bandura

1977; Harter 1983). Likewise, models of self, other, and *relationships*, which are constructed from relationship experiences, powerfully influence ongoing selection of social experiences (environments); expectations concerning the availability, responsiveness, and attitudes of others; and the complementary expectations concerning the self in relationships (Main and Hesse in press; Sroufe and Fleeson 1986; Egeland *et al.*, in press). This is the crux of Bowlby's attachment theory (1969/82, 1973, 1980). Others are selected, responded to, and influenced in directions compatible with previous relationship learning. As Bowlby referred to attachment behaviour as 'goal-corrected', we would argue that reproduction of a relationship system with qualities similar to those previously known is also goal-corrected. As with any goal-related behaviour, there may be considerable flexibility in modes and means utilized, and efforts will tend to persist until the goal is realized:

'Expectations are the carriers of relationships. Carrying forward all of the specific behaviors and response chains from previous interactions would be an overwhelming task, but a limited set of expectations can generate countless behavioral reactions, flexibly employed in a variety of situations. One's orientation concerning others, one's expectations concerning their availability and likely responses, and what, in general terms, one can do (or cannot do) to increase the likelihood of familiar responses are strongly shaped by early relationships.' (Sroufe and Fleeson 1986, p. 68)

The goal is not reproduction of specific previous behaviours with a new partner. The individual may respond with the *other's* previous behaviour should a partner be encountered who exhibits his own previous pattern. Novel behaviour patterns may be generated if they are complementary to the new partner's behaviour in ways formally similar to the previous relationship's complementarity. For example, exploiter–exploited relationships may take countless forms which may be quite dissimilar at the level of particular expressed behaviours, as when a physically abused child is verbally hostile toward a peer partner (Troy and Sroufe 1987). Even opposites may be seen as similar, as when an individual from a previously explosive relationship participates in a relationship characterized by total control over expression of anger. Despite such complexity, probabilistic statements based on this proposition may be derived and tested, in which researchers can specify in advance a limited set of outcomes hypothesized to be more likely for target cases versus controls.

   These four principles apply not only to dyads but to larger relationship systems such as families. *Relationship systems are wholes.* As such they are more than the sum of the parts. The whole is a complex system, including subsystems of dyadic and triadic relationships as well as individuals, each of which is interdependent with the others. *Relationship systems have continuity and coherence.* Even when individuals or subrelationships change, changes in other individuals or relationships will tend to maintain certain pre-existing qualitative features of the system. *The whole system is reflected in each subrelationship.* Each relationship within a system is constrained by and reflects the total organization. The overall system is assumed to be part of each relationship due to the fact that every relationship and every individual is touched by every other individual and relationship, usually through direct interaction. This feature enables relationships to respond to changes in other relationships in ways that typically maintain integrity of the whole. *Entire systems are carried forward.* New family systems reflect not only the partners' previous histories in child–caregiver relationships, but their experience of sibling relationships, adult–sibling relationships, and adult–adult relationships in their family, as well as other close relationships in which they directly participated. The task of forging a new system, which reflects the complex systems histories of each partner, could thus be quite complex. Often the task is simplified through mate selection (that is, selection of a compatible internalized system). We are beginning to relate friendship selection in 10-year-olds to attachment relationship history within the family. Early results suggest that such choices are congruent with the relationship histories of the two partners.

The task of the present volume is to examine the linkages among relationships in the family. We approach this task within the framework of our four relationship principles. In the present paper emphasis will be on the cardinal principle, namely, the family system as a totality. Relationships within the family are viewed as necessarily related because of their hierarchical organization within the total system. While dyads are products of individuals and families the products of individuals, dyads and so forth, it is also the case that dyads, for example, function to maintain the larger system. From this point of view we would move beyond the idea of one relationship influencing another (which obviously is the case) to the level of relationship organization within the family. Relationships within the family are constrained by the organization of the whole. We use the analogy, though it is imperfect, of 'degrees of freedom'. Given the assumption of system coherence, when one relationship in the system is specified other relationships lose some freedom to vary. Were two relationships specified, others become even more constrained. In short, it is possible to make probabilistic statements about the nature of one relationship in the family from assessments of qualities of another, not simply because the researcher has learned about how some individuals behave, but because total systems are organized and all relationships within the same system are constrained by that organization. Causal concepts are thus replaced by organizational concepts.

We will elaborate on this perspective in discussion. First, however, we will present some empirical data illustrating our relationship principles. The first examples, which take us outside the family to peer and child–teacher relationships, are none the less powerful illustrations of the coherence of relationships. Our final example will show that, in fact, qualities of one relationship in the family can be predicted from the presence of distinctly different qualities in another relationship, when the research is guided by the assumption of coherence among relationships in a system.

Relationships among pre-school peers and teachers

Several years ago, 40 children from the Minnesota Parent–Child Project (Egeland and Sroufe 1981; Sroufe 1983; Erickson *et al.* 1985) were brought together into two nursery school classrooms. This was an especially important opportunity to examine relationship systems because participating children could be categorized in terms of internal representations of relationships carried into the situation. Thus, one could ask questions about the kinds of peer relationships formed by children with varying attitudes and expectations concerning relationships, and similar questions about relationships between children and teachers. A major aim for the present paper is to examine the holistic qualities of these relationships, that is, how each relationship is a complex product of the particular members' contributions.

Ainsworth Strange Situation Classifications of infant–caregiver attachment relationships were used to infer the nature of the child's developing beliefs and attitudes about relationships (what Bowlby calls 'inner working models'). In attachment theory the emerging self is based in relationship history and may be defined as the organization of expectations concerning self, other, and relationships (Sroufe 1986; Sroufe and Fleeson 1986). With young children, a behavioural measure, based on observations of a salient relationship, is probably superior to interview techniques for inferring such constructions. Moreover, the project yielded substantial corroboration of these assessments from conversations between children and teachers (Sroufe 1986), from analysis of fantasy play themes (Rosenberg 1984), and from behaviour with peers (Sroufe 1983; Pancake 1985). Finally, an advantage of using the Ainsworth procedure is that relationships and, we assume, the nature of expectations derived from them, are grouped into three categories. By including a sizeable number of children within each category, a certain amount of error variance can be tolerated.

Descriptions of Ainsworth's patterns of attachment relationships are widely available (Ainsworth *et al.* 1978; Sroufe 1985). Simply, *secure* infant–caregiver relationships (pattern B) are manifest by confident expectations by the infant, ready exploration and ease of comforting in the caregiver's presence, positive greetings, and interaction, or, when distressed, active contact seeking. Such relationships are presumed, with ample evidence, to be rooted in reliable care, especially sensitivity and responsiveness to expression of need (Ainsworth *et al.* 1978; Sroufe 1985; Belsky and Pensky, this volume; Grossmann *et al.*, this volume). *Anxious/resistant* relationships (pattern C) are revealed in poverty of exploration, even in the caregiver's presence, low thresholds for threat, extreme separation distress and, especially, difficulty in being comforted by the caregiver, commonly accompanied by petulance and angry rejection of caregiver overtures. The mixture of preoccupation with the caregiver and strong contact seeking with refusal to settle and angry rejection (ambivalence) conveys an internalized relationship model based upon inconsistent, hit or miss, or chaotic care. The infant, while not giving up on the mother, is not firmly confident concerning her availability. The developing expectations are of other as available only with vigilance, and inconsistently so at that, and the self as ineffective in eliciting care. Finally, *anxious/avoidant* attachments (pattern A) are marked by failure to acknowledge or seek contact with the caregiver following distress of separation. Within limits, the more stressed (with a presumptive increase in activation of attachment), the more avoidance. Such infants give the illusion of nonchalance concerning caregivers or interchangeability of caregivers with others. (This is belied by the fact that avoidance is reserved for the caregiver.) Underlying such a paradoxical response to brief separations is a history of chronic emotional unavailability and/or rejection. In Bowlby's terms the infant's model is of the caregiver as unavailable and self as unworthy.

Into relationships with others, then, children with histories of secure attachment take inner beliefs of others as available and responsive, self as both effective and worthy, and relationships as rewarding. Those with anxious histories take less positive attitudes.

Victimizing relationships among pre-schoolers

Olweus (1980) had shown previously that both bully and 'whipping boy' statuses were stable among elementary school children and that each status had meaningful correlates in parental behaviour; that is, that such a relationship required the confluence of two histories. Here we report associations between the more specific attachment relationship measures and later peer relationships. Previously, quality of attachment has been shown to predict peer competence, sociometric status, and empathy (Sroufe 1983), as well as 'depth' of friendship (Pancake 1985). Here, as one part of pre-school, children were paired for at least 14 15-minute play sessions. In accord with Olweus' work, the major finding was that some children are exploitative, some can be exploited, and only when both come together in a relationship is there victimization, where one child systematically exploits, demeans, or otherwise mistreats a partner (Troy and Sroufe 1987).

These relationship patterns have specific links to particular attachment relationship histories. Children with secure histories neither victimize nor are they the victims of other children. When paired with an oppressive child they either engage in counter-assertiveness or a mutual distance is maintained (Pastor 1981; Troy and Sroufe 1987). Those with resistant histories are vulnerable to victimization, and those with avoidant histories are prone to victimize unless paired with a more powerful partner.

Most interesting are the results for particular pairings. When the pairing contained a child with an avoidant history and another child with a history of anxious attachment (*either* avoidant or resistant), victimization resulted, either physical exploitation or systematic sarcasm, derision, and rejection of one child by the other. Such patterns generally were established within two or three sessions. There were five such pairs in a total of 19 observed. Each was seen by two independent coders as a victimizing relationship and no other pair was so viewed. Such strong predictability was possible only when both relationship histories were considered. What is required is one child with an orientation toward exploitation and another child with an orientation toward being victimized and some vulnerability (mental slowness, frailty, etc.). Interestingly, such a relationship occurred with either avoidant/resistant pairs or avoidant/avoidant pairs. The latter case suggests that those with avoidant histories, themselves rejected, know both the victim and victimizing aspect of the relationship history. In one pair, the roles actually reversed several times over the 6-week period of study, as one child, then the other, experienced periods of special vulnerability. While numbers are small, relationships between two children with histories of resistant attachment were characterized by immaturity and social ineptitude, but not exploitation. These children were perfect foils for those with oppressive inclinations, but they themselves did not seem inclined to victimize. When paired with a child with a secure history, they often elicited nurturance and leadership, the secure child directing the play.

We believe that these results illustrate that attachment relationships are internalized and carried forward, with children who have been consistently rejected now rejecting or being rejected by their play partners. We emphasize here the pertinence of these data for understanding the integrity, coherence, and continuity of relationships. Detailed analyses of victimization pairs revealed roles for both oppressor and victim. An oppressor may repeatedly bait his partner ('It won't hurt. I promise'). On the other hand, victims repeatedly reinitiate contact that results in rejection or exploitation. In one session a child with a resistant history made 137 bids for contact that resulted in demeaning rejection. In another case the 'victim' plaintively asked his routinely exploitative partner: 'Aren't you going to tease me today, RJ?' These relationships, then, are the joint products of the two partners. Characteristics of one person are not sufficient for fully specifying relationships, nor are relationships simple sums of two individuals' characteristics. Resistant children are exploited by those with avoidant histories, not at all by those with secure histories. Some victimizers showed none of this behaviour in the classroom setting where they tended to be emotionally isolated. Only when out from under the eye of teachers and only when paired with a vulnerable partner did such behaviour emerge. When it emerged, usually by two or three sessions, it then remained stable across sessions. It seems clear to us that relationship properties, not individual characteristics alone, have been identified.

Child–teacher relationships

The peer victimization results dovetail nicely with findings concerning child–teacher relationships. The same two adults were principal teachers in each class; therefore it was possible to explore the interaction of their styles with children of varying attachment history. More than 100 videotapes made in the classroom provided numerous examples of interaction between all child–teacher pairs. Fifty interactive samples were drawn randomly from these tapes for each teacher–child dyad and were the basis for ratings of teacher behaviour or, in our view, teacher–child relationships. Nurturance, involvement, affection, control, expectations for compliance, 'tolerance', and anger were coded (Motti 1986). Brief definitions of these constructs are provided in Table 2.1. As can be seen, nurturance is distinguished from affection in that the former concerns caregiving behaviour, comforting, and the like. Expectations for control and tolerance are especially noteworthy because of their clear relationship connotations. Expectations for compliance are reflected in the teacher's behaviour surrounding a directive to a child. It is presumed that the teacher's turning to other business with no follow-up draws upon a history of experience with that given child; that is, an *expectation* that the child will comply. A strong imperative tone or immediately taking action to reinforce the directive suggests negative expectations concerning compliance. Likewise, when a teacher consistently allows (tolerates) one child to engage in minor infractions of classroom rules or to exhibit immature behaviour, this suggests a different set of standards for this child, again we presume based upon experience and expectations concerning this child.

Several aspects of the child–teacher data are specifically pertinent to the proposition that relationships are wholes and may be treated as the level of analysis. First, scales such as these, including 'expectations' and 'tolerance', may be rated with acceptable reliability (see Table 2.2). Secondly, in addition to usual coder reliability, where identical segments are scored by independent coders, for 12 pairs these reliabilities also were done in the manner of a split half reliability; that is, *two sets* of 50 non-overlapping interactions were randomly sampled from the videotapes and each set was rated by an independent coder. As seen in Table 2.2, agreement was as high as when coders viewed the same segments. Relationship qualities transcend specific interactions, Thirdly, there were significant differences between teachers, even though they were viewed with the same children. Ratings of relationships

Table 2.1   *Brief description of teacher–child relationship variables*

Teacher–child engagement—the degree to which the teacher is emotionally engaged with the child and is motivated to be engaged. Hedonic tone may be positive or negative, a low score implies indifference.

Warmth and affection—the degree to which teacher expresses positive, loving feelings toward the child. Physical affection, positive facial expressions and voice tones, expressed pleasure in seeing the child are all signs.

Nurturance–support—the degree to which the teacher takes care of the child's various needs (physical or emotional) and protects the child from real or perceived threats.

Anger—angry facial expressions, angry voice tones, sharp scolding, rough handling, or impatience and irritation all enter into this scale.

Tolerance—the degree to which the teacher makes allowances for the child; that is, permits infractions of classroom rules or immature behaviour. Tolerance is inferred when the teacher is aware of and yet does not curtail such behaviour (failing to follow directions, not waiting his/her turn, etc.).

Expectations for compliance—the degree to which the teacher expects the child to listen and comply with a directive, prohibition, or instruction. This is inferred from the way the teacher gives the directive, the timing and nature of follow-up behaviour (e.g. not waiting for the child to perform), and the use of physical or verbal reinforcement of the directive.

Degree of control—the degree to which the teacher attempts to control the child's behaviour, from minimal to persistent, consistent, and planful. Includes both guidance and discipline, as well as efforts to head off discipline situations.

involving the male teacher were characterized by less affection, less tolerance, and more control than those for the female teacher. Fourthly, there also were dramatic effects of the child's attachment history. Such effects were parallel for the two teachers. Thus these relationships, like all relationships, are products of both child and teacher characteristics or, we would presume, their relationship histories. The relationship could be specified from neither child nor teacher alone. Relationships are complex products of their individual members.

What do children with histories of secure attachment elicit from teachers? One would expect these relationships to be warm, mutually respectful, agreeable, age-appropriate, and matter of fact. This is exactly the pattern of results revealed in Table 2.3. Collapsing across teachers, children with secure histories did not differ significantly from the other two groups on engagement or affection (scores being high for all three groups); yet teachers exercised significantly less control over children with secure histories, they gave them (saw them as needing) significantly less nurturance, made significantly fewer allowances for inappropriate behaviour, and had significantly higher expectations for compliance. This is, of course, a coherent (interdependent) set

Table 2.2 *Inter-coder reliability: Pearson Product Moment Correlations and percent agreement for the same; non-overlapping observations in parentheses*

	Correlations		Percent agreement when allowed difference is	
Scale	$(n = 24)$	$(n = 12)$	0 or 1 pt	0, 1, or 2 pts
Tolerance	0.44*,[1]	(0.60)**	70% (71)	91% (94)
Nurturance	0.67**	(0.76)***	83% (71)	91% (94)
Control	0.81***	(0.74)***	83% (65)	100% (88)
Expectations	0.90***	(0.83)***	90% (81)	100% (94)
Engagement	0.68***	(0.47)*	78% (82)	100% (88)
Affection	0.50**	(0.54)*	65% (82)	91% (88)

* $p < 0.05$; ** $p < 0.01$; *** $p < 0.001$.

[1] For two of 24 pairs rated there was total disagreement (five-point discrepancies on a seven-point scale). These disagreements were resolved by a third coder. For the other 22 cases the correlation rises to 0.77.

of findings. Teachers, too, formed expectations and constructed models of their relationships with children.

A distinctly different but equally meaningful pattern obtained for the relationships within the resistant group. Theoretically, these children are oriented toward adult care but doubtful of its availability and their own potency. They also are somewhat inept in their efforts to achieve care or, as we have seen, to establish relationships with peers. What did their represented and currently instantiated models bring forth from competent, skilled, and caring teachers? High control, low expectations for compliance, and strikingly high engagement, nurturance and tolerance were characteristic. While they were getting care that they seemed to need, they also were confirming inner models of themselves as immature and incompetent, as also was the case in their relationships with peers. Those with avoidant histories elicited high control, relatively low expectations for compliance, and, not shown in Table 2.3, anger. Anger was a low-frequency behaviour and was scored only as 'ever seen' or not. Only children with avoidant histories elicited anger from these teachers. Thus, in some ways their relationships with teachers explicitly recapitulated aspects of relationships experienced with caregivers. Even so, their relationship history alone did not determine the teacher–child relationship. Anger and rejection from teachers were rare, and tolerance and nurturance were relatively high compared with the secure group.

The phenomenon of interacting relationship histories, or in our terms the wholeness and integrity of relationships, also is revealed in Table 2.4. Here we see the differences between the male and female teacher broken down across

Table 2.3 *Means and standard deviations on the teacher rating scales by attachment classification group (both teachers combined)*

	Avoidant A ($n=10$)	Secure B ($n=13$)	Resistant C ($n=6$)
Scale	X	X	X
Tolerance	3.95	2.35	4.75[2]
Nurturance	4.15	3.31	5.25[2]
Control	4.35	2.27[1]	4.17
Expectations	3.60	5.81[1]	3.33
Engagement	5.50	5.04	6.08
Affection	4.25	4.54	4.42

[1]Group B significantly different from groups A–C combined, as predicted a priori ($p < 0.001$, two-tailed).
[2]Group C significantly different from groups A–B combined, as predicted a priori ($p < 0.001$, two-tailed).

the A (avoidant), B (secure), and C (resistant) groups. Both teachers were tolerant of the 'C' children, whereas only the female teacher was tolerant of the 'A's. Likewise, the female teacher was dramatically more affectionate with the 'B's. While both teachers were caring and competent, warmth and nurturance were the primary province of the female, and firmness and authority were the province of the male. These interacted with child history.

Table 2.4 *Means comparing the two teachers on the rating scales for the three attachment groups, combined and separately*

	ABC ($n=29$)		A ($n=10$)		B ($n=13$)		C ($n=6$)	
Scale	M	F	M	F	M	F	M	F
Tolerance	3.07	3.72*	3.4	4.5*	2.0	2.7	4.7	4.6
Nurturance	3.83	4.17	3.5	4.8	3.1	3.5	5.0	4.5
Control	3.82	2.96***	4.0	3.8	2.5	1.5	4.7	3.7*
Expectations	4.57	4.28	3.8	3.7	5.7	5.6	3.5	2.8
Engagement	5.24	5.58	5.4	5.6	4.7	5.4	6.2	6.0
Affection	4.00	4.82**	3.7	4.8	3.5	5.2**	4.8	3.6

* $p < 0.05$; ** $p < 0.01$; *** $p < 0.001$.

To some extent this behaviour was preconceived on the part of the teachers. They believed that the children needed both warmth and firmness and sought to provide these through different but coherent styles. They described themselves as working well together this way. Nonetheless, it is probably not coincidental that these patterns are congruent with cultural stereotypes of adult males and females, and even stereotypes of the family. They chose roles with which they were comfortable. Our main point remains that to understand the relationship between teacher and child, in contrast to the teacher's style or the child's disposition, one needs to take into account *both* partners. This relationship, as is true for others, cannot be reduced to characteristics of each member added together. The 'A's do not elicit a certain amount of tolerance. Tolerance characterized their relationship with the female teacher but not very much their relationship with the male teacher. Tolerance and affection did characterize the relationship of the male teacher with the 'C's. It is not simply that he would never show such behaviours. We also would presume that the relationships of both male and female teachers with the children in this class were in fact constrained by the total system; that is, that the relationships of each of these teachers with children would be somewhat different if they were in a class with a different co-teacher, or with classes having different proportions of children with histories of secure attachment.

Interdependencies among family relationships

In our family research the primary goal at this stage is to illustrate the integrity and coherence of the family system. How such entire systems are internalized and carried forward by individuals will probably represent a major research theme in the field for the next decades. But as we view it, understanding how various dyadic relationships in the family are interdependent and how they serve and yet are influenced by the organized family system is an important foundation for the larger task. When applied beyond dyads to relationship systems, the principles of coherence and continuity we have outlined imply that each dyadic relationship is interdependent and each is capable of change in the service of overall stabilization. This interdependency may often be most apparent when dyads have distinctly different properties or when one dyad undergoes change. But it also may be seen clearly when dyadic patterns are notably atypical.

We have previously reported that when a mother behaves seductively towards her son she behaves in a hostile, derisive manner towards her daughter (Sroufe *et al*. 1985). Both seductiveness and derisiveness, even though based on codings of maternal behaviour, were viewed as *relationship* measures. Were seductiveness, for example, a simple trait of the mother it might be expected to be manifest towards daughters, which it was not, nor was it predictive of seductiveness toward other sons. Were seductiveness due only to some inherent child behaviour, then one would have expected no predictability to maternal behaviour toward the female sibling. As a relationship quality these patterns could not be reduced to properties of the individual members considered separately.

This network of relations was predicted from a view emphasizing the integrity of family relationships and capitalizing on the uniqueness of the seductive pattern. This gender-based, role-inappropriate behaviour was presumed to be based upon the mother's relationship history. Mothers who are seductive with their sons must have learned that adults cannot meet their needs with other adults, and that adults may seek to meet emotional needs through children (and that such efforts are gender-based). It was presumed (and empirically confirmed) that such mothers would report histories of paternal emotional exploitation, including, but not restricted to, incest. It was further inferred that these women were distant from their own mothers, without which the paternal exploitation would be unlikely to occur, and that the original marital pair also was characterized by distance (thus accounting for father's unmet needs). It was on this basis that it was hypothesized that these mothers would be hostile toward their daughters, recapitulating not only their own relationship with their mother but the total family configuration. Such behaviour also would reflect their low self-esteem and specific attitudes of female unworthiness. We would now hypothesize that male partners of these women will be at risk for sexually and/or emotionally exploiting the current daughters. Such cases have been identified, but as yet there are insufficient numbers for statistical confirmation with the Egeland and Sroufe sample.

We are pursuing the problem of coherence within the family relationship system by examining dyadic and triadic relationships in families with a 13-year-old child during a series of interaction tasks from the longitudinal study of Block and Block (1980). The initial focus of the adolescent family work was to see if qualities of the triadic relationship could be predicted from qualities of the two child–parent dyadic relationships. A series of rating scales were developed by J. Fleeson for either dyadic or triadic relationships (Table 2.5). For example, any member of a dyad or triad may express hostility/cynicism. The score for the relationship depends only on how much hostility is expressed, not on how many members express it. A few measures are focused on individuals in the dyads (e.g. 'child-like parent'). And one measure, *triangulation*, applies only to triads.

The first hypothesis predicted that if there was seductiveness in the opposite gender parent/child dyad (a cut-off score of 3 or higher on a 7-point scale), and if there was greater emotional engagement in the opposite gender dyad than the same gender dyad (a discrepancy on engagement scores of 2 points or higher), the independently assessed triad would be higher on triangulation

Table 2.5   *Rating scales for dyads or triads in adolescent families*

Emotional engagement—the degree to which members of the dyad or triad share a unique affective base. It may be positive, negative, or both, and it marks the depth or level of intimacy of the relationship.

Positive affective tone—the degree to which pleasure is taken in the shared process and in the other's contribution to the process.

Negative affective tone—a combination of signs of sadness, anxiety, anger, and other manifestations of negative affect, which also are scored separately.

Hostility–cynicism—derision, scorn, sneers, critical tones, hurtful comments. In contrast to anger there are direct and indirect comments that devalue the person's character. The focus seems to demean rather than to re-engage.

Conflict—disagreements and discord both concerning how to proceed and concerning the partner's behaviour.

Conflict resolution—degree to which members are able to reach solutions to conflicts that are satisfying to all persons.

Triangulation—the degree to which the major alliance appears to be between one parent and the child with the other parent occupying an outside (even detached) position.

Seductive relationship—'Courtship' behaviour between parent and child, manifest in physical behaviour (sitting very close, stroking, etc.), coyness, flirting, 'special' exchanges, and the like. There may be lingering looks, whispering, tones of privacy or preciousness.

Child-like parent—degree to which parent abdicates the adult role and behaves like a child.

Adult-like child—degree to which the child adapts an air of authority and status equal to the adult. The child adopts an adult voice and attitude.

Global scale 1—the security of each member within the relationship.

Global scale 2—the degree to which the relationship supports and promotes individual development.

Global scale 3—the degree to which the system promotes task engagement.

---

than triads not so characterized. Given the stronger connection and special nature of the relationship with the opposite gender parent (usually boys and mothers), it was a straight-forward prediction that fathers would occupy the out position in the triad and that the members of the other dyad would actively promote this status. The difference in the triangulation scores of the six cases so identified and the other 34 cases was in fact highly significant ($t = 4.79$, $p < 0.001$). The mother–son—father–son engagement discrepancy alone (nine cases) also yielded a highly significant results. In fact, for boys, maternal seductiveness in the dyad ($n = 9$) yielded a significant result ($t = 2.05$, $p < 0.05$).

Preliminary analysis also reveals other interesting findings. While sons in these families tended to be distant from their fathers in dyadic interaction, they were actively hostile to a greater degree when in the triad, thus promoting the exclusionary process. Moreover, in the triad the relationship between mother and father, assessed entirely independently, tended to be distant and/or hostile (for emotional engagement, $t = 2.69$, $p = <0.05$; for negative affectivity, $t = 2.02$, $p < 0.10$). Therefore, not only did dyadic interactions predict the nature of the triad as a whole, as required by the assumption of systems as hierarchically organized totalities, but qualitative aspects of child behaviour with the parent were shown to be influenced by the presence or absence of the other parent, and aspects of the mother–father relationship were predicted from the mother–child relationship. One knows something of importance about the mother–father relationship having only seen the relationship of either with their child. These are manifestations of the interdependence of relationships.

When these data are considered in combination with the previous findings that mothers who behave seductively toward their sons are derisive toward their daughters and report sexual or emotional exploitation by their fathers, the total relationship system outlined above seems well supported. We have a system of relationships where mother and father are distant, and there appears to be a cross-generational pair-bond between mother and son and, where present, father and daughter. Relationships between children and their same gender parents are distant or hostile.

An organizational perspective on family relationships

All systems are characterized by organization and integrity, with a co-ordination among levels and constraints upon subsystems with reference to the functioning of the whole. Social systems have, in addition, particular features, such as developing and volitional members and the simultaneous operation of multiple levels of organization. Unlike physical systems, like the drive train of a car, where the parts or elements of the system are readily defined, the parts of a social system may be considered to include the people, the roles which varying members may occupy, the rules which govern their behaviour, or, preferably, all of these at once. Social systems have both process and entity properties. Finally, family systems have further unique features. That is, there is a particular nature to the coherence and unity of family systems.

In trying to specify central systemic features of family organization, with the aim of understanding normative and pathological variations, we begin with the question of function. We will argue that function constrains family organization, and the nature of the particular organization has ramifications for the functions it serves. An organizational problem often will compromise the service of a function. We accept as general principles that organizations, like the termites' digestive system or the social organization of ants, arise in evolution to serve certain functions, and that certain patterns of relationship organization are more or less suitable for serving various functions. Thus, while pathology or maladaptation within families is usually defined in terms of the functioning of the system, an alternative is to consider whether particular patterns of family organization are optimally suited to the functions to be served.

Major functions of the family are the rearing of children and the meeting of adult intimacy/support needs. When these functions are considered simultaneously, the common organization of two adults of different genders and children under their care may be seen as a logical form. Moreover, generational boundary issues, gender relationships within the family, and rules concerning them, become prime foci for assessment.

To carry out these major family functions, certain distinctions must be maintained. First there are age distinctions. Adults must be distinguished from children, and all cultures distinguish at least infants, children, adults, and the aged. Secondly, all cultures distinguish males and females. We refer here not to a differentiation of roles, but to a distinction in terms of psychological identity. While a great deal of variety exists in terms of how such distinctions are maintained, we assume that significant deviation from the culture's general plan in this regard is commonly a sign of family disturbance. Separation of these functions is deeply rooted. In fact, developing a nurturing relationship with a child seems to be incompatible with developing a sexual relationship.

In the usual case an adult's intimacy needs are met by other adults and cross-gender intimacy needs are met within the parental pair-bond. Adults nurture children, and even where children are involved in child-care, caregiving is from older to younger child and under the ultimate supervision of adults (Whiting and Whiting 1975). Cultural and subcultural variations (extended families, etc.) add complexity but typically do not alter these organizational features, and the common pattern well serves the central family functions. In the prototype mother–father–child case, the adult pair-bond not only serves adult intimacy needs but also provides the emotional support and resilience for nurturing children. Children are not provided with the adult form of intimacy but neither are they obliged to nurture the adults. Adults must nurture children but they do so supported by their intimate adult relationship. Thus, when the typical family relationship pattern of our culture exists, the organization is suitable for fulfilling family functions. For this reason we emphasize assessments of generational boundary maintenance, gender-related expressions of intimacy, and patterns of nurturance in our family research.

Within our developmental/relationship theory we assume that adult intimacy needs can only truly be met by adults and that children develop the capacity to nurture by being nurtured. In the well-functioning family system, with intimate adults and well-nurtured children, children internalize and take forward into adulthood both the capacity and inclination to nurture children and the capacity for adult intimacy. In the major deviation we have explored, children are pressed into the service of adult intimacy needs. This is a function which they cannot fulfill, because the complexity of affect regulation in adult intimate relationships is beyond their cognitive and emotional capacity. When such a pattern exists, it typically indicates a failure of the adult pair to meet intimacy needs and also suggests that the adult-to-child nurturing function has been compromised. Children internalizing and carrying forward such a system would be limited both in the capacity for adult intimacy and the capacity to nurture children. These considerations again point to the importance of generational boundary maintenance and related organizational aspects in assessing families.

Another function of families concerns the learning of basic patterns of affect regulation. We mention this last because it does not have the same conceptual status as the other two functions. Nonetheless, it is closely related to them and marks another key arena for family assessment. In fact, affect regulation may be seen as serving the other family functions. Both adult intimacy and child-rearing, with its twin emphases of nurturance and control, are affectively laden. Adult intimacy is not possible without expression, sharing, and regulation of the full range of emotions, including feelings of anger, disappointment, and hurt. Adequate nurturing of children requires that adults both accept and limit the child's expressions of affect. In addition, they must minimize expressions of negative affect toward the child which derive from other relationships. This is an issue of affect regulation within the total system. Likewise, conflict is inherent in normal family functioning, with both conflict avoidance and the inability to resolve conflicts reflecting deviations from optimality. We assume that the child takes forward not only the general capacity for intimacy and nurturance but the particular patterns of affect regulation practiced in the family.

Organizational features of the family and affect regulation may be thought of as two sides of the same coin with respect to family assessment. If there are organizational anomalies, there will be problems with affect regulation. Likewise, difficulties in affect regulation will interfere with maintenance of functional family organization. When there are primary alliances across generations, that is, a failure to maintain generational boundaries, either distance or high negative affect between parents will result; either direct confrontation with conflicts will be avoided or conflict will be unresolved. In a circular manner, in the face of unresolved conflict or emotional distance (unregulated tension), marital partners will turn elsewhere for intimacy. Family pathology may be accessed either in the organizational or affect regulation domains; commonly these would be complementary.

In our initial efforts at family assessment, therefore, we have assessed affect expression and affect regulation, organizational variables (triangulation, parental seductiveness, child-like parent, parent-like child, comparative relations between mother–son, father–son, and mother–daughter, father–daughter variables), and certain 'balance' scales which are aimed at the interplay among these features. One scale focuses on the spontaneity–fearfulness of each member as an effort to get at the degree to which security or intimacy needs are being met. A second balance scale addresses the degree to which individuation of the child is promoted, with keys being elaboration, enthusiasm, and creativity in the interaction. A final scale is addressed to the coherence of the whole. The flexibility, persistence, and resourcefulness of the family in resolving conflict (and not being threatened by conflict), as well as the tolerance for ambiguity and capacity for exploring possibilities, are considered.

Certain predictions follow from considering simultaneously the child-rearing and intimacy functions of families. The intergenerational transmission of child exploitation is a well-demonstrated example. In our work we showed that mothers who were emotionally exploited by their own fathers were seductive with their sons and derisive toward their daughters (Sroufe *et al.* 1985). The prediction of derisiveness to daughters from the other two variables followed from the organizational and functional considerations discussed above. For fathers to be emotionally exploitive of their daughters, parental intimacy needs must not be met and the mother must not be fulfilling the childrearing functions (i.e. mother and daughter are distant or estranged). The daughter carries forward the lack of understanding of parent–child nurturance, the belief that adults may attempt to meet their needs with children (in a gender-based manner), and a non-optimal ability to regulate affect (especially angry feelings towards herself and her mother).

Two other predictions that have not yet been tested are:

1. When mothers cross boundaries with sons, fathers will do so with daughters (and vice versa). Clinically, this is seen commonly. For example, the mother of a child diagnosed as 'pervasive developmental disorder' reported to her therapist that the boy's father, her husband, had complained about the amount of attention she gave this son. He felt she was 'over-involved' with the boy. The mother went on to say that just recently her husband's daughter from a past relationship had come back into his life. The girl was spending weekends with him and the father devoted his time exclusively to her, a source of distress for the mother (see also Chapter 3, of this volume).

2. When there are parent–child boundary crossings, sibling relationships will fail to show the usual patterns of organization. For example, where a mother is seductive with a first-born son, this child will show parentification in some form (e.g. be unduly nurturant without the usual self-assertiveness of first-borns with sibs, or constantly play the 'teacher', or show role-reversal by

deferring to the younger child, or carry over the pattern of seductiveness into the sibling relationship). We believe that all of these will occur, and that as a set they will be more probable in sibling dyads where mother is seductive with the first-born. Preliminary analyses of 10 cases from the Egeland/Sroufe study suggest this is so.

Summary

Principles which govern relationships are illustrated with several empirical examples, and are then applied to relationships within the family. A primary principle concerns the coherence, integrity, or 'wholeness' of relationships. In part, this means that qualities of relationships, whether victimization in pre-school play-pairs, nurturance, and control in relationships between teachers and children, or emotional distance between marital partners, cannot be reduced to characteristics of individual participants. At the family level, coherence means that there is a total organization that may not be reduced to qualities of the relationship units within the family and that relationships within the family are constrained by the total organization. Moreover, given certain qualities in one relationship, other relationships in the family are further constrained in the service of maintaining the larger organization. This view is distinct from emphases on 'influences' of one relationship upon another. Rather, within this organizational perspective interdependency among relationships in the family is emphasized. The task of assessing family relationship organization may be guided by considerations of family functions (nurturing children, meeting adult intimacy needs). An emphasis on patterning in intergenerational and gender relationships follows. Illustrations of the usefulness of the approach are provided, including predictions of husband–wife relationship qualities from parent–child relationship qualities.

References

Ainsworth, M. D. S., Blehar, M. C., Waters, E., and Wall, S. (1978). *Patterns of attachment: a psychological study of the strange situation*. Erlbaum, Hillsdale, NJ.

Bandura, A. (1977). Self efficacy: toward a unifying theory of behavioral change. *Psychological Review* **84**, 191–215.

Block, J. H. and Block, J. (1980). The role of ego-control and ego-resiliency in the organization of behavior. In *Minnesota Symposia on Child Psychology*, Vol. 13 (ed. W. A. Collins). Erlbaum, Hillsdale, NJ.

Bowlby, J. (1969). *Attachment and loss*, Vol. 1, *Attachment*. Basic Books, New York.

Bowlby, J. (1973). *Attachment and loss*, Vol. 2, *Separation*. Basic Books, New York.

Bowlby, J. (1980). *Attachment and loss*, Vol. 3, *Loss sadness and depression*. Basic Books, New York.

Bowlby, J. (1982). *Attachment and loss*, Vol. 1, *Attachment*, (2nd edn.). Hogarth, London.

Caspi, A., Elder, G., and Bem, D. (1987). Moving against the world: life course patterns of explosive children. *Developmental Psychology* (in press).

Cottrell, L. (1969). Interpersonal interaction and the development of the self. In *Handbook of socialization, theory and research* (ed. D. Goslin). Rand McNally, Chicago.

Egeland, B. and Sroufe, L. A. (1981). Attachment and early maltreatment. *Child Development* **52**, 44–42.

Egeland, B., Jacobvitz, D., and Sroufe, L. A. (1987). Breaking the cycle of abuse. *Child Development* (in press).

Epstein, S. (1973). The self-concept revisited, or a theory of a theory. *American Psychologist* **28**, 404–16.

Epstein, S. (1980). The self-concept: a review and the proposal of an integrated theory of personality. In *Personality: basic aspects and current research* (ed. E. Staub), pp. 82–131. Prentice Hall, Englewood Cliffs, NJ.

Erickson, M., Egeland, B., and Sroufe, L. A. (1985). The relationship between quality of attachment and behaviour problems in preschool in a high risk sample. In *Growing points in attachment theory and research* (ed. I. Bretherton and E. Waters). *Monographs of the Society for Research in Child Development* **50** (1–2, Ser. no. 209), pp. 147–86.

Harter, S. (1983). Developmental perspectives on the self system. In *Handbook of child psychology* Vol. 4, *Socialization, personality, and social development* (ed. E. H. Hetherington, Series ed. P. Mussen), pp. 275–385. Wiley, New York.

Hinde, R. A. (1979). *Towards understanding relationships*. Academic Press, London.

Main, M. and Hesse, E. (in press). Lack of resolution of mourning. Its effects upon the second generation. In *Attachment in the preschool years* (ed. M. Greenberg, D. Cicchetti, and M. Cummings.) University of Chicago Press.

Main, M. and Weston, D. (1981). The quality of the toddler's relationship to mother and father. *Child Development* **52**, 932–40.

Matas, L., Arend, R. A., and Sroufe, L. A. (1978). Continuity of adaptation in the second year: the relationship between quality of attachment and later competence. *Child Development* **49**, 547–56.

Minuchin, S. (1974). *Families and family therapy*. Harvard University Press, Cambridge, Mass.

Motti, F. (1986). Relationships of preschool teachers with children of varying developmental histories. Unpublished doctoral dissertation. University of Minnesota.

Nelson, K. and Gruendel, J. (1981). Generalized event representations: basic building blocks of cognitive development. In *Advances in developmental psychology*, Vol. 1 (ed. M. Lamb and A. Brown) pp. 131–58. Erlbaum, Hillsdale, NJ.

Olweus, D. (1980). Bullying among school boys. In *Children and violence* (ed. R. Barnen). Academic Litterature, Stockholm.

Pancake, V. R. (1985). *Continuity between mother–infant attachment and ongoing dyadic peer relationships in preschool*. Biennial meeting of the Society for Research in Child Development, Toronto.

Pastor, D. (1981). The quality of mother–infant attachment and its relationship to toddlers; initial sociability with peers. *Developmental Psychology* **17**, 326–35.

Rosenberg, D. M. (1984). The quality and content of preschool fantasy play: correlates in concurrent social-personality function and early mother–child attachment relationships. Unpublished doctoral dissertation. University of Minnesota.

Rotter, J. (1966). Generalized expectancies for internal versus external locus of control of reinforcement. *Psychological Monographs: General and Applied* **80**, (1), 1–28.

Sroufe, L. A. (1979). The coherence of individual development. *American Psychologist* **34**, 834–41.

Sroufe, L. A. (1983). Infant-caregiver attachment and patterns of adaptation in preschool: the roots of maladaptation and competence. In *Minnesota Symposium in Child Psychology* (ed. M. Perlmutter), Vol. 16, pp. 41–81. Erlbaum, Hillsdale, NJ.

Sroufe, L. A. (1985). Attachment classification from the perspective of infant–caregiver relationships and infant temperament. *Child Development* **56**, 1–14.

Sroufe, L. A. (1986). Bowlby's contribution to psychoanalytic theory and developmental psychopathology. *Journal of Child Psychology and Psychiatry* **27**, 841–9.

Sroufe, L. A. and Fleeson, J. (1986). Attachment and the construction of relationships. In *Relationships and development* (ed. W. Hartup and Z. Rubin). Erlbaum, Hillsdale, NJ.

Sroufe, L. A. and Waters, E. (1977). Attachment as an organizational construction. *Child Development* **48**, 1184–99.

Sroufe, L. A., Jacobvitz, D., Mangelsdorf, S., DeAngelo, E., and Ward, M. J. (1985). Generational boundary dissolution between mothers and their preschool children: a relationship systems approach. *Child Development* **56**, 317–25.

Troy, M. and Sroufe, L. A. (1987). Victimization among preschoolers: The role of attachment relationship history. *Journal of the American Academy of Child Psychiatry*, **26**, 166–72.

Ward, M. J. (1983). Maternal behavior with firstborns and secondborns in the same family: evidence for consistency in family relations. Unpublished doctoral dissertation. University of Minnesota.

Whiting, B. and Whiting, J. (1975). *Children of six cultures: a psychocultural analysis.* Harvard University Press, Cambridge, Mass.

3

Child development in a network of relationships*
MARIAN RADKE-YARROW, JOHN RICHTERS, AND W. ELBERT WILSON

This essay is an exploration of the promise and problems in a relationships approach to investigating child development within the context of the family. A focus on relationships challenges psychology's customary ways of thinking about the child. The long-prevailing orientation in child-development research has been a view of the child as an independent entity. Kessen (1979) has captured this orientation very well:

'The child—like the pilgrim, the cowboy, and the detective on television—is invariably seen as a free-standing isolable being who moves through development as a self-contained and complete individual . . . Impulses are in the child; traits are in the child; thoughts are in the child; attachments are in the child.' (p. 219)

In the study of relationships, as defined by Hinde and Stevenson-Hinde (1987), the individual is dealt with 'not as an isolated entity but as a social being, formed by and forming part of a network of relationships which are crucial to its integrity.' (pp. 1–2):

'When two individuals interact on successive occasions over time, each interaction may affect subsequent ones, and we speak of them as having a relationship. Their relationship includes not only what they do together, but the perceptions, fears, expectations and so on that each has about the other and about the future course of the relationship, based in part on the individual histories of the two interactants and the past history of their relationship with each other. . . . While the nature of an interaction depends in part on the individuals involved, it is affected also by the relationship in which it is embedded. . . . However, that is not all . . . Each relationship is influenced by the social nexus of other relationships in which it is embedded. . .' (pp. 2–3)

This formulation presents a challenge. What are the implications for research of proceeding with a relationships orientation? Can one translate

*This work was supported by the National Institute of Mental Health, Bethesda, Maryland and by the John D. and Catherine T. MacArthur Foundation, Research Network on the Transition from Infancy to Early Childhood, Chicago, Illinois.

these conceptualizations into empirical data and analyses? Our plan of inquiry is first to comment briefly on where the field now stands in the study of relationships. Next, we use data from current studies in our laboratory to explore relationships. Finally, we review the venture by restating some key relationships issues.

Relationships in psychology

The concept of relationships is not new in psychology. In psychoanalytic theory, explanations of behaving and experiencing, and, indeed, development in terms of the id (wants and desires), ego (the 'knowing' self), and super-ego (knowledge of societal values) are cast in relationship terms; so, also, is the structure of intra- and interpsychic processes between patient and therapist. In Lewinian field theory, the equation, behaviour is a function of person and environment, is formulated in terms of meaning to the individual (e.g. the perceptions of the present field, the reconstructions of the past, and the expectations for the future), and includes the embeddedness and overlap among psychological situations. Similarly, the underpinning of family systems theory is a formulation of multiple relationships.

Thus, psychology has traditions in which a relationships perspective is central. However, relationships have not been an organizing research emphasis over the past decades. Rather, various elements of experience— intrapsychic processes, behaviour, cognition—have been investigated separately, always with the individual as the primary unit of study.

Developmental psychology has tended to follow the rest of psychology. Relationships (with a few exceptions, such as attachment) have not been a prominent focus. In the substantial body of research concerning parental influences on the child, where one should expect to find a relationships approach well represented, such is not the case. Investigations have been focused primarily on behavioural interactions. Researchers have not been much concerned with the perceptions, affects, and expectations of the individual; nor, with notable exceptions, have they emphasized the embeddedness of the child in family relationships and family social contexts (Bronfenbrenner 1979).

Recent reviewers of this field have drawn dreary conclusions, voicing deep disappointment in the less-than-convincing empirical evidence of family influences on the child (Maccoby and Martin 1983). In many studies no statistical associations have been found; where links have been established they have often been very weak. One conclusion has been that the effects of family experiences on children are so variable as to be of little use in understanding child outcomes, and that further research efforts to specify family influences are likely to go unrewarded.

Before accepting this position, we need to be aware that the critiques of progress in our knowledge of family influences are based largely on disappointments in the *results* of research. They have not, by and large, addressed the *theoretical* and *methodological* structures on which the research has been based. Dismay over the size of effects may be a direct result of our lack of clearly stated theoretical presumptions, a point to which we will return later. That the consequences of early conditions are not uniform is by no means unique to the study of family influences. Nor does the lack of uniformity in developmental outcomes suggest a weak or transient influence of early experience. As Cohen and Parmelee (1983) have pointed out, early signs of neurological or physiological deficits in infants do not predict a uniformity of dysfunction in later childhood. For some children there is continuity; for many others, later functioning is well within the range of normal; in both cases, later functioning may be moderated by a host of intervening influences. Importantly, though, one does not set aside the significance of early signs and the need to understand the bases for their different effects on children's functioning. The case is similar for family influences on offspring.

Also, the research data of developmental psychology do not seem to be capturing what appears obvious to the naïve observer of society: children are not immune to family disorganization and behavioural pathology, or to family integrity; children do not respond in a random fashion to these conditions; there are substantial predictable consequences for children's development (Segal and Yahraes 1978). Perhaps in our desire to document carefully these specific influences, we have lost the whole.

By placing the study of relationships back on the research agenda, Hinde has presented the discipline with a challenging perspective for addressing these resistant research problems. A relationships approach offers promise, provided it can be translated into paradigms and procedures that allow us to integrate different elements and levels of experiencing and behaving. The concrete challenge to research is

(1)   to acquire data on interactions between and among family members— over time, across relevant situations, and in relation to social contextual factors;

(2)   to develop data sources that provide insight into the meaning of these experiences to the participants; and

(3)   to consider interactions and relationships from a developmental point of view.

Our objective in this paper is to attempt an application of this relationship perspective to an existing body of data on young children and their families.

Interactions and relationships—findings from NIMH studies

We are drawing on current research at NIMH (Radke-Yarrow in press) in which we are studying families with and without a history of psychiatric disorder. Our interest is in studying the processes of child rearing and child development in these families. For this purpose, we have developed a paradigm through which we assess a range of parental functioning over time, and we follow the children's social and emotional development over the same time—from early childhood to adolescence. At present, assessments have been carried out at two points in the children's development. We have data at many levels, across situations, and over time, giving us rich opportunities for examining interactions and relationships.

For most of this paper, our sample was 108 pairs of siblings and their parents. The older sibling in each pair was 5–7 years of age when the study began; the younger sibling was between 2 and 3.5 years of age. Middle-class families ($n = 97$) were selected as our primary focus; a small number ($n = 11$) of very low-income families were also included. Except in this latter group, most families were intact. Mothers were either without psychiatric disorder ($n = 42$), or had a diagnosis of unipolar ($n = 51$) or bipolar ($n = 15$) depression.

Our research strategy was to obtain extensive observations of family functioning. During the first assessment period, the mothers and their two children were observed and videotaped in a research apartment (a suite of rooms with an adjoining bathroom and kitchenette) for a series of three half-days for mother and younger child, and one half-day for mother with both children. Time in the apartment was scripted to include a sequence of controlled but natural situations representative of ordinary day-to-day family experiences. Situations were chosen and created on the basis of their relevance to crucial domains of child-rearing and family functioning, including those that would allow us to evaluate patterns of parental control, caregiving, teaching, managing daily routines, decision making, responding to new experiences, and reacting to stressful as well as pleasant circumstances. Children were observed with their mother, with a sibling, with mother and sibling together, and with non-family adults. Similar observational procedures were repeated during the second assessment period, three years later, when the father, too, was present for observations in the flat, and when the younger child was observed with a peer. In addition to the videotaped observations, there were interviews with mother and father, various tests of the children (cognitive, neuropsychological, and physical), psychiatric evaluations of all participants, and teacher reports.

We are limited in our analyses of relationships by the current stage of the study. For present purposes, we have focused mostly on mothers and children from the initial assessment period. From the follow-up, the available data were derived from psychiatric assessments, interviews with the fathers, and observations of peer interactions.

The route we will follow through our data is mapped by the Hinde and Stevenson-Hinde concept of relationships and a relationships approach (quoted earlier). We begin with the construction of an affect-based index of the mother–child relationship, which we then use to examine:

(1)   how the mother–child relationship is associated with other family relationships and interactions;

(2)   how it is influenced by larger social group contexts;

(3)   how it depends on characteristics of both mother and child;

(4)   how the children's early relationships with mother predict their later relationships outside the family;

(5)   how relationships with father also contribute; and

(6)   the meaning of relationships to children.

An affective dyadic relationship

Parents and children relate to each other on many dimensions (e.g. love, authority, dependence) and in many kinds of interaction (involving care, control, instruction, companionship). Through all of these run some core themes for the participants, such as security, trust, closeness, etc. We reasoned that an important element of the *meaning* of interactions between partners in a relationship is reflected in their expressed affect. We therefore developed a measure through which we might tap into a significant aspect of these underlying themes. To capture this information, we obtained a minute-by-minute record of the dominant moods and emotions expressed by mother and child during their time alone together in the flat (for details, see Radke-Yarrow *et al.* 1987). Negative mood, specific negative emotions (fear, anger, sadness, anxiety, tension), specific positive emotions (happiness, tenderness, pleasure, affection), and neutral states were coded. These records were based on approximately 400 minutes, obtained on three days, typically scheduled within a two- to three-week period. Thus, a profile of affect was obtained for child and for mother while in each other's company. For present purposes we used the percentage of minutes in which negative affect (i.e. negative mood plus specific negative emotions) was expressed as our index measure.

This procedure yielded separate negativity scores for mother and child. The distributions of affect scores were positively skewed. Therefore, they were represented in the analyses that follow in terms of quartile placement. On the basis of these scores, we next derived a measure of concordance between partners by comparing their quartile scores. Using this same procedure, we also derived a relationship index for mother and older child, as well as for siblings. This affect measure begins to satisfy criteria for a relationship index by being based on interactions over time, across varied situations, with a history, and expectations for a future. In interpreting our assessment of affect as an index of relationship, we recognize that we are dealing with one aspect of the mother–child relationship, and at quite a global level. However, the dimension of affect is, we assume, a central quality of a relationship at any developmental level.

Affective relationships within the family

We begin by presenting some defining qualities of the mother–young child relationship in the families we studied: the absolute levels of negative affect they expressed in each other's company, and the stability of this negativity in their interactions. Not surprisingly, mothers and children varied considerably on this index, ranging from those who expressed negative affect during less than 1 per cent of their time together, to those who were negative during more than 50 per cent of their time. Across settings in which mother and child were alone together, the mean level of negative affect expressed by mothers was 22 per cent. Similarly, the mean level of negative affect expressed by children was 20 per cent. This index taps a fairly characteristic tone of mother–child interaction, showing stability over a three-week period between visits to our laboratory $(r = 0.62)$.

Within-dyad concordance

Expressed as the percentage of dyads in which partners were concordant at either high or low levels of negativity (based on a median split), the concordance was 66 per cent, with the remaining 34 per cent falling into discordant categories. When mothers were in the lowest quartile on negativity, only 15 per cent of their children were above the median in negativity. However, when mothers were in the highest quartile of negativity, 79 per cent of their children fell above the median in negativity. Of 108 mother–child pairs, in only two pairs were mother and child in opposite outside quartiles. Overall levels of negativity were significantly higher within dyads in which the mother had a history of depression; this resulted in a significantly higher number of dyadic relationships that were concordant in negativity.

Aside from supporting the meaningfulness of an affective code for the mother–child relationship, the high accord within the dyad indicates a rather remarkable interdependence between members of the pair. One might regard this accord as maternal influence, and, if so, it suggests an avenue for very early learning by the toddler of an affective view of the world. The impact of the child on the mother must also be a contributor, as must their mutual influences on one another. Only detailed longitudinal study can dissect these processes.

Between-dyad concordance in negativity

A central theme in family systems theory and in the Hinde and Stevenson-Hinde relationship perspective is one of interdependencies among subsystems within the family. There is a dynamic element to this perspective, an over-time process. With the present data, we were able to examine only cross-sectional associations between dyads that might reflect such a dynamic. The mother–child dyad was examined in relation to sibling systems. In 67 per cent of the families with a relationship between mother and younger child that was concordant in negativity, there was also a concordant–negative relationship between mother and older child, ($\chi^2 = 13.38$, $p < 0.01$). Not only did parent and child relationships correspond with one another, there was also an intergenerational link. In 83 per cent of the families with a concordant–negative relationship between mother and child, the sibling interaction pattern was also concordant negative, ($\chi^2 = 15.23$, $p < 0.01$).

The triadic situation (mother and both children together) did not greatly change the concordance within relationships, although introduction of the older child did significantly increase mothers' levels of negative affect. Dyadic mother–child relationships that were positively concordant remained so in the triadic context in 64 per cent of the cases. Those that were discordant remained so in only 45 per cent of the cases.

These group tendencies provide a sense of close interdependencies of subsystems within families in general. They also alert one, however, to the possible differences in patterning within individual families. If one is interested in characterizing the individual child as a member of the family, we see that his or her relationship with mother alone leaves out of consideration various kinds of within-family variations that might materially influence the meaning of the child's relationship with the mother. For example, if a positive mother–child relationship exists in a totally harmonious family context, if it exists in the context of a rivalrous sibling relationship, or if it is embedded in a very negative relationship between mother and sibling, we should expect that other dimensions (e.g. security, trust) of the mother–child relationship would be altered, and thereby its significance in the development of the child would be changed.

In focusing on the affective dimension of the mother–younger child relationship, we underscore the fact that this is but one dimension of their relationship. Other dimensions, such as reciprocity, caregiving, supportiveness, trust, intimacy, and security, hold potential for explaining variance in the quality of relationships not necessarily accounted for by the others.

Processes underlying associations

We have seen that there is a kind of affective interdependency among subsystems within families. We have paid little attention, however, to processes that underlie the associations within and across dyads that we have described. The investigation of processes requires not simply describing associations but following through to establish the mechanisms they reflect. In a limited way, our data allow us to explore sources of influence on the mother–child relationship.

Social class and the mother–child relationship

The social context that most visibly differentiates families is social class. Class is a factor that has consistently been associated in the literature with differences in family functioning and child development. We therefore examined class differences as a possible influence on the affective relationship. We divided our sample at the median on the Hollingshead classification, and also compared our group of 11 mothers of very low socio-economic (SES) status with 11 mothers from middle-class families, matched for age and gender of child, as well as diagnosis of mother. The low-SES group was exclusively Black, and eight mothers were single parents; we were not able to match groups in these factors. In both comparisons, mothers' relationships with their children were significantly more negative in the lower-SES families. Mothers in the impoverished SES group were negative 59 per cent of the time with their younger children, while mothers in the matched middle-class group were negative only 28 per cent of the time. Similarly, low-SES mothers were negative with their older children 71 per cent of the time, compared with middle-class mothers who were negative only 25 per cent of the time.

It is important to try to understand what underlies this association between maternal negativity and lower SES. Inspection of the specific emotion components of mothers' negative affect provides a lead; there was a difference in the negative content of the lower- and middle-SES groups. Although frequency indices of tension, anxiety, and sadness did not differ by social class, anger was significantly more frequent in the low-SES mothers. Still, for most mothers, anger represented only a small proportion of the total time that they were with their children. It seems likely, however, that anger in low-SES families may smoulder into the affect that we assess as negative mood, and dominate this mood, which accounts for a much larger percentage of the time. There was some support for this idea of underlying anger when we examined the profiles of anger in some of the very low-SES mothers: the frequency of their anger, *per se*, was extremely and uniquely high, sufficient to interpret it as the major and unrelenting context of family interactions. Moreover, in these families, compared to middle-class families, anger was not relieved by the occurrence of occasional positive interactions.

Family stability and the mother–child relationship

We have interpreted the data just presented as suggesting the possibility that the link between low-SES and negative mother–child relationships may be through the factors that give rise to anger. We know that conditions of poverty and border-line existence bring instability and unpredictability to everyday living, and that irritability and anger may certainly fester in such chronic conditions. Therefore, we looked to patterns of daily living in our families that reflected instability and unpredictability in life circumstances. On the basis of an intensive family life events interview with the mother, families were classified as stable ($n = 48$) or chaotic ($n = 35$). A third group ($n = 25$) of families fell between these extremes and was not included in this analysis.

Negative affect in relation to each other was found to be significantly higher in mothers (34 per cent) and children (29 per cent) from chaotic homes than in mothers (12 per cent) and children (21 per cent) from stable homes. Importantly, this difference between chaotic and stable families was maintained when social class was held constant. However, when the link between social class and a negative mother–child relationship was examined with level of chaos held constant, the association was no longer significant. One avenue of linkage between social class and negativity in the mother–child relationship thus appears to be through the corrosive hardship of unpredictability and disorganization.

The demonstrated influence of social–contextual factors on the mother–child relationship raises one of the most interesting questions for analyses of intrafamily influences or associations; namely, is the entire pattern of influences or associations within the family altered by context? Are factors that influence the child (or is the magnitude of the influences) changed by the context in which they occur? We used this social contextual factor of family stability to explore how it affects the influence of the mother–child relationship on accomplishing socialization goals. In the analyses that follow, we examine how the mother's success in regulating and controlling her child's behaviour is related to her affective relationship with the child, and whether this association is influenced by the stability–chaos dimension of family life.

Family stability and maternal influence attempts

An important developmental task for 2–3-year-olds is coming to terms with the control required by society, initially in the person of the caregiver. Mothers' success in socializing their children should, according to the child-rearing literature, be associated with positive, nurturing mother–child relationships. We inquired whether this association held regardless of the family context in which these interrelations were played out. Drawing on data from the NIMH study (Kochanska *et al.* 1987), we examined two indices of control interactions as they related to both the mother–child relationship and family stability.

The first was an index of the extent to which the mother was successful in gaining initial compliance from her child following an influence attempt. Our second index reflected the extent to which the mother used strong or harsh enforcement techniques without explanation as a strategy for dealing with her child's non-compliance. We focused on this technique as a strategy more likely to be employed by less adept and less sensitive mothers. Our expectations were that:

(1)   high rates of initial compliance would be associated with more positive mother–child relationships; and

(2)   maternal use of harsh enforcement in the face of non-compliance would be associated with negative mother–child relationships (see also Hetherington, this volume).

Neither expectation was supported without taking family context into consideration as a mediating factor. In particular, higher rates of initial child compliance were related to more positive mother–child relationships only in stable families ($r = 0.42$). Similarly, maternal use of harsh enforcement was associated with more negative mother–child relationships only in chaotic families ($r = 0.49$).

Thus, the quality of the mother–child affective relationship is linked differently to various rearing processes and outcomes, depending on the broader contexts of the family living pattern. The mechanisms of linkage between family stability–chaos and specific patterns of influence within the family are a matter of speculation at this point. However, it is clear that neither the child, nor the parent, nor their relationship can be regarded as completely 'isolable', 'free-standing' entities uninfluenced by the contexts in which they are embedded.

Gender as a mediating factor

In a manner analogous to our inquiry into factors in the social context as modifiers, we have also investigated gender of the child as a person-variable possibly influencing the mother–child affective relationship, and tried to understand some of the underlying factors. In our earlier analyses of the mother–child dyad, gender of child did not appear to influence either absolute level of, or concordance in, negativity within or across dyads. But to ask simply whether boys and girls relate differently to, or elicit different responses from, their mothers is a question too coarsely grained. It may be necessary to inquire whether mothers relate in the same way to boys and girls who behave similarly, or whether the same behaviour of a mother is responded to similarly by boys and girls? Thus, we have asked questions of our data similar to those posed by Simpson and Stevenson-Hinde (1985) concerning gender. In particular, we have focused on the societally defined, gender-typed characteristics of shyness and aggression, and have asked whether mothers' affective responding is differentially influenced by these qualities as a function of whether their toddlers are girls or boys. Our assessment of shyness was based on observer ratings of child behaviour during a home visit before the family was seen in our laboratory. Aggression, because of its relatively low occurrence during the home visit and in our laboratory was a summed score of aggression-related problems reported by mothers on the Achenbach Checklist (1983). On neither variable did the means for boys and girls differ. Other measures of child and mother behaviours that we examined in connection with gender, aggression, and shyness were based on our observations of them in the apartment.

Our first question was whether mothers responded similarly to aggression in boys and girls, and to shyness in boys and girls. The answer is 'no'; mothers behaved differently with children who were aggressive or shy, depending on the gender of the child. For boys, aggression was significantly associated with mothers' anger and unhappiness; aggression in girls, however, was not significantly associated with maternal affective expression in the apartment. Turning to shyness, we found again that a picture of differential maternal responding emerged. Mothers seemed not to be pleased with shyness in boys. Boys' shyness was associated with less joyfulness in their mothers. Mothers' interactions with shy girls, in contrast, were characterized by tenderness, affection, and sadness (see also Chapter 4).

To consider possible origins of mothers' differential responses, we analysed the behavioural correlates of aggression and shyness in boys and girls. We found that for boys, aggression was significantly associated with numerous unfavourable characteristics in their own behaviour; it was positively related to their anger and negative moods, and inversely related to their joyfulness, affectionate behaviour, and social competence. In contrast, for girls, aggression was unrelated to these or to other characteristics of their behaviour that we were able to assess. Shyness, too, had different correlates for boys and girls. Shyness in boys was associated with tension and negative mood—a pattern consistent with their mother's lower levels of joyfulness. In girls, however, shyness was associated with a more complex set of personal qualities, including tension, sadness, lower levels of anger and social competence, and higher levels of affection and compliance. Mothers might reasonably be expected to have ambivalent reactions—of concern for the shy daughters' tension, sadness, and lack of social competence, and of pleasure and affection for the shy, affectionate, and compliant girl.

One conclusion might be that mothers respond not to aggression or shyness, *per se*, but to the patterns of interrelated behaviour of which aggression and shyness are a part. In such an interpretation, we have inferred a direction of influence. An alternative direction might be considered; namely, mothers' anger and unhappiness may generate aggression from boys, but not from girls; mothers' joylessness may produce shy responding from boys, and similarly mothers' sad but affectionate behaviour may produce shyness in girls.

By drawing on another source of data in our study, we learned a bit more about the processes involved. We found that a characteristic of the mother also entered into this relationship, and we learned *how* tenderness and sadness occurred in mother–child interactions. Namely, a subgroup of depressed mothers in our sample (Radke-Yarrow *et al.* 1987) engaged in prolonged physical affection with their daughters in what appeared to be a kind of 'security blanket' sense. This affection was often mixed with mothers' sadness and tension, which appeared to draw the daughters into their mothers' own depressed states. Of course it may be that shy girls are predisposed to this kind of relationship with their mothers, or perhaps mothers' enmeshing behaviour with their daughters actually engenders withdrawn/shy behaviour. Both are plausible candidates for an interpretation of the gender-linked correlations. A point to emerge from our consideration of gender in relation to mothers' and children's responding to each other is that ostensibly simple gender-linked associations are not easily interpreted and cannot readily be extracted from their contexts.

Predictions from toddlerhood to six years of age

Developmental psychologists have had a long-standing interest in what one is able to predict about the child's development from information concerning earlier experiences. The data that we have presented on the mother–child relationship and its associations with other relationships and variables during the toddler period provide a base from which we can explore this question. Does the relationship at the toddler level predict behaviour at 6 years? Within the constraints imposed by our current stage of analyses, we have made assessments at 6 years of a theoretically relevant outcome, the children's competence and comfort in interpersonal relationships. One assessment was of competence with a peer, based on observations of a period of play with an unfamiliar peer. A second assessment was made from a standard psychiatric interview, the Child Assessment Schedule (Hodges *et al.* 1981), which includes questions about family, self, and friends. We limited our analyses here to information about the child's problems and skills in relating to others, and to the child's perceptions of his/her family. Thus, two somewhat different links over time are examined. Because the psychiatric interview probes especially into family relationships, associations across time represent continuities within the family system. By examining the child's behaviour with a peer, we were following the line of theory and the findings of other research (Matas *et al.* 1978) in which it is assumed that the young child, through his/her experience in the mother/child relationship, acquires the security and the skills needed in moving out into peer relationships.

Linkages were found between the child's affective relationship with mother and social competence with a peer three years later ($r = 0.40$). This association was based on the concordance measure of the mother–child relationship and a composite score on peer social competence. When mother and child were positively concordant in affect, the children's mean score on competence was 1.27 (range -2.4 to 1.68); when child was positive and mother was negative, or when mother was positive and child was negative, the means were 0.48 and 0.36, respectively; when both mother and child were negative, the child's mean level of peer competence was 0.08 (significantly different from positive concordance).

Individual scores on negative affect (i.e. mother's affect with child, child with mother, sibling with sibling) were also examined in relation to child's status at 6 years. For both boys and girls, the *child's* affect with mother was the best predictor of competence in the peer situation: the child's negative affect was significantly negatively correlated with later social competence ($r = -0.35$). It was the *mother's* negative affect in the toddler period that (meagrely) predicted the psychiatrist's assessment of the child's problems with relationships.

Although we have spoken of these associations as links between relationships in toddlerhood and competence at 6 years, they can not, of course, be interpreted solely as influences of earlier upon later relationships. Concurrent relationships at 6 years and conditions or contexts spanning the years undoubtedly also play a role. Some of these possible contributions were examined.

Links between father–child and mother–child behaviour at 6 years were also analysed. Based on interviews, fathers were rated on their planfulness and involvement in their parenting role. Mothers' behaviour was rated, based on 40 minutes of observation in the flat and on their general competence in handling interpersonal interactions with adults and children. Favourable ratings on each parent were positively and *independently* associated with children's compatible and positive initiating behaviours with the peer. Thus, both early relationships and concurrent good parental functioning contributed to the social functioning of the child.

The context of family chaos, which earlier was shown to relate to negative affect in the mother–toddler relationship, was re-examined as an enduring and intervening family condition, possibly modifying the linkages from 3 years to 6 years. And, indeed, we found such a modification to be the case. Within stable families only, the association between a negative mother–child relationship at 3 years and impaired competence with the peer at 6 years was maintained, and appeared over a range of indices of interpersonal skills in the peer setting. In chaotic families, however, all over-time associations had disappeared. Why should this be the case? Is it because in chronic conditions of chaos, a mother's positive availability may be too variable and unpredictable? Is it because other disruptive relationships within the family (e.g. between parents, between siblings) assume magnified importance? Or, do the stressful events and circumstances (not relationships) threaten the child's psychological integrity and interfere with developmental processes regardless of the mother–child relationship? Answers to these types of questions will not be easy to come by, emphasizing in one more way the interdependency of variables and relationships out of which the child's behaviour develops.

The child's perspective

The interview with the children from which psychiatric assessments were made also allowed us to sample the 'meaning' of parent–child relationships from the child's perspective. Each child answered direct questions about mother, father, and family. One of the challenges in investigating relationships is to try to assess not only the behaviour of the participants but also the experience or meaning that the interactions have for them (Hinde and Stevenson-Hinde 1987). How one conceives of meaning is, of course, a first hurdle (see Chapter 18). Assessing how children experience themselves and their social worlds presents very considerable difficulty.

Because of the paucity of this kind of information, it seems reasonable to communicate the small inklings that we tapped in our data. Interviewing our 6-year-olds about their families and themselves was informative. In the concreteness of their representations, the children often conveyed experience quite vividly (e.g. 'I'm not proud of me but I'm proud of my dad'; 'I'm afraid when my mother and father fight that they could hurt themselves'; 'I get a stomach ache when I come home from school and I'm with my dad'). From such responses, we believe we have begun to see their relationships at another level, which if carefully interpreted should refine assessments. However, there are complexities in obtaining these data, as young children are more and less verbally fluent, more and less open, and more and less insightful. A simple distinction among children on the basis of their verbal representations of their parents would not optimally capture meaning for the individual child. Even with this coarse classification, however, we found that this distinction was associated with differences in fathers' parenting. Those fathers rated from an interview as least planful and involved with their children were represented less favourably in their children's descriptions of them than were fathers who were rated as planful. We would take this as some encouragement for the reinstatement of interviews with children as adjuncts to behavioural observations—with the caution that the content of children's reports be interpreted carefully.

Something similar might be said for giving consideration to indirect approaches to ascertaining the meaning of relationships to the child. Projectives have been 'out of date' in mainstream psychology for several decades. Their contribution in partnership with behavioural data, however, deserves another look. Our data provided anecdotal evidence on this point. The older children (6-year-olds at initial assessment) responded to a set of pictures of ambiguous scenes of family interaction. We focused here on their interpretation of the picture of an older child approaching a younger child as the mother enters the room (Zahn-Waxler *et al.* 1987). They were asked what the mother would do. Of 96 children, 21 expected the mother to act as a punishing agent. When the affective mother–child relationships of these children and of those children who interpreted mother's entrance benignly were compared, the former group of children in reality had mothers who were significantly more negative with them (44 per cent of the time) than the children who interpreted the picture with a neutral or happy theme (18 per cent of the time). This difference was repeated when other dyadic and triadic interactions of the mother were compared. Importantly, those children who described a theme involving mother-as-punisher were *not themselves* more negative when interacting in any of the contexts in which we observed them, i.e. they were apparently not projecting their own negativity. Rather, the images or models that they brought to the interpretation of the picture seemed to reflect accurately the levels of maternal negativity to which they had been exposed.

Further, the children who represented the mother-as-punisher compared with those who did not were significantly more likely to be rated by the psychiatrist as having problems in the domain of relationships, and significantly more often described their families in problem terms. Although our data relating to meaning are fragmentary, the children's representations of their parents and family in response to direct questioning and in indirect ways, provide approximations of meaning which contribute to an understanding of the child's experiences of relationships with parent. From their expressed perceptions, fears, and expectations of parent, we come closer to the working images that children carry around with them.

Comments and conclusions

A relationships approach to understanding child development introduces complexity with respect to research models, data that are gathered, and analytic strategies that are applied. Using the framework presented by Hinde and Stevenson-Hinde (1987) we have explored such an approach, drawing on data from our ongoing study of young children and their families. We have found redundant evidence that significant incremental information is gained by considering the child in contexts and relationships. The child is not a pilgrim, detached and self-contained, but very much influencing and being influenced. We have seen that the mother–child relationship, indexed by the affect in their interactions, is related to characteristics of the child's functioning, both concurrently and over time. We have also seen that the nature of the mother–child relationship and its linkages to child functioning may be altered in important ways by contextual factors such as social class and family stability. We have noted how the context of family chaos, in particular, alters the quality of relationships in the family, the ways in which networks of relationships are organized in the family, and the factors that are critical influences on the child. Analyses of gender-of-child influences on relationships illustrated the significance of contexts in another way. Here it is the context of person variables in which a specific characteristic is embedded. It was shown that person variables are differently organized in boys and girls. This finding has implications for how gender differences and mothers' responses to gender differences are interpreted.

We would like to conclude with some thoughts concerning methods that are highlighted by these explorations of a relationships approach. An investigation of relationships inevitably takes one into a whirl of associations, and just as inevitably presents the problem of interpreting them. It is here that serious pursuit of mechanisms or processes versus hazardous theorizing about exploratory associations divides research. In the first instance, there is systematic follow-through to test alternate explanations of associations. In our data we have made a small start by unwrapping SES and identifying at least one process underlying its association with mother–child relationships. Also, exploration of the differing contexts of maternal affect experiences by sons and daughters of depressed mothers is another such effort. Such testing of alternative theories regarding associations is well illustrated in the papers by both Engfer and Rutter (this volume). The strongest approach to process questions is truly longitudinal data, as opposed to follow-up data or retrospective organizations of experience by the individual. Spaced follow-up assessments may miss critical events and developments. In retrospective accounts, the individual almost inevitably will create coherence within his/her own perspective and needs (Radke-Yarrow et al. 1970). In other words, research into developmental processes probably has no short cuts.

To emphasize the need for exploration of research methods for investigating developmental processes we will use our own research to raise questions and support possibilities. Our research interest is in understanding the divergent developmental courses of children whom we have been studying since early childhood. From the rich body of data available on these children, we are able to identify many patterns of associations and relationships. For example, clinically depressed mothers, compared with well mothers, are more likely to be ineffective in controlling their children (Kochanska *et al.* 1987), are less able to handle stressful situations involving their children (Breznitz and Sherman 1987), are more likely to make negative attributions to their children (Radke-Yarrow *et al.* 1987), and their children are less likely to have a secure attachment relationship (Radke-Yarrow *et al.* 1985). Each of these dimensions accounts for some variance on initial assessments and for some significant associations with later behavioural status. However, such findings, although informative, are still associations and products of conventional analyses of group differences. An additional level of research, of course, follows—one that utilizes the predictive or explanatory strength that comes from consideration of the combinations of conditions and relationships that make a difference in the developmental trajectories of individual children. But still another strategy is needed that fosters a process of discovery. It is the utilization of individual case histories. The case study has connotations that turn away the researcher. But we would suggest that there is a systematic way in which a case approach can be used.

For example, from our data, we have identified small groups of children who satisfy stringent criteria of homogeneity with respect to a given 'outcome', e.g. children who are highly and stably shy and inhibited (Bridges-Cline and Kochanska, unpublished manuscript), or children who by middle childhood are preoccupied with thoughts of suicide, or children who are coping competently despite conditions of both high genetic and environmental risk (Radke-Yarrow and Sherman in press). We are searching their developmental histories individually, for conditions and relationships that appear to have mattered in their development. There is an important difference between these case studies and conventional case studies. We are using the data (observations, experimental and test data, interviews, informant reports) that we have systematically obtained on all children, *prospectively*. In these data are the details and nuances of relationships within the family, the introspections of the child, the variations in their responding from which one can formulate hypotheses. Such individual cases and individual hypotheses, overlaid on one another, can identify factors apparently shaping children toward given outcomes. The case studies are thus the starting points, and often new starting points, for hypotheses that provide the bases for formulations that can then be tested on group data.

Earlier, we presented a rationale for viewing the affective tone of mother–child interactions as an index of the quality of their relationship. In so doing we—and similarly others in this volume—have proceeded without fully resolving some of the fundamental issues raised by a relationships perspective. How should relationships be operationalized and measured? How can they be distinguished from the interactions and characteristics of individuals? What criteria will suffice for a demonstration that an individual has influenced and/or has been influenced by a relationship? These are questions that require answers if we are to clarify the link between relationships and individual development. It may not be necessary to have answers in advance of our exploratory efforts. By initially employing a relatively open definition of the relationship construct proposed by Hinde and Stevenson-Hinde, one can proceed toward evolving a valuable approach for organizing and interpreting research on development.

We have only begun to approach relationships with a developmental perspective. The developmental capabilities and concerns of the child must have bearing on the dimensions of a relationship that are most important, on how a relationship is experienced, and on what its course will be. A developmental perspective on the parent is similarly relevant in a parent–child relationship.

Finally, a developmental perspective also focuses our attention on the importance of specifying what it is that individuals learn from earlier relationships that might account for continuities in development. Although issues of continuity, discontinuity, and transformation are certainly not new to the study of development, the concept of relationships has generally not been a central focus. A relationships perspective offers much in the study of development, which is still struggling with its theoretical presuppositions, methods, and avenues of inquiry.

Summary

Data from an ongoing longitudinal study of young children and their parents are used to explore a relationships approach to understanding child development. It is demonstrated that significant incremental information is gained by considering the child within relationships (mother–child, sibling–sibling, mother–siblings) and contexts (social class, family stability, child gender, maternal psychiatric status). It is also shown that patterns among variables are differently organized depending on the network of relationships and contexts in which they are embedded.

Acknowledgements

We would like to thank our colleagues, Grazyna Kochanska, Tracy Sherman, and Carolyn Zahn-Waxler, for their helpful comments. We gratefully acknowledge Rita Dettmers for her assistance in the preparation of this manuscript, Barbara Belmont and Jean Welsh for their management and analyses of data, and both April Vogel and Teresa Ingram for their help in designing and administering the peer interaction coding system.

References

Achenbach, T. M. (1983). Manual for the child behaviour checklist. University of Vermont, Dept. of Psychiatry, Burlington, Vermont.

Cohen, S. E. and Parmelee, A. H. (1983). Predictions of five-year Stanford–Binet scores in preterm infants. *Child Development* **54**, 1242–53.

Breznitz, Z. and Sherman, T. (1987). Speech patterning of natural discourse of well and depressed mothers and their young children. *Child Development* **58**, 395–400.

Bridges-Cline, F. and Kochanska, G. (1987). Personality development of children reared by normal and depressed mothers. Unpublished manuscript.

Bronfenbrenner, U. (1979). *The ecology of human development: experiments by nature and design.* Harvard University Press, Cambridge, Mass.

Hinde, R. A. and Stevenson-Hinde, J. (1987). Interpersonal relationships and child development. *Developmental Review* **7**, 1–21.

Hodges, K., Kline, J., Fitch, P., McKnew, D., and Cytryn, L. (1981). The child assessment schedule: a diagnostic interview for research and clinical use. *Catalogue of Selected Documents in Psychology* **11**, 56.

Kessen, W. (1979). The American child and other cultural inventions. *American Psychologist* **34**, 815–20.

Kochanska, G., Kuczynski, L., Radke-Yarrow, M., and Welsh, J. D. (1987). Resolutions of control episodes between well and affectively ill mothers and their young children. *Journal of Abnormal Child Psychology* **15**, 441–56.

Maccoby, E. E. and Martin, J. A. (1983). Socialization in the context of the family: parent–child interaction. In *Handbook of child psychology*, Vol. 4, *Socialization, personality, and social development* (ed. E. M. Hetherington, Series ed. P. H. Mussen), pp. 1–101. Wiley, New York.

Matas, L., Arend, R., and Scroufe, L. (1978). Continuity of adaptation in the second year: the relationship between quality of attachment and later competence. *Child Development* **49**, 547–56.

Radke-Yarrow, M. (1988). Family environments of depressed and well parents and their children: issues of research methods. In *Family social interactions: content and methodological issues in the study of aggression and depression* (ed. G. R. Patterson and E. Blechman). Erlbaum, New Jersey.

Radke-Yarrow, M. and Sherman, T. (1988). Hard growing: children who survive. In *Risk and protective factors in the development of psychopathology* (ed. J. Rolf, A. Masten, D. Cicchetti, K. Nuechterlein, and S. Weintraub) Cambridge University Press.

Radke-Yarrow, M., Campbell, J. D., and Burton, R. V. (1970). Recollections of childhood: a study of the retrospective method. *Monographs of the Society for Research in Child Development* **35**, (5), Series No. 138.

Radke-Yarrow, M., Cummings, E. M., Kuczynski, L., and Chapman, M. (1985).

Patterns of attachment in two- and three-year-olds in normal families and families with parental depression. *Child Development* **56**, 884–93.

Radke-Yarrow, M., Belmont, B., Nottelmann, E., and Bottomly, L. (1987). Young children's self-conceptions: origins in the natural discourse of depressed and normal mothers and their children. In *The development of the self during the transition from infancy to the early school years* (ed. D. Cicchetti and M. Beeghly), in press. University of Chicago Press.

Radke-Yarrow, M., Kuczynski, L., Belmont, B., Stilwell, J., Nottelmann, E., and Welsh, J. D. (1987). Affective interactions between normal and depressed mothers and their children. Unpublished manuscript.

Segal, J. and Yahraes, J. (1978). *A child's journey.* McGraw-Hill, New York.

Simpson, A. E. and Stevenson-Hinde, J. (1985). Temperamental characteristics of three- and four-year-old boys and girls and child–family interactions. *Journal of Child Psychology and Psychiatry* **26**, 43–53.

Zahn-Waxler, C., Kochanska, G., Mayfield, A., and Krupnik, J. (1987). Young children's interpretations of interpersonal stress and conflict. Unpublished manuscript.

4

Individuals in relationships
JOAN STEVENSON-HINDE

Individual characteristics: *consistency* across contexts and across time

Any effects of relationships on relationships must operate through individuals, as indicated in Fig. 4.1. The two-way arrows linking A⟷R indicate that aspects of an individual influence, and are influenced by, relationships (see Hinde 1979; Hinde and Stevenson-Hinde 1987). The individual's contribution to the relationship (A⟶R) may be broken down into aspects that are either uncharacteristic of A (i.e. relatively short-lived and/or attributable to some temporary influence on A) or *characteristic* of A (i.e. consistent across contexts and across time). The relationship's influence on the individual (A⟵R) may be short-lived or *relatively long-lasting*. In each case it is the latter, the consistent or long-lasting influences, that are the concern of this chapter, as opposed to what may be called 'contemporaneous influences' (see the Epilogue to this volume). To avoid too much theoretical baggage (e.g. see McCall 1986), consistency within the individual will be referred to, in a purely descriptive sense, as 'individual characteristics'.

The dialectic between an individual A, interactions with B, and aspects of the dyadic relationship with B:

A ⟷

B ⟷   Interactions ⟷ Aspects of the relationship

Arrows leading to A (A ⟵) provide a means for one relationship, such as A with B, to influence another, such as A with C:

A ⟷

C ⟷   Interactions ⟷ Aspects of the relationship

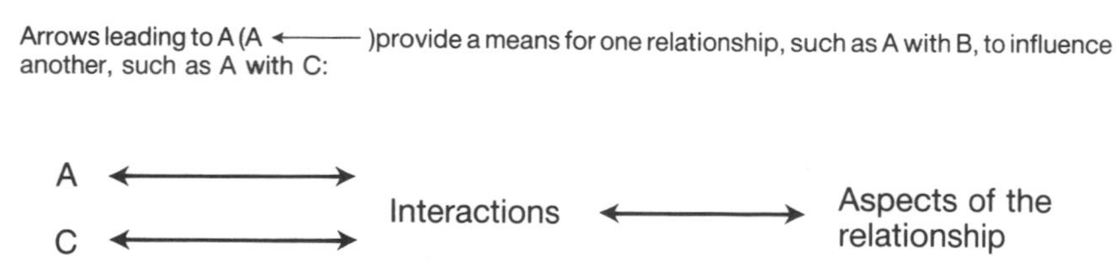

FIG. 4.1.   The way in which one relationship (A–B), operating through an individual (A), may affect another (A–C).

Individual characteristics, temperament and personality

More theory-laden terms than 'individual characteristics' are 'temperament' and 'personality'. The term 'temperament', suggested by Rutter for the characteristics defined by Thomas and Chess (1977), is now widely used to refer to a set of relatively stable traits that are present early in life. For Thomas and Chess, temperament is 'basically a personological construct'; for Rothbart, temperament exists 'within the person'; and Buss and Plomin similarly hold a 'personological position' (in Goldsmith *et al.* 1987). However, all point out that holding such a position is not incompatible with an interactive model of development. Thus, temperament may determine what situation is selected, how one reacts to a particular situation, and the nature of a social interaction. The situation might influence how temperament is expressed, and there may be a match or mismatch between the person and the environment, including the social environment. Nevertheless, the temperament construct conventionally remains personological, as if it were 'there', perhaps to be regulated by the social environment, but distinct from it.

It is generally accepted that '"personality" is a far more inclusive term than "temperament" ... Additional personality structures and strategies are developed in the course of maturation and subsequent interaction with the environment. Thus, temperament and personality are seen as broadly overlapping domains of study, with temperament providing the primarily biological basis for the developing personality.' (Rothbart, in Goldsmith *et al.* 1987, p. 510.) 'Although there are no clear demarcations between temperament and personality, the latter refers to dimensions influenced by more sophisticated cognitions and a more fully developed sense of self' (Goldsmith and Campos 1986, p. 239). After agreeing with Thomas and Chess's (1977) view of temperament as behavioural style, Rutter goes on to state that 'personality refers to the coherence of functioning that derives from how people react to their given attributes, how they think about themselves, and how they put these together into some form of conceptual whole' (1987, p. 454). There is certainly room here for relational properties of an adult's individual characteristics.

Individual characteristics in infancy and early childhood: fear of the unfamiliar

Although using different terms, most temperament theories contain a trait dealing with fear of the unfamiliar. 'Fear' is used by Goldsmith and Campos (1986), 'shyness' by Buss and Plomin (1984), and 'initial approach/withdrawal' by Thomas and Chess (1977). Turning to an ethological approach, fear may also refer to a behaviour system. 'Behavioural systems distinguished on the basis of common causation are usually found to subserve a particular biological function' (Baerends 1976, p. 731). Traditionally a behaviour systems approach has not been related to the study of individual differences, but there is no reason why it should not be. That is, consistent individual differences could reflect different thresholds for activation of any or all behaviour systems. Furthermore, 'Differences in responsiveness of one individual at different times can be understood on the basis of variations in the balance between different motivational systems' (Baerends 1976, p. 733). By combining a temperament approach, which emphasizes consistent individual differences, with a behaviour systems approach, which emphasizes motivational context, one may achieve flexibility and predictability.

If fear (or 'wariness', see Bronson and Pankey 1977; Sroufe 1977) is viewed as a behaviour system as well as a temperament dimension, then significant but low correlations between different contexts would be expected. In our current longitudinal study of fearful behaviour from 2.5 to 7 years (41 girls and 41 boys), one measure of fear of strangers is based on mothers' ratings of behaviour to unfamiliar adults and children in naturally-occurring situations (three items from the McDevitt and Carey (1978) scale and three similar items which we constructed). This was completed at 2.5 years, and children were then assessed in an Ainsworth strange situation (Ainsworth *et al.* 1978), followed by a test involving strange animals (Mongolian gerbils) (for further details, see Stevenson-Hinde and Shouldice, in preparation). The correlation between fear of strangers outside the lab and fear of stranger in the lab was 0.44 (Pearson, $p < 0.001$, two-tailed). Within the lab, the correlation between ratings of fear of stranger (episode 2) and fear of strange room (episode 1) was 0.39 ($p < 0.001$, two-tailed), and between fear of stranger and fear of strange animals 0.24 ($p < 0.05$, two-tailed). Thus, individuals were significantly consistent across context but they were also inconsistent, in that less than 20 per cent of the variance from one context to another was explained. A temperament approach combined with a behaviour systems approach would predict both consistency and inconsistency, over and above any measurement error. For example, a child's past experience of strange animals may have been more or less frightening than meeting a stranger. The same fear system would be activated, but activated to a different degree, in each situation.

Fear and relationships

Within the framework of attachment theory, activation of a fear behaviour system leads to activation of an attachment behaviour system (e.g. Bretherton and Ainsworth 1974; Sroufe 1977; Bowlby 1982; Greenberg and Marvin 1982). *How* a child uses an attachment figure as a secure base is best seen under higher stress than meeting a stranger, namely upon reunion with mother after a period of separation from her (Ainsworth *et al.* 1978). This reunion behaviour is taken by most developmentalists (e.g. Hinde 1982; Bretherton 1985; Sroufe 1985) to index an aspect of the *relationship* with the attachment figure that is present. For example, the behaviour shown upon reunion with one parent does not predict the behaviour shown with the other (Main and Weston 1981). Therefore, asking if fear (a characteristic of an individual) is associated with *how* the child uses mother as a secure base (an aspect of a relationship) is a question which fits the A←→R dialectic discussion above (Fig. 4.1).

In our current study with 2.5-year-olds, fear of stranger was rated in the Ainsworth strange situation with mother present (episode 2), immediately after mother and child had been in the strange room on their own for three minutes (episode 1). Ratings on a 4-point scale were made when the stranger entered the room, when she sat down, when she invited the child to approach and see what she had in her hand, and when she sat on the floor to play with the child. The four ratings were then averaged, to obtain a fear of stranger score. Following maternal separation, reunion behaviour by the child to the mother (episodes 4 and 7) was examined for hesitation, avoidance, and/or resistance (a security rating of 1) as opposed to the use of mother as a secure base in a free, direct, and straightforward way (a security rating of 4). To assess the relation between fear and security, each sex was divided into three subgroups, according to low, medium, or high fear of stranger, and their security ratings were compared. Children with low or medium fear had significantly higher security ratings on reunion than did children with high fear (*t*-tests, $p < 0.05$, two-tailed). As this implies, correlations between fear and security were negative, although not always significant, since the *medium* fear group sometimes had the highest security ratings. Here, the non-significant correlations indicated only non-linearity, rather than absence of a relation between two variables (see also Hinde and Dennis 1986).

Direction of effects

This relation between a characteristic of a child that is significantly consistent across situations and an aspect of the mother–child relationship indicates that one may make a prediction from an individual to a relationship or vice versa (A←→R in Fig. 4.1). The direction of effect, i.e., whether the child's characteristic drove the relationship, or whether the relationship influenced the characteristic, is an issue which requires a precise formulation, in terms of *differences* between the participants at one particular time or *changes* in the participants across time (see Hinde 1979, Chapter 19).

From a theoretical view, the importance of early relationships for development of the individual is a key assumption of attachment theory

(Bowlby 1982). The above finding, that the most positive secure base behaviour went with low or moderate fear, fits the prediction that a secure relationship should produce a less fearful, more confident child than an insecure relationship. The importance of any relational influence on fear, and indeed some other individual characteristics, probably increases initially. That is, over the first six months a relational influence may not be as important as over the second six months, when clear-cut attachment relationships are formed, or later, as the child develops 'working models' of relationships (e.g. Bowlby 1982; Bretherton 1985; Main *et al.* 1985) and becomes more susceptible to family expectations and social pressures (Maccoby and Jacklin 1975, pp. 303–48; Huston 1983). Following Kagan's intriguing suggestion that by about 7 years of age inhibition becomes relatively fixed, as if connections were 'soldered in' (Kagan, 1988), relational influences on a fear system may be greatest from 1 to 7 years.

Evidence in the other direction, for the child driving the relationship, is suggested by studies which identify an individual characteristic early on, and which demonstrate some consistency and heritability. In particular, fear of strangers (e.g. Schaffer 1966) or behavioural inhibition (e.g. Rothbart, 1988) develops over the second half of the first year of life; consistency of behavioural inhibition and its physiological correlates has been shown in a variety of contexts (Kagan *et al.* 1985; Reznick *et al.* 1986); and behavioural genetic studies 'suggest that shyness in both infancy and adulthood is heritable and that genetic variance in infancy continues to affect individual differences in adulthood' (Daniels and Plomin 1985, p. 121), with possible changes in heritability across age (Rose and Ditto 1983).

Furthermore, the predominant direction of effects may change with age. An example comes from an earlier study of 42- and 50-month-old children. With shyness rated from maternal interview questions about initial approach/withdrawal to strange people, consistency from 42 to 50 months was 0.61 (Spearman, $n = 41$, $p < 0.001$, two-tailed). For girls, shyness was significantly positively correlated with: mother sensitive to child, mother enjoys child, joint activities with mother and with father, a positive relationship with the older sibling, and conversational questions to mother; and shyness was negatively correlated with: child actively hostile to mother, child passive (i.e. not engaged) with mother, mother–child activity changes (implying that they did not do one thing for long), child reactively hostile to peers in nursery school, and both peers and adults disconfirming the child. The opposite held for 50-month-old boys (for details see Hinde and Tamplin 1983; Hinde *et al.* 1985; Simpson and Stevenson-Hinde 1985).

At 42 months, only four correlations between shyness and measures at home and school differed greatly (i.e. by > 70 points) between boys and girls, whereas at 50 months, 12 correlations differed greatly (Stevenson-Hinde and Hinde 1986). Mothers' comments during interviews suggested why such differences were more common at the later age. Some mothers complained that their sons should have grown out of their shyness, having been in nursery school for a year, while others commented with pleasure that their daughters still preferred being at home with them. Indeed, when asked to label adjectives as masculine or feminine, mothers tended to label 'shy' as a feminine characteristic, but 'assertive' as masculine (Maccoby and Sants, personal communication). Thus, mothers (and fathers) may have different attitudes towards shyness in boys and shyness in girls, with shyness in boys becoming less acceptable as they get older. Here, we have a possible influence of socio-cultural structure on the value systems of individuals, which in turn affects interactions and relationships. This suggests that shyness may be driving social interactions one way for shy girls and another way for shy boys (see also Radke-Yarrow et al. this volume). No sex differences in the absolute levels of shyness had appeared, at either 42 or 50 months. If interactions were driving the shyness, one would expect, from a reinforcement model, that girls in the sample should become more shy than boys. We are testing this prediction in our present study.

In summary, a plausible scenario is that a fear system may have different levels of activation for different individuals. The threshold will be affected by the quality of close relationships (e.g. raised by secure relationships). When a child is about to start primary school, a low threshold for a girl will be more socially acceptable than for a boy. If social reinforcement operates, girls should eventually be more fearful than boys. Finally, following Kagan's model of inhibition, any setting of a fear behaviour system may become more difficult to alter by about 7 years of age.

Relational properties of individual characteristics

In considering effects of relationships on an individual (A$\longleftarrow$R), it is likely that the development of some individual characteristics will be more influenced by relationships than others. That is, within-the-person character-istics may lie along a continuum, which approaches 0 per cent dependence on relational influences at one end and 100 per cent at the other (Fig. 4.2). For example, in some contexts activity might be less relational than a temperamen-tal characteristic concerning emotionality (e.g. Buss and Plomin 1984; Goldsmith and Campos 1986) or negative mood (e.g. Thomas and Chess 1977). Indeed, affect has been used as an important element in the meaning of relationships (e.g. Easterbrooks and Emde, this volume; Radke-Yarrow et al. this volume), and in the attachment literature there is an explicit connection between emotions and behaviour to an attachment figure.

'No form of behaviour is accompanied by a stronger feeling than is attachment behaviour. The figures toward whom it is directed are loved and their advent is greeted with joy. So long as the child is in the unchallenged presence of a principal attachment-figure, he feels secure. A threat of loss creates anxiety, the actual loss sorrow: both, moreover, are likely to arouse anger.' (Bowlby 1982, p. 209)

Thus, experiencing and expressing emotions form an integral part of the child–attachment figure relationship.

Furthermore, within a context of secure attachment, positive mood would be predicted. Two sets of data support this. First, criterion sorters, asked to characterize security of attachment in 3-year-olds, gave the item 'predominant mood is happy' the seventh *highest* placement out of 100 items, while 'cries often' got the 14.5th *lowest* placement. (These two items also got extreme placements in sorts for 1-year-olds; see Waters and Dean 1985.) We correlated these criterion sorts with sorts done by mothers of 2.5-year-olds, to obtain a security of attachment score ranging from -1.00 to $+1.00$. In addition, mothers and fathers independently completed the McDevitt and Carey (1978) questionnaire, to provide scores on the nine temperament dimensions of Thomas and Chess (1977). The highest correlations between security of attachment and temperament involved the *mood* dimension. Mothers' ratings of negative mood was significantly correlated (Pearson r's; $p<0.05$, two-tailed) with security scores, at -0.39 for boys ($n=41$) and -0.34 for girls ($n=41$). Fathers' ratings of negative mood were similarly significantly correlated with security scores, at -0.32 for boys ($n=39$) and -0.30 for girls ($n=41$). Thus, emotionality, and in particular positive mood, went both conceptually and empirically with security of attachment (Stevenson-Hinde 1986).

The above discussion of individuals and relationships is not incompatible with a view of either 'fear' or 'mood' as individual characteristics, with some consistency across situations and across time. The suggestion is that characteristics of individuals may be influenced by relationships, not only in the short term, for their expression, but also in the long term, for their development.

The place of individual characteristics in the effects of relationships on relationships

Finally, let us return to our initial question, of how to conceptualize the *individual* in studying the effects of relationships upon relationships (Fig. 4.1). This may be summarized as:

Relationship A–B→Individual characteristics of A→Relationship A–C

In moving from the next subsection to the following one, it is helpful to imagine the continuum of 'within-the-person' characteristics, from those that

0% [< ->] 100%

Influence of Social relationships

Different characteristics may lie at different places on the continuum
    e.g. In some contexts, activity may lie towards the left and affect towards the right

The position of any given characteristic may change during development
    e.g. Fear may be relatively **independent** of relationships from 0–6 months, then **modified** by attachment relationships and social reinforcement, and finally **relatively fixed**

A characteristic need not fall in any particular domain
    e.g. Emotionality, mood, or affect are common to both **temperament** theory and **attachment** theory

FIG. 4.2. A continuum to indicate the influence of social relationships on temperamental characteristics.

are little influenced by relationships to those that are primarily relational in origin (Fig. 4.2).

Mediators arising from temperament and personality theories

It is probably no coincidence that where temperament or personality variables are cited as mediators between relationships, those variables lie towards the relational end, with many concerning 'affect'. This is indeed a theme of the chapter by Belsky and Pensky (this volume), where the mediators between relationships are 'dispositional or personality characteristics of individuals that are affective and social in character' (pp. 198–99). In particular, Belsky and Pensky view personality as a mediator between relationships in one generation and those in the next generation. They argue that the developmental history→personality→family functioning process holds not only for parenting but for marital relationships as well. As the first arrow indicates, characteristics of individuals develop, in part, as a result of their experiences in their family of origin. Drawing from classical personality theory, Belsky and Pensky argue that two dimensions, concerning positive affectivity and negative affectivity (e.g. Tellegan 1984), are powerful mediators between one relationship and another.

Other mediators have involved difficult behaviour, as when antisocial traits become a part of coercive family cycles of interaction (Patterson and Dishion, this volume), or when children develop problem dispositions and carry them into marital and parent–child relationships many years later as adults (Caspi and Elder, this volume).

Mediators arising from learning theory and attachment theory

However, Caspi and Elder (this volume) also argue 'that it is not so much a personality trait . . . that is maintained across time, but an interactional style that evokes reciprocal maintaining responses from others' (p. 231). Thus, constructs arising from theories of temperament or personality are not always necessary as mediators. Although not incompatible with personality variables, mediators do arise from other theoretical orientations (see also Belsky and Pensky, this volume).

For example, mediators may come from learning theory, with behaviour patterns learned in one relationship generalized to another relationship. Thus, a child may model antisocial behaviour patterns of his/her parents and carry these into his/her own parenting behaviour as an adult (e.g. Patterson and Dishion, this volume).

More complex within-the-person variables, which may well involve modelling, arise from attachment theory. An infant's 'felt security' depends upon how sensitively responsive the mother is to the infant's needs (see Grossmann *et al.*, this volume). This maternal sensitivity might in turn depend upon a within-the-person concept such as 'maternal integration' (see Belsky and Pensky, this volume). Furthermore, individuals are said to internalize important early relationships and those internalizations or 'working models' are carried forward to influence future relationships (e.g. Bowlby 1982). Thus, the nature of the child's attachment to mother is held to be internalized into a working model of relationships, which then influences behaviour in other relationships.

'Once the infant has been involved in the attachment relationship, its inherent dispositions are both subsumed and transformed by the relationship. These dispositions cannot be reclaimed as the infant moves forward to new relationships. Congenital temperament, could it be assessed, in large part ceases to exist as a separate entity. . . . The child brings forward *only* an organization of feelings, needs, attitudes, expectations, cognitions, and behaviour; that is, only the relationship history as processed and integrated by the developing individual.' (Sroufe and Fleeson, 1986, p. 52)

Sroufe and Fleeson (this volume) show how such an approach can give coherence to apparently disconnected interactions, from a 'seductive' mother's early history to her present behaviour with sons and daughters, and from a child's attachment relationship with mother to peer–peer relationships. For example, a child presumed to have one kind of working model, based on insecure, avoidant attachment to mother (classification A), would be apt to bully an insecure, resistantly attached child (classification C), while a securely attached child (classification B) would tend to nurture and lead. Similarly, an adult attachment interview may be seen as indexing an adult's working model of early relationships, which in turn influences how that adult behaves as a parent to his/her own children (see Grossmann *et al.*, this volume).

Mediating constructs as unnecessary

With a family systems approach, relationships affect relationships directly, and individual constructs are unnecessary. The irreducible unit is not the individual but the *cycle of interaction* (or *interactive unit*, see Minuchin, this volume) so that our initial diagram loses the individual and becomes a feedback loop:

Relationship A–B→Relationship A–C→Relationship A–B→etc.

Individuals and relationships are subsystems within an organized whole. Constructing a measure of temperament or personality by summing measures across different situations has no meaning within this approach. 'If the individual is part of an organized family system, he or she is never truly independent and can only be understood in context.' (Minuchin 1985, p. 290, and this volume). Nevertheless, Minuchin (this volume) does raise the issue of how to take account of the perspectives of different members while assessing the family as an organized system. This seems close to saying that some assessment of the individual is necessary in order to understand fully the functioning of the family system.

Thus, to study effects of relationships on relationships, we must come to terms with the individual, including the 'meaning . . . in the sense of individual representations and affective themes' (Emde, this volume, p. 354) of different relationships to the individual. Where one can identify particular individual characteristics, it is suggested that the characteristic itself will be at least somewhat relational in origin. While it is necessary to be clear about our concepts of temperament, personality, modelling, and working models, we must at the same time not focus on only one of these but remain open-minded and eclectic in our approach to studying the individual and his/her role in all the possible combinations of family relationships.

Summary

Individual characteristics have been discussed in terms ranging from behaviour systems and temperament to internal working models of relationships. In considering the interplay between individual characteristics and relationships (Fig. 4.1), directions of effect may be inferred from longitudinal data, as illustrated by our own study of fearfulness. It is argued that some individual characteristics may be influenced by relationships more than others, and that relational influences may change during development (Fig. 4.2). Finally, those characteristics that are themselves influenced by relationships, such as an individual's affect or internal working model of relationships, may also be the ones that mediate influences of relationships on relationships.

References

Ainsworth, M. D., Blehar, M. C., Waters, E., and Wall, S. (1978) *Patterns of attachment*. Erlbaum, Hillsdale, NJ.

Baerends, G. P. (1976). The functional organization of behaviour. *Animal Behaviour* **24,** 726–38.

Bowlby, J. (1982). *Attachment and loss*, vol. 1, *Attachment*, (2nd edn.). Hogarth, London.

Bretherton, I. (1985). Attachment theory: retrospect and prospect. In *Growing points of attachment theory and research* (ed. I. Bretherton and E. Waters). *Monographs of the Society for Research in Child Development* Serial No. 209, **50,** (1–2), 3–35.

Bretherton, I. and Ainsworth, M. D. S. (1974). Responses of one-year-olds to a stranger in a strange situation. In *The origins of fear* (ed. M. Lewis and L. A. Rosenblum). Wiley, New York.

Bronson, G. W. and Pankey, W. B. (1977). On the distinction between fear and wariness. *Child Development* **48,** 1167–83.

Buss, A. H. and Plomin, R. (1984). *Temperament: early developing personality traits*. Erlbaum, Hillsdale, NJ.

Daniels, D. and Plomin, R. (1985). Origins of individual differences in infant shyness. *Developmental Psychology* **21,** 118–21.

Goldsmith, H. H. and Campos, J. J. (1986). Fundamental issues in the study of early temperament: the Denver twin temperament study. In *Advances in developmental psychology*, Vol. 4 (ed. M. E. Lamb, A. L. Brown, and B. Rogoff). Erlbaum, Hillsdale, NJ.

Goldsmith, H. H. *et al.* Roundtable: What is temperament? Four approaches. *Child Development* **58,** 505–29.

Greenberg, M. T. and Marvin, R. S. (1982). Reactions of preschool children to an adult stranger: a behavioral systems approach. *Child Development* **53,** 481–90.

Hinde, R. A. (1979). *Towards understanding relationships*. Academic Press, London.

Hinde, R. A. (1982). Attachment: some conceptual and biological issues. In *The place of attachment in human behavior* (ed. C. M. Parkes and J. Stevenson-Hinde). Basic Books, New York.

Hinde, R. A. and Dennis, A. (19867). Categorizing individuals: an alternative to linear analysis. *International Journal of Behavioral Development* **9,** 105–19.

Hinde, R. A. and Stevenson-Hinde, J. (1987). Interpersonal relationships and child development. *Developmental Review* **7,** 1–21.

Hinde, R. A. and Tamplin, A. (1983). Relations between mother–child interactions and behaviour in preschool. *British Journal of Developmental Psychology* **1,** 231–57.

Hinde, R. A., Stevenson-Hinde, J. and Tamplin, A. (1985). Characteristics of 3–4 year olds assessed at home and interactions in preschool. *Developmental Psychology* **21,** 130–40.

Huston, A. (1983). Sex-typing. In *Handbook of child psychology* Vol IV, (4th edn.), *Socialization, personality, and social development* (ed. E. M. Hetherington, Series ed. P. H. Mussen). Wiley, New York.

Kagan, J. (1988). The concept of behavioral inhibition to the unfamiliar. In *Perspectives on behavioral inhibition* (ed. J. S. Reznick). University of Chicago Press.

Kagan, J., Reznick, J. S., and Snidman, N. (1985). Temperamental inhibition in early childhood. In *The study of temperament: changes, continuities and challenges* (ed. R. Plomin and J. Dunn). Erlbaum, New Jersey.

McCall, R. B. (1986). Issues of stability and continuity in temperament research. In *The study of temperament: Changes, continuities and challenges* (ed. R. Plomin and J. Dunn). Erlbaum, New Jersey.

Maccoby, E. E. and Jacklin, C. N. (1975). *The psychology of sex differences*. Stanford University Press and Oxford University Press.

McDevitt, S. C. and Carey, W. B. (1978). The measurement of temperament in 3–7 year old children. *Journal of Child Psychology and Psychiatry* **19**, 245–53.

Main, M. and Weston, D. (1981). The quality of the toddler's relationship to mother and to father: related to conflict behavior and the readiness to establish new relationships. *Child Development* **52**, 932–40.

Main, M., Kaplan, N., and Cassidy, J. (1985). Security in infancy, childhood, and adulthood: a move to the level of representation. In *Growing points of attachment theory and research* (ed. I. Bretherton and E. Waters). *Monographs of the Society for Research in Child Development* Serial No. 209, **50**, (1–2), 66–104.

Minuchin, P. (1985). Families and individual development: provocations from the field of family therapy. *Child Development* **56**, 289–302.

Reznick, J. S., Kagan, J., Snidman, N., Gersten, M., Baak, K., and Rosenberg, A. (1986). Inhibited and uninhibited children: a follow-up study. *Child Development* **57**, 660–80.

Rose, R. J. and Ditto, W. B. (1983). A developmental–genetic analysis of common fears from early adolescence to early adulthood. *Child Development* **54**, 361–8.

Rothbart, M. K. (1988). The early development of behavioral inhibition. In *Perspectives on behavioral inhibition* (ed. J. S. Reznick). University of Chicago Press.

Rutter, M. (1987). Temperament, personality and personality disorder. *British Journal of Psychiatry* **150**, 443–58.

Schaffer, H. (1966). The onset of fear of strangers and the incongruity hypothesis. *Journal of Child Psychology and Psychiatry* **7**, 95–106.

Simpson, A. E. and Stevenson-Hinde, J. (1985). Temperamental characteristics of three- to four-year-old boys and girls and child–family interactions. *Journal of Child Psychology and Psychiatry* **26**, 43–53.

Sroufe, A. L. (1977). Wariness of strangers and the study of infant development. *Child Development* **48**, 731–46.

Sroufe, A. L. (1985). Attachment classification from the perspective of infant–caregiver relationships and infant temperament. *Child Development* **56**, 1–14.

Sroufe, A. L. and Fleeson, J. (1986). Attachment and the construction of relationships. In *Relationships and development* (ed. W. W. Hartup and Z. Rubin). Erlbaum, NJ.

Stevenson-Hinde, J. (1986). Towards a more open construct. In *Temperament discussed* (ed. D. Kohnstamm). Swets and Zeitlinger, Holland.

Stevenson-Hinde, J. and Hinde, R. A. (1986). Changes in associations between characteristics and interactions. In *The study of temperament: Changes, continuities and challenges* (ed. R. Plomin and J. Dunn). Erlbaum, NJ.

Stevenson-Hinde, J. and Shouldice, A. E. (in preparation). Fear, mood and security in 2.5-year-old boys and girls.

Tellegan, A. (1984). Structures of mood and personality and their relevance to assessing anxiety, with an emphasis on self report. In *Anxiety and anxiety disorders* (ed. A. Tuma and J. Moser). Erlbaum, NJ.

Thomas, A. and Chess, S. (1977). *Temperament and development*. Brunner/Mazel, New York.

Waters, E. and Deane, K. E. (1985). Defining and assessing individual differences in attachment reltionships: Q-methodology and the organization of behavior in infancy and early childhood. In *Growing points of attachment theory and research* (ed. I. Bretherton and E. Waters). *Monographs of the Society for Research in Child Development*, Serial No. 209, **50,** (1–2), 41–65.

II

Marital and parent–child relationships

5

Marital and parent–child relationships: the role of affect in the family system
M. ANN EASTERBROOKS and ROBERT N. EMDE

Since Bronfenbrenner's (1979) conceptualization of an ecological approach to the study of child development, researchers have made a pointed attempt to identify aspects of the family environment that influence the quality of parenting and development. The recent growth in prominence of family systems theories in developmental psychology has strengthened the interest in examining interactional processes within the family (Parke *et al.* 1979; Belsky 1981) as the basis for individual differences in children's social and personality development. Within this sphere, recent note has been made of the influence of the marital relationship on parenting attitudes and behaviour, and on children's development (Pedersen *et al.* 1977; Belsky 1984; Goldberg and Easterbrooks 1984; Brody *et al.* 1986).

Marriage and parenting

The focus of this paper is on the links between marital and parent–child relationships, particularly affective dimensions of marital functioning. In this chapter, we will draw together representative findings from the literature on marital and parent–child associations, including developmental psychology, family sociology, and clinical psychology. Secondly, we will present illustrations from our own research on early family development.

In large measure, ecological and family systems theory and research support the idea that the quality of the marital relationship and that of the parent–child relationship are interdependent (Pedersen 1975; Parke 1979; Belsky 1981, 1984; Goldberg and Easterbrooks, 1984). To illustrate, early studies of the transition to parenthood determined that marital quality (indexed by extent of marital conflict, husbands' reported support of their wives, the affective quality of the interaction) was related to mothers' competence in infant feeding, as well as the quality of expressed maternal affect in the first year of life (Pedersen 1975; Pedersen *et al.* 1977).

Influence processes

There is general agreement concerning the notion of interdependence between marriage, parenting, and child development. The dilemma is in determining the nature of these associations. One model portrays the primary pathway as a direct, positive connection between marital quality and the child's development. Parents who have satisfying, supportive marital relationships will be more available to respond sensitively to the needs of their child, will provide a warmer affective climate in the home, and will constitute more positive role models, thereby facilitating optimal child development. Correspondingly, a negative or discordant marital relationship may be a source of stress or preoccupation for parents, rendering them less available for sensitive parent–child interactions. In this view, marital relationships serve as supports or impediments in the sensitive parenting of young children. The literature that links marital discord and adult psychopathology (Bloom *et al.* 1978; Stroebe and Stroebe 1983) suggests that parents who are stressed by marital discord may also be compromised emotionally in parent–child interactions.

A contrasting paradigm predicts that in families where pre–birth marital quality is high, the birth of a child may be viewed as a hindrance or intrusion in the marital relationship, thereby creating strain in parent–child relationships. The converse model (the compensatory hypothesis) states that as a result of a poor marital relationship, parents will become more invested in the parent–child relationship, becoming more responsive and available to the child.

Based on the available theoretical and empirical evidence, we and others (Pedersen *et al.* 1977; Feldman *et al.* 1983; Belsky 1984; Goldberg and Easterbrooks 1984) suggest that while in some cases parental involvement and investment may increase as a result of marital dissatisfaction (Minuchin *et al.* 1978), the quality of parenting typically will not be optimized (see also Chapter 6, this volume). While parents may be involved and absorbed in parenting they simultaneously may be drained by marital conflict or distress. An illustration is found in a recent study of school-aged children and their parents (Brody *et al.* 1986) which reported that mothers in distressed marriages became more structuring in their problem-solving interactions (asking more questions, managing the interaction more); fathers were more intrusive and provided less positive feedback to their children.

Mechanisms of influence—marriage to child

If we embrace the proposition that marital quality influences child development, we are still faced with the task of elucidating the mechanisms by which these effects occur. Several processes of influence have been suggested, and indeed it is probable that multiple processes operate simultaneously. Explanatory processes may be classified under the rubrics of social learning, socialization, and family systems models (Emery, 1982; Camara and Resnick, in press).

Social learning explanations emphasize the role that child modelling of behaviour displayed by dissatisfied parents may have in child maladaptation. According to observational learning processes, children acquire negative behavioural strategies (for instance, of conflict negotiation, affect expression) by exposure to parental models. Further, children may identify less strongly with a parent due to marital discord, thus affecting parents' potential as positive models. However, this may moderate their potential as negative models as well.

The socialization hypothesis proposes that parents experiencing marital discord will engage in different, more inconsistent, and less optimal socialization practices than will happily married couples, and that these differences in parenting behaviours affect children. Importantly, parents' emotional availability to their children may be compromised as a result of marital discord and dissatisfaction. In order to monitor sensitively and respond to a child's needs and desires, parents must be emotionally open and available (Emde and Easterbrooks 1985).

In addition to affective dimensions, marital distress may be related to parental disciplinary styles (both quality and consistency). Inconsistent discipline is known to be related to child behaviour problems, particularly lack of impulse control (Becker 1964; Patterson 1977). There is also some indication that parents who air disagreements about discipline in front of their children are indeed more inconsistent in carrying out discipline (Rutter 1972; Hetherington et al. 1976). A study by Block and colleagues (Block et al. 1981) underscores the influence of parental agreement regarding child-rearing values and practices on the marital environment and child functioning. In this study, the lack of a jointly held 'couple' orientation toward child-rearing predicted marital disruption and child behaviour problems at a subsequent point in development.

The third model, guided by clinical family systems theory, focuses on the role of the child in alleviating marital distress (or in deflecting attention from the distress) by 'taking on the symptom'. In this way, family attention is refocused on the problems of the child, which relieves the tension of marital discord (Minuchin et al. 1978). Deviations in child behaviour, then, serve an adaptive function in the family.

It is our belief that each of these models may operate at different times, and to a different extent in diverse family systems. To date, the socialization hypothesis has engendered the greatest amount of research activity. The majority of the research conducted in the infancy period supports the idea that variations in marital quality affect the child by modifying parental attitudes and behaviour in interaction with the child (Pedersen 1975; Pedersen et al. 1977; Feldman et al. 1983). As noted by Goldberg and Easterbrooks (1984), a positive marital relationship provides important emotional support to fuel parents for the tasks of sensitive parenting.

Developmental considerations

It is probable that there are developmental components in the relation between marriage and parenting quality, suggesting that at certain developmental periods the support of the marital relationship is more crucial than at other times. This support may be especially acute during the transition to parenthood and in parenting the first child, while parenting roles are being developed. Such periods of transition invoke maximum instability in family relationships. It could be that certain developmental periods (for example, the first few months of infancy, or toddlerhood, or early adolescence) are more stressful for families, requiring greater levels of sustenance. Evidence strengthening this proposition is found in the work of Brown and Harris (1978) citing a peak in the incidence of depression among mothers of young children.

Developmental considerations also mediate the process by which marriage affects child development, as the child gains greater cognitive sophistication and cumulative exposure to marital interaction styles. For example, children's attention to parents as models increases across the initial years of childhood, as children actively strive to assume behaviours exhibited by parents. We should be careful, though, not to assume a simplistic relation between quality of marriage and quality of parenting. Parenting sensitivity is multiply determined, in part by historical factors such as parents' own child-rearing history or quality of their own parents' marital relationship, and in part by resources available to the family, such as social network support and economic resources (see Main *et al.* 1985; Chapters 2, 11, and 12, this volume).

Marriage and child development

Suggestions regarding the impact of the marital relationship on major indices of child development follow from the clinical literature asserting that marital discord results in increased risk of behavioural and emotional disorder in children. There is a growing body of evidence suggesting that the marital bond affects the socio-emotional development of very young children. Goldberg and Easterbrooks (1984) reported associations between marital adjustment and security of toddler–parent attachment. In families where mothers and fathers reported low marital adjustment there were more insecure toddler– mother and toddler–father attachments than in families where mothers and fathers reported high marital adjustment. In a similar vein, Belsky (1984) found that mothers of infants who were insecurely attached to them at 1 year of age evidenced more decline in positive marital activities and sentiments and more increase in negative aspects of the marital relationship from pregnancy to the end of the first year than did mothers whose infants were securely attached at 1 year.

The most substantial body of research linking marital and child characteristics concerns school-aged children, much of which focuses on clinical samples. This literature demonstrates that in two-parent families as well as in cases of divorce, in clinical and non-clinical samples, marital discord is related to non-optimal child adaptations, particularly in the areas of behaviour conduct problems or impulse control (Hetherington *et al.* 1976; Porter and O'Leary 1980; Rutter 1980; Block *et al.* 1981; Emery 1982; Camara and Resnick, in press). In general, children in families experiencing marital stress are seen by parents and teachers as having more behaviour problems than children whose parents report marital satisfaction. Marital conflict appears as the most salient factor in children's post-divorce adjustment. Further, children whose parents were divorced but not in conflict show less evidence of behaviour problems than do those in conflicted two-parent families (McCord *et al.* 1962; Power *et al.* 1974).

Several factors may mediate the extent to which marital quality affects children's development. Characteristics of the marital discord (the child's exposure to open hostility versus emotional withdrawal, duration of marital dissatisfaction), the child's age and cognitive level, gender, temperamental factors, the presence of marital co-operation as well as marital conflict, and the availability of other supportive adults close to the child (Ross 1980; Block *et al.* 1981; Emery 1982; Camara and Resnick, in press) are likely to modify responses to the stress of marital discord. Of particular importance may be the potential 'buffering effects' of other positive relationships, both within and outside the family (Rutter 1980).

While the issue of child gender differences in response to marital distress and dissatisfaction is not well researched, one study (Block *et al.* 1981) reported that the results of marital conflict on impulse control were manifest in a disparate manner for boys and girls. In line with gender role stereotypes, boys became more undercontrolled in the presence of marital conflict, while girls became more overcontrolled. Classic studies of divorce (e.g. Hetherington *et al.* 1976; Hetherington, this volume) also report gender differences in children's responses to divorce, suggesting the greater vulnerability of males (though these findings are complicated by traditional patterns of custody arrangements). In general, then, boys demonstrate problems of non-compliance and acting out, while girls may internalize the problems, becoming more withdrawn and depressed.

Child characteristics as instigators or mediators of marital distress

Although we have given prominence to the influence of marital quality on parenting attitudes and behaviour and thereby on child characteristics, there are other ways to conceptualize the interdependencies in the family system. Particular attributes of the child may influence marital quality (see Chapter 6, this volume). For example, a 1-year-old who does not sleep through the night and who is taken into the parental bed may influence marital satisfaction, communication, and intimacy. Indeed, the link between child sleep disturbances and marital functioning is prominent in clinical work.

Characteristics of the child (such as temperament or gender) may also play a role in mediating the effects of marriage and parenting on other aspects of children's development (e.g. attachment, cognitive development). Child temperamental difficulty and marital quality may also interact to influence the nature of parenting. To illustrate, one study of young infants documented negative changes in parental personality characteristics from pre-natal to infancy periods only when infants were perceived as difficult (Sirignano and Lachman 1985). Positive changes in parental personality were associated with perceptions of the infant as easy. Taken further, it can be seen that parenting efficacy, marital satisfaction, and, in turn, child development may be influenced by this process. Further support for the coupling of marriage, child characteristics, and parenting is found in Zeren and Wallace's (1985) study of fathers of 2-year-olds. In this study, high paternal nurturance and 'purpose in life' were present in environments characterized by marital satisfaction and a child who was positively reinforcing of paternal interaction, suggesting an interaction between child and marital characteristics.

The literature concerning perinatal risk status (for example, critical illness, mental retardation, low birth-weight, physical abnormalities), may also address the impact of child characteristics on the marital relationship. Early studies in this area proposed that non-normative developmental status promoted marital discord (Seashore et al. 1973; Korn et al. 1978; Pawl and Petarsky 1983). Another body of data advances the view that the child's risk or developmental status may in some cases bear no relation to marital quality, and in other instances may enhance the marriage relationship by increasing support and communication (Korn et al. 1978; Harmon 1980; Easterbrooks and Harmon 1986). The prevailing sentiment seems that individual differences in marital adjustment may be related to pre-birth marital quality rather than simply child status (Gath 1978; Belsky et al. 1983).

While it may be the case that certain characteristics of children may instigate marital distress and discord, results of a more experimental study suggest that the representative direction of effects is from marriage to child (Oltmanns et al. 1977). In this study, parents did not report increased marital satisfaction concomitant with improvements in their child's behaviour problems. Correspondingly, Margolin and Christensen (1981) found that marital therapy improved marital and parent–child problems, but that family therapy was not successful in alleviating marital difficulties.

If we view the parent–child relationship as intermediate between characteristics of the child and the marital relationship, we may not always witness direct linkages of child and marriage. In cases of atypical or difficult child characteristics, an ethological view suggests that the parenting system would be robust and flexible enough to accommodate a variety of child behaviours. In other words, while there are some biological constraints on the ability of the caregiving system to adapt to extremes in child characteristics (such as very difficult temperament or risk conditions), it also makes sense that there is enough flexibility built into the system (from a biological standpoint) that parents are able to adapt to a host of different characteristics in their children before the quality of other relationships (i.e. the marriage) is compromised.

The role of affect

In Martin's (1975) review of studies linking parenting and child development, he concluded that the affective dimensions of these relationships demonstrate the strongest and most consistent associations (when compared with variables such as cognitive style, for example). Similarly, in a review of the clinical family interaction literature, Jacob (1975) offered a parallel conclusion, namely, that affective quality was a better predictor of family interaction than knowledge of dominance or communication clarity. In the marital interaction field of study, indices of affect reliably discriminate between couples who are experiencing marital distress and non-distressed dyads (Billings 1979; Gottman 1979). Distressed couples share more negative affect and, to a more limited degree, there is less evidence of positive affect. Further, there is indication that negative affect between spouses becomes shared within the family system: in one study, parents experiencing marital conflict showed increased negativity toward their children (Johnson and Lobitz 1974). These data are consonant with the literature on general styles of parenting that emphasizes the role of parental warmth in optimal child development (Baumrind 1971), and with findings, such as those of Pedersen and his associates, linking husband support with maternal–child affect in infancy (Pedersen et al. 1977).

Research in the family system: illustrations from a longitudinal study of marriage and parent–child relationships

With a few exceptions, the most elaborate research investigating associations between quality of marriage, parenting, and child development has focused on the early period of infancy (the first months or year). As noted above, the data support the idea that positive marital adjustment facilitates sensitive parenting, and in turn is manifest in some dimensions of child adaptation (particularly attachment). One drawback of a considerable number of studies reported above is the lack of longitudinal designs and, in some cases, the failure to include fathers as well as mothers. Since the toddler period provides new challenges and reorganizations for the child and the parents, in our present work we are investigating the relations among marital adjustment, parenting behaviour and attitudes, and child behaviour in a longitudinal study of generally well-functioning families during the first two years.

In the present report, the following hypotheses are addressed:

1. We expected positive associations between marital quality and indices of parenting (positive affect sharing, positive parenting attitudes and behaviours) for mothers and fathers.

2. According to this hypothesis, we predicted that there would be differential association between various dimensions of parental behaviour and marital adjustment. For example, we predicted that marital quality would be more strongly associated with negative parental emotions than positive emotions. This prediction was made on the basis of stronger predictive ability of negative affect in the marital literature (Gottman 1979).

3. Next, we expected that self-report measures of emotion and parenting would demonstrate stronger associations with self-report (rather than observational) measures of marital quality for two reasons, namely that both were self-report measures, and that our laboratory observations of parenting may not assess as broad a range of parenting.

4. We also expected positive associations between marital quality and parental perceptions of child characteristics. For example, we expected that parents with low marital quality would perceive their infant as more difficult temperamentally, and thereby as more of an interference in their marriages. Correspondingly, happily married parents were expected to report easier temperamental characteristics of their children than couples whose marriages were less well functioning.

5. Finally, we explored whether children of more happily-married couples would exhibit more compliance to parental prohibitions than children of less satisfied couples. This analysis was considered exploratory, since compliance was measured in the limited context of the laboratory, and the 12–24 month age period may reflect just the beginning of issues of compliance and control in the family.

Subjects and procedures

Subjects were 35 married middle-class couples with their first-born infants, seen in a laboratory playroom when the infants were 6, 12, 18, and 24 months of age. The playroom was furnished with toys for the child, a small table with magazines, and a small table with a box of tissues, mechanical clock, and a vase with dried flowers. The format for each 1–1.5 hour visit consisted of a parental interview, followed by questionnaire completion by each parent, and a couple discussion interaction task. Because our desire was to see naturalistic interaction patterns, parents were free to interact with their children in whatever way they felt most comfortable. For example, parents responded differentially to their children's play and distress signals.

Measures

Marital assessments. Two measures of the marital relationship were assessed: one observational and one parental self-report. Husbands' and wives' perceptions of the quality of marital adjustment were assessed with the Dyadic Adjustment Scale (DAS) questionnaire (Spanier 1976). Spouses independently completed the questionnaire at the 6-month and 24-month laboratory visits. An observational measure of marital harmony was rated from a couple discussion task conducted at the 6-, 18-, and 24-month laboratory visits. Using a 'revealed difference technique' (Strodtbeck 1951) the couple compared responses on a questionnaire that each had completed independently, and attempted to resolve differences of opinion by discussion. Each couple was rated on a 5-point scale of marital harmony, focusing on affective expression (positive and negative), the extent to which they approached the task as a 'team', the frequency of careful and supportive listening, and the frequency of interruptions and critical comments made to the spouse.

Parental behaviour.   Due to our interests in the affective environment in the family, we assessed the frequency of positive affect sharing between parents and child at each of the laboratory visits, as well as the frequency of physical affection and approval directed from parent to child. Positive affect sharing was defined as mutual gaze between parent and child, combined with mutual expression of positive affect (smile, laugh). Physical affection involved behaviours such as hugs, stroking, pats, that did not occur in the context of caregiving, and behaviours scored as approval included statements such as 'Yes, that's the way' and 'You're a good girl' meant to convey praise to the child. For these variables, joint measures for the family were constructed combining maternal and paternal behaviour toward the child, in order to assess family influence.

Parental perceptions.   At each of the visits, parents independently completed several questionnaires which were designed to assess characteristics of parenting quality and the family environment. The Parental Attitudes toward Child Rearing questionnaire (PACR) (Easterbrooks and Goldberg 1984; Goldberg and Easterbrooks 1984) was completed at the 24-month visit. Present analyses utilize the PACR subscales of warmth, strictness, and aggravation, for which we had specific hypotheses in relation to marital adjustment.

The Bother Scale (Easterbrooks and Goldberg 1984; Goldberg and Easterbrooks 1984) was used at the 24-month visit to assess parents' perceptions of the child's interference in their lifestyle. The scale is a modification of a scale designed for early infancy by Wente and Crockenberg (1976).

Emotions. There were both behavioural observations and questionnaire measures of emotions at the laboratory visits. Behavioural observations of mother, father, and child hedonic tone were coded from the video-tapes of the interview component of the playroom visit at 6 and 18 months. During three five-minute observations, the facial and vocal expressions of each individual were coded for positive and negative hedonic tone. Four-point ratings were made at 30-second intervals (see Emde and Easterbrooks 1985 for scoring details). Present analyses use mean positive and negative composites for each individual.

The questionnaire assessment of emotional experience was the Differential Emotions Scale (DES) (Izard *et al.* 1974). The DES measures the frequency of 10 basic emotions (joy, interest, surprise, anger, fear, disgust, contempt, shyness, distress, and guilt). At the 12- and 24-month visits, parents independently reported on their own emotional experience. Composite variables were formed for mother and father at each age, measuring positive emotions (mean of joy, interest, and surprise) and negative emotions (mean of anger, fear, disgust, contempt, shyness, distress, and guilt).

Child temperament. Mothers' and fathers' perceptions of their infant's temperament were assessed when the infants were 6 months old, using the Infant Behavior Questionnaire (IBQ) (Rothbart 1981). At 18 months, parents completed a modification of Goldsmith's Toddler Behavior Questionnaire (Goldsmith *et al.* 1986). This questionnaire is a modification of Rothbart's IBQ used for younger infants. Based on previous research (Frodi *et al.* 1981), we created composite measures of mothers' and fathers' perceptions of infant difficulty by summing the scores for negative emotions (fear and anger/frustration) and subtracting scores for positive emotionality (smiling and laughter).

Child compliance. Compliance with parental prohibitions was assessed at 18 and 24 months during the laboratory visits. Toddler compliance was defined as incidents in which a parent prohibited the child (either verbally or physically), and the child complied within the next 10 seconds. Compliance was expressed as a proportional measure, ranging from 0.00 to 1.00.

Results

Marital consistence across time and measures. In order to examine the consistency of the different measures of marital quality, we conducted Pearson correlations to assess the consistency and stability of the self-report measure (DAS) of marital adjustment and the observational measures of marital harmony assessed in the laboratory discussion across time and measures.

Significant associations were found between self-report (using a combined score for mother and father) and behavioural observation at 6 months ($r = 0.28$, $p < 0.05$; $n = 34$) and 24 months ($r = 0.41$, $p < 0.05$; $n = 31$). Table 5.1 presents characteristics of marital consistency across the study period. There was evidence of temporal continuity for both measures of marriage. No differences in the means for reported marital adjustment or observed marital harmony were found over time. Means for maternal reports of marital adjustment were 118 (6 months) and 114 (24 months); fathers' scores were 116 (6 months) and 112 (24 months) at the two time periods. Similar consistency was demonstrated in the behavioural observation of couple marital interaction (means were 3.79, 3.89, and 3.65 at 6, 18, and 24 months, respectively).

Table 5.1 *Temporal consistency (Pearson r) of marital adjustment (reported) and marital harmony (observed)*

	Marital adjustment		
	Mother	Father	Marital harmony
6–18 months			0.34*	(n = 33)
18–24 months			0.59***	(n = 31)
6–24 months	0.70***	0.76***	0.29$^+$	(n = 31)

p values, two-tailed: $^+$ $p < 0.10$; * $p < 0.05$; *** $p < 0.001$.

In all reported analyses using marital harmony in the conflict resolution task, we divided couples into two groups ($n = 15$ each group) based on their position relative to the composite mean for marital harmony at 6, 18, and 24 months. This strategy allowed for a more meaningful analysis (using analyses of group differences instead of correlations), since the scores were not normally distributed, and differences between scale points such as 3.60 and 3.65 were not considered meaningful.

Marriage and parental perceptions.   In order to examine the overall influence of the quality of the marital relationship on the parenting environment, a series of correlational analyses were conducted (Pearson *r*) examining relations between the composite measure of marital adjustment (mean of mother and father DAS at 6 and 24 months), the extent to which parents perceived their child as an interference in their lives (using the Bother Scale at 24 months), and two variables from the PACR, measuring mothers' and fathers' warmth and aggravation, at 24 months. We also examined relations between parents' marital environment and perceptions of their child's temperament, predicting that parents in happier marriages would perceive their children as easier than parents in less concordant marriages (see Table 5.2).

Table 5.2   *Correlations (Pearson* r *) of marital adjustment (reported) and parental perceptions*

	Mother	Father	
Child-rearing attitudes:			
Warmth	ns	0.31*	(n = 31)
Aggravation	ns	−0.34*	(n = 31)
Parental Perceptions of:			
Child interference	−0.32*	−0.31*	(n = 31)
Child temperamental difficulty			
6 months	−0.26+	−0.22+	(n = 34)
18 months	−0.45*	−0.34*	(n = 33)

p values, two-tailed: + *p* < 0.10; * *p* < 0.05.

Parents who reported greater marital adjustment perceived their toddler as less of an interference in their lives. Fathers in happier marriages were warmer and less aggravated about their children. Marital adjustment was not related to mothers' child-rearing attitudes. Couples' scores on our observational assessment of marital harmony (grouped above and below the mean) were not related to child-rearing attitudes.

Correlations linking parents' perceptions of their child's temperament (6 months and 18 months) and marital adjustment (6 months and 24 months) demonstrated that when reported marital quality was high, parents perceived their child as less difficult. Associations between parents' perceptions of child temperament and the observational measure of marital harmony also showed developmental trends. While there were no significant relations at 6 months (means for mothers: low harmony 6.33, high harmony 6.35; means for fathers: low harmony 6.21, high harmony 6.00), at 18 months mothers in high harmony couples perceived their toddlers as easier than mothers in less harmonious marriages (means for mothers: low harmony 6.91, high harmony 6.07, $t = 2.1$, $p < 0.05$; means for fathers: low harmony 6.48, high harmony 5.95, $t = 1.6$, ns).

Marriage and parental behaviour.   In the laboratory we observed the extent of positive affect sharing (mutual gaze and smiling displayed by both parent and child), and physical affection and approval expressed from parents to child. The joint measure of reported marital adjustment was not significantly related to either of our composite measures of parent–child interaction (affect sharing, or joint physical affection and approval). On the other hand, marital harmony (couple discussion task) was associated with the composite of physical affection and approval expressed from parents to child in the laboratory. Children whose parents were more harmonious tended to receive more approval and physical affection (means: low harmony 48.14, high harmony 64.22, $t = 1.75$, $p < 0.10$).

Further, our observational measure of marital harmony was related to observations of shared positive affect between parents and child in the laboratory (composited over the 12-, 18-, and 24-month visits). In families characterized by high marital harmony in couple discussion (indicated by positive affective exchanges) there was also evidence of greater positive affect exchanged between parents and child (mean frequency of positive affect sharing in the low harmony group = 24, high harmony = 32, $t = 1.71$, $p < 0.10$). *Parental agreement on strictness and the marital environment.* We tested directly the specific hypothesis, proposed by Block *et al.* (1981), that higher levels of parental agreement on child-rearing (specifically in regard to discipline) are associated with greater marital and child functioning. In our examination of this hypothesis, we examined whether parental agreement (assessed via correlations) on the child-rearing subscale of strictness was related to reported overall marital adjustment, observations of marital harmony, affect sharing, and child compliance (using the composite measures for these variables). We found a very strong significant association only between parental agreement and the composite (12, 18, 24 months) of positive affect sharing between parents and child ($r = 0.75$, $p < 0.001$). When parents were in greater agreement on attitudes about strictness, there was more frequent sharing of positive affect between parents and child over the period from 12–24 months.

Marriage and parental emotions. We explored the hypothesis that couples reporting higher marital adjustment would experience less negative emotions and more positive emotion than would unhappily married couples. Data from the 6-month and 12-month measures of emotion were correlated with the 6-month reports of marital adjustment (encompassing early infancy), while the 18- and 24-month data were correlated with the 24-month report of marital adjustment (indexing the late infancy period).

Results of the analyses supported our predictions. Marital adjustment was not related to either mothers' or fathers' observed hedonic tone observed in the laboratory. However, marital adjustment was related to self-report measures of emotional experience. Table 5.3 presents the results of these analyses. By early toddlerhood, the data supported the predictions for negative emotions, and demonstrated positive trends linking marital adjustment and positive emotions for both mothers and fathers. Observed marital harmony was related only to mothers' reports of positive emotion at 12 and 24 months (means: low harmony 53.31, high harmony 63.40, $t = 2.79$, $p < 0.01$); harmony was not related to mothers' negative emotions, or to paternal emotions.

Marriage and child compliance. Pearson correlations were conducted to test for relations between self-report and behavioural observations of the quality of the marital environment and child compliance to parental prohibitions (a

Table 5.3   *Correlations (Pearson* r *) of marital adjustment (reported) and parental emotions*

	Positive emotions		Negative emotions	
	6 months $(n = 34)$	18 months $(n = 33)$	6 months $(n = 34)$	18 months $(n = 33)$
Mothers	ns	0.29^{+}	-0.24^{+}	-0.43^{**}
Fathers	ns	0.27^{+}	-0.27^{+}	-0.38^{**}

p values, two-tailed: $^{+}$ $p < 0.10$; ** $p < 0.01$.

percentage measure of the frequency of child compliance with parental requests to stop). There was a significant association between the two observational measures in the laboratory: an overall measure of marital harmony (assessed in the couple discussion tasks at 6, 18 and 24 months) was related to child compliance (composite at 18 and 24 months). In families where marital harmony scores were above the mean, children were highly compliant (92 per cent of the time), compared with 74 per cent for children whose parents demonstrated less marital harmony across the 18 months of the study ($t = 2.25$, $p < 0.05$). There was not a significant relation between parents' reports of marital adjustment and compliance.

Discussion and conclusions

In accordance with the principles outlined by family systems theories (Minuchin 1985), we examined the affective nature of family bonds in explaining possible connections between marital and parent–child relationships. The longitudinal design of our study allowed us to examine development in the family system across the transition from infancy to toddlerhood (6–24 months), a period of rapid developmental changes and challenges for the family. For both parents and child, these challenges revolve around increasing independent competence and autonomy (displayed in locomotor, linguistic, and affective realms). For the marriage, important tasks include integrating the needs of individual and couple functioning in stride with facilitating independent child development (requiring alterations in the expression of intimacy, and schedules of sleeping, enjoyment of leisure time, and socializing with friends, for example). For most couples in our sample, the life changes associated with a developing young child were not reflected in major changes in marital quality, nor were they experiencing severe marital distress. Nevertheless, marital quality within this range did differentiate the nature of parent–child relationships, which adds credence to the presence of these links in more extreme samples.

In summarizing our major findings, we found some support for the socialization model linking marital quality and parent–child relationships. A composite measure of marital adjustment (based on maternal and paternal reports at 6 and 24 months), and an observational measure of marital harmony in couple discussion during a conflict resolution task, were related to parents' perceptions of the child (interference in parents' lifestyles, temperamental difficulty). In addition, for fathers, marital adjustment was also related to child-rearing attitudes about warmth and aggravation. Fathers who felt they had happier marriages were warmer and less aggravated about their children than other men. To our surprise, we did not find similar patterns for mothers. Perhaps it was the case that for mothers (who in our sample were the primary caregivers even though many were also employed outside the home), parenting attitudes are more strongly buffered biologically against minor variations in the caregiving environment than for fathers, since the sensitive ministrations of a primary caregiver are vital to infant survival and optimal development. Evidence for the stronger buffering of the maternal caregiving system (specifically affectionate behaviour) is found in a study of newborns undergoing a routine medical procedure (Butterfield et al. 1982).

Aspects of the marital relationship were also examined with regard to family behaviour in the laboratory. The sharing of positive affect between parents and child was very strongly related to the extent of parental agreement about child discipline and control, and to marital harmony in couple discussion. In addition, marital harmony was related to the expression of approval and physical affection from parents to children. Each result favoured families demonstrating higher marital quality. Moreover, parents who reported happier marriages also reported feeling less negative emotion and more positive emotion in their everyday lives. In these data, developmental trends were evident, showing stronger associations in the second year and, as expected, stronger links with negative emotions than positive emotions. Finally, there was support for the notion that observed marital harmony was linked with child compliance.

In an earlier study, Block and colleagues (1981) found that the extent to which parents held consistent attitudes toward child-rearing predicted later marital distress and children's adaptation. Results of our study did not offer strong support for the thesis that parental agreement about strictness of discipline was associated with contemporaneous marital adjustment. However, we did discover a very strong relation between parental agreement and the frequency of positive affect sharing between parents and children. There are several possible explanations for the different pattern of results in the two studies, including developmental considerations as well as the importance of continuing longitudinal investigations.

In addition to affective experience in families, parents' reports of marital adjustment also were related to their perceptions of the child (interference in parents' lifestyles, temperament), their emotional experiences, and parenting attitudes (fathers only). Similarly, observed marital harmony was related to dimensions of parenting (particularly parental emotions and perceptions of child temperament). In families characterized by a positive marital climate, parents viewed their children as less of an interference in their lifestyles, and as less difficult temperamentally. The latter finding was most significant for mothers. The stronger connection between marriage and maternal perceptions may be related to the fact that all of our mothers were primary caregivers, thus temperamental difficulty would be more salient for them than for fathers who are less directly or intensively involved in caregiving.

Our observations of marital harmony in the couple discussion task also were related to affect sharing, physical affection and approval from parents to child, and child compliance in the laboratory, while parental reports of marital adjustment did not show similar associations. We understand this pattern of results in methodological terms, namely that these variables have in common the fact that they are assessed via behavioural observations in the same laboratory setting.

By knowing the overall quality of the marital environment, we were also informed about the characteristics of the emotional/affective climate to which the child was exposed. As predicted, we found that there was a coherent association between mothers' and fathers' self-reports of their own emotional experience and reported marital quality, particularly in regard to negative emotions. Parents who reported more positive marital adjustment also experienced fewer negative emotions (e.g. anger, sadness, guilt, contempt). Over the course of the study, there was a tendency for higher marital adjustment to be linked with more positive emotional experience (e.g. joy, interest, surprise). Taken further, this trend suggests that as family development proceeds, these emotion effects will exert a stronger influence on parenting behaviour and on the child, by way of parental emotional unavailability (see Emde and Easterbrooks 1985; Chapter 3, this volume). Parents who chronically experience high levels of negative emotion and little positive emotion may feel emotionally drained, and will not be optimally emotionally available to their children. Moreover, they may demonstrate a different pattern of affect socialization in interaction with their children, or convey a more negative veneer in general.

The results of our study underscore the importance of studying affect and emotion in the family context. The quality of the marital relationship is an important source of variation in the emotional climate of the family, parents' views of their children, and their role in the family system. Children in families characterized by tension in the marriage are exposed to different affective environments, even within families who generally are not experiencing severe marital discord. Thus, one might anticipate differential socialization of emotions in these families, and different patterns of emotional development in their children. Indeed, the data examining shared positive affect between parents and children illustrate the links between marital adjustment and emotional availability. In families characterized by high marital harmony in couple discussion, there was more positive affect communicated in parent–child interaction. These findings are consonant with those of Johnson and Lobitz (1974) who found, in a study of older children, that marital conflict was related to increased negative affect communicated from parents to child. The patterns manifest support both the socialization and observational learning hypotheses of marital–child influences. These data suggest that what children are learning about emotions in the context of the family varies according to the characteristics of their parents' marriage. At the same time, young children are constructing their models of interpersonal affective communication in the context of early family relationships (Sroufe and Fleeson 1986; Chapter 2, this volume).

Parents presented a consistent view of their perceptions about family relationships (marital and parent–child). Those parents who perceived their marriages as more satisfying also viewed their children in a more positive light (easier temperaments, less of a bother in their lives). These data are fully consonant with the idea that parents hold a 'perceptual bias screen' which influences their views of their family life (Jones-Leonard 1985). A dissatisfying marriage fosters a negative emotional state (a 'negative screen') which colours perceptions of the child as well as the marriage. On the other hand, maritally satisfied parents hold a 'positive screen' about their interpersonal relationships, which can lead them to interpret child behaviours as more positive than do objective observers. As suggested by Jones-Leonard (1985), the pattern exemplified by parents in less happy marriages, of viewing the child in a negative light, is shared by abusing parents and depressed individuals (Ruehlman et al. 1985; Wolfe 1985). According to this model, marital distress (or other major life stressors) produces altered (and more negative) perceptions of the child which eventually may result in dysfunctional parent–child interaction.

The present findings suggest several interesting avenues for further research, including the use of clinical samples (for example, parents with affective disorders) and families experiencing more extreme marital discord. The use of an 'extreme groups' research strategy, in which one would compare specific subsamples of the population (with very high and very low levels of marital quality, for example) has been a fruitful approach in other areas of developmental research (e.g. Garcia Coll et al. 1984). Further research endeavours may also find it fruitful to examine mediators of parental and children's adjustment to stressful family interaction (specifically with reference to marital distress). For example, the presence of other intimate and supportive interpersonal relationships may serve as a buffer for the effects of marital distress on parenting. Finally, there is strong support for continuing our longitudinal investigation of the influence of marital and affective parent–child relationships on the socialization of emotions and for children's emotional development.

Summary

In this chapter, we have reviewed evidence from the growing body of literature linking marital and parent–child relationships in families with young children. There is now sufficient evidence to suggest that infants are exposed to different affective environments while growing up in families differing in marital quality. We have also presented some results from our ongoing longitudinal study of early family development. Our data support the tenets of ecological and family systems theories, namely that marital and parent–child relationships are interdependent in the early years of development. In the majority of cases, the transference between these two subsystems is of a positive nature. Parents who characterized their marriages in more positive terms provided a warmer affective climate in the family. We have examined a process model of the linkages between marital relationships and early child development in the family. These data promote a socialization explanation of family interaction, suggesting that parents modify their behaviour in parent–child relationships in accord with other current life stresses and experiences, and illustrate the importance of examining child development in the family context.

References

Baumrind, D. (1971). Current patterns of parental authority. *Developmental Psychology Monographs* **4**, (1, Part 2).

Becker, W. C. (1964). Consequences of different kinds of parental discipline. In *Review of child development* (ed. M. L. Hoffman and L. W. Hoffman). Russell Sage Foundation, New York.

Belsky, J. (1981). Early human experience: a family perspective. *Developmental Psychology* **17**, 3–23.

Belsky, J. (1984). The determinants of parenting: a process model. *Child Development* **55**, 83–96.

Belsky, J., Spanier, G., and Rovine, M. (1983). Stability and change in marriage across the transition to parenthood. *Journal of Marriage and the Family* **45**, 553–66.

Billings, A. (1979). Conflict resolution in distressed and nondistressed married couples. *Journal of Consulting and Clinical Psychology* **47**, 368–76.

Block, J. H., Block, J., and Morrison, A. (1981). Parental agreement–disagreement on child-rearing orientations and gender-related personality correlates in children. *Child Development* **52**, 965–74.

Bloom, B. L., Asher, S. J., and White, S. W. (1978). Marital disruption as a stressor: a review and analysis. *Psychological Bulletin* **85,** 867–94.

Brody, G. H., Pillegrini, A. D., and Sigel, I. E. (1986). Marital quality and mother–child and father–child interactions with school-aged children. *Developmental Psychology* **22,** 291–96.

Bronfenbrenner, U. (1979). *The ecology of human development: experiments by nature and design.* Harvard University Press, Cambridge.

Brown, G. W. and Harris, T. (1978). *Social origins of depression.* Tavistock, London.

Butterfield, P. M., Emde, R. N., Svejda, M., and Naiman, S. (1982). Silver nitrate in the eyes of the newborn: effects on parental responsiveness during initial social interaction. In *The development of attachment and affiliative systems* (ed. R. N. Emde and J. R. Harmon). Plenum, New York.

Camara, K. A. and Resnick, G. (in press). Interparental conflict and cooperation: effects on children's social behavior. In *Divorce, single-parent, and step-parent families* (ed. E. M. Hetherington and J. Arastek).

Easterbrooks, M. A. and Goldberg, W. A. (1984). Toddler development in the family: impact of father involvement and parenting characteristics. *Child Development* **55,** 740–52.

Easterbrooks, M. A. and Harmon, R. J. (1986). *Perinatal risk, attachment, and the transition to parenthood.* Paper presented at the International Conference on Infant Studies, Los Angeles.

Emde, R. N. and Easterbrooks, M. A. (1985). Assessing emotional availability in early development. In *Early identification of children at risk: an international perspective* (ed. W. K. Frankenburg, R. N. Emde, and J. Sullivan). Plenum, New York.

Emery, R. E. (1982). Interparental conflict and the children of discord and divorce. *Psychological Bulletin* **92,** (2), 310–30.

Feldman, S. S., Nash, S. C., and Aschenbrenner, B. G. (1983). Antecedents of fathering. *Child Development* **54,** 1628–36.

Frodi, A. M., Lamb, M. E., Frodi, M., Hwang, C-P., Forstrom, A., and Corry, T. (1981). Stability and change in parental attitudes following an infant's birth into traditional and nontraditional Swedish families. *Scandinavian Journal of Psychology.*

Garcia Coll, C., Kagan, J., and Reznick, J. S. (1984). Behavioral inhibition in young children. *Child Development* **55,** 1005–19.

Gath, A. (1978). *Down's Syndrome and the family: the early years.* Academic Press, New York.

Goldberg, W. A. and Easterbrooks, M. A. (1984). The role of marital quality in toddler development. *Developmental Psychology* **20,** 504–14.

Goldsmith, H. H., Elliott, T. K., and Jaco, K. L. (1986). *Construction and initial validation of a new temperament questionnaire.* Paper presented at the meetings of the International Conference on Infant Studies, Los Angeles.

Gottman, J. G. (1979). *Empirical investigation of marriage.* Academic Press, New York.

Harmon, R. J. (1980). Infant behavior and family development. In *Primary health care of women* (ed. L. Sonstegard, B. Jennings, and K. Kowalski). Duxbury Press, New York.

Hetherington, E. M., Cox, M., and Cox, R. (1976). Divorced fathers. *Family Coordinator* **25,** 417–28.

Izard, C., Dougherty, F., Bloxom, B., and Kotsch, W. E. (1974). The differential emotions scale: a method of measuring the subjective experience of discrete emotions. Unpublished manuscript, Dept of Psychology, Vanderbilt University.

Jacob, T. (1975). Family interaction in disturbed and normal families: a methodological and substantive review. *Psychological Bulletin* **82**, 33–65.

Johnson, S. M. and Lobitz, G. K. (1974). The personal and marital adjustment of parents as related to observed child deviance and parenting behaviors. *Journal of Abnormal Child Psychology* **2**, 193–207.

Jones-Leonard, D. (1985). Perceptual bias as a possible mechanism in the relationship between marital discord and child behavior problems. Unpublished master's thesis. University of Denver.

Korn, S. J., Chess, S., and Fernandez, P. (1978). The impact of children's physical handicaps on marital quality and family interaction. In *Child influences on marital and family interaction* (ed. R. Lerner and S. Spanier). Academic Press, New York.

Main, M., Kaplan, N., and Cassidy, J. (1985). Security in infancy, childhood, and adulthood: a move to the level of representation. In *Growing points of attachment theory and research* (ed. I. Bretherton and E. Waters). *Monographs of the Society for Research in Child Development*. Serial No. 209, **50**, (1–2), 66–104.

Margolin, G. and Christensen, A. (1981). *The treatment of families with marital and child problems*. Paper presented at the meeting of the Association for the Advancement of Behavior Therapy, Toronto.

Martin, B. (1975). Parent–child relations. In *Review of child development research*, Vol. 4 (ed. F. D. Horowitz). University of Chicago Press.

McCord, J., McCord, W., and Thurber, E. (1962). Some effects of paternal absence on male children. *Journal of Abnormal and Social Psychology* **64**, 361–9.

Minuchin, P. (1985). Families and individual development: provocations from the field of family therapy. *Child Development* **56**, 289–302.

Minuchin, S., Rosman, B. L., and Baker L. (1978). *Psychosomatic families: anorexia nervosa in context*. Harvard University Press, Cambridge, Mass.

Oltmanns, T. F., Broderick, J. W., and O'Leary, K. D. (1977). Marital adjustment and the efficacy of behavior therapy with children. *Journal of Consulting and Clinical Psychology* **45**, 724–9.

Parke, R. D. (1979). Perspectives on father–infant interaction. In *Handbook of infant development* (ed. J. D. Osofsky), pp. 549–90. Wiley, New York.

Parke, R. D., Power, T., and Gottman, J. (1979). Conceptualizing and quantifying influence patterns in the family triad. In *Social interaction analysis: methodological issues* (ed. M. Lamb, S. Suomi, and G. R. Stephenson). University of Wisconsin Press, Madison.

Patterson, G. R. (1977). Accelerating stimuli for two classes of coercive behaviors. *Journal of Abnormal Child Psychology* **5**, 335–50.

Pawl, J. H. and Petarsky, J. H. (1983). Infant-parent psychotherapy: a family in crisis. In *Infants and parents* (ed. S. Provence), pp. 39–84. International Universities Press, New York.

Pedersen, F. (1975). *Mother, father and infant as an interactive system*. Paper presented at the annual convention of the American Psychological Association, Chicago.

Pedersen, F., Anderson, B., and Cain, R. (1977). *An approach to understanding linkages between the parent–infant and spouse relationships*. Paper presented at the biennial meeting of the Society for Research in Child Development, New Orleans.

Porter, B. and O'Leary, K. D. (1980). Marital discord and childhood behavior problems. *Journal of Abnormal Child psychology* **80,** 287–95.

Power, M. J., Ash, P. M., Schoenberg, E., and Sorey, E. C. (1974). Delinquency and the family. *British Journal of Social Work* **4,** 17–38.

Ross, A. O. (1980). *Psychological disorders of children*. McGraw-Hill, New York.

Rothbart, M. K. (1981). Measurement of temperament in infancy. *Child Development* **52,** 569–78.

Ruehlman, L. S., West, S. G., and Pasahow, R. J. (1985). Depression and evaluative schemata. *Journal of Personality* **53,** 46–68.

Rutter, M. (1972). Relationships between child and adult psychiatric disorders. *Acta Psychiatrica Scandinavia* **48,** 3–21.

Rutter, M. (1980). Protective factors in children's responses to stress and disadvantage. *Primary prevention of psychopathology: III. Promoting social competence and coping in children* (ed. M. W. Kent and J. E. Rolf). University Press of New England, Hanover, NH.

Seashore, M. J., Leifer, A. D., Barnett, C. R., and Leiderman, P. H. (1973). The effects of denial of early mother–infant interaction on maternal self-confidence. *Journal of Personality and Social Psychology* **27,** 369–78.

Sirignano, S. W. and Lachman, M. E. (1985). Personality change during the transition to parenthood: the role of perceived infant temperament. *Developmental Psychology* **21,** 558–67.

Spanier, G. B. (1976). Measuring dyadic adjustment: new scales for assessing the quality of marriage and similar dyads. *Journal of Marriage and the Family* **38,** 15–32.

Sroufe, L. A. and Fleeson, J. (1986). Attachment and the construction of relationships. In *Relationships and development* (ed. W. W. Hartup and Z. Rubin). Erlbaum, Hillsdale, NJ.

Strodtbeck, F. L. (1951). Husband–wife interaction over revealed difference. *American Sociological Review* **16,** 468–73.

Stroebe, M. S. and Stroebe, W. (1983). Who suffers more? Sex differences in health risks of the widowed. *Psychological Bulletin* **93,** 279–301.

Wente, A. S. and Crockenberg, S. (1976). Transition to fatherhood: Lamaze preparation, adjustment difficulty and the husband–wife relationship. *The Family Coordinator* **25,** 351–8.

Wolfe, D. A. (1985). Child-abusive parents: an empirical review and analysis. *Psychological Bulletin* **97,** 462–82.

Zeren, A. S. and Wallace, J. R. (1985). *The prediction of paternal characteristics from their children's temperament*. Paper presented at the meeting of the Society for Research in Child Development, Toronto.

6

The interrelatedness of marriage and the mother–child relationship*
ANETTE ENGFER

Introduction

Research on the 'transition to parenthood' is generally anything but encouraging concerning the course of the marital relationship. Although some decline in marital satisfaction has also been observed over time in young couples who are not parents (see Huston *et al.* 1984; Markman *et al.* 1987), the arrival of a child seems to be a serious test for the marital relationship. One perspective addressing the erosion of marriage at the transition to parenthood suggests that the growing disparity in the roles and responsibilities of the spouses precipitates this decline in marital satisfaction (see Waldron and Routh 1981; Cowan *et al.* 1985; Goldberg *et al.* 1985; Worthington and Buston 1986). According to this view, the responsibilities of parenting induce profound and often stressful changes into the marital relationship which must be negotiated by husband and wife.

Another perspective is offered by Belsky (1981, 1984) who claims that the marital relationship serves as the main support for competent parenting. According to this hypothesis, the support received from the spouse is seen as critical for parental functioning. There is a growing body of research documenting the links between marital satisfaction and parenting (Goth-Owens *et al.* 1982; Goldberg and Easterbrooks 1984; Cowan *et al.* 1985; Cox *et al.* 1985; Goldberg *et al.* 1985; Heinicke 1985; Oates and Heinicke 1985; see also Chapters 5 and 7, this volume) and, in general, these studies have corroborated the assumption that marital satisfaction enhances the quality of parenting.

Few studies, however, have been guided by explicit hypotheses concerning the mechanisms linking the marital and the parent–child relationship. This

*This research was supported by a grant from the *Deutsche Forschungsgemeinschaft*. I would like to thank Maria Gavranidou for her help with the computer work and Brenda Volling for her help in preparing the English version of this chapter.

shortcoming cannot be solely attributed to the fact that such hypotheses did not exist, since Easterbrooks and her co-workers have reviewed repeatedly the ways in which marriage and parenting may mutually affect each other (see Easterbrooks and Emde 1984; Goldberg and Easterbrooks 1984; and Chapter 5, this volume). Instead, many of these hypotheses proved difficult to test because methodologically adequate longitudinal studies were, until recently, rare, and few studies combined self-report measures from both spouses with observational assessments. Although a number of studies have recently filled this gap (see Goth-Owens et al. 1982; Cox et al. 1985; Heinicke 1985; Oates and Heinicke 1985), only a few studies examined the relations between marriage and parenting over a time-span extending beyond the second year of the child's life. Accordingly, then, the picture depicting the links between marriage and parenting may be incomplete since some of these links may be revealed only after a longer span of time (see Cowan et al. 1985; Easterbrooks and Emde in this volume). Therefore, it seems worthwhile to inquire into these relations over a longer time-period.

The purpose of the present investigation was to examine four hypotheses about the interrelatedness of marriage and the mother–child relationship using data from a longitudinal study extending over the course of four years after the birth of a child. Since this study has focused mainly on mothers and their children, the hypotheses have been stated in terms of *maternal* feelings and competencies and their relation to the quality of marriage. These four hypotheses are presented graphically in Fig. 6.1.

Four hypotheses about the interrelatedness of marriage and the mother–child relationship

The 'spill-over' hypothesis

One would expect that a warm and supportive marital relationship not only helps the mother to cope with the stresses connected with pregnancy and the transition to parenthood, but that such support would also enhance her enjoyment of the child as the tangible outcome of marital love. This is referred to as the 'spill-over' hypothesis, and implies that the quality of marriage directly affects the way in which the mother relates to her infant in both positive and negative ways.

This 'spill-over' hypothesis is by and large supported by the results of studies showing that happily married mothers feel more pleased and competent in their maternal role (Brüderl 1982; Goth-Owens et al. 1982; Goldberg and Easterbrooks 1984; Cox et al. 1985; Heinicke 1985) and were also observed to relate more positively to their infants (Goth-Owens et al. 1982; Heinicke 1985; Oates and Heinicke 1985; Chaptes 5 and 7, this volume).

1. The 'Spill-over' hypothesis:

2. The compensatory hypothesis:

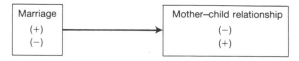

3. The mother–child relationship affecting the course of marriage

4. The 'common-factor' hypothesis:

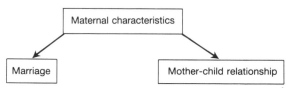

FIG. 6.1.   Four hypotheses about the interrelatedness of marriage and the mother–child relationship.

The compensatory hypothesis

On the other hand, the compensatory hypothesis suggests that the mother who does not find her needs for love and intimacy fulfilled in her marital relationship may attempt to satisfy these in her relationship with her child. According to this view, a stronger involvement with the child would be likely to occur if the mother experienced deficits in the quality of her marriage.

Consistent with this line of reasoning is recent clinical evidence suggesting the formation of strong parent–child coalitions in families with a distressed marital relationship (see Chapters 2, 5, and 14, this volume). Empirical results supporting the compensatory hypothesis for the very early mother–child relationship are rare, however. Whilst Goldberg *et al.* (1985) found mothers' marital dissatisfaction to be related to higher maternal involvement with the baby, the question pertaining to the direction of influence still remains. Is it the case that marital dissatisfaction produced the higher involvement with the infant, or that mothers being highly involved in the responsibilities of care-giving felt increasingly dissatisfied with their marriage, particularly if they received too little support from their husbands?

It seems less likely that one would see a *decrease* in maternal sensitivity toward her child when a mother's needs are fulfilled within her marital relationship. Yet some results support this unexpected reversal (Goldberg and Easterbrooks 1984), although mostly in the case of happily married husbands who tend to interact less with their infants (Goth-Owens *et al.* 1982).

The mother–child relationship influencing the course of the marital relationship

Most of the research on the transition to parenthood assumes the mother–child relationship to influence the course of the marital relationship. That is, the stresses and responsibilities connected with the care of young infants are thought to be the major causes for the decline in marital satisfaction reported by young couples parenting their first child. According to Easterbrooks and Emde (1984), the stresses of parenting and the subsequent decline in marital quality may be exacerbated if the mother is faced with a temperamentally difficult child. Therefore, I used mother's perceptions of difficult temperament as an indicator of stress in the mother–child relationship and examined whether this would contribute to problems and conflicts in the marital relationship.

The 'common-factor' hypothesis

While in the preceding hypotheses it was assumed that marriage influences mothering or that stresses associated with mothering influence marriage, a third possibility should not be dismissed. Specifically, maternal personality characteristics may be the common determinants of the quality of both the marital and the mother–child relationship (see Chapter 12, this volume).

Emotionally stable, optimistic, warm, and empathic characteristics of women may not only contribute to the success of their marital relationship, but may also be responsible for good mothering. Therefore, we call the simultaneous impact of maternal characteristics on the marital and the mother–child relationship the 'common-factor' hypothesis.

Methods

The data presented here come from a larger longitudinal study on the development of distressed mother–child relationships.

The sample consisted of 36 families living in Munich or its surroundings. At delivery the mothers were between 23 and 43 years of age with a median of 30 years. At this time the duration of marriage was between 1 and 13 years with a median of 5.2 years. At 43 months we had complete data-sets for 35 mothers and 33 fathers in the assessment of the marital relationship. The families were mainly middle and lower middle class. 43 months after delivery there were 24 boys and 12 girls in our sample, 11 boys and 7 girls being first-born, the rest second- or later-born children.

Maternal sensitivity in the interaction with the infant was observed and rated twice:

(1)   on the maternity ward, doctors and nurses judged maternal sensitivity; and

(2)   eight months after delivery, maternal sensitivity was observed and judged in a free-play situation of 30 minutes' duration in the homes of the families.

Maternal personality characteristics were measured twice—4 and 18 months after delivery. By use of the Freiburg Personality Inventory (FPI, see Fahrenberg *et al.* 1978) we assessed the following dimensions of maternal personality: nervousness, depressiveness, emotional irritability, neuroticism, and composure.

Maternal feelings and child-care attitudes in relationship with the infant were assessed 4 and 18 months after delivery. Here we utilized several scales of a questionnaire pre-tested in a sample of 170 mothers (*Fragebogen zu den Einstellungen von Müttern mit Kindern im Kleinstkindalter*, EMKK, see Codreanu 1984; Engfer 1984). Here we refer to the following scales:

1. *Empathic Enjoyment of the Child.* This scale describes maternal feelings of self-efficacy, of warm and empathic interest in the child. A typical item is: 'If my baby cries, I know at once what is wrong with him.'

2. *Anxious Over-protectiveness.* This scale describes an almost irrational fear that something may happen to the baby in terms of accidents, diseases, etc. A typical item is: 'Sometimes I cannot sleep at night for the fear that something may happen to the baby.'

3. *Role-reversal.* This scale describes the maternal expectation to receive love, comfort, and affection from the child. As such it focuses more on the needs of the mother than on the needs of the child. A typical item is: 'My child should make me very happy.'

Perceived behaviour problems of the child were assessed three times: 4, 18, and 43 months after delivery. In prior analyses we had used maternal feelings of anger and aggravation as a criterion for defining child difficultness (see

Engfer 1986; Engfer *et al.* 1986). Therefore child difficultness involved different measures at different ages of the child, taking such age-dependent changes in maternal assessments of child behaviour problems into account. At 4 and 18 months we used 5-point rating scales modelled after the scales developed by Broussard and Hartner (1970). These include 10 items such as 'How frequently does your baby cry?' At 4 months, perceived child difficultness was measured by a compound score of frequent crying, restlessness, and lack of soothability; at 18 months this compound score consisted of frequent crying, restlessness, and sleeping problems; at 43 months, perceived child difficultness was measured by a scale of six items describing the aggressive non-compliance of the child.

The *quality of the marital relationship* was assessed twice from the perspective of the mothers, i.e. 4 and 43 months after delivery. For the fathers, however, we have this assessment only once, 43 months after delivery. Here we utilized the Relationship Inventory by Hahlweg (1979) measuring three dimensions of marital interaction:

1. *Conflict.* This scale describes the frequency and intensity of marital arguments. A typical item is: 'If we fight, he/she yells at me.'

2. *Communication.* This scale describes the amount of communication and mutual disclosure between the spouses. A typical items is: 'He/she tells me openly what he/she feels and thinks.'

3. *Affection.* This scale describes the active exchange of affection including physical caressing. A typical item is: 'He/she caresses me affectionately.'

The methods of evaluation included bivariate (Pearson) correlations, t-tests, and path analysis with latent variables as developed by Lohmöller and Wold (1980) (for a more detailed description of this method see Engfer and Gavranidou 1987; and Chapter 7 this volume). According to our sample size of 35 mothers and 33 fathers, the level of significance for bivariate correlations was 0.10 for $r \geq 0.22$; 0.05 for $r \geq 0.28$; 0.01 for $r \geq 0.41$; 0.001 for $r \geq 0.51$. For ease of presentation levels of significance are omitted in the text, but they are included in the presentation of the results in Table 6.1.

Results

Before I examine the four hypotheses I would like to present some information about the data in general. For the sample as a whole we found a significant decline in the quality of marriage from 4 to 43 months. From the perspective of the mothers there was a significant increase in the amount of marital conflict ($t = 1.98$, $p < 0.05$), and an even more depressing *decrease* in the positive aspects of the relationship, i.e. in the openness for communication ($t = -4.37$,

$p < 0.001$) and the expression of affection ($t = -9.32$, $p < 0.001$). These results are in harmony, then, with those of other studies in which a decline in marital satisfaction during the initial years of parenthood has also been found. The following sections will focus on the four hypotheses about the ways in which the marital and the mother–child relationship may be related.

Empirical results supporting the 'spill-over' hypothesis

The following results are in harmony with the 'spill-over' hypothesis. Mothers who described their marital relationship as communicative and affectionate at 4 months enjoyed their babies and felt self-confident and happy in their maternal role: the Empathic Enjoyment of the Child scale was significantly related to Communication ($r = 0.36$) and Affection ($r = 0.41$) in the Relationship Inventory. These positive qualities of the marital relationship were also related to Empathic Enjoyment of the Child at 18 months ($r = 0.48$ and 0.33).

Further support for the 'spill-over' hypothesis was provided by the finding that maternal sensitivity as observed on the maternity ward was positively related to marital Communication ($r = 0.46$) and negatively to Conflict ($r = -0.28$) in the Relationship Inventory at 4 months. A harmonious marital relationship was also associated with sensitive mothering observed 8 months after delivery as the correlations for Conflict ($r = -0.37$) and Communication ($r = 0.35$) indicate.

Empirical results supporting the compensatory hypothesis

We also found some support for the compensatory hypothesis in our results. Mothers in marital relationships involving a considerable amount of conflict were particularly prone to show 'role-reversal' in relationship with their babies, i.e. they considered their child as a compensatory source of comfort, love, and affection: at 4 months the contemporaneous correlation between the Conflict scale of the Relationship Inventory and the Role-reversal scale of the Maternal Child-care Attitudes Questionnaire was $r = 0.42$. Also, these mothers in distressed marital relationships tended to feel anxiously over-protective of their babies ($r = 0.30$), as if they were afraid that they might lose the child as a last source of love and affection. While mother-perceived marital Conflict at 4 months ceased to predict maternal Role-reversal at 18 months ($r = 0.19$), it did continue to predict maternal Over-protectiveness ($r = 0.35$).

One would expect that mothers expressing such intense involvement with their babies should also show more involvement and sensitivity towards their babies in the view of outside observers. This was not the case, however: mothers expressing this kind of emotional over-involvement with their babies (i.e. scoring high on the Role-reversal and Over-protectiveness scales) were judged to be significantly less sensitive in the interaction with their newborn babies as observed on the maternity ward. The correlations were $r = -0.43$ for the Role-reversal scale and $r = -0.36$ for the Over-protectiveness scale (for details see Engfer and Gavranidou 1987).

Empirical results supporting the hypothesis that stresses in the mother–child relationship affect the quality of the marital relationship

The third hypothesis involves a reverse route of influence: the mother–child relationship affecting the quality of the marital relationship. Mothering may be particularly stressful if the mother is faced with a temperamentally difficult child. Therefore we need to examine whether a difficult child may be a source of conflict and problems in the marital relationship.

According to prior analyses (see Engfer 1986; Engfer *et al.* 1986), child difficultness involved different measures at different ages of the child, as described above. Perceived child difficultness at 4 and 18 months was significantly related to marital conflict as perceived by mothers ($r = 0.45$ and 0.42) and by fathers ($r = 0.30$ and 0.60) at 43 months. For mothers we found only a weak and non-significant correlation between the aggressive non-compliance of the child and the amount of conflict they reported themselves as having with their husbands at the same point in time. But for the husband-perceived marital conflict this empirical relation of $r = 0.37$ was significant.

This may mean that if the mothers found their children aggressively non-compliant at 43 months, the husbands reported themselves as having more aggressive quarrels with their wives. Since the couples mainly described the behaviour of the spouse on the Conflict scale of the Relationship Inventory we used, it looks as if the mothers who were stressed from the aggressive non-compliance of their children were more aggressive and irritable in interaction with their husbands—or at least they were perceived that way by their husbands.

But the strongest empirical relation of $r = 0.60$ was between mother-perceived child difficultness at 18 months and husband-perceived irritable quarrels with their wives at 43 months. This may mean that the behaviour problems of the children at this particular age triggered maternal feelings which had long-term consequences for the course of the marital relationship.

What were the feelings and behavioural propensities of mothers that were associated with perceived child difficultness at 18 months and which had this profound effect on the marital relationship? Generally speaking, mothers who perceived their children as being difficult at 18 months showed on all scales of our personality inventory concurrent symptoms of irritability, depressive exhaustion, and declined well-being. Therefore the profound effect of early child difficultness on marital conflict later on could have been mediated by the feelings that the mothers showed in response to these problems.

We tested this hypothesis by using path analysis with latent variables (see

Lohmöller and Wold 1980). In this case, the highly related personality measures were used as indicator variables for the measurement of the latent variable of maternal irritability.

The results presented in Fig. 6.2 substantiated the assumption that the effect of perceived child difficultness on marital conflict was almost exclusively mediated by the feelings of overload and irritability which the mother showed in response to the behaviour problems of the child. These maternal feelings of overload and irritability predicted father-perceived marital conflict at 43 months even better than mother-perceived marital conflict, as the path coefficients and the amount of variance accounted for in the criterion variables indicate.

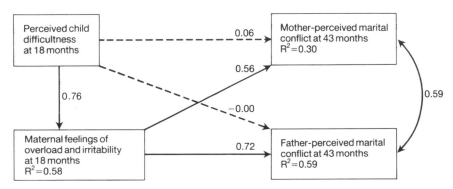

FIG. 6.2   The empirical path model of the influence of perceived child difficultness on mother-perceived and father-perceived marital conflict at 43 months, as mediated by maternal feelings of overload and irritability at 18 months.

It therefore seems warrantable to conclude that a difficult child could affect the marriage in a negative way, that the behaviour problems at 18 months after delivery had these long-term consequences in particular, and that these consequences were mainly mediated by the feelings and behavioural tendencies the mothers showed in response to the problems.

Results supporting the 'common-factor' hypothesis

The last hypothesis concerns the possibility that the personal resources of the mother may be the common determinant of both the marital and the mother–child relationship. Our data lent abundant support for this last hypothesis.

1. Maternal personality characteristics, which at 4 and 18 months were only moderately related to the quality of marriage as assessed 4 months after delivery, were very strong predictors of the quality of the marital relationship as assessed at 43 months from the perspective of both spouses (see Table 6.1).

Wives' self-descriptions as depressed, moody, irritable, and unstable were significantly associated with the amount of marital conflict and the lack of communication and affection reported at 43 months. And these same characteristics were also found to be significantly related to symptoms of distress in the mother–child relationship (see Engfer 1984, 1986).

2. But even more surprising was the result that mothers who showed a lack of sensitivity in interaction with their new-born and 8-month-old infants were also the mothers whose marriages seemed to go awry in the long run. The initial rating of maternal sensitivity on the maternity ward was negatively related to the amount of Conflict ($r = -0.74$) and positively to Communication ($r = 0.50$) and Affection ($r = 0.31$) in the marital relationship as perceived by the husband 43 months after delivery. The observed sensitivity of the mother in interaction with her 8-month-old child showed a similar pattern of correlations to the dimensions of the marital relationship at 43 months, although somewhat smaller in magnitude (see Table 6.1).

Therefore it looks as if maternal sensitivity as observed in the interactions with the young infant not only allowed prediction of the future course of the mother–child relationship (see Engfer 1986; Engfer and Gavranidou 1987), but also was highly predictive of the course of the marital relationship.

Discussion

It is a widely accepted assumption that marriage and parenting are interrelated. It seems less clear, however, just how the relations between these two relationships should be conceived. Therefore, it was a major aim of this chapter to explore the various ways in which marriage and the mother–child relationship affected each other.

For the 'spill-over' hypothesis which states that marriage directly affects mothering we found some empirical evidence. Mothers in affectionate and communicative marital relationships enjoyed their babies and felt happy and competent in their maternal roles. Furthermore, we found that lack of conflict and openness for communication in the marital relationship were associated with sensitive mothering as observed on the maternity ward and again 8 months after delivery.

We also found some support for the compensatory hypothesis, which implies that the mother–child relationship has to make up for deficits experienced in the marital relationship. Specifically, mothers in marital relationships involving a considerable amount of conflict were prone to interpret the relationship with their infants as a substitute source of love and affection as well as being over-anxiously worried about the health and well-being of their infants.

Table 6.1 *Dimensions of marital quality as related to maternal sensitivity, personality characteristics, and perceived child difficultness measured at different points in time*

Variables measured	4 months after delivery Mother-perceived marital			43 months after delivery Mother-perceived marital			43 months after delivery Father-perceived marital		
	conflict (n=36)	communication	affection	conflict (n=35)	communication	affection	conflict (n=33)	communication	affection
On the maternity ward:									
Maternal sensitivity	−0.28*	0.46**		−0.55***	0.51***	0.46**	−0.74***	0.50**	0.31*
4 months after delivery:									
Maternal personality									
nervousness				0.32*		−0.38*	0.28+		0.25+
depressiveness		−0.34*		0.39*	−0.33*	−0.26†	0.44**	−0.34*	−0.31*
emotional irritability				0.26†		0.37*	0.46**		−0.39*
composure				−0.41**	0.33*	−0.50**	−0.59***	0.32*	0.33*
neuroticism		−0.21†		0.43**	−0.33*	−0.46**	0.45**	−0.38*	−0.50**
Perceived child difficultness	0.31*	−0.27†		0.45**	−0.41**		0.30*	−0.43**	−0.36*
8 months after delivery:									
Maternal sensitivity	−0.37*	0.35*		−0.42*	0.39*	0.29*	−0.60**	0.37*	
18 months after delivery:									
Maternal personality									
nervousness				0.43**			0.29*	−0.26†	
depressiveness	0.23†	−0.34*		0.46**	−0.61***	−0.56***	0.47**	−0.56***	−0.46**
emotional irritability	−0.26*	−0.25*		0.33*	−0.32*	−0.32*	0.53***	−0.44**	−0.39*
composure		0.32*		−0.40**	0.44**	0.56***	−0.47**	0.43**	0.54***
neuroticism		−0.28*		0.33*	−0.46**	−0.48**	0.48**	−0.46**	−0.43**
Perceived child difficultness	0.48**	−0.46**	0.21†	0.42**	−0.50***	−0.36*	0.60***	−0.46**	−0.36*
43 months after delivery:									
Perceived aggressive non-compliance of the child				0.24†	−0.31*		0.37*		

†p=0.10; *p=0.05; **p=0.01; ***p=0.001.

We also found very convincing evidence for the third hypothesis which states that a child who is difficult to care for may present a risk for the course of the marital relationship. Our path-analytic evaluation made clear, however, that child difficultness had this detrimental effect on the marital relationship only if the mothers responded to it with irritability and depression.

The strongest and most convincing evidence seems to be for the 'common-factor' hypothesis. Both maternal personality characteristics and maternal sensitivity in interaction with the new-born and 8-month-old infant were highly predictive of the quality of marriage as assessed 43 months after delivery from the perspective of both spouses. Thus, by and large we found empirical support for all our hypotheses.

It seems difficult, however, to make a clear-cut distinction between these competing hypotheses in spite of the fact that they imply opposite and, therefore, mutually exclusive assumptions about the direction of effects. This ambiguity was due partly to the fact that some of our results supporting the first and second hypotheses were based on contemporaneous correlations coming from the same data source—the mother. Therefore, no conclusive evidence is possible concerning the question whether marriage influenced the mother–child relationship or whether the mother–child relationship influenced marriage. Furthermore, these same results could also be considered as support for the 'common-factor' hypothesis. On the other hand, these ambiguities may present an accurate picture of how these two relationships are associated in the minds of mothers who participate in, and have to assess, both relationships.

Considering other results of our study, it seems noteworthy, however, that in some cases the longitudinal correlations exceeded the contemporaneous ones. This applies to the relations between marital conflict and child difficultness in particular. Here we found that at 4 and 43 months these contemporaneous correlations were moderate at best, but marital conflict as assessed at both times was significantly related to perceived child difficultness at 18 months. This result may indicate that the links between marriage and the mother–child relationship change according to the stage of family development and that there are certain critical phases of parenting when marital support is particularly important.

Our results, and likewise those of Easterbrooks and Emde (Chapter 5, this volume), suggest that the very early stage of mothering may not be the time when marriage and the mother–child relationship are most closely linked. Instead, the quality of marriage appeared to be much more relevant for the stresses experienced in the mother–child relationship at 18 months. Since, unfortunately, we did not have assessments of marriage at 18 months, we do not know what occurred in the marital relationship at that time. For instance, was the mother receiving support from her husband or did she feel left alone or even criticized for her ineptness as a mother? We do know, however, that maternal feelings of depression and irritability triggered during this stressful stage of mothering were significantly related to marital outcome at 43 months.

In considering the impact of maternal characteristics on the course of marriage, a number of things should be noted. First, although maternal sensitivity was related to some personality characteristics of the mother (the relations were between $r = 0.20$ and 0.50 and generally around 0.25; for details see Engfer and Gavranidou 1987), these were in no way tautological measures as it might initially appear from our results. Instead, both the maternal sensitivity and personality measures seemed to tap different aspects of maternal functioning and both seemed to be relevant for the course of marriage and the mother-child relationship.

Secondly, the fact that it was the affective aspects of maternal personality which were so very predictive of the quality of the marital relationship is consistent with the results of other longitudinal studies on the development of early marriage. Here it has been found repeatedly that women are more aware of marital decline than are their husbands and more inclined to express their discontent in marital interaction (see Markman 1984; Christensen 1987; Notarius and Pellegrini 1987). These results concerning the impact of maternal personality on the course of marriage are also in harmony with those of other studies showing that the main route of influence appears to run from personality to marital quality rather than the reverse (see Elder *et al.* 1984 Kelly and Conley 1987; Markman *et al.* 1987; Chapter 12, this volume). We would be in error, however, to conclude from these results that the wife is solely responsible for the state of the marital relationship.

We have no measures of the personality characteristics of the husbands which, according to the finding of other studies, also influence the course of the marital relationship (see Elder *et al.* 1984; Kelly and Conley 1987; Markman *et al.* 1987; Chapter 11, this volume). Furthermore, the chapter by Caspi and Elder (Chapter 12, this volume) shows that characteristics of the husbands may be a powerful corrective for the less than optimal characteristics which wives with negative developmental histories bring into marriage and parenting. Thus, without the information on the characteristics of the husbands, our analysis about the factors determining the course of marriage remains incomplete. It does seem, though, given the associations we did find, that the interrelation of the marital and the parent–child relationship deserves further empirical investigation.

Summary

Data from a longitudinal study on the development of mother–child relationships were used to examine four hypotheses of how the mother–child relationship may be related to the marital relationship. These were the 'spill-over' hypothesis, the compensatory hypothesis, the mother-child relationship affecting the marital relationship, and the 'common-factor' hypothesis. The findings lent support to all these hypotheses on how the mother–child and the marital relationship may affect each other.

References

Belsky, J. (1981). Early human experience: a family perspective. *Developmental Psychology* **17**, 3–23.

Belsky, J. (1984). The determinants of parenting: a process model. *Child Development* **55**, 320–35.

Broussard, E. R. and Hartner, M. S. S. (1970). Maternal perceptions of the neonate as related to development. *Child Psychiatry and Human Development* **1**, 16–25.

Brüderl, L. (1982). Formen der Bewältigung des Übergangs zur Elternschaft. Unpublished masters thesis. Giessen University.

Christensen, A. (1987). Detection of conflict patterns in couples. In *Understanding major mental disorders: the contribution of family interaction research* (ed. K. Hahlweg and M. Goldstein). Family Process Press, New York.

Codreanu, N. (1984). Kindbezogene Einstellungen von Müttern mit Kleinkindern. Unpublished masters thesis. Munich University.

Cowan, C. P., Cowan, P. A., Heming, G., Garrett, E., Coysh, W. S., Curtis-Boles, H., and Boles III, A. J. (1985). Transition to parenthood. His, hers, and theirs. *Journal of Family Issues* **6**, 451–81.

Cox, M. J., Owen, M. T., Lewis, J. M., Riedel, C., Scalf-McIver, L., and Suster, A. (1985). Intergenerational influences on the parent–infant relationship in the transition to parenthood. *Journal of Family Issues* **6**, 543–64.

Easterbrooks, M. A. and Emde, R. 1984. Marriage and infant: different systems linkages for mothers and fathers. Unpublished manuscript. University of Colorado Health Sciences Center.

Elder, G. H., Liker, J. K., and Cross, C. E. (1984). Parent–child behavior in the Great Depression: life course and intergenerational influences. In *Life-span development and behavior*, Vol. 6 (ed. P. B. Baltes and O. G. Brim). Academic Press, New York.

Engfer, A. (1984) Entwicklung punitiver Mutter-Kind-Interaktionen im sozioökologischen Kontext. Arbeitsbericht zum Antrag an die Deutsche Forschungsgemeinschaft auf Gewährung einer Sachbeihilfe. Unpublished manuscript. Munich University.

Engfer, A. (1986). Antecedents of behaviour problems in infancy. In *Temperament discussed. Temperament and development in infancy and childhood* (ed. G. A. Kohnstamm). Swets and Zeitlinger, Lisse.

Engfer, A. and Gavranidou, M. (1987). Antecedents and consequences of maternal sensitivity. A longitudinal study. In *Psychobiology and early development* (ed. H. Rauh and H. C. Steinhausen). North Holland, Amsterdam.

Engfer, A., Gavranidou, M., and Heinig, L. (1986). Stability and change in perceived characteristics of children 4 to 43 months of age. Paper presented at the Second European Conference on Developmental Psychology, Rome, Italy.

Fahrenberg, J., Selg, H., and Hampel, R. (1978). *Freiburger Persönlichkeitsinventar*. F-P-I. Hogrefe, Göttingen.

Goldberg, W. A. and Easterbrooks, M. A. (1984). The role of marital quality in toddler development. *Developmental Psychology* **20**, 504–14.

Goldberg, W. A., Michaels, G. Y., and Lamb, M. (1985). Husbands' and wives' adjustment to pregnancy and first parenthood. *Journal of Family Issues* **6**, 483–503.

Goth-Owens, T. L., Stollak, G. E., Messé, L. A., Peshkess, I., and Watts, P. (1982). Marital satisfaction, parenting satisfaction, and parenting behavior in early infancy. *Infant Mental Health Journal* **3**, 187–97.

Hahlweg, K. (1979). Konstruktion und Validierung des Partnerschaftsfragebogens, PFB. *Zeitschrift für Klinische Psychologie* **8**, 17–40.

Heinicke, C. M. (1985). Pre-birth couple functioning and the quality of the mother-infant relationship in the second half of the first year of life. Paper presented at the Biennial Meeting of the Society for Research in Child Development, Toronto.

Huston, T. L., McHale, S. M., and Crouter, A. C. (1984). When the honeymoon's over: changes in the marriage relationship over the first year. In *Key issues in personal relations* (ed. R. Gilmour and S. Duck). Erlbaum, Hillsdale, NJ.

Kelly, E. L. and Conley, J. J. (1987). Personality and compatibility: a prospective analysis of marital stability and marital satisfaction. *Journal of Personality and Social Psychology* **52**, 27–40.

Lohmöller, J. B. and Wold, H. (1980). Three mode path models with latent variables and partial least square (PLS) parameter estimation. Forschungsbericht 80.03, Fachbereich Pädagogik, Hochschule der Bundeswehr München.

Markman, H. J. (1984). The longitudinal study of couples' interactions: implications for understanding and predicting the development of marital distress. In *Marital interaction. Analysis and modification* (ed. K. Hahlweg and N. S. Jacobsen). Guilford, New York.

Markman, H. J., Duncan, S. W., Storaasli, R. D., and Howes, P. W. (1987). The prediction and prevention of marital distress: a longitudinal investigation. In *Understanding major mental disorders: the contribution of family interaction research* (ed. K. Hahlweg and M. Goldstein). Family Process Press, New York.

Notarius, C. I. and Pellegrini, D. S. (1987). Differences between husbands and wives: implications for understanding marital discord. In *Understanding major mental disorders: the contribution of family interaction research* (ed. K. Hahlweg and M. Goldstein). Family Process Press, New York.

Oates, D. S. and Heinicke, C. M. (1985). Pre-birth prediction of the quality of the mother–infant interaction. *Journal of Family Issues* **6**, 523–42.

Waldron, H. and Routh, D. K. (1981). The effect of the first child on the marital relationship. *Journal of Marriage and the Family* **43**, 785–8.

Worthington, E. L. and Buston, B. G. (1986). The marriage relationship during the transition to parenthood: a review and a model. *Journal of Family Issues* **7**, 443–73.

7

Marital and mother–child relationships: developmental history, parent personality, and child difficultness*
HANS-JÜRGEN MEYER

Introduction

The mother–child relationship is thought to be of formative significance for personality development. Accordingly, one of the central issues in infant as well as personality research is the identification of those factors that play a crucial role in the development of the early mother–child relationship. Whereas most researchers agree that the mother–child relationship is multiply determined, there is no consensus about which factors are essential or about the direction of their influence. However, it is increasingly accepted that at least two types of factors have an important impact on the mother–child relationship; individual characteristics of the mother and the child, and characteristics of maternal and child relationships with other family members.

As for maternal characteristics that are thought to have an impact on mother–child relationships, two distinct aspects can be distinguished: relatively stable personality traits and child-related attitudes and feelings, particularly those of competence in child-rearing (Goldberg 1977). The child characteristic that has received the most attention in terms of its impact on the mother–child relationship is temperament, in particular those aspects that parents find difficult to deal with (Bates 1980).

Concerning the influence of other family relationships, discussions focus on the impact of the marital on the mother–child relationship. The marital relationship has mainly been conceptualized as the principal source of support for parents (Belsky 1984). A third predictive domain of family relationships which has only recently been addressed empirically is the developmental history of the caregiver, especially his or her experience in the family of origin. It is argued that at least some patterns of marital and parental behaviour are

*This research was supported by a grant from the *Deutsche Forschungsgemeinschaft*.

transmitted from one generation to another (see Chapters 11–13 and 15, this volume). In this chapter our main aim is to explore the relative importance of these domains as predictors of one dimension of the mother–child relationship, namely the harmony of the dyads' handling of control issues.

Theoretical model of the antecedents of the mother–child relationship

Before describing the study in more detail, I will explain the guiding model and refer to some of the recent empirical findings concerning the links between the major constructs involved. As the global model summarizes aspects that are reported in more detail in other chapters in this volume (see the contributions by Belsky and Pensky; Engfer; Easterbrooks and Emde; Caspi and Elder, and Rutter). I shall describe it only briefly here. A more detailed description can be found elsewhere (Voss and Meyer 1986). The postulated causal pathways that link developmental history, marital quality, and characteristics of the mother and the child to the mother–child relationship are presented in Fig. 7.1.

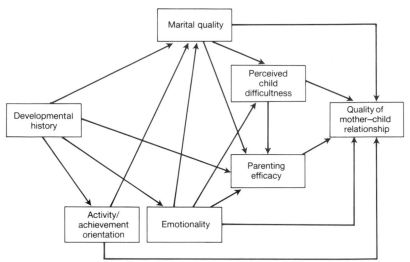

FIG. 7.1   Theoretical model of the antecedents of the mother–child relationship.

Developmental history.   Several recent studies support the view of cross-generational continuity, not only in the case of parent–child, but also of marital relationships. As for the marital relationship, there is some evidence from studies on divorce, as well as from studies on 'normal' marital functioning, of transmission from one generation to the other (e.g. Pope and Mueller; 1976; Rutter and Madge 1976).

Concerning the parent–child relationship, a number of studies also lend support to the notion of cross-generational continuity. Research on child abuse documents an assocation between the experience of violence and abusive disciplinary practices in the parents' family of origin and mistreatment of children in the family of procreation (for reviews see Herrenkohl and Herrenkohl 1981; Engfer 1986). Recently, studies on mother–child attachment also found evidence for transmission across generations (Main *et al.* 1985; Sroufe *et al.* 1985).

It was hypothesized that the exposure to a harmonious marriage in one's own childhood and the experience of nurturant and supportive parenting in the family of origin would forecast higher marital satisfaction and less conflict in the marital relationship. In addition, we expected that parental personality traits and parenting self-efficacy would be influenced, at least in part, by a person's developmental history.

Parental personality.   In the literature, personality characteristics are treated as salient determinants of parenting and mother–child relationships. Negative emotionality is probably the trait that has received most attention in this regard. There is evidence, not only from studies of psychologically disturbed adults but also from the range of 'normal' psychological functioning, that depressiveness, anxiety, and inhibitedness interfere with optimal parenting (e.g. Field *et al.* 1985).

In addition, irritability and the tendency to become easily upset and angry have been found to be related to less sensitive and affectionate caregiving and an insecure mother–child relationship (Ainsworth *et al.* 1978; Weber *et al.* 1986). Less is known about the influence of other personality traits. However, it seems reasonable to speculate that parents characterized by high levels of tempo and vigour, a sense of time, urgency, and impatience, and competitive achievement–striving tendencies are less sensitive and responsive in caring for their infant. I also expected these basic personality traits to predict not only perceived effectance in child-rearing function and difficultness of the child, but also the quality of marital relationships.

Parenting efficacy   Besides common personality traits, experienced stress by the mother resulting from her daily responsibility for the infant and her perception of parenting self-efficacy are likely to influence her child-rearing behaviour. There is some evidence, not only from dysfunctional families but also from the more usual range of variation, that low self-esteem and dissatisfaction with the parental role has a negative impact on competent parenting (e.g. Crnic *et al.* 1983). It was hypothesized that negative experience in the family of origin, maternal depressiveness, and temperamental difficultness of the child cause a lower sense of parenting competence. It was further hypothesized that marital quality has a positive impact on perceived self-efficacy in the parental role.

Marital relationships   It is widely assumed that marital relationships and parent–child relationships are interrelated. However, there is some controversy concerning the direction and the nature of this interdependence. The majority of recent empirical results support the notion of a positive influence of marital quality on parent–child relationships (Goldberg and Easterbrooks 1984; Cutrona and Troutman 1986). Accordingly, we predicted positive associations between marital quality, maternal perception of her efficacy as a parent, and mother–child interaction.

Perceived child difficultness.   In recent years arguments have been advanced concerning the significance of a child's temperamental characteristics for mother–child interaction (Thomas and Chess 1977). Among the temperament constructs that have received the most attention with respect to their impact on parenting and the mother–child relationship is the child's difficultness or negative affectivity. Although empirical findings are somewhat contradictory, most studies indicate that difficult temperament has an impact on parenting and the mother–child relationship, particularly on those aspects that centre on control issues (Lee and Bates 1985).

In view of several findings concerning the relations between maternal personality, particular maternal anxiety, and negative perception of the child's temperament (Vaughn *et al.* 1980; Bates and Bayles 1984), we expected perceived difficult temperament to depend, at least partly, on negative emotionality in mothers. In addition, we hypothesized that the perception of a child's difficultness would be influenced by marital quality. This direction of effect has been favoured in preference to regarding marital adjustment as depending on the child's characteristics (Easterbrooks and Emde 1984).

Mother–child relationship   Hinde (1976) suggested that categories of dimensions important in characterizing interpersonal relationships are the content and the quality of the interactions between the individuals involved. In order to characterize the relationship between mother and child, attachment, play, and control components of interactions have been widely used. For present purposes we have focused on control issues that are increasingly important after the first year of the child's life (Schaffer and Crook 1980). The way dyads handle situations where the mother and the child have to co-ordinate their individual plans and wishes and co-operate with each other are conceptualized as important precursors of later childhood behaviour problems (Bates *et al.* 1985).

The study

The present study is part of an ongoing longitudinal study on maternal relationships with first- and second-born children. The aim of this project is to describe the linkage between the relationships of a mother with each of her two children, and in studying processes that are likely to be involved in mediating these relations. For the present analyses, we have included only data from the beginning of our study when the first-borns were 14 months old, and none of the 35 families participating in the study had a second child. Eighteen of the infants were male and 17 were female. The sample was predominantly middle class, and the parents were well educated (8 mothers and 16 fathers graduated from college). The average age of the parents was 29 years for fathers (range = 21–36) and 26 for mothers (range = 19–33). Seven mothers were working part-time and one had a full-time job.

The families were seen in a laboratory playroom setting. The laboratory session, lasting 30 minutes, consisted of a number of episodes. Since the present report relies on observations of the family members during only two episodes, these will be reviewed here.

1. Clean-up (present: mother, child): the co-operative quality of mother–child interactions were observed in a clean-up episode. After a 6-minute exploration episode where the child explored the room and handled several play objects, a signal was given by a knock on the one-way mirror. The mother was told to leave her chair and to clean up the room by putting the play materials in a basket. She was told not to do the clean-up alone, but to integrate the child 'as far as possible'.

2. Couple discussion task (present: mother, father, child): the quality of couple's interaction was observed in the last episode of the family's visit. The discussion task was similar to that of Easterbrooks and Emde (1984). The couple was presented with a set of six drawings of infants' facial expressions of emotions. These drawings were taken from Izard's 'Maximally Discriminative Facial Movement Coding Manual' (Izard 1979). The couple was told that we were interested in establishing whether parents agree in their judgments about the emotions expressed. Parents were instructed to discuss which emotions they felt were represented and to record their joint decisions. The infant was present during the task. The parents had no instructions concerning their behaviour towards the child. The length of the discussion was 12 minutes on the average (range 6–20 min).

The entire laboratory session was videotaped using a split-screen video-recorder. After the laboratory session, parents were given questionnaires concerning their developmental history, personality, marital satisfaction, child-related feelings, and the temperament of the child. They were asked to complete them at home independently and to send them to our institute.

Table 7.1. summarizes the constructs, indicator variables, and measures employed in the study. Observational and questionnaire measures are described below.

Measures

Developmental history   In order to gather data on developmental history we applied two questionnaires. Marital satisfaction of the parents in the families

Table 7.1 *Latent and indicator variables of a causal model on antecedents of the mother–child relationship*

Latent variables	Indicator	Measures
Developmental history	Marital satisfaction	Romantic Relationship Questionnaire (Domittner 1979)
	Experience with mother (G1) ⎫ Experience with father (G1) ⎬	Modification of the subscale 'happiness of childhood' of the EMKK (Engfer 1984)
Parental personality	Achievement orientation	Subscale 'achievement orientation' of the FPI-R (Fahrenberg *et al.* 1984)
	Activity	Subscale of the EAS Temperament Survey (Buss and Plomin 1984)
	Anger	Subscale of the EAS
	Emotionality	Subscale of the EAS
Parenting self-efficacy	Overstrain Frustration Depressiveness	Subscales of the EMKK
Marital relationship	Marital satisfaction	Romantic Relationship Questionnaire (Domittner 1979)
	Harmony of interaction	Discussion task: Marital Harmony Score (rating-scale, Goldberg and Easterbrooks 1984)
Perceived difficultness	Perceived difficultness	Infant Characteristics Questionnaire (Bates 1978)
Mother–child relationship	Quality of assistance	Clean-up task: quality of assistance (rating-scale)
	Child compliance	Percentages of compliance

of origin was measured with a modification of the Romantic Relationship Questionnaire developed by Domittner (1979). This 16-item scale covers aspects of marital satisfaction, communication, and consensus. (Typical item: 'Did your parents agree in their attitudes and opinions?').

The parent's own childhood experiences with their mothers and fathers were measured with a 12-item scale. The items of the scale were derived from the subscale 'Happiness of childhood' of a more comprehensive child-rearing-attitude questionnaire developed by Engfer (1984). The items which originally referred to the child-rearing behaviour of the parents as a dyad were changed to refer to the behaviour of the mother and father separately. (Typical item: 'When I was a child, I felt I was at my father's mercy.') Consequently, two scores were derived from the scale: childhood experience with mother, and childhood experience with father. It is important to note that these scores reflect parents' current perception of their childhood relationships and not actual childhood experiences.

Parental personality   Parental personality was measured with selected scales of the FPI-R—the most common German personality inventory (Fahrenberg *et al.* 1984), and the Adult EAS Temperament Survey (Buss and Plomin 1984). From the FPR-R, we used two scales. The subscale 'frankness' has been included to control the social desirability response bias that is pertinent when employing self-report measures. (Typical item: 'Every now and then I show off a little bit.') The scale 'achievement orientation' refers to behaviour characterized by competitive achievement-striving, a sense of time urgency, and a preference for a job instead of private life engagement. The EAS 'activity' scale refers to the energetic level (tempo and vigour) of behaviour. The EAS 'emotionality' and 'anger' scales address the tendencies to become upset and/or annoyed easily.

Parenting efficacy   In order to assess maternal perception of her efficacy as a caretaker and her feelings of disappointment concerning her maternal role, we applied the following three subscales of the EMKK developed by Engfer (1984): 'overstrain', 'frustration', and 'depressiveness'. (Typical item: 'I feel as if I am doing something wrong with my baby.)

Perceived difficultness   Child difficultness was measured by a German version of the Infant Characteristic Questionnaire (ICQ) developed by Bates (1978). The original questionnaire consists of 32 seven-point ratings concerning characteristics such as the child's activity level, amount of crying, persistence in completing a task, and demandingness. For this study we added scores from the discriminating items only for the first factor that resulted from a factor analysis on the ICQ-ratings of our sample. The first factor, called 'difficultness', corresponds closely to the factor definition of difficult temperament obtained by Bates. The score reflects the mother's perception of her infant's negative emotionality.

Marital relationship   Two kinds of measures were used to assess the marital relationship. The first measure was the Romantic Relationship Questionnaire developed by Domittner (1979). The original questionnaire contains 18 items that encompass parental feelings concerning the functioning of the marriage, such as marital satisfaction, consensus, and communication.

The second measure was derived from our observation of the couple discussion task. The harmony of interaction between the mother and the father was assessed by a five-point rating scale developed by Goldberg and Easterbrooks (1984). Scores mainly reflect the kind of affective sharing and the patterning of verbal communication during the discussion task. Couples who received high scores of 5 (high harmony of interaction) were friendly towards each other, arranged the situation so that both could equally participate in the task, demonstrated mutual respect, and shared pleasure. Couples who received a low score demonstrated spousal conflict by making sarcastic comments, ignoring proposals, blaming each other for not being competent, and working separately. This score reflected the quality of interaction: the content of individual contributions was not addressed.

Quality of the mother–child interaction   Two scores of the quality of the mother–child interaction were derived from behavioural observations of mother and child during the clean-up episode. The first score assessed the quality of maternal assistance. The major criteria were the timing and the way in which the mother introduced the task to the child, the clarity and pacing of her verbal cues, the way of arranging the play material and basket, and the flexibility demonstrated by changing instructions and strategies according to the child's behaviour. A high score was given according to the extent these criteria were met.

In addition, the clean-up episode was scored for the child's compliance with maternal controls. Maternal controls were defined and scored according to the manual 'On coding controls' developed by Schaffer and Crook (1979). Only the frequency of the mother's control behaviour and the child's compliance to the controls were counted. Frequency counts of the child's compliance were converted to percentage of maternal controls.

Method of evaluation

To evaluate our causal model about the predictors of the mother-child relationship, we used path analysis with latent variables as the primary means of analysis. The LVPLS (Latent variables path analysis with partial least-squares estimation) causal modelling procedure, developed by Wold (1982) and transformed into computer programs by Lohmöller (1984), is similar to LISREL in that it distinguishes between a measurement model (relations between several indicator variables and the latent variable or factor) and a structural model (causal predictive relations or paths among the latent variables). Unlike LISREL, LVPLS does not require measurement at the interval-scale level and is not sensitive to violations of multivariate normality and small sample sizes. In addition, we used bivariate and partial correlations between selective indicator variables.

Before the correlations of the indicator variables were entered in the LVPLS causal analysis, self-report measures used in the study were correlated with parental frankness scores. As anticipated, parental frankness correlated significantly with several aspects of parents' developmental history, personality, and marital satisfaction, as well as with women's sense of competence as parents. Hence the matrix included in the LVPLS analysis consisted of partial correlations controlling for parental frankness scores, which are used as a measure of social desirability response bias (see above).

Results

Antecedents of the marital relationship

As a first step towards answering our main question, we evaluated our predictions concerning the determinants of marital quality. It was hypothesized that parental developmental history predicts, at least in part, personality characteristics of the parents as well as their marital satisfaction. Personality characteristics and marital satisfaction were regarded as causal links between developmental history and quality of couple interaction. In addition, it was predicted that marital satisfaction depends on personality characteristics. Concerning the relation between marital satisfaction of mothers and fathers, we assumed a bidirectional influence.

Factor loadings obtained for all nine constructs indicate a satisfactory fit of the measurement model. However, the result of the latent variable 'developmental history' reveals some differences between mothers and fathers. For mothers, the highest loading on the developmental history factor was marital satisfaction of parents (0.89), followed by childhood experiences with mother (0.79) and with father (0.23). Whereas for fathers, childhood experiences with their own fathers yielded higher loadings (0.83) than experiences with mothers (0.53) and marital satisfaction of their parents (0.20).

The results for the structural model indicating the interrelations between the latent variables are given in Fig. 7.2. The model explains a considerable proportion of variance in the three variables indicating marital quality (0.56 and 0.49 for marital satisfaction of mothers and fathers and 0.45 for quality of couple interaction). The main findings can be summarized as follows:

1. Although the paths from marital satisfaction to the observed quality of marital interaction do show a positive sign, they are lower than expected, particularly as far as the impact of fathers' marital satisfaction is concerned.

2. Not surprisingly, mothers' and fathers' marital satisfaction correlate significantly with each other ($r = 0.57$, $p < 0.001$).

3. The substantial path coefficients leading to marital satisfaction and quality of interaction are similar for mothers and fathers although somewhat different in strength.

4. The impact of the predictors depend on the aspect of marital quality in question.

Developmental history, as measured by marital satisfaction of the parents in their families of origin and the parents' childhood experiences with their own

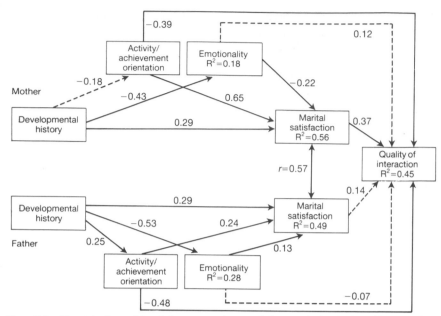

FIG. 7.2 Empirical model of the antecedents of the marital relationship (marital satisfaction and quality of couple interaction).

parents, has an important impact on the emotionality aspect of their personality. According to the zero-order correlations, childhood experiences with mothers seem to be of particular importance for maternal emotionality ($r = -0.46$, $p < 0.01$ for anger scale; and $r = -0.32$, $p < 0.05$ for emotionality scale), whereas childhood experiences with fathers seem to be more important for paternal emotionality ($r = -0.41$, $p < 0.01$ for emotionality scale).

Compared with the influence on emotionality, the impact of developmental history on the activity/achievement/orientation component is lower and different for mothers and fathers. According to our hypothesis, developmental history of wives and husbands does affect marital satisfaction in the family of procreation, although only to a moderate degree. In line with our expectations, there are substantial path coefficients leading from individual characteristics of the parents to marital quality. However, the strength of their influence varies depending on the dimension of personality in question. Contrary to our expectations, maternal and paternal emotionality do not strongly influence either marital satisfaction or the quality of mother–father interaction.

On the contrary, the activity/achievement dimension is particularly important as a predictor of marital quality. However, its impact on marital satisfaction is positive whereas it is negative on the quality of interaction. This pattern is similar for mothers and fathers, although for mothers the predictive power of activity/achievement orientation on marital satisfaction is higher, and on the quality of interaction it is lower, as compared with the fathers.

Antecedents of the mother–child relationship

As a second step of our analysis, we estimated the complete model of the antecedents of the mother–child relationship. Because of the relatively low associations found between reported marital satisfaction and observed quality of couple interaction, both variables were separately included in our model. It must also be noted that the variable indicating marital satisfaction includes the total couple satisfaction score (created by adding both parents' marital satisfaction scores). Thus both scores are measures of the parents as a dyad and not of the mother alone. The result for the measurement model again demonstrated a satisfactory fit. The factor loadings in the model are high. As to our criterion variable, the quality of mother–child interaction, factor loadings for child compliance were higher than for the quality of maternal assistance (0.99 and 0.53 respectively).

In the proposed model (shown in Fig. 7.1) both marital quality and maternal personality were hypothesized to affect the mother–child relationship, not only directly but also through the mediation of mother's parenting self-efficacy. It was further hypothesized that the impact of temperamental difficultness on the quality of the mother–child relationship, as indicated by the co-operative quality of interaction, is primarily direct but also mediated by perceived self-efficacy in the parenting role.

As shown in Fig. 7.3, the total model provides only a moderate fit to the data. Whereas the majority of findings were in line with our expectations there were also some unexpected results.

The results indicate moderate direct effects of maternal personality and marital quality on the quality of mother–child interactions. Contrary to the pattern observed for harmony of marital interaction, the emotionality aspect of maternal personality contributes significantly to the quality of mother–child interaction. A comparison of the respective bivariate correlations indicate that the relations between maternal anger and child non-compliance may have contributed particularly to this finding ($r = 0.45$, $p < 0.01$).

The positive relations between both aspects of marital quality and the quality of mother–child interactions are also in line with our expectations. The bivariate correlations reveal that child compliance is significantly related to both measures of marital quality ($r = 0.33$ for marital satisfaction, $r = 0.37$ for quality of couple interaction, $p < 0.05$), whereas the quality of maternal assistance is related to harmony of couple interactions only ($r = 0.30, p < 0.05$). It is interesting to note that in this model the summary score for marital satisfaction has a particularly strong predictive power on observed quality of marital interaction.

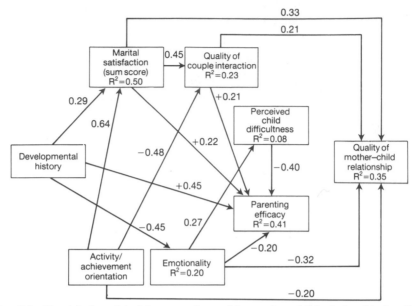

FIG. 7.3   Empirical model of the antecedents of the mother–child relationship (quality of mother–child interaction). Only path coefficients >0.20 are shown.

In the proposed model, maternal emotionality, marital relationship, and child difficultness were assumed to affect the mother's sense of competence in child-rearing functions. According to the path coefficients, parenting self-efficacy appears to depend particularly on positive experience in the mother's family of origin and in infant temperament, whereas marital satisfaction, the quality of couple interaction, and maternal emotionality have only a moderate impact. As for the influence of maternal emotionality, a comparison of the bivariate correlations indicates that the anger component of emotionality is not related to parenting efficacy, and thus might have reduced the predictive power of emotionality on feelings of helplessness in the child-rearing situation.

Contrary to the paths proposed in the theoretical model, neither child's difficultness, as perceived by the mother, nor her parenting efficacy had an impact on the mother–child relationship as measured by the co-operative quality of interaction.

Discussion

The discussion of the data first focuses on methodological issues and then on the implications of the findings concerning our model.

Methodological considerations

One methodological problem of the present study concerned the reliance on maternal self-report data as indicators for developmental history, marital satisfaction, personality traits, and parenting self-efficacy. Thus, the observed association between these variables could be attributed to consistency in aspects of the mothers' perceptions and evaluations alone. However, as I controlled for maternal frankness these links cannot be interpreted as merely reflecting such a general response bias. Further analysis suggested that a bias in maternal perception due to depression also does not contribute much to the observed relations.

Another problem concerns the inconsistency of the path coefficients estimated by our analysis procedure. This is not a characteristic of the method itself, but results when rather complex models are estimated on the basis of relatively small sample sizes. Although the path coefficients do show some change in magnitude from one model to the next, this change is not substantial. So the model estimates can be regarded with some confidence.

Finally, LVPLS, like LISREL, uses correlational data. Thus LVPLS is ill-suited to identify non-linear sorts of relations among variables included in the model.

Possible mechanisms mediating the links between marital and mother–child relationships

With respect to the interrelatedness of the quality of marriage and the mother–child relationship, the results were in line with expectations. Both aspects of marital quality, that is marital satisfaction and the quality of couple interaction, did predict the quality of mother–child interaction, though only to a moderate degree. The question arises as to the mechanism underlying such associations. Since it is the mother who is the same element in both dyads, one might argue that her personality characteristics were responsible for the observed similarity. The findings suggest that maternal activity/achievement orientation accounted for the observed similarity, whereas the effect of emotionality was specific to mother–child interaction. One explanation for the generalized effect of the activity/achievement orientation dimension is that couple discussion and the cleaning-up episode were similar in so far as both situations included problem-solving tasks and might be conceived as tests of competence. Accordingly, these situations might have provoked achievement-orientated behaviour towards the other member of the respective dyad.

Contrary to the activity/achievement dimension, maternal emotionality was predictive only of mother–child interaction. However, consistent with recent findings by Crockenberg (1985), it was only the anger, not the emotionality component, that was particularly important in predicting mother–child conflict. The missing link between maternal proneness to distress (typically described as frustration) and the harmony of couple and mother–child interaction is contrary to expectation and suggests some specificity in the role of subclinical depressiveness as a predictor of intrafamilial relationships. It seems that in cases where marital or mother–child conflict are criteria for the quality of a relationship, the predictive power of this passive aspect of personality functioning is limited. On the contrary, frequent expression of anger is incompatible with sensitive responsiveness and thus may produce a less compliant child, as research by Stayton et al. (1971) suggests.

In addition to maternal personality, mothers' marital satisfaction contributes to the quality of couple interaction as well as to mother–child interaction. Marital satisfaction itself depends largely on the personality dimensions—activity and achievement orientation—that have been found to have a negative impact on the quality of interactions. Mothers who described themselves as active, always on the run, and competitive also considered themselves as happy and satisfied with their marital relations. Research has shown that persons displaying high levels of achievement orientation and activity are more satisfied with their job and family situations on the whole, and are less inhibited and more interested in their surroundings as compared with individuals with lower scores (Fahrenberg et al. 1984). Thus, one might interpret marital satisfaction as another aspect of this positive socio-emotional adjustment.

The impact of marital satisfaction on the harmony of mother–child interaction was confirmed by an additional analysis. When we evaluated a causal model for the prediction of the quality of mother–child interaction, substituting marital satisfaction (sum score) and quality of couple interaction for marital satisfaction of the mother alone, this score was slightly more predictive ($p = 0.48$) of the mother–child interaction than her activity/achievement orientation ($p = -0.23$) and emotionality ($p = -0.35$). Partial correlations controlling for activity/achievement orientation revealed that the correlations between mother's marital satisfaction and her quality of assistance as well as child compliance were significant ($r = 0.31$, $p < 0.05$; $r = 0.47$, $p < 0.01$). Thus, besides maternal personality characteristics, marital satisfaction also accounts for a considerable proportion of the variance in harmony of mother–child interaction, supporting the notion of interdependence of familial relationships.

The role of developmental history

As for the impact of developmental history, the findings are mainly consistent with our hypothesis. Mothers and fathers who reported supportive childhood experiences and who recalled high couple adjustment between their parents were more satisfied with their own marriage. However, since marital satisfaction is affected by marital adjustment in the family of origin only for mothers ($r = 0.34$, $p < 0.05$), the notion of a cross-generational continuity in marital quality is only partly supported. Developmental history was also related to the parents' personality characteristics. However, the reports of how parents were reared in their families of origin and how their parents got along as a couple only predicted the emotionality but not the activity/achievement aspect of their personality. Given the literature on socio-emotional development, one might argue in retrospect that it seems more reasonable to assume that children's relationship experiences in the family of origin are more predictive of affect-related traits, such as anger and emotionality, in later adulthood than of behavioural styles, such as activity and achievement striving. The results indicate, too, that maternal developmental history was predictive of women's sense of competence and well-being as a parent (see Chapter 13, this volume). Addressing the question of which indicator variable of developmental history was particularly important, partial correlation controlling for maternal emotionality revealed that only childhood experiences with their mothers predicted maternal self-efficacy significantly (mean: $r = 0.33$, $p < 0.05$). Recall that the mothers' relationship with their own mothers was also more predictive of maternal emotionality than the relationship with their fathers. Taken together these data support the notion that experiences in the family of origin (at least as recollected) affect mothers' personal, marital, and parental functioning (perceived parental competence). Parallel to findings concerning the development of representations of relationships (Main et al. 1985), the data indicate that mother's childhood relationships with their own mothers seem to be particularly important. However, as this portion of the analysis relied on retrospective reports, generalizations drawn from these findings must be made with caution. Recent research has shown that the validity of reports of childhood relationships depend, at least partly, on how the mother has integrated her experiences and feelings regarding attachment (see Chapters 1 and 13, this volume). These current representations seem to be better predictors of maternal functioning than her actual experiences in her family of origin. More research needs to be done on the validity of retrospective accounts and processes underlying cross-generational continuity and discontinuity.

The interrelatedness of child difficultness and parenting self-efficacy

In addition to developmental history, child difficultness accounted for a substantial proportion of the variance in the women's sense of competence and well-being as a parent. With emotionality controlled, perceived difficultness still significantly predicted maternal self-efficacy (mean: $r = 0.30$, $p < 0.05$). This finding parallels Cutrona and Troutman (1986) who showed that, at three months after delivery, perceived self-efficacy of mothers is affected in important ways by infant difficultness. However, as the possibility still remains that, aside from maternal emotionality, maternal self-efficacy might have an impact on perceived child difficultness, this was tested by a revised model. In this modified model, accounting for 37 per cent of the variance in the outcome variable, the path coefficient from maternal self-efficacy to perceived child difficultness was even higher ($p = -0.49$). We may infer from these findings that the influence between both constructs might be best conceived of as bidirectional. If one accepts the notion that perception of child difficultness consists, at least partly, of objective components (Bates and Bayles 1984), one may argue that infants' characteristics, such as intense and frequent crying and lack of response to soothing, have an impact on parents' perceived effectiveness. In turn, little confidence in parenting ability may lead to a suboptimal performance in parental skills, and subsequently to infant's behaviour which might be viewed as difficult.

Child difficultness and parenting self-efficacy as related to mother–child relationship

Perhaps the most unexpected findings of the study were that neither maternal self-efficacy nor child difficultness affected the quality of mother–child interaction in important ways ($p = 0.15$ for maternal self-efficacy, and $p = -0.15$ for child difficultness). As for the impact of parenting self-efficacy, it may well be that it is more predictive for other aspects of control behaviour, such as persistence in controlling efforts. It may also be that maternal feelings of competence are predictive only for those types of interactions that are crucial with respect to the development of feelings of inadequacy in child rearing function, i.e. handling negative emotionality for 1-year-olds. Thus, the influence of parenting competence on control and compliance issues might be apparent by the time the child is 2 or 3 years of age, when these kinds of interactions become particularly important.

Concerning the role of perceived difficultness, we were not as confident regarding the direction and power of it's impact on mother–child interaction as we were with the other variables included in our study. The result confirms a number of earlier research findings that child temperament has little or no effect on mother–child interaction (e.g. Vaughn *et al.* 1981; Meyer 1985) but is opposite to findings by Lee and Bates (1985), who reported associations between perceived difficultness, maternal control behaviour, and child non-compliance. Several explanations could account for the different patterns observed. First, our control measure did not distinguish between positive or proactive controls and negative or reactive controls, which seem to be particularly important for conflict in mother–child interaction. Secondly, in our study mother–child interaction was observed when the children were 14 months old, instead of 2 years as in the study cited above. It might be that mothers have more flexible attitudes about what a 14-month-old child should or can do, so that coercive patterns of interaction (Patterson 1982) are not yet established. Furthermore, it may be that the relation between difficultness and harmony of interaction depends on a third variable, i.e. sex of the child. However, owing to the small sample size the model was not tested for specific subgroups. Finally, it may be that the relations between difficultness and mother–child control interaction are non-linear so that path analysis is inappropriate to discover this kind of association. Checking for this possibility, we split the children into three groups according to their difficultness scores, with child compliance being the dependent variable. Children rated as 'easy' were more compliant (49 per cent) than the moderate (32 per cent) or difficult (40 per cent) group. t-tests of the mean differences between the groups indicated that only the difference between 'easy' and the 'moderate' groups were statistically significant ($t(23) = 2.78$, $p < 0.01$, two-tailed). A similar analysis with the quality of maternal assistance as the independent variable, however, revealed no group differences. Obviously, there is a need for a more thorough analysis of the impacts of maternal child-related feelings and attitudes and child's characteristics on the quality of mother–child interaction. With respect to mother's and child's characteristics, it might be useful to consider other kinds of variables, such as maternal power-assertive and rigid attitudes, and child persistence in trying things out.

Conclusion

The data from our exploratory study provided moderate support for the idea that reported experiences in the family of origin affect parental personality as well as fathers' and mothers' marital relationship. The results also indicate that for further reasearch it might be useful to distinguish the generalized from the more specific effects, and to investigate these pathways for females and males separately.

The findings presented are consistent with the notion that the quality of marital and mother–child relationships, as indexed by the harmony of interactions, are interrelated. There is evidence for at least two hypotheses: one suggests a direct link from marriage to mother–child relationship, and the other refers to personality characteristics of the mother as the common ingredient in both kinds of relationship. Maternal activity and her achievement oriented tendencies seem to be important when conflict of interaction indicates the quality of relationship. On the contrary, the influence of maternal anger was predictive of the quality of mother–child interaction only. As with the impact of marital quality, the effect of maternal personality on mother–child interaction is mainly direct and not mediated through feelings of self-efficacy and well-being in the maternal role. The role of parenting self-efficacy as well as the child's difficultness as mediating factors in our proposed model did not prove to account for the data. It could be that those factors are not predictive at this age of the child and for this particular index of mother–child relationship. For future research it might be useful to consider different meanings of conflict in mother–child interaction. For example, patterns of predictors seemed to be different when child's compliance is adaptive for problem-solving, as compared with the type of situation we included in our study. Finally, it must be noted that harmony of interaction is only one index of the mother–child relationship. For a better understanding of the intra- and interpersonal influences on the mother–child relationship, additional models with other outcome variables need to be tested.

Summary

In the present study, an attempt was made to assess the relative status of experience in the family of origin, parental personality characteristics, marital quality, and child's difficultness in predicting the co-operative quality of the mother–child relationship.

Participants were 35 families with their 14-month-old first-born children. The contemporaneous assessments included: independent observations of mother–child interaction in a clean-up episode, and mother–father interaction in a couple discussion task. Parents completed questionnaires concerning their child-rearing history, personality, and marital satisfaction. In addition, the mother's perception of her self-efficacy in the parenting role and child difficultness were investigated with questionnaires. The data were analysed with a causal modelling approach based on latent variables (LVPLS). Two path models were tested. Results of the first path analysis with experience in family of origin, parental personality, and marital satisfaction as predictors of co-operative quality of couple interaction indicated that parents' activity and achievement-striving tendencies, as well as mother's marital satisfaction, were the most successful predictors.

Results of the second path analysis, with co-operative quality of mother–child interaction as outcome, revealed that both marital quality and maternal characteristics had a moderate effect. Bivariate correlations suggested that maternal anger is particularly predictive of conflict in mother–child interaction. Methodological questions associated with the causal modelling approach, and theoretical implications for understanding the interrelatedness of co-operative quality of couple and mother–child relationship are discussed. Furthermore, reasons for some unexpected results, such as the non-significant roles of child difficultness and parenting self-efficacy for harmony of mother–child interaction, are suggested.

References

Ainsworth, M. D. S., Blehar, M. C., Waters, E., and Wall, S. (1978). *Patterns of attachment: a psychological study of the strange situation*. Erlbaum, Hillsdale, NJ.

Bates, J. E. (1978). Infant characteristics 13 month. Unpublished manuscript. Indiana University.

Bates, J. E. (1980). The concept of difficult temperament. *Merill–Palmer Quarterly* **26**, 299–319.

Bates, J. E., and Bayles, K. (1984). Objective and subjective components in mothers perceptions of their children from age 6 months to 3 years. *Merrill–Palmer Quarterly* **30**, 111–30.

Bates, J. E., Maslin, C. A., and Frankel, K. A. (1985). Attachment security, mother–child interaction, and temperament as predictors of behavior problem rating at age three years. In *Growing points of attachment theory and research* (ed. I. Bretherton and E. Waters). *Monographs of the Society for Research in Child Development* **50**, (1–2), Serial No. 209, 167–93.

Belsky, J. (1984). The determinants of parenting: a process model. *Child Development* **55**, 83–96.

Buss, A. H. and Plomin, R. (1984). *Temperament: early developing personality traits*. Erlbaum, Hillsdale, NJ.

Crnic, K. A., Greenberg, M. T., Ragozin, A. S., Robinson, N. M., and Basham, R. B. (1983). Effects of stress and social support on mothers and premature and full-term infants. *Child Development* **54**, 209–17.

Crockenberg, S. (1985). Toddlers' reactions to maternal anger. *Merrill–Palmer Quarterly* **31**, 361–73.

Cutrona, L. E. and Troutman, B. R. (1986). Social support, infant temperament, and parenting self-efficacy: a mediational model of postpartum depression. *Child Development* **57**, 1507–18.

Domittner, G. (1979). Zum Einfluß der Fremdes- und Elternmeinung auf die Entwicklung heterosexueller Paarbeziehungen. Unpublished doctoral dissertation, University of Graz, Graz.

Easterbrooks, M. A. and Emde, R. N. (1984). *Marriage and infant: different systems linkages for mothers and fathers*. Unpublished manuscript, University of Colorado, Health Sciences Center, Denver, Col.

Engfer, A. (1984). Entwicklung punitiver Mutter-Kind Interaktionen im sozioökonomischen Kontext. Arbeitsbericht zum Antrag an die Deutsche Forschungsgemeinschaft auf Gewährung einer Sachbeihilfe, Unpublished manuscript, University of Munich, Munich.

Engfer, A. (1986). *Kindesmißhandlung. Ursachen, Auswirkungen, Hilfen.* Enke, Stuttgart.

Fahrenberg, J., Hampel, R., and Selg, H. (1984). *Das Freiburger Persönlichkeitsinventar FPI*. 4., revidierte Auflage. Hogrefe, Göttingen.

Field, T., Sandberg, D., Garcia, R., Vega-Lahr, N., Goldstein, S., and Guy, L. (1985). Pregnancy problems, postpartum depression, and early mother–infant interactions. *Developmental Psychology* **21**, 1152–6.

Goldberg, S. (1977). Social competence in infancy: a model of parent–infant interaction. *Merrill–Palmer Quarterly* **23**, 163–77.

Goldberg, W. A. and Easterbrooks, M. A. (1984). Role of marital quality in toddler development. *Developmental Psychology* **20**, 504–14.

Herrenkohl, R. C. and Herrenkohl, E. C. (1981). Some antecedents and developmental consequences of child maltreatment. *New Directions for Child Development* **11**, 57–76.

Hinde, R. A. (1976). On describing relationships. *Journal of Child Psychology and Psychiatry* **17**, 1–19.

Izard, C. E. (1979). The maximally discriminative facial movement coding system (Max). University of Delaware Instructional Resources Center, University of Delaware, unpublished manuscript. Newark, Delaware.

Lee, L. C. and Bates, J. E. (1985). Mother–child interaction at age two years and perceived difficult temperament. *Child Development* **56**, 1314–25.

Lohmöller, J.-B. (1984). *LVPLS 1.6 program manual—latent variables path analysis with partial least-squares estimation*. Zentralarchiv für Empirische Sozialforschung, University of Cologne, Cologne.

Main, M., Kaplan, N., and Cassidy, J. (1985). Security in infancy, childhood and adulthood: a move to the level of representation. In *Growing points of attachment theory and research* (ed. J. Bretherton and E. Waters). *Monograph of the Society for Research in Child Development* **50**, (1–2), Serial No. 209, 66–104.

Meyer, H.-J. (1985). *Zur emotionalen Beziehung zwischen Müttern und ihren erst- und zweitgeborenen Kindern*. S. Roderer, Regensburg.

Patterson, G. R. (1982). *Coercive family process*. Castalia Publishing, Eugene, Oreg.

Pope, H. and Mueller, C. W. (1976). The intergenerational transmission of marital instability. *Journal of Social Issues* **32**, 49–66.

Rutter, M. and Madge, N. (1976). *Cycles of disadvantage: a review of research*. Heinemann, London.

Schaffer, H. R. and Crook, C. K. (1979). On coding controls. Unpublished manuscript. University of Strathclyde, Glasgow.

Schaffer, H. R. and Crook, C. K. (1980). Child compliance and maternal control techniques. *Developmental Psychology* **16**, 54–61.

Sroufe, L. A., Jacobvitz, D., Mangelsdorf, S., DeAngelo, E., and Ward, M. J. (1985). Generational boundary dissolution between mothers and their preschool children: a relationship systems approach. *Child Development* **56**, 317–25.

Stayton, D. J., Hogan, R., and Ainsworth, M. D. S. (1971). Infant obedience and maternal behavior: the origins of socialization reconsidered. *Child Development* **42**, 1057–70.

Thomas, A. and Chess, S. (1977). *Temperament and development*. Bruner/Mazel, New York.

Vaughn, B. E., Deinard, A., and Egeland, B. (1980). Measuring temperament in pediatric practice. *Journal of Pediatrics* **96**, 510–18.

Vaughn, B. E., Taraldson, B., Crichton, L., and Egeland, B. (1981). The assessment of infant temperament: a critique of the Carey Infant Temperament Questionnaire. *Infant Behavior and Development* **4**, 1–17.

Voss, H.-G. and Meyer, H.-J. (1986). Zur Stabilität emotionaler Beziehungsmuster zwischen Müttern und ihren erst- und zweitgeborenen Kindern. Unpublished manuscript. Dept of Psychology, Technische Hochschule Darmstadt, Darmstadt.

Weber, R. A., Levitt, M. J., and Clark, M. C. (1986). Individual variation in attachment security and strange situation behavior: the role of maternal and infant temperament. *Child Development* **57**, 56–65.

Wold, H. (1982). Softmodeling: The basic design and some extensions. In *Systems under direct observation: causality, structure, prediction*, Vol. 2 (ed. K. G. Jareskog and H. Wold), 1–54. North Holland, Amsterdam.

III

Parent–first-born–second-born relationships

8

Changes in dyadic relationships within a family after the arrival of a second child
KURT KREPPNER

Introduction

A student of human development interested in how relationships influence other relationships is confronted with a gap in current knowledge: since Bell (1968) created the concept of bidirectionality in socialization, the developing individual has been studied in a number of dyadic relationships, such as mother–child (Lewis and Freedle 1973), father–child (Lamb 1975; Parke 1979) or sibling–sibling (Pepler *et al.* 1981; Dunn and Kendrick 1982), but how these relationships inside the family influence each other has not been investigated. Moreover, a consistent theoretical model of how one relationship may affect another is still lacking. Apart from Clarke-Stewart's (1978, 1980) studies on second-order effects and Belsky's (1981; Belsky and Isabella 1985) conclusions about parental and marital relationships in the family, only sparse empirical work is available in which whole families with their relational networks were investigated systematically (Maccoby and Martin 1983; Minuchin 1985; Chapter 1, this volume). However, turning to the domain of family research, one encounters another difficulty: the more relationship-oriented work on families has often neglected the developmental aspect and delineated individual development and the associated crises only globally (Kantor and Lehr 1975; Reiss 1981). Only in recent years have longitudinal conceptions about a family's development been formulated: these have been based upon the developmental tasks concept (Duvall 1971; Aldous 1978; Olson *et al.* 1983). In another area, the transition to parenthood, several studies of the changes in relationships after the arrival of the first child (LaRossa and LaRossa 1981; Cowan and Cowan 1983; Osofsky and Osofsky 1984) showed that stress increases during the years after pregnancy, for both mothers and fathers.

Approaching the field of developing relationships by using a double access, such as family research and developmental psychology, the student is confronted with another dilemma: whereas in family research the family is viewed as a system, with boundaries against the outside world, strategies for coping with problems, and patterns according to which communication among members is shaped, the changes in these different aspects as they occur over the life course have not yet been investigated. Although the family as a whole has been conceptualized as going through a life cycle with various stages, the variations of single relationships and the impact of these possible variations upon the network of the family's relationships have not been emphasized.

To overcome at least some of these problems, the linking of family research with longitudinal developmental studies offers promise for the investigation of continuity and change in relational networks. In addition, theoretical conceptions used in the respective domains may facilitate access to the complex interplay among relationships. One of these concepts is the idea that a family as a whole has tasks to accomplish for its successful transitions through the life cycle (Duvall 1971; Aldous 1978). Although the task concept refers to transitions in the roles and positions of individual family members, changes and continuities in their cognitive representations have not been conceptualized in terms of relationships. As recent research has shown, cognitive representations of social relationships can be assumed even in small children (Ford and Thompson 1985; Main et al. 1985). By regarding this cognitive representation as a kind of 'internal working model' (Bowlby 1969) of social relationships, one can view the question of how relationships influence other relationships as a psychological issue, and thereby combine relational with developmental aspects (Dix et al. 1986).

Relationships and development

Research on the interplay between individual and family development may highlight at least some of the components of constancy and change in the family's relationship network. The linking of individual human growth with transitions in family interaction can perhaps contribute to a new view of these intertwined processes. According to a family-oriented, development-in-context perspective, changes in extant relationships are essential for attaining a new balance after the arrival of a new child (Kreppner et al. 1982). However, at the same time, consistency in family interaction is a prerequisite for maintaining a kind of 'family identity', into which the new member is to be integrated and to which he or she has to adapt during the developmental course. This complicated process of equilibration includes not only establishing relationships with the new child, but also rearranging all existing relationships inside the family.

The family is often thought of as a paradigmatic example of context having its own dynamic character. The conceptualization of an interplay between the developing individual and a context which follows a developmental course raises a number of questions which to date have been considered relevant only for dyadic relationships (e.g. mother and child), or for the developing individual (e.g. maternal sensitivity, familial characteristic of interaction, etc.). In our approach, we attempt to emphasize the developmental nature of the context in which the individual is producing his or her own development (Lerner 1982). Thus, in addition to the traditional view of individual development as two directional but static (where the context does not change), changes induced by the acting individual are seen as influencing the context's own dynamics which in turn are creating a matrix of probabilistic conditions for individual development (Featherman and Lerner, 1985). In this respect, the interplay between individual and context development appears to be an issue which is extremely sensitive to alterations.

To describe these interdependent processes adequately, recent studies have strongly recommended a multimethod approach. For the study of interpersonal relationships, both the more general system-related considerations and behaviour-oriented micro-analyses must be included (Hinde 1979, 1982). In the following section, a methodological approach is described in which changes in relationships over time were explored by a combination of two methods: a qualitative delineation of the family's efforts to integrate a new member served as the first step, followed by a quantitative analysis of the family's changes in interaction patterns over time.

The expansion of the family system after the arrival of a second child

To explore changes in the relational network of a family, the arrival of a second child was taken as a kind of 'natural experiment'. A one-child family establishes a triadic relational network (mother–father–child) with a spousal relationship between father and mother, and two parental relationships, mother–child and father–child. This triad has to be expanded to a tetradic relational system when the second child arrives (mother–father–child 1–child 2), now encompassing six dyadic relationships. Not only can the establishing of interaction patterns with the new family member be abstracted as being one of the family tasks that must be accomplished during the course of development, but also the accomplishing of this task implies that all extant relationships are subject to possible alterations. However, the expansion process is only one component of the family system's discontinuity; the adaptation to the changing needs and abilities of the growing second child represents another. The family's efforts to find new interaction forms is also influenced to a large degree by the developmental steps of the child. As the new-born infant runs through its developmental course, the biological growth of locomotor and expressive abilities seems, at least in part, to determine the rhythm of family interaction. For example, during the child's first years of life, rapid and fundamental changes occur, impinging on the family's relational pattern. In the first months, the new child demands much care and attention. This almost inevitably leads to less care and attention for the older sibling. As a consequence, either the sibling him- or herself tries to attract more attention, or one of the parents (usually the father) has to spend more time with this child than before. During this period, both parents are more involved in caretaking activities, and this has, of course, consequences for their marital relationship as well. The follow-up of the new addition's integration and socialization into the family can serve as an approach for investigating the development-in-context process more thoroughly.

Methodological problems

A longitudinal study of a whole family with two small children poses a number of methodological questions. Expansion and adaptations to individual development can be investigated in single dyadic as well as more complex relational patterns. The inclusion of a rapidly developing child yields the possibility of observing changes in interaction and efforts towards mutual adaptation in the making. The necessary shift from a triadic to a tetradic system after the arrival of the new child can be seen by following the whole family system over a longer period of time. In a triadic family, three dyadic and one triadic relationships are possible; in a tetradic family, six dyadic, four triadic, and one tetradic constellations are possible. Thus, constellations representing the family's relational network as well as the several dyadic relationships can be studied as they change over time. However, when one attempts to pin-point such an expansion and adaptation, one is faced with a multitude of problems. Changes in a dyadic relationship can be denoted by a set of behavioural items, but alterations in a relational network are far more difficult to grasp. Moreover, the delineation of the system's own development and how the implicit changes in this process may influence the individual's developmental course on the one hand, and how it may itself be influenced by the individual's specific growth on the other, appears to be another tricky issue for empirical research.

A parallel analysis of all possible dyadic relationships (six relationships in a two-child family or 12 different initiative–target combinations), encompassing changes in family dynamics over time, would overcome this problem at least partially. Data from such an analysis could indicate general trends (independently of whether they were generated by an individual's or by the system's development) and provide a baseline for succeeding single case analyses. In such an empirical approach, interaction patterns of families could be compared with one another at specific times by using formal items such as the varying constellations of family members or the frequencies of initiating interactions. On the level of single case analysis, the particular solution for the family task (like the integration of a new child) can be traced back to typical interaction episodes; conclusions can then be drawn about the families' 'internal working model' for expectations about the children's developmental changes or the establishment of new relationships.

For the longitudinal study of families with small children, an additional problem must be mentioned: no specific instrument exists with which interaction in these young families could be measured properly. Whereas several observational methods have been developed for describing mother–child or father–child interaction, no comparable instruments are available for depicting whole families' interaction patterns and their possible changes over a longer time period. For instance, what may appear to be an excellent instrument for measuring parent–child interaction at 4 months may be irrelevant at, say, 18 months. The solution to this problem lies in choosing indicators that on the one hand are suitable for including all members of a family, but on the other also 'grow' with the children's developing capacities to initiate interactions.

Data sampling in family research is based mostly on either inquiries encompassing all family members or observations of lab-performed family communication (for example, as the family discusses a common task [Olson *et al.* 1983] or resolves an induced problem situation [Reiss 1981]). Both methodological approaches demand families with children who can answer an inquiry or who can at least talk and express verbally their own position in the family. Consequently, the family occupied with integrating a new member (i.e. caring for a baby which needs attention) cannot be studied by applying the same devices that are used when investigating families with school children or young adolescents.

Empirical study of expanding families

Sampling method and analysis of observational material

The observation of families with small children over a period of time was initiated as an exploratory study, in which a series of analytical approaches to the delineation of a family's expansion and socialization processes were attempted.

Sixteen families were observed over a two-year period. Each family had one child between 1 and 3 years old and a second child born at the beginning of the study. The families were visited in their homes every month and observed in their everyday interactions when one or both parents were dealing with one or both children. Observations took place in the later afternoon hours, when usually fathers had returned from work and could participate in family interactions. Videotapes covering 30 min to 1 h of family life were made from every visit.

For further analysis, interpretations of the family's interactions were guided by the concept of task accomplishment (having a new member who needs attention and care), by considering changes in the relational network (six instead of three possible dyads, new triadic constellations), and by focusing upon specific solution patterns of families in similar situations. This led to a global description of a three-phase model of the integration process during the two-year period. The changes in the expanding system were found to follow the developmental course of the new child as he or she grew and acquired new sensorimotoric, cognitive, and social skills. The most salient changes occurred at 8/9 months when the second child entered the crawling age, and at 16/17 months, when he or she became a 'real' member of the family by virtue of his or her expanded communication abilities. From a structural and family-oriented point of view, the common changes were interpreted as a kind of systemic expansion and development (Fig. 8.1; Kreppner *et al.* 1982).

Age of second child	Phases of family development	Structural changes of family system	Family tasks
0–8	Intergration for new member	Triadic system plus new member 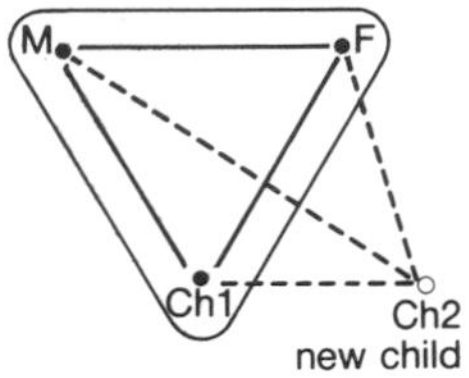	Introduction of the new member into the family Distribution of attention Involvement of father Maintaining of a spousal relationship
9–16	Achieving for new calibration	Negotiating positions 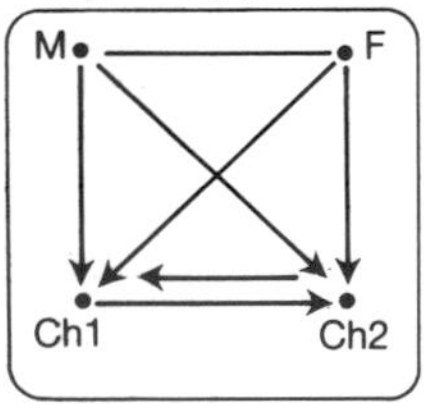	Transmission of social rules Setting of sanctions for transgressions of rules Language training Handling of sibling rivalry
17–24	Generation differentiation	Two subsystems 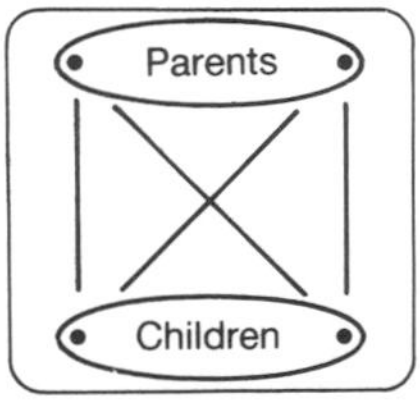	Establishment of parent and sib subsystems Individual relationships between parent and both children Affirmation of individual interests of parent Balancing parent's and children's interests

FIG. 8.1   Family development during the first two years.

After this first, more hermeneutic approach to analysing the family, we wished to supplement the global portrait of family expansion with a more refined analysis of single components of family interaction and socialization. Before proceeding further, we needed to make some decisions in order to be able to quantify various features of the socializing and integrating family system. First, units of analysis according to which certain elements could be classified had to be defined; secondly, a category system that could cover specifics of the family expansion process over the whole time period had to be created (Kreppner 1984).

After reviewing family interactions from videotapes encompassing the entire time span and participation of all family members, we found a 20–40 second interval (episode) to be the most appropriate unit. Whereas in most studies dealing with single mother–father–child interaction 5–10 second intervals are used, the potential complexity of interactions with two parents and two children present requires a longer time interval. The longer time interval allows the action–reaction–action–reaction cycle to be seen as the interchange involving the whole family network rather than just a single action–reaction dyad.

In the quantification of family interaction, the following dimensions were included for analysis:

(1) family constellation—number of members present in an episode, configuration among present members, specification of members;

(2) family dynamics—initiative of action, target of action.

On every dimension, up to 10 items were specified. For example, the initiative in an episode can be taken by the mother, by the father, or by another member of the family. By the same token, the target of action can be any member or a specific configuration (e.g. a dyad).

For the present empirical analysis, the video material for 13 families covering the two-year period was partitioned into seven segments covering three or four months each. The segments were labelled according to their respective central periods: birth to 12 weeks (6/8 weeks), 3–6 months (4/5 months), 7–10 months (8/9 months), 11–14 months (12/13 months), 15–18 months (16/17 months), 19–21 months (20/21 months), 22–24 months (23/24 months). Two videotaped observations from each time segment (observations on different occasions, each observation lasting 32 minutes) were combined to balance situational effects and then used as a basis for quantitative analysis. These samples of family interaction (64 minutes for each time segment from each of the 13 selected families) were split into episodes lasting between 20 and 40 seconds, yielding 160–180 episodes per segment and family, or about 1100 episodes per family, covering the whole period. Each episode was scored by trained raters; inter-rater reliabilities (Cohen's Kappa) ranged from 0.90 to

0.98 for the constellation categories, from 0.80 to 0.89 for the dimensions of family dynamics. In the following section, the focus will be on changes in family relationships over time.

General trends of changes

Family constellations   Changes in family constellations over time as a rather formal depiction of family interaction provide information about general trends in the expansion process of the family and the integration process of the new child. For the analysis of general trends in the changes, those constellations seemed to be of greatest interest in which all four family members were present.

Family constellations were coded by a three-digit number. The first digit indicates the number of persons present in an episode (1, 2, 3, 4); the second digit stands for the configuration among family members (1 = no, 2 = dyadic, 3 = triadic, 4 = tetradic interaction); and the third digit specifies the family members actually interacting in this configuration (for details see key of Fig. 8.2).

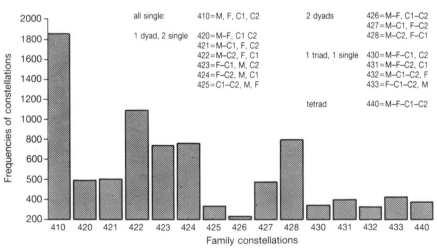

FIG. 8.2   Aggregated frequencies of family constellations with all four members present ($n = 13$).

As Fig. 8.2 shows, the most frequently occurring constellations were 410 (F, M, C1, C2), 420 (M–F, C1, C2), 421 (M–C1, F, C2), 422 (M–C2, F, C1), 423 (F–C1, M, C2), 424 (F–C2, M, C1), 427 (M–C1, F–C2), and 428 (M–C2, F–C1). The median of the families' distribution of frequencies was taken as an indicator for general trends of change over time. Looking at the time-specific course of those constellations which showed significant deviations from an equal distribution over time (see Table 8.1, first column), one can see, for example, that the constellation in which no interaction among members was scored although all were present (410: F, M, C1, C2), seldom occurred during the first months after the second child's arrival. It occurred increasingly during the second half of the first year, reaching a peak at its end, slightly decreasing, perhaps toward a new level, during the second year (Fig. 8.3). The course of this single constellation suggests that the arrival of the second child does indeed have an impact upon the family's interaction pattern during the first months after the child's birth. Its course indicates that in the expanded family a kind of stability is not regained earlier than during the second year. Moreover, looking at constellations in which the mother was interacting with the second child, while the father was either dealing with the first child (428: M–C2, F–C1) or having no interaction (422: M–C2, F, C1), one can see, particularly in 422, a pattern that was complementary to the 410 constellation: high frequencies prevailed during the first eight months, but thereafter decreased sharply, indicating the levelling of this mother–child 2 family constellation (Figs 8.4 and 8.5). The medians of father–child 2 constellations with mother having no interaction with the first child (424: F–C2, M, C1) showed a deviation from equal distribution only during the 4/5 months time segment, pointing to a rather short period in which the new constellation was established; afterwards it remained at a constant level in the expanded family (Fig. 8.6). The constellations depicting mother's interaction with the father and no interaction between the two children (420: M–F, C1, C2), and mother's interaction with the first child and no interaction between the father and the second child (421: M–C1, F, C2) did not deviate significantly from an equal distribution, the frequencies remained at an overall low level. The father's interaction with the first child, when mother and second child were present but not interacting (423: F–C1, M, C2) did not reach a moderate level until the 8/9 months period (Fig. 8.7). This indicates the relatively difficult situation confronting the first child in its family during the first 8–9 months after the sibling's arrival.

From these time-specific constellation patterns one can draw the conclusion that, at least during the first eight months after the second child's arrival, the family's interaction network is changing as a whole, not only in establishing relationships with the new child, but also in altering extant relationships between the parents and the first child.

Family dynamics   In order to pursue the relational imbalance more closely during the time after the second child's arrival, changes in dyadic relationships in terms of their internal dynamics were considered in more detail. Medians (q2) as well as upper (q1) and lower (q3) quartiles of the families' frequency distribution of initiative–target pairs in all dyadic configurations yielded a

Table 8.1   *Results of Kolmogorov–Smirnov tests*

Family constellations over time (one-sample test)	Initiative–target combinations over time (one-sample test)	Initiative–target comparison over time (two-sample test)
410: M, F, C1, C2**	M–C2**	M–C1/C2**
420: M–F, C1, C2(ns)	M–C1*	F–C1/C2(ns)
421: M–C1, F, C2(ns)	F–C2(ns)	C1–M/F(ns)
422: M–C2, F, C1**	F–C1**	C2–M/F(ns)
423: F–C1, M, C2*	C1–M*	C1/C2–M(ns)
424: F–C2, M, C1**	C1–F(ns)	C1/C2–F*
427: M–C1, F–C2(ns)	C2–M**	C1–C2/C2–C1*
428: M–C2, F–C1**	C2–F**	M–F/F–N**
	C1–C2*	
	C2–C1(ns)	
	M–F*	
	F–M(ns)	

(ns) $p > 0.05$; *$p < 0.05$; **$p < 0.01$; ***$p < 0.001$, two-tailed.

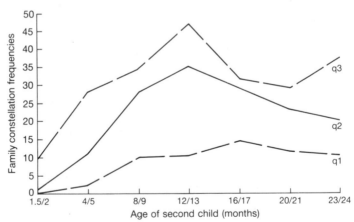

FIG. 8.3   Family constellations over time ($n = 13$). Constellation 410; median, upper, and lower quartiles.

picture of changes over time. Deviations of medians from an equal distribution over the entire two-year period were tested for all initiative target pairs (Table 8.1, second column). Interestingly, a number of medians did not deviate significantly from equal distribution, namely the father–child combinations F–C2, and C1–F, that is, when the father is initiating interaction with his

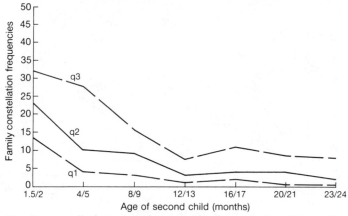

FIG. 8.4   Family constellations over time ($n = 13$). Constellation 422; median, upper, and lower quartiles.

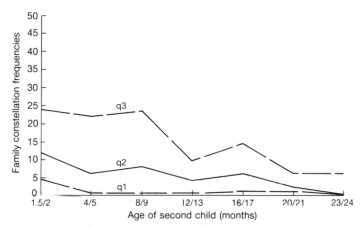

FIG. 8.5   Family constellations over time ($n = 13$). Constellation 428; median, upper, and lower quartiles.

second child as well as when the first child is turning to his or her father. Moreover, two subgroup combinations C2–C1 and F–M, where the second child and the father are initiators, did not display significant variations over time. Moderate significances showed up, however, when in the two generational subgroups the first child and the mother as initiators were considered (C1–C2 and M–F). In addition, moderately significant deviations appeared in the two configurations involving mother and the first child, M–C1 and C1–M. Highly significant deviations stood out in four combinations,

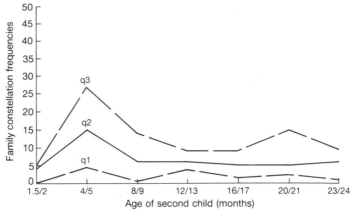

FIG. 8.6   Family constellations over time ($n = 13$). Constellation 424; median, upper, and lower quartiles.

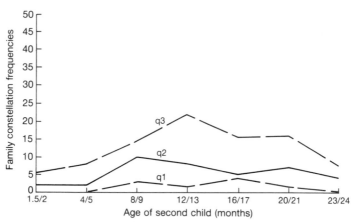

FIG. 8.7   Family constellations over time ($n = 13$). Constellation 423; median, upper, and lower quartiles.

three of which included the second child— M–C2, C2–M, and C2–F —one the father and the first child.

To find out more about general tendencies in the influence of relationships on other relationships during the period of family expansion, comparisons of selected combinations were conducted with the Kolmogorov–Smirnov two-sample test (Table 8.1, third column). First of all, the mothers' initiatives toward their two children (M–C1/C2) were highly different, and the same holds for the husband–wife/wife–husband comparison. Thus, the mothers apparently did not only show differences in their initiatives to their two children (preferring the second child over the first one), but they were also in an imbalanced situation with their husbands (they showed more initiatives toward their husbands than vice versa). Furthermore, moderately significant disparities among initiative–target pairs existed between the siblings' initiations to their father (C1/C2–F) as well as to each other (C1–C2/C2–C1). As the second child's developmental status during the first months has to be taken into account, this divergence caused by a higher rate of the first child's initiatives is hardly astonishing. However, the siblings obviously did not differ when their initiatives toward their mother were compared (C1/C2–M). When the two children were considered separately, the initiatives toward both parents did not show significant differences. This means that, even for the second child, the father seems to be an important target during this early period.

To illustrate selected changes in parent–child dyadic interactions within the family, the four courses of the mothers' and fathers' dyadic initiatives toward their two children as well as the first child's initiatives toward both parents are presented in more detail (Figs 8.8–8.13).

Inspection of these selected curves reveals that mother–child 2 initiatives occurred frequently during the first months, declined to the 8/9 months period, and remained at a constant level thereafter (Fig. 8.8). The frequencies of the mothers' initiatives toward their first-born children remained at an overall lower level, even during the period after 8/9 months when a new intrafamilial balance appeared to be reached (Fig. 8.9). The fathers' initiatives toward their new children remained at a generally lower level than the mothers' initiatives, but showed equally distributed frequencies over time (Fig. 8.10). Moreover, the fathers' initiatives toward their first children indicated a high degree of attention during the first eight months (Fig. 8.11), perhaps compensating the mothers' preoccupation with the new baby and contributing to a new balance.

Finally, looking at the first children's own initiatives in turning toward their parents, an increased effort to interact with the mother can be seen, particularly between the 8/9 and the 16/17 months period (Fig. 8.12). Though the median does not deviate significantly from an equal distribution, the course of the distribution of the first child's initiatives toward the father, as indicated by q1 and q3 values, displays a remarkable peak at 8/9 months (Fig. 8.13). Taking together the four courses that depict the child 1–parent relationships, two interesting tendencies can be noticed: first, child 1–father and father–child 1 interactions showed a similar pattern with a common peak at 8/9 months and a rather constant rate of frequencies thereafter, indicating a kind of balance over time in this relationship. Secondly, the child 1–mother and mother–child 1 interactions displayed a contrasting tendency. Whereas the first children appeared to increase their initiatives after the 8/9th month

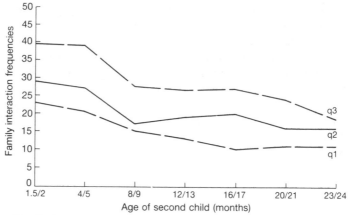

FIG. 8.8   Family interaction over time ($n = 13$). Mother–Child 2; median, upper, and lower quartiles.

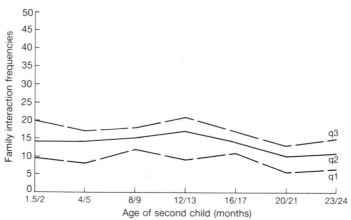

FIG. 8.9   Family interaction over time ($n = 13$). Mother–Child 1; median, upper, and lower quartiles.

period to reach their mothers, the mothers' initiatives moved in the opposite direction.

To summarize, the analysis of general trends in changes in relationships revealed a rather complex pattern with regard to different family constellations as well as with single dyadic interactions. A comprehensive picture of the family's general trends in establishing and re-establishing both extant and new relationships among members could be drawn by using an exhaustive set of

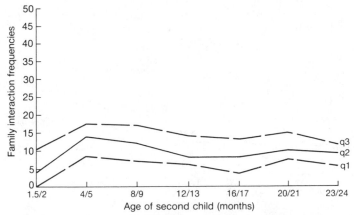

FIG. 8.10   Family interaction over time ($n = 13$). Father–Child 2; median, upper, and lower quartiles.

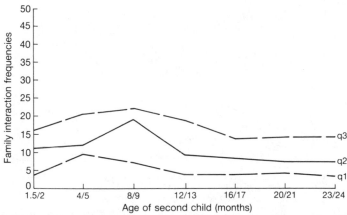

FIG. 8.11   Family interaction over time ($n = 13$). Father–Child 1; median, upper, and lower quartiles.

dyadic patterns. These patterns provided, in addition to an overall description, a baseline from which the deviations of single cases could be compared. Because the family's expansion and adaptation process is manifested in the changes of the constellations over time as well as in the single dyadic relationships, these indications of changes in family interaction provide a kind of window through which new aspects of the influences among relationships become visible.

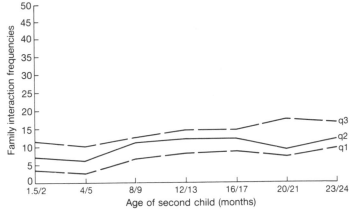

Fig. 8.12   Family interaction over time ($n = 13$). Child 1–Mother; median, upper, and lower quartiles.

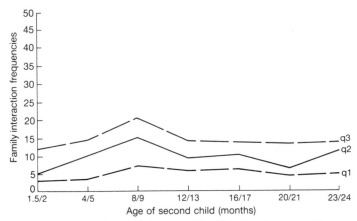

Fig. 8.13   Family interaction over time ($n = 13$). Child 1–Father: median, upper, and lower quartiles.

Single case analysis of relational interference

The achievement of family expansion and the manner in which the new child is integrated can be investigated in more detail by analysing single cases. In the following section I discuss a family that shows salient deviations from the other families in the specific constellations and initiative–target patterns. These indices of family interaction are taken as a starting point to find out more about specifics in family communication, which in turn could point to inner representations or 'internal working models' that contribute to the generation of these patterns.

The distributions of the single families' constellations (see Fig. 8.14) revealed in general higher frequencies for mother–child 2 configurations, 422 (M–C2, F, C1) and 428 (M–C2, F–C1), than for mother–child 1 configurations, 421 (M–C1, F, C2) and 427 (M–C1, F–C2). In one family (no. 6, black bars) the opposite situation occurred, and in the double-dyadic constellation mother–child 1/father–child 2, this family no. 6 exceeded all other families, whereas it remained within the distribution's range for the mother–child 2/ father–child 1 configuration. The analysis of configurations with only one dyadic interaction makes the difference in this mother's dealing with the two children even more obvious: a comparison between this family's constellation 421 (M–C1, F, C2) and 422 (M–C2, F, C1) showed an excessive rate of mother–child 1 frequencies and a rather low rate of mother–child 2 frequencies. In comparing these maternal interaction patterns with the father's configurations, no such deviations could be found.

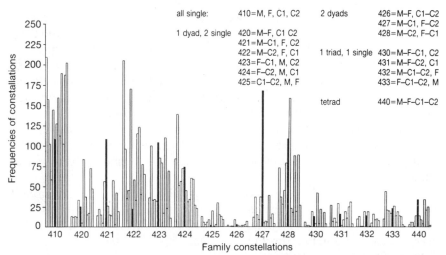

FIG. 8.14   Frequencies of single families' constellations with all four members present $(n = 13)$.

In addition, when the time-specific courses of the relevant mother–child 2 constellations were compared with mother–child 1 constellations, the lack of higher frequencies in the mother–child 2 constellations during the first months was apparent. The general trend for the mothers' initiatives toward both children showed that mothers were mostly occupied with their second children during the first months (Fig. 8.8). Examination of the course of no. 6 family's directed mother–child 1/child 2 interactions made the deviation of the mother–second child interaction obvious. In contrast to the other families, the mother here shared her attention between two children rather equally during the first months. During the second year, however, the pattern of interaction followed the general trend of the other families.

This abstract pattern, indicating a peculiar set for handling relationships in the expanding family, must be brought to life. One question, for example, is how the maintenance of the old relationship influenced the new relationship between the mother and her second child. Relationships are constructed by individuals and realized through particular formats of verbal and non-verbal exchange. It seemed, therefore, that it would be interesting to follow the communication between the mother of family no. 6 and her first and second children during the first months, when she deviated strongly from the general pattern. The analysis of a sample of everyday communication could perhaps shed some light upon the model this mother had for the relationship with her second child as compared with that for the first child. In other words, keeping in mind the extreme position of this family in the mother–child 1 and mother–child 2 relationships, information could be gathered about the possible internal model that allowed the mother–child 1 relationship to continue *although* a second child demanded attention and a new relationship had to be established. Knowledge about the deviation from 'baseline' behaviour can guide the interpretation of communication patterns to reveal the mechanisms that produced the specific format of relationships. In the present case, one could presume that the attempt to maintain the mother–child 1 relationship must have had manifestations in the maternal communications to both children. The clinging to an exlusive relationship with the first child even after the second child's arrival must have entailed a kind of retardation in the establishment of a new relationship with the second child.

The modality and direction of communication can highlight both parents' efforts to leave the old triadic relationship pattern untouched by the new member. To demonstrate this kind of 'enriched interpretation' of this family's everyday interaction, two short episodes have been selected (see Appendix).

In the first episode, the mother is talking to the first child about the new baby in a rather impersonal way, suggesting that her crying has to be borne, is unchangeable like a natural phenomenon ('she always cries'). In her conversation with the older child, the mother even anticipates more crying and suggests a tool for stopping it. Interestingly, the mother never directly addresses the new child, and neither does the father who is undressing the baby. He joins the mother's and the first child's discussion about the new baby's unchangeable behaviour, thus restoring the old triadic formation.

In the second episode, as the mother is directly involved in a caretaking activity with her second child, she obviously expects trouble although the baby is lying quietly in her arms. Again, the old triadic formation encompassing father, mother, and first child is apparently being re-established. At the end of this episode, the mother passes the baby on to the father who is going to dress her. She is now renewing her old relationship with her first child.

Summing up, this enriched interpretation of a family's everyday interaction episode may redirect attention to the relevance of quantitative results. The simple interpretation of an episode without additional information concerning the recurrence of typical aspects may appear somewhat arbitrary and perhaps even hazardous. Results of the quantitative analysis of typical relationship patterns, however, stay on a rather abstract level unless a piece of 'real' communication can clarify their meaning on the level of everyday communication. In our case, the integration of two different approaches can highlight the interplay between the maintenance of a special relationship and the effect this has on another relationship which remains in a way 'undeveloped' compared to other mothers' activities to stimulate their babies during the first months. From this perspective, the mother's communications about the new 'intruder' can be taken as a kind of recurring pattern which tends to maintain the old equilibrium (triadic formation).

Conclusion and outlook

This study's results point to complex interaction patterns among relationships within the family, but to date no consistent framework exists which could help specify those components of the network that have a major impact upon either individual or family development. This study's attempt to combine these two aspects was intended to gain more fruitful access to the process of development in context. With this linkage, a genuine developmental perspective is introduced into family research. As a possible contribution to the construction of a framework, two components commonly used in the study of individual development were transferred to the development-in-context domain: developmental tasks and the internal working model. Developmental tasks have been used as a device for exploring relational changes in families during the life course, and the concept of an 'internal working model', known mainly from attachment research, has been adapted to grasp the cognitive representations of relational experiences. An integrated view of developmental and relational aspects on the one hand, and of outside and more general delineations (family tasks) as well as internal and more specific features (internal working models) on the other, may guide us to a more comprehensive framework for understanding the development-in-context process.

Beyond a linear and perhaps mechanistic view of how single relationships in a family influence each other, one can imagine the existence of a higher-order effect providing a sort of 'meta'-perspective of how relationships exert influence upon each other. If one assumes a developmental course for the family system, then single dyadic relationships inside the system may change not only from being directly affected, but also as a result of a higher-order influence giving rise to a new format of interaction in the expanded family's relational network.

Thus, changes occurring in relationships can be regarded as being generated not only by other specific single relationships, but also by possible transitions in the network as a whole, as they occur at specific 'turning points' during the family's life course.

As an heuristic tool for a better understanding of such a higher-order transformation on the level of interacting individuals and on the level of internal representations, perhaps Bateson's (1973) notion of a 'deutero-learning' (or 'meta-learning') process provides a useful guide. With this concept Bateson tries to delineate the compilation of social experience in the individual, a process which is assumed to be different from the process by which object-related learning takes place ('proto-learning'). In this, the individual is seen as taking into account the situational conditions in which he or she learns. The relational context in which proto-learning occurs is itself learned by a kind of second-order learning process. By the same token, situational conditions of a whole family's network may have an impact upon the establishment of new single relationships in the expanding system.

The notion of an interdependent set of developing relationships brings a new perspective to the question of how relationships influence relationships. The process of accumulation in a child's internal working model may be conceived of as a second-order learning process about how to act in a complex relational network, which can be described as being similar to Bateson's notion of a 'larger entity'. Enrichment in the accumulation process can sometimes be found without any influence coming from outside the system's boundaries, but rather being induced by the process delineated as a higher-order learning process. Thus, changes in single dyadic relationships (e.g. mother–child 1 (A) and father–child 1 (B)) inside the same network might be triggered by the process described by Bateson as 'practice':

'There is thus a larger entity, call it *A plus B*, and that larger entity, in play, is achieving a process for which I suggest that the correct name is *practice*. This is a learning process in which the system A plus B receives no new information from outside, only from *within the system*. The interaction makes information about parts of A available to parts of B and vice versa.' (1979, p. 138)

It can be suggested that this kind of learning process may occur in an expanding (developing) family system, and perhaps better characterizes the accumulation of complex internal models than does the description of learning in single dyadic relationships. In addition, the concept of family tasks may serve as a valuable, supplementary framework for describing specific development-dependent situational conditions under which the deutero-learning processes occur. For example, as the family has to accomplish the expansion and integration task, the mother–father and mother–first child relationships may be changed (perhaps enriched) by the establishment of relationships with the new child. The compilation of social experiences is the basis for the family members' cognitive representations affecting the practice of establishing relationships (see Chapter 2, this volume). Finally, the situational condition whereby a stock of experience concerning relationships is built can be classified according to the specific modality by which the family tries to accomplish their tasks. With this combination of the family task and internal working model concepts, the analysis of the mutual influence of one relationship upon another could perhaps be guided by a set of more differentiated and sophisticated hypotheses than is the case in today's research.

Thus, as a final consideration when exploring mutual influences in a relational network, one could ask the question as to how individual and family development synchronize with each other. Does the accomplishment of family tasks generate an alteration in social exchange that in turn gives rise to specific deutero-learning processes, building up an internal working model for the establishment of further relationships? Or, going the other way around, does the meta-learning process lead to changes in the family's internal representation of social reality which trigger the accomplishment of the new task, thereby spurring the development process of the family. Could there be a kind of asynchrony in these two processes in pathological development? Further research needs to deal with these kinds of problems more thoroughly.

Summary

Bridging the gap between developmental psychology and family research has been the aim of studies of changes in dyadic relationships within the family. Whereas single mother–child and father–child relationships have been preferred targets in infancy research, a comprehensive picture of the entire family's relational network and its changes during children's development is still lacking. Moreover, family research, though stressing the complex dependency of the single relationships within the family's communication network, has neglected developmental processes of family members as a factor for relationship changes.

After the birth of a second child, all extant dyadic relationships in a family have to be rearranged, and new relationships with the new member have to be established. The necessary expansion of the triadic family to a tetradic formation was used as a kind of 'natural experiment', providing a basis for comparison in an observational study and a starting point for the analysis of changes in relationships.

Thirteen families were investigated as they changed in constellations and dyadic interactions during the two years after a second child's arrival. For the quantitative analysis, videotaped family interactions in everyday life were partitioned into small episodes and scored according to a number of categories covering structural and dynamic aspects.

Analyses point to an intense mother–child 2 interaction during the first 8–9 months and a continuous preference for the new child over the older sibling for the whole period. Differences were found in the balance in the relationships the first children had with their mothers and fathers. While the first children displayed an increasing tendency to interact with their mothers after the 8/9 months period, the mothers' initiatives to turn toward their first children decreased. The first children's and the fathers' tendencies to initiate interaction seemed to concur over the entire two years.

The accomplishment of a family task in everyday interaction was illustrated in a single case analysis. A family was selected which showed deviating patterns with untypically low frequencies of mother–child 2 constellations and interactions during the first months, the time when the activity of mothers to integrate the new child into the family's relational network is usually very high. In this case, the parents' dealings with their two children were taken as exemplifying a general family task (integration of the new child) and this family's everyday interaction and communication were interpreted as being specific accomplishments of that task (maintenance of the extant triadic constellation).

Acknowledgements

The empirical research reported in this chapter is part of a project which was carried out in collaboration with Yvonne Schütze. I gratefully acknowledge the helpful contribution of Alexander von Eye to the statistical analysis of the data. I want to thank Christiane Brunke and Holger Wessels for their assistance in computing the data, and I appreciate all the raters who helped to produce the data from the videotapes.

Appendix

Episodes: recurring patterns of family interaction concerning mother–child 2 and mother–child 1 interactions.
(Family M is preparing, conducting, and ending the ritual of bathing the children. Age of second child: 16 days/period 1).

The family is in the nursery, M is undressing C1, F is with C2. C2 begins to whine while F is beginning to undress her.

C1:   Ulla (*C2*) is crying!

M: (*to C1*) Ulla is crying. Well, you know. In the first place she is a little hungry, I suppose.

F: And she doesn't like to be undressed.

M: And in the second place she doesn't like to be undressed, you know. If one dresses and undresses her, she always cries. And later on, after the bath, she is going to cry even more! One should try to give her the pacifier.

F: Exactly.

M: (*to C1*) You know.

Family is in the bathroom. M is holding the baby in a small tub, F is standing beside her, bending over the front area of the main tub in which C1 takes her bath.

M: (*to C2 who is lying quietly in the tub*) Please, don't cry after the bath when you'll be dressed, It's so nerve-racking! (*After a while*) Hello! (*M moves the baby softly back and forth in the water and wets her hair*) Hair-wash!

F: (*to C1*) Look, Ulla's hair is being washed!

M: And she doesn't even cry.

F: (*to C1, pointing to C2*) Look, there!

C1:   She still isn't crying.

After M has finished hair-wash and bathing the baby.

M: (*to C2*) Now, you could stay a little longer, couldn't you? If we leave the tub, you are going to yell terribly, won't you? You are not crying here, so I better let you stay here until tomorrow morning.

F is turning from C1 to C2, and both parents are now looking at C2. C1 calls F back.

M: (*to F*) Would you please hold the towel? (*for C2*)

F holds the towel in which C2 is going to be wrapped. M lifts C2 out of water, C2 begins to whine.

M: (*to C2*) You don't like to be taken out of the tub, do you?

Both M and F are wrapping C2 in the towel, M passes C2 to F.

M: (*to F*) Please take her over.

F leaves with C2 for the nursery, M turns to C1 who is still in the bath and begins a relaxed conversation with her.

References

Aldous, J. (1978). *Family careers*. Wiley, New York.

Bateson, G. (1973). The logical categories of learning and communication. *Steps to an ecology of mind* (ed. G. Bateson), pp. 133–44. Paladin, Frogmore.

Bateson, G. (1979). *Mind and nature*. Dutton, New York.

Bell, R. Q. (1968). A reinterpretation of the direction of effects in studies of socialization. *Psychological Review* **75**, 81–95.

Belsky, J. (1981). Early human experience: a family perspective. *Developmental Psychology* **17**, 3–23.

Belsky, J. and Isabella, A. (1985). Marital and parent–child relationships in family of origin and marital change following the birth of a baby: a retrospective analysis. *Child Development* **56**, 342–9.

Bowlby, J. (1969). *Attachment and loss*, Vol. 1, *Attachment*. The Hogarth Press, London.

Clarke-Stewart, K. A. (1978). And daddy makes three: the father's impact on mother and young child. *Child Development* **49**, 466–78.

Clarke-Stewart, K. A. (1980). The father's contribution to children's cognitive and social development in early childhood. In Pedersen, *The father–infant relationship* (ed. F. A. Pedersen), pp. 111–46. Praeger, New York.

Cowan, P. A. and Cowan, C. P. (1983). *Quality of couple relationships and parenting stress in beginning families*. Paper presented at the Biennial Meeting of the Society for Research in Child Development, Detroit.

Dix, T., Ruble, D. N., Grusec, J. E., and Nixon, S. (1986). Social cognition in parents: inferential and affective reactions to children of three age levels. *Child Development* **57**, 879–94.

Dunn, J. and Kendrick, C. (1982). *Siblings: love, envy, and understanding*. Harvard University Press, Cambridge, Mass.

Duvall, E. (1971). *Family development*, (4th edn.). J. B. Lippincott, Philadelphia.

Featherman, D. L. and Lerner, R. M. (1985). Ontogenesis and sociogenesis: problematics for theory and research about development and socialization across the life span. *American Sociological Review* **50**, 659–76.

Ford, M. E. and Thompson, R. A. (1985). Perceptions of personal agency and infant attachment: toward a life-span perspective on competence development. *International Journal of Behavioral Development* **8**, 377–406.

Hinde, R. A. (1979). *Towards understanding relationships*. Academic Press, New York.

Hinde, R. A. (1982). The uses and limitations of studies of nonhuman primates for the understanding of human social development. In *Parenting: its causes and consequences* (ed. L. W. Hoffman, R. Gandelman, and H. R. Schiffman). Erlbaum, Hillsdale, NJ.

Kantor, D. and Lehr, W. (1975). *Inside the family*. Jossey Bass Publications, San Francisco.

Kreppner, K. (1984). Kategoriensystem zur Beschreibung familialer Interaktionen. Unpublished manuscript, Max Planck Institute for Human Development and Education.

Kreppner, K., Paulsen, S., and Schütz, Y. (1982). Infant and family development: from triads to tetrads. *Human Development* **25**, 373–91.

Lamb, M. (1975). Father: forgotten contributers to child development. *Human Development* **18**, 245–66.

LaRossa, R. and LaRossa, M. M. (1981). *Transition to parenthood. How infants change families*. Sage, Beverly Hills.

Lerner, R. M. (1982). Children and adolescents as producers of their own development. *Developmental Review* **2**, 343–70.

Lewis, M. and Freedle, R. (1973). Mother–infant dyad: the cradle of meaning. In *Communication and affect* (ed. P. Pliner, L. Krames, and T. Alloway), pp. 127–55. Academic Press, New York.

Maccoby, E. E. and Martin, J. A. (1983). Socialization in the context of the family: parent–child interaction. In *Handbook of child psychology: socialization, personality, and social development*, Vol. 4 (ed. P. H. Mussen), pp. 1–101. Wiley, New York.

Main, M. B., Kaplan, N., and Cassidy, J. (1985). Security in infancy, childhood, and adulthood: a move to the level of representation. In *Growing points of attachment theory and research* (ed. I. Bretherton and E. Waters). *Monographs of the Society for Research in Child Development* **50**, (1–2), Serial No. 209, 66–104.

Minuchin, P. (1985). Families and individual development: provocations from the field of family therapy. *Child Development* **56**, 289–302.

Olson, D. H. McCubbin, H. I, Barnes, H. L., Larsen, A., Muxen, M. J., and Wilson, M. (1983). *Families: what makes them work*. Sage, Beverly Hills.

Osofsky, J. D. and Osofsky, H. J. (1984). Psychological and developmental perspectives on expectant and new parenthood. In *Review of Child Research* Vol. 7, *The Family* (ed. R. D. Parke), pp. 372–97. The University of Chicago Press.

Parke, R. D. (1979). Perspectives on father–infant development. In *Handbook of infant development* (ed. J. D. Osofsky), pp. 549–90. Wiley, New York.

Pepler, D. J., Abramovitch, R., and Corder, C. (1981). Sibling interaction in the home: a longitudinal study. *Child Development* **52**, 1344–7.

Reiss, D. (1981). *The family's construction of reality*. Harvard University Press, Cambridge, Mass.

9

Connections between relationships: implications of research on mothers and siblings

JUDY DUNN

Although it is generally accepted that the relationships a child forms are influenced by—and in turn influence—other relationships within his or her social world, we still know very little about the nature and extent of such influences. This ignorance is in one sense surprising: it is, after all, a central tenet of Freud's formulation of personality development that the early mother–child relationship influences in a profound way an individual's later relationships. Most discussion of the effects of relationships upon other relationships in development has, in fact, centred on this issue of the sequelae of the child's relationship with the primary caregiver, either in the context of the consequences of differences in attachment between child and mother for children's behaviour with peers (Easterbrooks and Lamb 1979; Sroufe and Ward 1980; Sroufe and Fleeson 1986), or in the context of trans-generational effects in parent–child relationships (e.g. Belsky and Isabella 1985; Dowdney *et al.* 1985). Interest has focused, too, on the significance of marital relations for parent–child relationships (Belsky and Isabella 1985), but the mutual influence of children's other close relationships—father–child, sibling–child, grandparent–child—and their links with the mother–child relationship have received much less attention. Moreover, it remains the case that features of the mother–child relationship other than security of the child's attachment have been little studied in relation to other relationships, and, most importantly, the nature of the processes that may be involved in mediating the links between relationships is little understood.

In this chapter I want to consider the connections between one trio of family relationships, those of a mother with each of her two children, and the relationship between those two children. A close look at the evidence for links between these three not only shows us something of the complexity of the interconnections between these relationships, but also suggests a number of different processes that may be involved in mediating the influence of one relationship upon another. And it highlights a number of issues that are relevant to thinking more generally about the relations among relationships, points that may be applicable to the connections between other relationships and to other phases of development.

Reflection on the evidence for links between the sibling–child and mother–child relationship makes clear, for instance, one central issue: that many different processes are probably involved in such connections, processes operating at very different levels of analysis. Which of these processes we choose to emphasize will depend on our own preferred approach to describing relationships, and upon the framework within which we attempt to understand development. I will consider in turn, in this chapter, five sets of findings from our studies on siblings and from those of others, each of which suggests processes of very different kinds that link mother–child and sibling–child relationships. The aim is to illustrate the variety of ways in which these three relationships inter-relate, and to provide a basis for considering how far these processes may be of developmental importance, and relevant for other relationships.

There is another more immediately practical reason for examining the links between these three family relationships. Relationships between siblings frequently involve uninhibited expression of aggression or hostility, and parents are commonly held to be responsible for such hostility between their children (e.g. Calladine and Calladine 1979). Given the concern and distress that many parents feel at the expression of hostility between their children (Newson and Newson 1968), and their own sense of helplessness about coping with it, it is important that we should examine the basis of these claims of parental responsibility for sibling conflict.

Three caveats about the material that I shall discuss should be noted. First, the data to be discussed chiefly concern *interaction* between siblings, and between child and parent, rather than more global dimensions of relationships. Extrapolation from such interactional data to discussion of relations among relationships should probably be done with caution. However, it should be noted that the series of interactions that I shall discuss are nested within long-term relationships, and influenced by the quality of those relationships. Secondly, it should be taken as a given that we can make inferences about direction of effects in very few of the sets of data that I shall discuss—a point to which I will return. Thirdly, for clarity of presentation, I shall discuss the data chiefly in terms of pairs of dyadic relationships; it is, however, important to acknowledge that each of the dyadic relationships is likely to be influenced by many other relationships.

A. Emotional disturbance as a connecting link

The first set of findings concerns the first child's relationship with the mother before and immediately following the birth of a sibling, and the relationship between the two siblings that develops over the ensuing year. Our first sibling study followed families from before the birth of a second child through the infancy of the second, and included observations of mother–child and sibling–child interaction, as well as interviews with the mother (Dunn and Kendrick 1982). The results (replicated in several recent studies) revealed that most first–born children showed signs of disturbance following the sibling's birth, and that there were also marked changes in the interaction between the first–born and their mothers, with a sharp decrease in maternal attention, and in play, and an increase in punitive and restrictive maternal behaviour. There was also a change in the responsibility for initiating and maintaining communicative interaction: after the sibling birth there was a sharp decrease in the proportion of initiations of interaction for which the mother was responsible, other than prohibiting exchanges. The signs of disturbance in the first-born children varied: some became more difficult and demanding, some more clinging and unhappy, and around a quartèr of the sample of first-born children responded to the sibling birth by a sharp increase in *withdrawn* behaviour. In these families the drop in communicative interaction between mother and first-born was particularly marked. We argued from these results that the experiences of dramatic shifts in the relationships of the children with their mothers were probably linked to the signs of disturbance in the first-borns.

Now as we followed the children over time we found striking differences in the quality of the relationship that developed between the siblings, ranging from sibling pairs whose every interaction was friendly and affectionate to pairs who were never observed to interact in a friendly way, but who were continually aggressive and hostile. Among the findings of the study there were two sets of connections between the mother–child relationship at the time of arrival of the sibling and these differences in the relationship that developed between the siblings, to which I want to draw attention.

The first of these connections was that the children who reacted to the changes in the mother–child relationship by becoming withdrawn, and whose relationships with their mothers were marked by a particularly sharp drop in interaction, were one year later particularly hostile and negative to their younger siblings, and their siblings were negative to them. One possible interpretation of this set of findings is that the experience of the sharp change in the mother–child relationship that accompanied the sibling birth led for some children to a general emotional insecurity and anxiety, a disturbance manifest in their extremely withdrawn behaviour, and that this *general emotional reaction* coloured the children's social behaviour and relationships with others, including their developing relationship with their siblings. According to this interpretation, then, the process linking the mother–child and sibling–child relationship is a general one, a connection mediated by the child's general emotional well-being. We would expect, if this interpretation (example A in Fig. 9.1) has validity, to find that these children had difficulty in a number of their social relationships: in their peer relationships, in their relationships with their fathers, grandmothers, and other important figures in their lives.

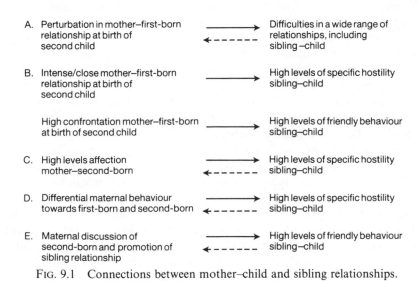

FIG. 9.1   Connections between mother–child and sibling relationships.

B. Response to displacement: siblings filling an emotional need?

A second set of findings linking the early mother–child relationship to the individual differences in the sibling relationship suggested rather more specific or focused connections. The families had differed greatly in the quality of the relationship between mother and first–born child before and immediately following the birth of the sibling. The differences were particularly marked in two aspects of the relationship: in the amount of play and joint attention between mother and first child, and in the frequency of confrontation and maternal prohibition. (There was a significant but not substantial negative correlation between these two aspects of interaction $(r_s(43) = -0.36)$.) In families with first-born girls in which there had been a relatively high frequency of joint play and attention between mother and daughter before and immediately following the sibling birth, the first-born girl was more likely to behave in a hostile way towards her sibling 14 months later than the first-born children in families in which the mother–child relationship had not been so close. In these families, moreover, the younger sibling, too, was by 14 months much less friendly toward the older sibling than the younger siblings in the other families. In contrast, in families in which there had been a relatively high frequency of confrontation between mother and first-born girl before the sibling birth, the daughters were, one year later, particularly friendly towards their siblings. The interview questions concerning the relationships of both girls *and* boys with their fathers suggested a very similar pattern of results. These results raise a number of different questions that are beyond the scope of this chapter (but see Dunn and Kendrick 1982). There is space here simply to consider briefly two interpretations of the pattern of findings.

One interpretation of the results is to view the hostile behaviour of those girls who had enjoyed a close relationship with their mother as a response to being supplanted—hostile behaviour directed at a usurper, an emotional response but one more specific in focus than that disturbance indicated in example A. We have argued, however, that there is another way to view this pattern, and that is to focus on the high level of warm and friendly behaviour directed toward the sibling by those children who had a more detached relationship, or a relationship with a high degree of conflict and confrontation, with their parents. In these families the developing relationship with the sibling can, it appears, contribute greatly to the emotional life of the child. The pattern of results suggests a connection (example B in Fig. 9.1) that is again of a general emotional kind—that a need for affection and attention is sometimes met *within the sibling relationship* for those children whose relationships with their parents are more distant or confrontational. Fitting with such an interpretation are other findings from the first sibling study, such as the data showing that in families in which the mothers were depressed and tired after the sibling birth, the relationship between the siblings developed in a particularly friendly fashion. These two interpretations are not, of course, incompatible. The two processes might each be operating within different families.

C. Focused hostility as a response to an affectionate relationship between others

Other findings from the studies suggest quite different kinds of processes linking the quality of the mother–child relationship with that of the siblings. This evidence suggests that for some children who develop a hostile relationship with their sibling, this hostility is linked to a particularly close, playful, and affectionate relationship between the mother and the second-born child. There are correlations, for example, over time between measures of the frequency with which mother and second-born play together and, six months later, the frequency of negative behaviour shown by the first–born to the second, and vice versa. There are also several lines of evidence showing that both first-born and second-born children monitor with vigilance the interaction between their mothers and their siblings. They respond with promptness to such interaction, they may attempt to disrupt or alternatively to join such interaction in a friendly way, but they rarely ignore it, and they often comment explicitly with hostility to it. The analysis of individual differences in how the first-born children respond to the interaction between their mothers and their siblings showed that those children who reacted to such playful interaction with direct attempts to disrupt the exchange were in other circumstances hostile and negative towards their siblings (Kendrick and Dunn 1982).

The findings indicate that for some children, witnessing affection and play between their mother and sibling is deeply upsetting, and is associated with the development of a hostile and negative relationship with the sibling, focused on that individual. Our third possibility, then, example C in Fig. 9.1, is that experiencing a close and affectionate relationship between the mother and younger sibling is linked to the development of a focused hostility towards that sibling. It is interesting to note that in a longitudinal study of mother–sibling triads recently completed in Canada, Howe (1986) reports very similar patterns of associations between mother–first child joint attention, mother–second child play, and positive and negative sibling interaction. That is, the greater the maternal involvement in play and attention to *either* child, the less friendly the interaction between the siblings.

D. Sensitivity to differential maternal behaviour

The evidence that children closely monitor the interaction between their mothers and siblings suggests a further process that links mother–child and sibling–child relationships. This is that siblings are sensitive to *differences* between the behaviour that their mother shows towards each of them. The suggestion here is that what influences the relationship between the siblings is not simply the experience of witnessing the mother behaving in an affectionate way towards the sibling. Rather, what matters to the siblings is the extent to which she is *differential* in her behaviour: according to this view (example D in Fig. 9.1) it is not the absolute but the relative affection, control, warmth, or punitiveness that she shows towards each one that matters to the children. Several studies of siblings who are slightly older than the pre–school children we have discussed so far indicate that differential maternal behaviour shown by mothers is indeed systematically linked to differences in interaction between the siblings (Bryant and Crockenberg 1980; Stocker 1986; Brody *et al.*, in press; Hetherington Chapter 16, this volume). And, in a study of the relations between emotional adjustment in adolescence and differential parental treatment, employing a very different methodology and working with a large nationally representative sample, clear links were found between individual's perceptions of how far they were treated differentially from their siblings and their emotional adjustment (Daniels *et al.* 1985).

A close examination of differential maternal behaviour in our Cambridge studies, and in the Colorado Adoption Project (Plomin and De Fries 1985) reveals that there are a number of factors that influence how far mothers behave differentially towards their children, and that these factors affect *different* aspects of maternal behaviour. Thus, while differences in a mother's physical affection shown towards her children were influenced by the age of each child (and disappeared if mother–child interaction with each child *at the same age* was examined), differences in her confrontational behaviour with the siblings were linked to differences in the children's temperament, and showed little consistency even when data taken at a similar age for each child were considered. Such results show us that differential maternal behaviour should not be considered as a global aspect of a mother's relationships with her children; the different aspects of differential behaviour are not only influenced by different factors but are likely to have different developmental significance for the children in the family (see Dunn and Stocker 1987, for a discussion of the evidence for this argument, and its importance in the origin of individual differences). Differential affectionate behaviour towards the two siblings may, of course, not be independent of the level of the affection shown by the mother towards the second child, and thus the process outlined in example C above.

E. Discussion of others as a mediating process

The evidence for the sensitivity with which children monitor the interaction between their mothers and siblings brought to our attention another issue, and suggests the possibility that a further process may link the behaviour of the mother to the quality of the relationship that develops between her children. This involves the ways in which the mother 'manages' the relationship between the two children—not solely her strategies for intervening in their disputes, but the ways in which she supports or 'promotes' their relationship, and the ways in which she discusses the feelings, actions, and intentions of each child with the other. At first sight it might seem quite inappropriate to consider such processes as relevant to the relationship between very young siblings. Siblings in middle childhood or adolescence clearly have powers of reflection about their own and others' behaviour, and it is therefore quite plausible to suggest that these aspects of maternal behaviour might contribute to the quality of the relationship between the siblings of this age group. It would appear much less likely that they are relevant to the relationship between siblings in infancy and the pre-school period. However, a number of different lines of evidence from our various studies of young siblings suggests that they may be important even in early childhood.

For instance, in our initial study of the arrival of a sibling, there were marked differences between the mothers in the extent to which, in the first two weeks after the baby was born, they discussed with their first-born children (aged on average 2 years) the new baby as a person with wants, needs, and feelings. In those families in which the mothers talked with their first-born in this way about the new-born sibling, the first-born were, one year later, much more friendly towards their sibling than the first-born in families in which the mothers had not discussed the new baby as a *person* in this way.

These differences between mothers were not significantly related to differences in their involvement in play, or in their permissiveness or controlling behaviour. Rather, they reflected differences in mothers' conversational behaviour with their toddlers that appeared to be independent of differences in the more 'conventional' aspects of maternal play or controlling behaviour. We have argued that while it would be quite inappropriate to infer from these associations that there is a simple causal connection between the mother's style of discussing the baby with her 2-year-old and the quality of the relationship that develops between the children, nevertheless we should take seriously the implication that our 2-year-olds were capable of a much higher degree of reflection about the baby as a person than would have been presumed likely in such young children, and that the mother's construction of the baby as a person, her interpretation of the baby's needs and behaviour, can indeed influence the older sibling's behaviour towards that baby.

Other findings from our subsequent studies support the view that children as young as 2 years old are indeed interested in, attend to, and take part in discussion of the feelings and actions of other family members (Dunn *et al.* 1987), and that differences in how these matters are discussed by mothers are systematically related to differences in the children's behaviour, over time, towards those family members. For instance, prosocial behaviour by second–born children towards their older siblings was shown more frequently by the children whose mothers six months earlier had talked about the feelings of their sibling, than by the children whose mothers had not discussed feelings in this way (Dunn and Munn 1986). And as a second illustration, children whose mothers in talking to the *older sibling* (when intervening in the siblings' quarrels) had referred to the younger's feelings, themselves were more likely to attempt to enlist their mothers' aid in later quarrels (Dunn and Munn 1985). Such findings suggest that in our attempts to specify the links between a mother's behaviour with her children and the relationship that develops between those children we should include the communication and discussion of other family members—the interpretation of others' behaviour and the articulation of that interpretation—designated in Fig. 9.1 as example E.

Cognitive processes would presumably be involved in such a connection to a considerably greater extent than in the examples A, B, and C.

Implications

These sets of data illustrate very different ways in which the quality of the mother–child relationship may be linked to the quality of the relationship between siblings in early childhood. They also raise three general issues, relevant to our thinking about relations between other relationships: first, the issue of the direction of effects; secondly, the importance of considering individual differences, when assessing the relations among relationships; thirdly, the relevance of the developmental stage of the child to these different processes.

Direction of effects

It was noted, initially, that in several of the sets of data considered here we cannot make inferences about the direction of effects. Thus in example A, it is likely that even if it was the perturbation in the mother–child relationship that led initially to disturbed behaviour in the child, such disturbed behaviour was likely to *increase* the difficulties in the mother–child relationship—a matter of positive feedback. In examples C and D, while the direction of effects was unquestionable in the immediate response of first-born children to affectionate play between mother and second-born, it is also possible that mothers increase their affectionate behaviour towards a younger sibling whose older sibling is continually hostile and aggressive—that is, that they attempt to 'make up' to the second-born for such negative experiences at the hands of their sibling. And in example E, it is very possible that mothers whose children get along well are more likely to talk to the children about each others' feelings than mothers who know that their children cannot stand each other. Each of these connections, that is, shows us ways in which the quality of the sibling–child relationship may affect the relationship between each child and the parent. Other data from the sibling study make this point particularly clear: for instance the finding that how mothers responded to sibling quarrels when their second-born was 14 months differed according to how the children had behaved towards each other six months earlier; the pattern of connections differed according to whether the first-born was a boy or a girl (Kendrick and Dunn 1983).

Individual differences

The second general issue raised by the examples concerns the significance of individual differences in determining the relative importance of the different processes outlined in Fig. 9.1. The findings show us that individual differences between children must be taken into account in any evaluation of the importance of these different processes. In example A, for instance, the temperament of the first-born child was of major importance in accounting for the form and extent of emotional disturbance, and in whether this was linked to difficulties in the sibling relationship. Examples B and C were connections that depended upon particular qualities of the relationship between a mother and her first or second child, respectively. And the different connections in example D, as we noted, depended on individual differences in the children, or in the mothers' personalities and attitudes. The general point to be emphasized is that which of these particular processes are likely to be developmentally important depends on individual differences in the children and in their relationships with their mothers.

Developmental stage of the child

The third general issue concerns the significance of the child's developmental stage for these different processes. It is possible, for instance, that the processes involved in example A are less likely to occur in the relationships of individuals beyond the vulnerable early years of childhood. It appears plausible, however, that the connections implied in examples B, C, D, and especially E *are* likely to occur in the relationships between family members who are older than the pre-school children that we have considered here.

Conclusion

In conclusion, the examples discussed demonstrate that there are both short-term and longer-term connections between the relationships of mothers with their individual children, and of those siblings within the family. Different kinds of processes are likely to be involved in such connections; individual differences between children in temperament and in the quality of their relationships, and the developmental stage of the child, will influence which of these processes are developmentally significant. For each of the examples considered, there may be different patterns for boys and for girls, and other relationships within the family may influence the associations. It is important that we should be sensitive to these complexities, and to the fact that which connections we emphasize as developmentally important will depend on how we study children—on the levels of description and analysis we select—and on what outcome measures we focus upon. It is also clear that it would be misleading to attribute frequent quarrels between siblings simply to a parent's handling of conflict between the children.

The delineation of connections between relationships that involve effects on the mother–child relationship stands by itself important. If we consider the mother–child relationship significant in a child's development, then we should take seriously the relationships that affect it, and those, as the connections discussed here demonstrate, may include the sibling–child relationship. But there are other more general implications in the links that have been described. The argument that individual differences and developmental stage of the child influence the significance of these different processes implies that we should move away from general claims about relations among relationships, and from attributing connections between these relationships to general and vaguely conceived mechanisms, such as inner working models, towards specifying from *which* children at *which* stage of development *particular* relationships are likely to have significance for *particular other* relationships. It is clear that the relationships discussed here have certain distinctive features: the mother–child relationship is special in its 'complementarity' (Hinde 1979), its combination of dependency–protection, and its intensity of emotion; while the sibling–child relationship is special in its dimensions of rivalry/competition, uninhibited emotional expression, and in its possibilities for co-operation and companionship. It seems likely, then, that some of the processes that have been outlined here would be relevant only to other relationships that share some of these particular features. We might predict, therefore, that examples A and B, for instance, would occur only in the connections between relationships one of which involves intense emotional dependency. (But could this not include some spousal relationships? Or adolescent friendship?) One obvious next stage in the exploration of the relations among relationships is to specify how far the dimensions of particular relationships determine the nature of the processes linking them to other relationships. What is presented here is only a first step, but it is to be hoped that it provides a context in which discussion and plans for research can begin to move towards that second stage.

Summary

The nature of the processes connecting different relationships within the family is discussed, in the context of evidence from longitudinal observational studies of three family relationships, those of a mother and her two children. The results suggest that a number of different processes are involved in mediating the influence of one relationship upon another. These processes differ in nature, and range from general emotional disturbance as a mediating link through a series of processes of increasing specificity and cognitive complexity, such as children's monitoring of differential maternal behaviour towards self and sibling, to processes involving maternal 'attributional style' and communication about others. It is argued that individual differences in children and the developmental stage of the child will influence which of these processes is developmentally significant.

Acknowledgements

The research discussed in this chapter was supported by the Medical Research Council and by a grant from the National Science Foundation (BNS-8643938).

References

Belsky, J. and Isabella, R. A. (1985). Marital and parent–child relationships in family of origin and marital change following the birth of a baby: a retrospective analysis. *Child Development* **56**, 342–9.

Brody, G. H., Stoneman, Z., and McKinnon, C. (1987). Contributions of maternal childrearing practices and interactional contexts to sibling interactions. *Journal of Applied Developmental Psychology* (in press).

Bryant, B. and Crockenberg, S. (1980). Correlates and dimensions of prosocial behavior: a study of female siblings and their mothers. *Child Development* **51**, 529–44.

Calladine, C. and Calladine, A. (1979). *Raising siblings*. Delacorte Press, New York.

Daniels, D., Dunn, J., Furstenburg, F. F. jun., and Plomin, R. (1985). Environmental differences within the family and adjustment differences within pairs of adolescent siblings. *Child Development* **56**, 764–74.

Dowdney, L., Skuse, D., Rutter, M., Quinton, D., and Mrazek, D. (1985). The nature and qualities of parenting provided by women raised in institutions. *Journal of Child Psychology and Psychiatry* **26**, 599–625.

Dunn, J. (1987). *Mothers and siblings: developmental implications of differences in relationships within the family*. Paper presented at Max Planck Institute Conference on 'Family Systems and Life-Span Development', December 1986.

Dunn, J. and Kendrick, C. (1982). *Siblings: love, envy and understanding*. Harvard University Press, Cambridge, Mass.

Dunn, J. and Munn, P. (1985). Becoming a family member: family conflict and the development of social understanding in the second year. *Child Development* **56**, 480–92.

Dunn, J. and Munn, P. (1986). Sibling quarrels and maternal intervention: Individual differences in understanding and aggression. *Journal of Child Psychology and Psychiatry* **27**, 583–95.

Dunn, J. and Stocker, C. (1987). The significance of differences in siblings' experience within the family. In K. Kreppner and R. Lerner (eds.). *Family systems and life span development*. Lawrence Erlbaum Ass., Hillsdale, New Jersey.

Dunn, J., Bretherton, I., and Munn, P. (1987). Conversations about feelings states between mothers and their young children. *Developmental Psychology* **23**, 132–9.

Easterbrooks, M. A. and Lamb, M. E. (1979). The relation between quality of infant–mother attachment and infant competence in initial encounters with peers. *Child Development* **50,** 380–7.

Hinde, R. A. (1979). *Towards understanding relationships.* Academic Press, London.

Howe, N. (1986). Socialization, social cognitive factors and the development of the sibling relationship. Ph. D. Dissertation. University of Waterloo, Canada.

Kendrick, C. and Dunn, J. (1982). Protest or pleasure? The response of firstborn children to interaction between their mothers and infant siblings. *Journal of Child Psychology and Psychiatry* **23,** 117–29.

Kendrick, C. and Dunn, J. (1983). Sibling quarrels and maternal responses. *Developmental Psychology* **19,** 62–70.

Newson, J. and Newson, E. (1968). *Four years old in an urban community.* Allen and Unwin, London.

Plomin, R. and De Fries, J. (1985). *Origins of individual differences in infancy: the Colorado Adoption Project.* Academic Press, New York.

Sroufe, L. A. and Fleeson, J. (1986). Attachment and the construction of relationships. In *Relationships and development* (ed. W. W. Hartup and Z. Rubin). Erlbaum, Hillsdale, NJ.

Sroufe, L. A. and Ward, M. J. (1980). Seductive behavior of mothers of toddlers: occurrences, correlates and family origins. *Child Development* **51,** 1222–9.

Stocker, C. (1986). Mothers' differential behavior and sibling conflicts. Unpublished M.A. thesis. University of Cornell.

10

Triadic interactions: mother–first-born –second-born

J. BARRETT AND R. A. HINDE

Introduction

The study of how relationships affect relationships is fraught with methodological difficulties. In principle, we can adopt either a long-term or a short-term approach. In the former case, we can assess, over a span of time, how far any change in A's relationship with B is correlated with a change in B's relationship with C. Studies of changes in the marital relationship on the birth of a first baby (e.g. Belsky and Isabella 1985) or of changes in the mother–first-born relationship on the arrival of a second-born (e.g. Dunn and Kendrick 1982) exemplify this approach. Such studies may involve either interview or questionnaire techniques and/or direct observation.

In the short term, we can study the triadic situation A–B–C. One approach is to compare interactions between A and B in the presence or absence of C. For example, Corter et al. (1983) found that maternal presence reduced the number of interactions between siblings and that their interactions were more agonistic when she was present than when they were on their own. Liddell and Collis (in press), taking this one step further, found that effects were due to the presence of the third person rather than his/her characteristics.

One may also compare dyadic interactions among the several dyads present (i.e. A–B, B–C, and A–C). This is one approach adopted by Dunn and Munn (1986) when they investigated maternal interventions in sibling conflict. They found that, when intervening, mothers behaved differently to elder and younger siblings. For example, behaviours like prohibition, suggesting conciliation, explaining actions, and references to social rules and feelings were more likely to be addressed to the elder than the younger sibling. Furthermore, mothers were twice as likely to prohibit the elder child than the younger, and mothers who gave many prohibitions to one sibling were unlikely to do so to the other.

The present contribution is primarily methodological, presenting a means for analysing the dynamics of certain types of triadic relationships—namely, those in which the effect of A's relationship with B on B's relationship with C is mediated by, or made apparent through, triadic interactions. It is, of course, possible for such an effect to occur even when A is never in C's presence, but such cases are not the present concern.

Such a methodology must involve a coding system capable of recording not only links between successive interactions involving the same individuals (e.g. A speaks to B and B speaks to A in answer), but also those between interactions involving a change in participants (e.g. A speaks to B and as a consequence C speaks to B). It must also take into account that such interactions may have an importance out of proportion to their frequency. An indication of this is available from the non-human primate literature. In rhesus monkeys, the dominance ranks of individuals depend to a considerable extent on triadic interactions involving coalitions between two individuals against a third, yet only about 10 per cent of agonistic interactions are triadic (Datta 1983, and personal communication).

Coding scheme

The coding scheme was adapted from a modification of Caldwell's (1969) coding scheme (Hinde *et al.* 1983). The coding is done from an audiotape of the observer's spoken description of behaviour and the participants' verbal behaviour. Interactions are coded as parsed sentences in the form: subject, verb, object, and qualifier. The qualifiers refer to the place of the sentence in a series of interactions (e.g. 'in initiation', 'in answer') and also to qualities of the verb (e.g. 'loudly', 'with hostility', 'with reason implicit'). Thus:

Mother: 'Would you like something else to play with?'
Elder child: 'Yes, I would.'
Mother: 'Go and look in the toy cupboard.'
Elder child: Child goes to the toy cupboard.

would be coded in the form:

Sentence 1: Mother inquires to child, initiating an interaction.
Sentence 2: Child speaks to mother, in answer.
Sentence 3: Mother suggests to child, with reason, in extension.
Sentence 4: Child locomotes in compliance with the mother.

Sentence 3 contains a control verb, and by convention the following sentence includes the issuer of the control as object. This facilitates a limited sequential analysis: frequency of compliance to mother can readily be related to the frequency of control. The above method is limited in two ways. First, at present it is possible only to analyse sequences of two related sentences. More complex sequences of interactions could be analysed by the addition of more qualifiers. However, such a procedure would require a very extensive data set to provide adequate samples of each type of sequence. Secondly, the method is limited to dyadic interactions involving a focal individual, in this case the elder child ($M \rightarrow E$ and $E \rightarrow M$, where E is the elder child and M the mother).

For triadic interactions, this system has been modified using the classification of triadic interactions provided by Parke *et al.* (1979). This is exemplified in the following examples, using cases where initially the mother talks to the elder child. The classification of the second sentence in the triadic interaction as circular, parallel, or transitive depends on its subject and object.

Circular triadic interactions
Here the subject of sentence 1 becomes the object of sentence 2, thus:

Mother to elder child: 'Go and find something to play with.'
Younger child (Y) to mother: 'Can I go too?'

Thus the sequence is $M \rightarrow E$, $Y \rightarrow M$.

Parallel triadic interactions
Here the object of sentence 1 becomes the object of sentence 2, thus:

Mother to elder child: 'Go and find something to play with.'
Younger to elder child: 'Can I come too?'

Thus the sequence is $M \rightarrow E$, $Y \rightarrow E$.

Transitive triadic interactions
Here the object of sentence 1 becomes the subject of sentence 2, thus:

Mother to elder child: 'Go and find something to play with.'
Elder to younger child: 'Will you come too?'

Thus the sequence is $M \rightarrow E$, $E \rightarrow Y$.

In coding two successive sentences involving mother, elder child, and younger child in terms of dyadic and triadic interactions, there are 15 possible combinations. Six of these are dyadic, with the same two individuals involved in both sentences, and nine are triadic. To be classed as triadic, a sentence must follow shortly after a previous sentence involving at least one of the same subjects and there must be evidence of a causal relation between the two. The possible triadic sentences are shown in Table 10.1 in the form $E \rightarrow M \Rightarrow M \rightarrow Y$. In this case, $E \rightarrow M$ represents the first sentence, $M \rightarrow Y$ represents the second sentence, and the symbol '$\Rightarrow$' the inferred causal relation between them. In coding, Sentence 1 and Sentence 2 represent two separate interactions and a triadic qualifier is attached to the second sentence indicating the category of triadic interaction involved. By calculating the frequency of triadic qualifiers, the frequency of each type of qualifier, and the subjects and objects of their sentences, it is possible to begin to study the dynamics involved.

Table 10.1   *Representations of triadic interactions between mother (M), elder child (E), and younger child (Y)*

Interactants in Sentence 1	Interactants in Sentence 2		
	E and M	E and Y	Y and M
Transitive sentences			
Y→E⇒	E→M		
Y→M⇒	M→E		
M→E⇒		E→Y	
M→Y⇒		Y→E	
E→M⇒			M→Y
E→Y⇒			Y→M
Parallel sentences			
Y→M⇒	E→M		
Y→E⇒	M→E		
M→Y⇒		E→Y	
M→E⇒		Y→E	
E→Y⇒			M→Y
E→M⇒			Y→M
Circular sentences			
M→Y⇒	E→M		
E→Y⇒	M→E		
Y→M⇒		E→Y	
E→M⇒		Y→E	
Y→E⇒			M→Y
M→E⇒			Y→M

Use of the coding scheme

To exemplify the coding scheme, some preliminary data have been extracted from an ongoing study of the mother–first-born–second-born triadic interactions. They were taken from home observations of 21 triads in two 20-minute observation sessions. The mother was asked to be present while the children played a board game. Her degree of participation was left to her. All interactions were recorded on audiotape and later coded.

The first question concerns the frequency of the three types of triadic interaction. To this end, the frequencies of all the dyadic and triadic interactions (identified as such by their qualifiers) were assessed. All children had some triadic interactions. The medians were 7.7 per cent (range 3.4–11.9 per cent) of all interactions for elder children and 8.5 per cent (range 2.9–14.1 per cent) for younger children.

Next, were triadic interactions equally likely between the various possible participants? Table 10.2 shows the frequency of triadic interactions for each possible combination of participants as a percentage of total triadic interactions for the child involved. Initiations by the younger child to the mother accounted for a smaller proportion of his/her triadic interactions (median 26.7 per cent) than was the case for the elder child (median 34.0 per cent) (Wilcoxon, $p < 0.001$, two-tailed).

Table 10.2 *Percentage of total triadic interactions for each pair of participants*

	Elder child (E) and mother (M)		Elder child (E) and younger (Y)		Younger child (Y) and mother (M)	
	E→M	M→E	E→Y	Y→E	Y→M	M→Y
Median	34.0	24.4	26.1	11.4	26.7	34.4
Range	17.3–54.4	7.7–57.5	4.4–50.0	0–26.5	9.1–51.4	5.7–50.0

Several points arise:

1. This could have been because the younger child was second-born or because younger children lack the sophistication to engage in triadic interactions. Some evidence against the latter possibility was provided by the fact that the frequency with which the younger siblings were initiators in triadic interactions was not significantly correlated with their age ($r = 0.12$, ns), though this could have been due to the small age range of the children concerned.

2. Child initiations to mother could occur after a sentence in which the one child was object and the other subject (transitive, e.g. Y→E⇒E→M), or the other child was subject and the mother the object (parallel, e.g. Y→M⇒E→M), or vice versa (circular, e.g. M→Y⇒E→M). For both the elder child and the younger, circular triadic interactions were most common (χ^2, $p < 0.005$ and $p < 0.025$ respectively). In other words, each child was more likely to speak to the mother after the mother had spoken to the sibling that

after the sibling had spoken to the mother, or the children had spoken to one another:

$M \rightarrow Y \Rightarrow E \rightarrow M$ more common than $Y \rightarrow M \Rightarrow E \rightarrow M$ or $Y \rightarrow E \Rightarrow E \rightarrow M$, and
$M \rightarrow E \Rightarrow Y \rightarrow M$ more common than $E \rightarrow M \Rightarrow Y \rightarrow M$ or $E \rightarrow Y \Rightarrow Y \rightarrow M$.

Furthermore, circular triadic interactions with the elder child as subject and mother as object were more common than those with the younger as subject (Wilcoxon, $p < 0.001$, two-tailed),

i.e. $M \rightarrow Y \Rightarrow E \rightarrow M$ more common than $M \rightarrow E \Rightarrow Y \rightarrow M$.

This suggests that the elder children were, in fact, making more effort to retain their mothers' attention than younger children. Data on the total interactions with the mother are in harmony with this view. Expressed as a percentage of total interactions involving each child, the elder initiated more interactions with the mother compared with the younger (E, 38.3 per cent; Y, 34.8 per cent; Wilcoxon, $p < 0.01$). However, maternal initiations to the elder and younger children, expressed as percentages of total interactions for each child, did not differ significantly (E, 38.9 per cent; Y, 38.4 per cent; Wilcoxon, ns).

Further evidence for this view is provided by analysing the behaviour of the siblings towards one another in the second sentence. First, triadic interactions by the elder child to the sibling accounted for a higher proportion of his/her interactions, 26.1 per cent, than was the case for the younger child, 11.4 per cent (Wilcoxon, $p < 0.01$, two-tailed). Secondly, the two siblings showed different patterns of triadic interactions. Parallel interactions with the elder child as subject and the younger child as object were more common than circular or transitive ones,

i.e. $M \rightarrow Y \Rightarrow E \rightarrow Y$ (parallel) more common than $Y \rightarrow M \Rightarrow E \rightarrow Y$ (Circular) or $M \rightarrow E \Rightarrow E \rightarrow Y$ (Transitive) (χ^2, $p < 0.01$).

This was not the same for the younger sibling where circular interactions with the younger as subject and the elder as object were more common than parallel or transitive. This may mean that elder children were attempting to distract maternal attention away from the younger children.

Pursuing the hypothesis that elder children try harder than younger children to keep maternal attention, we may next consider the nature of these interactions with the mother and, in particular, circular triadic interactions. If they were primarily bids for maternal attention, their content would be likely to differ from that of dyadic interactions. Accordingly, circular triadic interactions were classified into five behavioural groups:

Dependent—e.g. 'Mummy, will you help me?'

Controlling—e.g. 'Do this, do that.'

Asserting—e.g. 'That's mine.'

Information processing—e.g. 'That's a red balloon.'

Other—behaviours that occurred too infrequently to have separate categories.

Of these, the first three categories are most likely to serve an attention-seeking function. In fact, dependent interactions were seldom used in this context. They were recorded only once each in only five of the elder children and four of the younger children. Furthermore, circular triadic dependent interactions formed a smaller percentage of total circular triadic interactions than did dyadic dependent interactions as a percentage of total dyadic interactions ($p < 0.05$ for the elder children and $p < 0.01$ for the younger; Wilcoxon, two-tailed).

A similar algorithm was used for investigating assertive and controlling behaviours. For the elder child, both controls and assertive behaviour formed a somewhat (but not significantly) higher percentage of circular triadic interactions than they did of dyadic interactions (controls: medians 7.1 per cent and 4.8 per cent respectively, Wilcoxon, ns; assertions: medians 9.1 per cent and 8.9 per cent respectively, Wilcoxon, $p < 0.10$, two-tailed). A high proportion of the younger children gave no controls or assertive triadic interactions and the medians could not meaningfully be compared.

This analysis indicates that bids for maternal attention are more subtle than merely becoming more dependent when mothers direct attention towards siblings. Elder children seemed to make more effort than younger siblings to retain maternal attention and became somewhat more controlling and assertive in these triadic situations than in normal dyadic interactions.

A similar type of analysis throws light on the mother's role in mediating between the siblings. In general, the sibling relationship, as compared with other peer relationships, is likely to be characterized by both co-operation and competition: we may expect the mother to be especially concerned with protecting the more vulnerable younger sibling from the elder child. The data from the analysis of triadic interactions which follow from one sibling interacting with the other sibling seem to support this hypothesis. Mothers were more likely to interact with the elder after the elder had initiated an interaction with the younger than after other types of interactions:

$E \rightarrow Y \Rightarrow M \rightarrow E$ (Circular) was more common than either $Y \rightarrow M \Rightarrow M \rightarrow E$ (transitive) or $Y \rightarrow E \Rightarrow M \rightarrow E$ (parallel) (χ^2, $p < 0.05$).

For the younger sibling, Y, by contrast, there was no significant difference in the frequencies of circular, transitive or parallel interactions:

$Y \rightarrow E \Rightarrow M \rightarrow Y$ (circular); $E \rightarrow M \Rightarrow M \rightarrow Y$ (transitive); $E \rightarrow Y \Rightarrow M \rightarrow Y$ (parallel) did not differ significantly (χ^2, ns).

Maternal circular interactions to one child occur after that child has interacted with the sibling. For example, the child may refuse to let the younger child have a turn in a game and, as a consequence, the mother may tell him to let the sibling have a turn. If mothers were defending younger siblings, it is to be expected that circular triadic interactions directed towards the elder children would be more frequent than those directed by the mothers to the younger children. The data used in this analysis concerned interactions initiated by the mother to one child as a percentage of the interactions initiated by that child to the other. The median frequency for circular triadic interactions initiated by the mother to the elder child (median 7.4 per cent) was greater than that to the younger (median 5.3 per cent) but the difference was not significant.

On the hypothesis that these maternal circular interactions involve interference between the siblings, their content is likely to be different from that of dyadic interactions. For each of the children, maternal circular control was expressed as a percentage of total maternal circular interactions, and maternal dyadic control was expressed as a percentage of total maternal dyadic interactions. Circular triadic control was significantly greater than dyadic control (medians: E, dyadic 16.2 per cent, triadic 44.4 per cent; Wilcoxon, $p < 0.001$, two-tailed: Y, dyadic 20.0 per cent, triadic 36.4 per cent; Wilcoxon, $p < 0.05$, two-tailed).

If mothers were defending the younger against the elder sibling, absolute maternal circular control would be greater for the elder child than for the younger child. Although the difference was not significant, the medians were in the right direction, with 1.8 per 40 minutes for the elder and 1.0 per 40 minutes for the younger.

To sum up, the pattern of triadic interactions that mothers initiated to the elder child differed from that with the younger child. Maternal triadic control was greater than dyadic control, which indicates that mothers behave differently to their children as a result of a previous sibling interaction. There is some evidence that mothers control the elder sibling more than the younger child after sibling interaction. This is in harmony with the view that mothers are defending the weaker younger sibling against the more powerful elder sibling.

Conclusion

In order better to assess the moment-to-moment influence of one relationship on another, it is necessary to extend the methods used for coding observations of dyadic situations to cope with triadic ones. In this contribution, some data from an ongoing study have been used to show how a triadic coding system permits exploration of the dynamics of the processes involved. Specifically, circular triadic interactions of the elder child to mother were found to be more common than those of the younger child, and several lines of evidence indicated that they represented bids for maternal attention. The analysis of triadic interactions initiated by mothers presented less clear-cut results, but there was some evidence to support the hypothesis that mothers defended the younger sibling from the elder (see also Chapters 8 and 9, this volume).

This type of analysis should have considerable power when applied to differences between families, as it will permit such differences to be related to other factors in the situation. For instance, there may be individual differences in how one mother 'defends' the younger against the elder child, which can then be related to differences in age gap between the sibling pairs, or to temperamental differences between mothers or children, or maternal family histories.

However, two limitations of the current method must be noted. First, there is a limit to the complexity of the interactions that can be coded. In some triadic interactions, an individual directs his/her behaviour to both the other participants. For instance, Kummer (1967) has described how a female in the harem of a hamadryas baboon male may simultaneously try to threaten off another female, present to the male, and position herself in such a manner that if the threatened female reciprocates, her threat will be interpreted by the male as directed towards him. Although comparable 'tripartite' interactions occur in man, they were observed infrequently in this study. The current coding scheme could be extended to cover them by the use of additional qualifiers.

Secondly, Parke et al. (1979) point out that this classification of triadic influences can be extended to less immediate events. What A does to B may have been influenced by what C did to A in the past. Although the recording method used in this study does not capture such effects directly, data on the effects of interactions on immediately following ones could act as pointers to more long-lasting influences.

References

Belsky, J. and Isabella, R. A. (1985). Marital and parent-child relationships in family of origin and marital change following the birth of a baby: a retrospective analysis. *Child Development* **56**, 342–9.

Caldwell, B. M. (1969). A 'new' approach to behavioural ecology. In *Minnesota Symposia on Child Psychology*, Vol. 2 (ed. I. P. Hill). University of Minnesota Press, Minneapolis.

Corter, C., Abramovitch, R., and Pepler, D. (1983). The role of the mother in sibling interaction. *Child Development* **54**, 1599–605.

Datta, S. (1983). Patterns of agonistic interference. In *Primate social relationships: an integrated approach* (ed. R. A. Hinde). Blackwell Scientific Publications, Oxford.

Dunn, J. and Kendrick, C. (1982). *Siblings: love, envy and understanding*. Harvard University Press, Cambridge, Mass.

Dunn, J. and Munn, P. (1986). Sibling quarrels and maternal intervention: individual differences in understanding and aggression. *Journal of Child Psychology and Psychiatry* **27**, 583–95.

Hinde, R., Easton, D., Meller, R., and Tamplin, A. (1983). Nature and determinants of preschoolers' differential behaviour to adults and peers. *British Journal of Developmental Psychology* **1**, 3–19.

Kummer, H. (1967). Tripartite relations in hamadryas baboons. In *Social communication among primates* (ed. S. A. Altman). University of Chicago Press.

Liddell, C. and Collis, G. M. (1987). Second-order effects—number or nature of companions? *Journal of Genetic Psychology* (in press).

Parke, R., Power, T., and Gottman, J. (1979). Conceptualising and quantifying influence patterns in the family triad. In *Social interaction analysis: methodological issues* (ed. M. Lamb, S. Suomi, and G. Stephenson). University of Wisconsin Press, Madison.

IV

Coherence across generations

11

Developmental history, personality, and family relationships: toward an emergent family system*
JAY BELSKY AND EMILY PENSKY

Introduction

This chapter is concerned with the origins of individual differences in relationship functioning in the family system in contemporary society, particularly marital and parent–child relationships. In it we adopt a life-course, developmental perspective; that is, we assume that the relationship practices in nuclear family units are, in part, derived from prior experiences of the individuals concerned both in and out of their families of origin. Thus, we view individuals as carrying forward, from their prior relationship experiences, skills, expectations, and behavioural practices that affect the way they function—as parents and as spouses—in their families of procreation. We refer to 'the emergent family system' to emphasize that individuals and family relationships establish developmental trajectories which affect how families subsequently function.

Evidence regarding three distinct family dysfunctions is considered in the first part of the chapter to demonstrate that some degree of continuity exists in marital and parent–child relationships across generations. Additional evidence on so-called 'normal families' is then examined to determine whether lessons learned from the study of dysfunction are more broadly generalizable. Upon finding that they are, we posit that emotionally-laden and socially-based learning shapes personality development and that personality plays a central, causal role in the intergenerational transmission process. Both cross-sectional and longitudinal evidence is then summarized to substantiate this assertion. In addition, evidence is examined which highlights the conditions under which discontinuity, rather than continuity, characterizes the intergenerational transmission process.

*Work on this chapter was supported by a grant from the National Institute of Child Health and Human Development (RO1HD15496) and by a NIMH Research Scientist Development Award (KO2MH00486).

The intergenerational transmission of family relationships

The case of family dysfunction

Family dysfunction in the current analysis is meant to imply only that the phenomena under consideration—child maltreatment, spouse abuse, and divorce—are routinely associated with pain and suffering (psychological and physical) that virtually all individuals would seek to avoid. No assumptions are made about the ultimate utility of such family phenomena, and divorce is not seen to share the pathological stigma routinely associated with abusive behaviour.

Child maltreatment. Numerous clinical reports, as well as more empirically-based investigations of child maltreatment, draw attention to the intergenerational nature of this family dysfunction. Even though limitations of the database (e.g. retrospective reports) are widely acknowledged, most reviewers agree that a history of maltreatment in childhood places the person at increased risk of mistreating his/her own offspring (Parke and Collmer 1975; Belsky 1978; Friedrich and Wheeler 1982; Burgess and Youngblade, in press). Kaufman and Zigler (1986) recently estimated the rate of transmission to be around 30 per cent lower than that reported in non-representative samples, even large ones (e.g. Herrenkohl *et al.* 1983; Egeland *et al.* 1984), but higher than the 17.6 per cent rate reported by Straus (1979; Straus *et al.* 1980) using a nationally representative sample of more than 1100 subjects which did not include single-parent families or those with children under two years of age. Although few studies chronicle the factors which enable individuals to escape the intergenerational cycle (but see Hunter and Kilstrom 1979; Egeland *et al.*, in press), it is generally acknowledged that it is principally in interaction with other aetiological factors (e.g. child temperament, marital quality, social support) that the risk associated with child-rearing history is 'realized'.

Spouse abuse. Though not as extensively documented as child maltreatment, spouse abuse emerges as intergenerationally repetitive, both in small sample studies and in those relying upon more nationally representative, large sample surveys (Gelles 1976; Steinmetz 1977; Straus *et al.* 1980; Pagelow 1981; Roscoe and Benaske 1985). Of particular interest is the finding by Gelles (1976) that women who witnessed spouse abuse are more likely to be victims of it in their own marriages. Also noteworthy are the results of Kalmuss' (1984) analysis of more than 2000 adults, indicating that exposure to both marital and parent–child aggression in childhood contribute to subsequent spouse abuse; that witnessing spouse abuse exerts a stronger effect; and that the effects of these distinct experiences are cumulative.

Marital instability. Investigations of the intergenerational transmission of divorce contrast with those on child maltreatment and spouse abuse, in that investigators typically rely upon nationally representative samples obtained through large national surveys rather than upon select samples of mistreated individuals. The evidence indicates, though not without exception (Duncan and Duncan 1969), that individuals whose parents divorced are more likely to experience divorce in their own marital relationships (Bumpass and Sweet 1972; Heiss 1972; Pope and Mueller 1976; Mueller and Pope 1977; Kulka and Weingarten 1979; Mott and Moore 1979; Glenn and Shelton 1983; Korbin and Waite 1984; Mueller and Cooper 1986). Although the variance accounted for by divorce in one's family of origin in predicting one's own divorce may not be great, the differences between percentages adjusted for background variables seems important. Glenn finds, for example, in his analyses of survey data compiled over a decade (1973–86), that the risk of divorce is more than 25 per cent greater for men from broken homes and more than 50 per cent greater for women from such families of origin (Glenn and Shelton 1983; Glenn and Kramer 1986).

It would seem, then, whether we consider marital or parent–child relationships, that dysfunction is transmitted across generations, though by no means is this inevitable. In a later section we consider the 'conditions of discontinuity' that seem to be responsible for redirecting developmental trajectories. For now we must determine whether the lesson learned from studying family dysfunction (i.e. that there is intergenerational transmission) can be generalized to non-disturbed families.

From pathology to normality

The issue of the interrelation of normal and abnormal development is one that is central to the emerging field of 'developmental psychopathology' (Rutter 1982; Cicchetti 1984; Sroufe and Rutter 1984). As Rutter (1982) has noted, caution must be exercised in generalizing from the abnormal or dysfunctional to the normal or functional, because 'causal processes for abnormality may not always be identical with those that underlie variations within the normal range' (Rutter 1982, p. 107). Is it appropriate, then, to generalize from the study of family dysfunction to so-called normal families in the case of the intergenerational transmission of parent–child and marital relationships?

Parent–child relationships. Studies of the antecedents of individual differences in the security of infant–mother attachment provide some of the most revealing evidence regarding cross-generational continuities in the quality of parent–child relationships in non–disturbed families. Morris (1980, 1981) found that mothers of securely attached children were more likely than mothers of insecurely attached children to be positively identified with their mothers and to perceive them as strong, nurturant, and emotionally available; and Ricks (1985) noted that mothers of securely attached 1-year-olds recalled significantly more acceptance and less rejection from their parents (see also Chapter 13, this volume).

Lawful continuity across generations in the nature and quality of parent–child relationships in non–disturbed families occurs not only in the area of attachment. In an intensive, longitudinal study of some 28 middle-class, Caucasian families, Cox and her colleagues (1985) found that mothers assessed as sensitive, responsive, accepting, and enjoying in their mothering when infants were 3.5 months old recalled, during pregnancy, having mothers and fathers who promoted their own individuality rather than being intrusive or over-controlling. In another study of 46 middle-class parents of young infants, Heinicke *et al.* (1983) found that those women who were more responsive to their 1-month-old infants reported less conflict in their relations with their parents while growing up. As a final example, Minde (1980) observed that women who interacted with their premature infants in less sensitive and contingently responsive manners recalled poorer relationships with their own mothers during their childhoods.

Marital relationships.   Associations between quality of family relationships across generations in non-disturbed families are also evident in the case of marriage. On the basis of an initial investigation of 341 middle- and upper-middle-class families, Terman (1938, pp. 34–4) observed that 'the happiness scores of respondents of either sex was positively associated with the marital happiness of their parents': such results led him to conclude that 'marital happiness appears to be a condition that tends to run in families'. In view of the prior discussion of the early family origins of attachment security and Kalmuss' (1984) previously cited study linking abusive parent–child relationships in one generation to spouse abuse in the next, it is also noteworthy that Terman (1938) discerned positive associations between the quality of parent–child relationships (retrospectively reported) and subsequent marital quality.

In a second, more extensive investigation of psychological factors associated with marital adjustment, Terman (1938) studied almost 800 couples from 'a fairly wide sampling of the married population of southern and central California' which, in his terms, 'probably underestimated the proportion of maladjusted couples that would be found in the generality of marriages in California' (p. 41). Despite this truncated range, the results of the initial study were replicated. Since Terman's time the positive association between marital and parent–child relationships in one's family of origin and the happiness of one's own marriage has been documented repeatedly (Goodrich *et al.* 1968; Snyder 1979; Eysenck and Wakefield 1981).

It would seem, then, that there are grounds for concluding that lessons drawn from the study of family dysfunction are clearly relevant for the understanding of families which are typically characterized as normal because they display no severe disturbances. Not only is it the case that relationship dysfunctions, such as child maltreatment, spouse abuse, and divorce are intergenerationally transmitted, but so, too, are the nature and quality of parent–child and marital relationships that fall within the normal range. This is not to say that what exactly is transmitted has been specified, or even that the conditions under which intergenerational continuity characterizes the process of individual, relationship, and family development have been articulated, but only that lawful relations have been chronicled repeatedly between relationship qualities of one generation and those of the next, in the case of both dysfunctional and normal families.

The process of transmission: developmental history, personality, and family relationships

Process considerations have not been the focus of the preceding discussion simply because most of the investigations cited failed to address them empirically. Nevertheless, the mechanisms by which participation in particular kinds of parent–child relationships (nurturant, abusive) and exposure to specific types of marital relationships (harmonious, distressed) in one's family of origin might affect relationship funtioning in one's family of procreation are routinely discussed in the course of interpreting the empirical evidence just summarized. Social learning processes of imitation and reinforcement figure importantly in such analyses, particularly in the cases of child maltreatment (e.g. Burgess and Youngblade, in press) and spouse abuse (e.g. Kalmuss 1984).

That acquisition processes other than these need to be considered is strongly suggested by recent research on young children's responses to witnessing positive and negative adult interactions. In studying the responses of 1–2.5-year-old children as bystanders to naturally occurring and simulated expressions of anger and affection by others, Cummings et al. (1981) observed that expressions of anger acted as environmental stressors, frequently causing distress, whereas affectionate responses between others (including spouses) were most often responded to with affection and overt signs of pleasure. But, 'children seldom exactly mimicked others' expressions of anger. When anger responses to naturally occurring anger episodes occurred they usually indicated a contagion of affect rather than a matching of behaviour' (Cummings et al. 1981, p. 1280). Furthermore, even though exposure to simulated angry adult interaction increased aggression between peers, especially when such exposure was repeated, children's behaviour 'did not appear to be a function of modeling in the strict sense of the concept' (Cummings et al. 1985, p. 505).

Cummings et al.'s findings and interpretative analysis convinces us that a more dynamic explanation of intergenerational transmission is called for than one which focuses simply upon overt behaviour and the social learning processes of imitation and reinforcement. What is required is a framework which, while including these processes, stresses emotion, arousal, and the developing self system as well. In this regard we find particularly attractive the concept of 'internal working models' initially advanced by Bowlby (1980) and recently elaborated by other attachment theorists (Bretherton 1985; Main *et al.* 1985; Sroufe and Fleeson 1986, and this volume). Internal working models are defined as affectively-laden mental representations of the self, other, and of the relationship, derived from interactional experiences, which function (outside of conscious awareness) to direct attention and organize memory in a way that guides interpersonal behaviour and the interpretation of social experience. Although these models have a strong propensity to resist change, given their role as organizers of experience and filterers of information, they are susceptible to modification. To be stressed, however, is the active role of the individual in interpreting the experienced world and the inclination to assimilate information into pre-existing models. Interpersonal development is likely to be conservative, as a result, as the individual disregards inconsistent information or reinterprets it, rather than modify his/her model.

Malatesta and Wilson's (1986) recent analysis of the role of emotion and cognition in personality development makes it eminently clear that much of the recent work on the development of discrete emotions (e.g. Izard 1977, 1984; Malatesta and Izard 1984; Lewis and Michalson 1985) and the socialization of emotional expression (Malatesta and Haviland 1982; Malatesta 1985; Malatesta *et al.*, in press), especially during the infancy and early childhood years, is not inconsistent with the concept of 'internal working models' in attachment theory. In reviewing the theoretical writings of Tomkins (1962, 1963), Izard (1977), and Lewis and Michalson (1985) on emotional development, Malatesta and Wilson (1986, p. 6) note that one common theme underlying this work is that 'individual people are predisposed to experience certain prevailing emotional states and to respond to the world in certain characteristic ways' and that 'these predispositions accrue by and large from experience'. Most significant in this regard is the extent to which children encounter particular affects, have their own emotions responded to (or ignored), and experience circumstances that evoke particular feelings. According to Izard (1977, p. 11), the repetitive experience and expression of emotion in the course of interaction with others 'inevitably produces distinct and significant personality characteristics'. Or, in the words of Tomkins (1963, p. 303), individuals develop personal 'affect theories' whose ideo-affective organization influence a broad spectrum of behaviours by fundamentally affecting 'the interpretation and disposition of information'.

The role of personality

To the extent that processes such as those outlined by Cummings *et al.* (1981), attachment theorists and discrete emotions theorists play an important role in the intergenerational transmission process, we should expect dispositional or personality characteristics of individuals that are affective and social in character to be systematically related to their rearing experiences in their families of origin and to their relationship functioning in their families of procreation. In the remainder of this chapter we summarize evidence consistent with this proposition. Before doing so, however, some comments are in order regarding 'personality'.

Ever since the publication of Mischel's (1968) influential book, *Personality and assessments*, if not before, the concept of personality has been under attack in the field of psychology. In arguing that behaviour is situationally specific and unstable over time, Mischel and others contended that the concept of personality traits had proven 'untenable'. Recently, Block and Epstein have demonstrated that individual differences are stable across situations and over time, at least when appropriate measurement procedures are employed, and thus that personality is 'alive and well' (Block 1977; Epstein 1977, 1979, 1980; Block and Block 1980; Epstein and O'Brien 1985). Some of the strongest evidence that this is indeed the case has been provided by McCrae and Costa (1984) who, on the basis of their own and others' longitudinal research, have concluded that:

a substantial body of literature unanimously shows that individuals change very little in self-reported personality traits over periods of up to thirty years and over the age range from twenty to ninety ... The idea that personality should be so deeply and permanently ingrained is revolutionary in a scientific climate in which growth and development are watchwords. (p. 91)

This work by McCrae and Costa, and that which is more directly behavioural in nature by Epstein and by Block, convinces us that it is not inappropriate to conceptualize individuals as possessing relatively stable inclinations to function in certain ways and to argue that such dispositions play a causal role in the developmental process.

Recent research is helpful in highlighting two independent and emotion-based dimensions of personality which account for much of the variation in individual differences chronicled across a wide variety of studies using a multitude of measurement tools, and which would seem to be systematically related to the developmental processes discussed by Malatesta and Wilson (1986) as well as by attachment theorists. McCrae and Costa (1980, 1984; McCrae 1982), following Eysenck and Eysenck (1969), use the terms *neuroticism* and *extraversion* to refer to these two higher-order constructs, whereas Tellegan and his associates who study transient mood prefer the labels *negative affectivity* and *positive affectivity*, respectively (Tellegan 1984; Watson and Clark 1984; Watson, Clark, and Tellegan 1984; Watson and Tellegan 1985). Neuroticism/negative affectivity reflects the inclination of an individual to be anxious, depressed, hostile, self-conscious, emotionally unstable, impulsive, and to have poor ego strength; that is, to be psychologically maladjusted. Persons displaying high levels of neuroticism 'are prone to violent and negative emotions that interfere with their ability to deal with their problems and to get along with others' (McCrae and Costa 1984, p. 43). Extraversion/positive affectivity reflects interpersonal warmth, attachment, and gregariousness (i.e. sociability) as well as activity and excitement seeking. Persons displaying high levels of extraversion tend to be friendly and compassionate, to have an intimately involved style of personal interaction in contrast to a cold, formal impersonal one; and to be busy, active, energetic, and to experience positive emotions frequently.

We shall see, in turning to examine work linking personality with parenting, marriage, and developmental history, that many dimensions of personality which have been studied in investigations of marriage and parenting fit nicely into the two emotion-based dispositions that have been identified in investigations of personality (e.g. Costa and McCrae 1980), transient mood (e.g. Tellegan 1982), and mental health (e.g. Veit and Ware 1983). It must be noted, in considering the work to be reviewed, that we think of personality in terms of a dynamic self system, not simply as a compilation of static traits. Personality, then, is deemed significant because of its interpersonal consequences. And such consequences are expected to ensue as a function of personality because individuals are predisposed to attend to certain affective-social information in the world (and not attend to other information) and to react in certain characteristic (i.e. dispositional) ways, all of which elicit responses from the social world that often have the (intended or unintended) consequences of maintaining the emotional, social-information processing and interpersonal proclivities of the individual in question.

Personality and parenting.   Depression, a component of neuroticism/negative affectivity, is probably the most extensively studied characteristic of psychological functioning that has been related to parenting. Whether clinically depressed individuals (Weissman *et al.* 1972; Field 1984) or those falling within the normal range of affective expression have been the focus of inquiry (Longfellow *et al.* 1982; Zelkowitz 1982; Colletta 1983; Conger *et al.* 1984; Cox *et al.* 1985; Crnic and Greenberg 1985; Forehand *et al.* 1985), research evidence consistently indicates that the propensity to experience negative affect states is associated with parental care that is less than optimal. This includes lower levels of attention and responsiveness in the case of fathers of infants (Zaslow *et al.* 1985), mothers of infants (Field *et al.* 1985), and mothers of pre-school and school-age children (Weissman and Paykel 1974), as well as more power assertive (as opposed to reason-based) and inconsistent disciplinary practices (Longfellow *et al.* 1982; Zelkowitz 1982; Weissman *et al.* 1972; Colletta 1983; Conger *et al.* 1984; Forehand *et al.* 1985). It is noteworthy that in many of these studies measures of depression correlate positively with, or relate to, assessments of parenting in the same way as measures of anxiety (Longfellow *et al.* 1982; Conger *et al.* 1984; Cox *et al.* 1985; Crnic and

Greenberg 1985), irritability (Conger *et al.* 1984), hostility (Crnic and Greenberg, 1985), and symptomology (Cox *et al.* 1985), just as McCrae and Costa's (1984) work on neuroticism and Watson and Clark's (1984) on negative affectivity would suggest.

Not all research linking psychological characteristics of parents with their child-rearing behaviour focuses upon neurotic-like traits. Heinicke (1985) reported, for example, that mothers rated higher on ego flexibility before their babies were born were more responsive and positively affectionate in their caregiving (see also Heinicke *et al.* 1983). Stevens (1986) observed maternal self-efficacy (as indexed by a measure of locus of control) to be positively related to black and white mothers' tendencies to be stimulating, responsive, and non-punitive in providing care to their 13–30-month-old toddlers (even after educational level was statistically controlled). Studying economically at-risk mothers and their 8-month-olds, Levine *et al.* (1984) found that those women who scored higher on a sentence-completion measure of ego development engaged in more positively affectionate and responsive interaction with their infants during face-to-face encounters than did mothers scoring lower on the scale.

These data are all consistent with Benn's (1985) findings that employed mothers scoring high on a composite measure of psychological integration, assessing the extent to which women were 'warm and secure in their sense of self . . . emotionally balanced and satisfied with themselves . . . and enjoy[ed] intimacy with those important to them' (p. 12), displayed high levels of sensitivity in caring for their infants. Indeed, these and other results led Benn to conclude, consistent with the line of reasoning being developed here, 'that the characteristics of acceptance and sensitivity are *overt manifestations* of maternal integration which become associated with child development outcomes because of their connection to this more *underlying property in mothers*' (p. 12, emphasis added).

Personality and marriage.   From the 1930s to the 1950s the relation between individual differences in personality and marital functioning was well studied. In the time since, this focus has fallen from favour, largely because students of the family have turned their attentions to what actually transpires between husbands and wives at the behavioural level.

Terman and Buttenwieser (1935) were among the first to document empirical associations between personality characteristics of spouses and the functioning of their marriage. Indeed, the results of this first study led Terman to assert, in describing the orientation of his second and more extensive investigation, that 'what comes out of marriage depends upon what goes into it and that among the most important things going into it are the attitudes, preferences, aversions, habit patterns, and emotional-reponse patterns which give or deny to one the aptitude for compatibility.' In this second study Terman (1938) compared the self-descriptions of the most and least happy couples (matched on age, years married, schooling, and husband occupation) and observed that happily married women possessed 'kindly attitudes towards others', 'expected kindly attitudes in return', were 'co-operative', self-assured, and optimistic, whereas unhappily married women were emotionally tense, moody, aggressive, irritable, and egocentric (pp. 145–6). The personality differences between happily married and unhappily married men revealed much the same; the former were co-operative, unselfconscious, extroverted, and emotionally stable, whereas the latter were 'moody, somewhat neurotic' and 'prone to feelings of social inferiority' (p. 155).

In the time since Terman's (1938) classic study a large quantity of data has been collected which are generally consistent with his findings and his basic thesis 'that successful adjustment in marriage is in part a function of personality variables' (Terman 1938, pp. 15–16). In fact, the results of a variety of studies support the conclusion that, in the terms of McCrae and Costa (1984), neurotic individuals are more likely to experience marriages as dissatisfying whereas the reverse is true of persons who are highly extroverted (Dean 1966; Pickford et al. 1966; Zaleski and Galkowska 1978; Eysenck 1980; Zaleski 1980; Frank et al. 1986).

One criticism which could be wielded against all such work, including Terman's, is that measures of personality and marriage were obtained at roughly the same point in time. Several longitudinal studies do indicate, however, that personality predicts future marital satisfaction (Bentler and Newcomb 1978; Cowan et al. 1986). Most impressive is Skolnick's (1981) analysis of the *adolescent* personality correlates of *midlife* marital satisfaction. Even though concurrent personality measures proved to be stronger predictors of marital satisfaction than adolescent personality, 16 per cent of the variance in women's marital satisfaction could be explained by their early personality scores after adult personality was statistically controlled. In the case of both men and women, a self-confident and nurturant (versus hostile) orientation positively related to marital satisfaction. Furthermore, individuals who eventually got divorced displayed less self-control and were more self-indulgent as teenagers than agemates whose marriages were to remain intact through midlife.

Personality and developmental history.   When it comes to considering the developmental origins, in terms of experiences in the family, of individual differences in adult psychological functioning, it is a component of neuroticism/negative affectivity, namely depression, which has received the most systematic empirical attention. Two different research strategies have been employed to examine the association between depression in adulthood and parent–child relationships during childhood. In one, retrospective reports of childhood experiences of clinically depressed patients are compared with non-patients 'matched' to the probands. In the other, samples of non-disturbed individuals are studied on the assumption 'that depression can be studied as a continuum ranging from subtle variations of normal affect states to severely disabling clinical conditions' (Blatt *et al.* 1979, p. 394).

The findings from both sets of studies are consistent in showing that depressed psychiatric patients, in comparison with non-patients, as well as more depressed non-patients in comparison with less depressed non-patients, report more negative and less positive child-rearing experiences in their families of origin (Abraham and Whittock 1969; Raskin *et al.* 1971; Jacobson *et al.* 1975; Blatt *et al.* 1979; Lyons-Ruth *et al.* 1984). As important as these findings are, even more significant are those from each set of studies indicating that severity of depression (among psychiatric patients and within non-patient samples) is systematically related to quality of parent–child relationships (Abraham and Whittock 1969; Jacobson *et al.* 1975; Blatt *et al.* 1979). Such data led Jacobson *et al.* (1975, p. 12) to conclude that there exists 'a gradation in the severity of depressive illness that relates to the severity of childhood rearing' (p. 12).

In view of our earlier discussion of the personality dimensions of neuroticism and the concept of negative affectivity, it comes as little surprise to learn that the very child-rearing-history correlates which have been linked repeatedly with depression are also associated with loneliness. In one large study, for example, lonely respondents recalled their parents as being remote, less trustworthy, and more disagreeable, whereas non-lonely respondents remembered their parents as warm, close, and helpful (Rubenstein *et al.* 1979). Similar results led Brennan and Auslander (1979, p. 200) to conclude that lonely adolescents come from families manifesting 'an absence of emotional nurturance, guidance, or support. The climate is cold, violent, undisciplined, and irrational.' An almost identical lack of positive involvement and lack of trust in parents has recently been shown to be a strong correlate of female college students' self-reported loneliness, which was itself strongly related to their scores on the Beck Depression Inventory (Lobdell and Perlman 1986).

In summary, the evidence reviewed provides a good deal of support for the contention that psychological or personality characteristics of adults are systematically related to the nature and quality of the parent–child and marital relationships in which they are involved and, at least in the case of depression and loneliness, are also associated with experiences they report having in their own childhoods in their families of origin. Moreover, these data are consistent with the assertion that the cross-generational continuities in marital and parent–child relationships documented earlier may well be mediated by psychological and behavioural characteristics of individuals that develop, in part, as a result of their experiences in their families of origin.

We would be remiss if we did not also note that the evidence just considered, as well as that summarized below, is also consistent with behaviour–genetic interpretations. That is, linkages between developmental history, personality, and family relationships may reflect the operation of genetic predispositions in different social contexts (parent–child and marital relationships) at different developmental periods (childhood, adulthood). Although the absence of behaviour–genetic research designs (twin and adoption studies, within-family comparisons) precludes the evaluation of this thesis, it must be noted that neuroticism and extraversion are among the most highly heritable individual traits (Plomin 1986). Despite this, we remain of the opinion that even strongly heritable dispositions, particularly those which are affective in nature (such as neuroticism/negative affectivity and extraversion/positive affectivity) are susceptible to regulatory influence from the social environment. Evidence consistent with this proposition will be considered shortly when we examine the conditions under which past is not prologue to the future in the case of family relationships.

Longitudinal evidence

Virtually all of the research summarized up to this point suffers from one major methodological weakness—reliance upon retrospective reports of experiences in the family during childhood. Fortunately, there exists a number of prospective longitudinal studies which generally substantiate conclusions drawn on the basis of this more limited database.

The first such investigations to be considered were conducted by Vaillant and his colleagues (Vaillant 1974; Vaillant and Milofsky 1980) and are deemed significant because they document theoretically meaningful associations between relationship experiences in the family of origin and psychosocial development and the capacity for relationships in adulthood. In attempting to predict adult mental health and social functioning at age 47 in a sample of men first studied as college students, Vaillant (1974) found that those individuals who characterized their family experiences in more negative terms (with regard to family relationships and their own functioning) were more likely at midlife to score high on traits of pessimism, passivity, and self-doubt. Of special importance was the strongest specific correlation—that between a warm home atmosphere and 'object relations', the latter assessed using both subjective and objective evidence of close friendships, good relationships with family, and a stable marriage.

Remarkably consistent with the general thrust of these findings are those emanating from an analysis of a group of inner-city male youths from another sample who, at age 47, scored in the top and bottom third of the sample on a health–sickness rating assessing global mental health, which was itself strongly correlated with measures of object relations (0.68) and maturity of ego defences (0.70). Of special importance are Vaillant and Vaillant's (1981) findings that a measure of adolescent industry/responsibility (after Erikson 1950), tapping household and paid work involvement and academic and extracurricular school performance, strongly predicted the establishment and maintenance of warm relationships with a wide variety of people in adulthood (as well as work success) and was itself strongly *predicted by* a composite measure of family environment, tapping cohesiveness of the home and maternal and paternal supervision and affection.

Several recent analyses of data gathered as part of the Oakland and Berkeley Growth Studies provide evidence that is generally consistent with the findings emerging from the Vaillant investigations. For example, Brooks (1981) discovered, using data obtained on more than 100 men and 100 women followed from adolescence through midlife, that when parents were happy people who provided warm and affectionate care as well as fair and consistent discipline, they tended to raise adolescents who were socially and psychologically integrated, productive, dependable, self-assertive, considerate of others, and non-impulsive. These personal traits, it was further observed, predicted social maturity at midlife, which itself forecast happy marriages and a positive emotional climate in the family.

Drawing on the same database, Elder *et al.* (1986) provide a more detailed analysis of intergenerational transmission across four generations. Using retrospective reports provided by the parents of the first children studied, Elder *et al.* found that growing up in a home in which parents' personalities could be described as unstable, in which marital conflict was frequent, and in which parental care was depicted as unaffectionate, controlling, and hostile, led to the development of unstable personalities in the children as adults. This personal instability on the part of the Berkeley parents (derived, as it seemed to be, from poor developmental experiences in their own families of origin) was itself related to tension in their own marriages, which contributed, along with personal instability, to their own administration of extreme and arbitrary discipline to their children. Exposure to such care resulted in their children (now third generation) developing behaviour problems that were themselves predictive of undercontrolled behaviour in adulthood. This developmental legacy was then predictive of functioning at work and at home, with the men with undercontrolled personalities, who had evidenced problems in childhood as a result of the poor care they received, displaying very erratic work histories and unstable marriages. The women, too, showed evidence of intergenerational deficit, participating in unaffectionate, explosive, and conflicted marriages, and being described by their own children as ill tempered and by their husbands as explosive in child-rearing. Not surprisingly, the children (fourth generation) of these parents developed undercontrolled behaviour styles, thereby recreating the behaviour patterns of their own parents (see also Caspi and Elder, Chapter 12 this volume).

Adding to our understanding of the intergenerational transmission process are the results of an ambitious study of the life courses of some 89 women from inner London who spent a good deal of their early and middle childhoods in high-quality residential facilities because of disorganization and conflict in their families of origin (Quinton *et al.* 1984; Rutter and Quinton 1984; Dowdney *et al.* 1985). In comparison to 41 women from the same neighbourhood but reared at home, the institutionally reared girls developed many more personal and relationship difficulties as young adults: they were more likely to evidence disturbance in personality development and psychosocial functioning (e.g. depression, anxiety, sleep, and eating disorders), to be less 'planful' in their mating (i.e. know their spouses for less than six months before cohabitation, be pre-maritally pregnant, marry for negative reasons like escaping from a discordant home), to marry men with problems, to experience marital problems and difficulties in love/sex relationships, and to rear their offspring in a less skilled manner (i.e. irritable, insensitive, and punitive care) (see also Chapter 17, this volume).

When these results and those of the other prospective longitudinal studies are considered together, they provide strong support for the contention that, at least insofar as the family is concerned, past is often prologue to the future. Developmental history appears to shape personality development and, thereby, future functioning. It would be mistaken, however, to consider the intergenerational transmissions of parent–child and marital relationships chronicled in these studies as inevitable. In fact, all the investigators whose work we have cited as evidence of lawful continuity make this point, often in the context of the relatively low associations documented in their research.

But it is one thing to assert that the modesty of some of the statistically significant relations that we have been considering indicates that there is a fair degree of unpredictability in the family system, and it is quite another to account for this discontinuity. In the absence of evidence documenting when and why prediction is modest or even nonexistent (i.e. lawful discontinuity), it remains impossible to distinguish error of measurement from actual discontinuity (cf. Bateson 1978; Hinde and Bateson 1984). Fortunately, the work of Rutter and Quinton (1984; Quinton *et al.* 1984; Quinton and Rutter 1985) illuminates the conditions under which discontinuity characterizes the processes of individual and family development.

Lawful discontinuity

In moving beyond a between-groups analysis of girls reared entirely at home and girls reared in residential settings to a *within-group* analysis of the latter group, Quinton and Rutter were able to document the circumstances under which early relationship difficulties did and did not undermine subsequent personality development, marriage, and parenting. Those ex-care girls who had positive school experiences were significantly less at risk for the development of personality disorder in adult life. In addition, these more fortunate girls were significantly more likely to be planful in the mate selection process (see above) and, as a result, to establish a harmonious relationship with a non-deviant spouse. The presence of such a supportive spouse, it is further worth noting, was significantly associated with parenting (Quinton *et al*. 1984), such that those ex-care women who spoke warmly of their spouse and/or indicated confiding in him were far more likely to be rated as good parents and far less likely to be rated as poor parents. On the basis of these findings Quinton *et al*. (1984, p. 115) noted that 'the spouse's good qualities exerted a powerful ameliorating effect on the parental functioning of the ex-care women' and went on to conclude that even though 'the findings run counter to the view that early experiences permanently and irrevocably change personality development', they do reveal 'that there are continuities in development that stem from the opening up or closing down of further opportunities—a train of events in which there are lasting sequelae as a result of a cumulative chain of indirect effects' (Quinton *et al*. 1984, p. 123).

What has yet to be determined in Rutter and colleague's most insightful analysis of life-course development is why it was that some ex-care girls found themselves in a position to experience school positively. One possibility is suggested by the antecedents of the industry/responsibility construct in Vaillant's studies, as his measure bears a striking resemblance to Quinton and Rutter's schooling variable and, like theirs, also proved to be a powerful predictor of future success in personal relationships. The fact that the strongest predictor of industry/responsibility in the Vaillant study turned out to be positive family relationships leads to the suggestion that the ex-care girls who gained most from school had more positive relationships (or less negative ones) with some member(s) of their families (nuclear or extended) or even with the staff at the residential centre than did their counterparts whose school experiences appear to have been less growth promoting.

Regardless of whether such a process was important in determining which ex-care girls found schooling to be a significant developmental experience, it is important to recognize the contribution of Rutter's work in documenting the role which mate selection and marriage, as well as school experience, play in maintaining or redirecting developmental trajectories established earlier in life. Of particular significance in this regard, especially given our earlier consideration of the intergenerational transmission of divorce, is the fact that Hetherington's (Hetherington *et al*. 1978) early work on the daughters of divorce and Mueller and Pope's (1977) analysis of survey data also underscore the importance of mate selection in the process of intergenerational continuity. Girls from disrupted families, both studies revealed, were likely to become pregnant pre-maritally and to marry, also at young ages, men with few resources (both psychological and economic), all of which resulted in relationships which were at high risk for dissolution and unsupportive of individual and family development (see Carlson 1979, for similar results).

The buffering role which marriage played in Rutter's studies in the life courses of girls at risk for relationship difficulties has also been documented in other research. Consider Egeland *et al.*'s (in press) recent finding that intergenerational cycles of child maltreatment are broken when women with abusive histories are involved in stable and emotionally supportive marital relationships. Consider also Crockenberg's (1986) recent findings that mothers with histories of parental rejection in their own childhoods are protected from becoming angry with and punitive toward their 2-year-old children when they experience high levels of social support from their spouse or some other significant individuals in their lives (see Carroll 1977, for similar results).

In view of these data demonstrating the buffering effect of marriages, we are forced again to wonder where these satisfying and supportive relationships come from in the lives of women whose relationship histories have placed them at risk with regard to both their marital and parent–child relationships. One possible answer to this question is found in Egeland *et al.*'s (in press) discovery that the women with abusive histories who did not mistreat their own offspring were disproportionately likely, relative to women who succumbed to the intergenerational cycle, to have had an emotionally supportive and non-abusive adult available during early childhood (see Hunter and Kilstrom 1979, for similar results) and to have undergone extensive therapy during their lives. What this suggests, of course, is that such relationship experience can serve as a corrective for individuals whose primary relationships in their families of origin were so problematical.

Conclusion

The evidence summarized in the preceding section and, indeed, throughout this chapter is generally consistent with the notion that cognitive–affective information about self, other, and relationships, derived as it seems to be from relationship experience in the family of origin, is 'not only internalized but carried forward to new relationships' (Sroufe and Fleeson 1986). This is accomplished through interrelated informational, emotional, and inter-actional processes which encompass personality development. In fact, as Sroufe and Fleeson (1986, p. 68) point out, 'It is because persons select and create later social environments that early relationships are viewed as having special importance.' Indeed, it is for this reason, Caspi and Elder (in press) argue, that 'attributing adult outcomes to proximal events is spurious because the effects derive from attributes of individuals, already evident in childhood . . .' (*ms.* p. 23).

The fact that individuals actively contribute to their own development through a rather conservative interpersonal process of seeking and interpret-ing experience in a manner consistent with their experientially-established and emotionally-laden understanding of self, other, and relationships does not, however, preclude the possibility of change. Discontinuity is considered as lawful as continuity: when discontinuity emerges it should be as a result of experiences which alter 'working models', that is cognitive–affective biases, and, in so doing, redirect developmental trajectories established earlier in life. When considered in this light, both the consistent relations from one generation to the next—as seemingly mediated by 'personality'—which were documented in the preceding sections of this chapter, as well as the discontinuities chronicled by Rutter, by Egeland *et al.*, and by Crockenberg, make eminent sense. In each case in which 'lawful discontinuity' was noted, it appeared to be related to relationship experiences, either with spouses, school-mates, or some non-parental adult, which probably enhanced the individual's feelings of worthiness while at the same time providing behavioural models of consideration and caring.

Without such 'corrective emotional experiences' it is difficult to imagine how a history of rejection and disregard would enable one to develop positive feelings about self and others, learn to manage emotional impulses, and take the perspective of and, as a result, develop the ability to care for and nurture another, be it a spouse or a child. Thus, when direct continuity is discerned from one generation to the next, we can presume that relationship experiences which might deflect a developmental trajectory that has been forged in earlier experiences and carried within a personality system have either not been encountered or have not been realized. What all this implies, of course, is that intergenerational transmission is by no means inevitable, even if probabilistically likely.

Summary

Investigation of child maltreatment, spouse abuse, and divorce reveals that these family dysfunctions are, to some degree, intergenerationally transmitted. Such evidence raises the question as to whether or not parent–child and marital relationships which fall within the 'normal' range are also transmitted across generations. A summary of pertinent research reveals that the intergenerational transmission of family relationships is not restricted to the pathological or dysfunctional range and, thereby, raises questions about the processes or mechanisms of intergenerational transmission.

It is argued the social learning theories which focus principally on imitation and overt behaviour cannot account for the complexity of the processes which must be involved. Recent research on the major dimensions of personality and mood draws attention to two broad and orthogonal dimensions—neuroticism/negative affectivity and extraversion/positive affectivity—which are posited as being important and dynamic, mediating processes which link prior experience in the family of origin with relationship functioning in the family of procreation.

Research is summarized which is consistent with this line of argument. More specifically, in an effort to garner support for the contention that relationship experience in the family of origin shapes personality development and, thereby, future relationship functioning, evidence is examined which documents linkages between developmental history and personality, personality and marital relationships, and personality and parent–child relationships. Recent prospective longitudinal research by Caspi and Elder and by Rutter (this volume) also provides support for the intergenerational transmission process under consideration.

Finally, evidence is considered which highlights the conditions under which discontinuity rather than continuity characterizes the developmental process. These data and other data are interpreted in terms of developmental processes articulated by attachment theory and by other theories of emotional and personality development.

References

Abraham, M. and Whittock, F. (1969). Childhood experience and depression. *British Journal of Psychiatry* **115,** 883–8.

Bateson, P. P. G. (1978). How does behavior develop? In *Perspectives in ethology*, Vol. 3 (ed. P. P. G. Bateson and P. H. Klopfer). pp. 55–66. Plenum, New York.

Belsky, J. (1978). Three theoretical models of child abuse: a critical review. *International Journal of Child Abuse and Neglect* **2,** 37–49.

Benn, R. (1985). *Factors associated with security of attachment in dual career families.* Paper presented at the Biennial Meeting of the Society for Research in Child Development, Toronto.

Bentler, P. and Newcomb, M. (1978). Longitudinal study of marital success and failure. *Journal of Consulting and Clinical Psychology* **46,** 1053–70.

Blatt, S. J., Wein, S. J., Chevron, E., and Quinlan, D. M. (1979). Parental representations in normal young adults. *Journal of Abnormal Psychology* **88,** 388–97.

Block, J. (1977). Recognizing the coherence of personality. In *Personality at the crossroads: current issues in interactional psychology* (ed. D. Magnusson and N. Endler), pp. 37–63. Erlbaum, Hillsdale, NJ.

Block, J. and Block, J. (1980). The role of ego control and ego-resiliency in the organization of behavior. In *Minnesota Symposia on Child Psychology*, Vol. 13 (ed. W. A. Collins). Erlbaum, Hillsdale, NJ.

Bowlby, J. (1980). *Attachment and loss*, Vol. 3, *Loss, sadness, and depression.* Basic Books, New York.

Brennan, T. and Auslander, N. (1979). *Adolescent loneliness.* (ERIC Document Reproduction Service No. 194 822).

Bretherton, I. (1985). Attachment theory: retrospect and prospect. In *Growing points of attachment theory and research* (ed. I. Bretherton and E. Waters). *Monographs of the Society for Research in Child Development* **50**, (1–2), Serial No. 209.

Brooks, J. (1981). Social maturity in middle-life and its developmental antecedents. In *Present and past in middle life* (ed. D. Eichorn, J. Clausen, N. Haan, M. Honzik and P. Musen), pp. 243–65. Academic Press, New York.

Bumpass, L. and Sweet, J. (1972). Differentials in marital instability: 1970. *American Sociological Review* **37**, 754–66.

Burgess, R. J. and Youngblade, L. (in press). Social incompetence and the intergenerational transmission of abusive parental behavior. In *New directions in family research* (ed. R. Gelles, G. Hotaling, D. Finkelhor, and M. Straus). Sage, Beverly Hills.

Carlson, E. (1979). Family background school and early marriage. *Journal of Marriage and the Family* **41**, 341–53.

Carroll, J. (1977). The intergenerational transmission of family violence: the long term effects of aggressive behavior. *Aggressive Behavior* **3**, 289–99.

Caspi, A. and Elder, G. (in press). Childhood precursors of the life course: early personality and life disorganization. In *Child development in lifespan perspective* (ed. E. M. Hetherington, R. Lerner, and M. Perlmutter).

Cicchetti, D. (1984). The emergence of developmental psychopathology. *Child Development* **55**, 1–4.

Colletta, N. (1983). At risk for depression: a study of young mothers. *Journal of Genetic Psychology* **142**, 301–10.

Conger, R., McCarthy, J., Yang, R., Lahey, B., and Kropp, J. (1984). Perception of child, childrearing values, and emotional distress as mediating links between environmental stressors and observed maternal behavior. *Child Development* **55**, 2234–47.

Costa, P. and McCrae, R. (1980). Still stable after all these years: personality as a key to some issues in adulthood and old age. In *Life-span development and behavior*, Vol. 3 (ed. P. Baltes and O. Brim), pp. 65–102. Academic Press, New York.

Cowan, P., Cowan, C., and Heming, G. (1986). *Risks to marriage when partners become parents: implications for family development*. Paper presented at the Annual Meeting of the American Psychiatric Association, Washington, DC.

Cox, M. J., Owen, M. T., Lewis, J. M., Riedel, C., Scalf-Michler, L., and Suster, A. (1985). Intergenerational influences on the parent–infant relationship in the transition to parenthood. *Journal of Family Issues* **6**, 543–64.

Crnic, K. and Greenberg, M. (1985). *Parenting daily hassles: relationships among minor stresses, family functioning and child development*. Paper presented at the Biennial Meetings of the Society for Research in Child Development, Toronto.

Crockenberg, S. (1986). *Maternal anger and the behaviour of two year old children*. Paper presented at the International Conference on Infant Studies, Beverly Hills, Calif.

Cummings, E., Zahn-Waxler, C., and Radke-Yarrow, M. (1981). Young children's responses to expressions of anger and affection by others in the family. *Child Development* **52**, 1274–82.

Cummings, E., Iannotti, R., and Zahn-Waxler, C. (1985). Influences of conflict between adults on the emotions and aggression of young children. *Developmental Psychology* **21**, 495–507.

Dean, D. G. (1966). Emotional maturity and marital adjustment. *Journal of Marriage and the Family* **28**, 454–7.

Downdey, L., Skuse, D., Rutter, M., Quinton, D., and Mrazek, D. (1985). The nature and qualities of parenting provided by women raised in institutions. *Journal of Child Psychology and Psychiatry* **26**, 599–625.

Duncan, B. and Duncan, O. (1969). Family stability and occupational success. *Social Problems* **16**, 273–85.

Egeland, B., Jacobvitz, D., and Papatola, K. (1984). *Intergenerational continuity of abuse*. Paper presented at the Conference on Biosocial Perspectives in Abuse and Neglect, York, ME.

Egeland, B., Jacobvitz, D., and Sroufe, L. (in press). Breaking the cycle of abuse: relationship predictors. *Child Development*.

Elder, G., Caspi, A., and Downey, G. (1986). Problem behavior and family relationships: life course and intergenerational themes. In *Human development: interdisciplinary perspectives* (ed. A. Sorensen, F. Weinert, and L. Sherrod), pp. 293–340.

Epstein, S. (1977). Traits are live and well. *Personality at the crossroads: current issues in interactional psychology* (ed. D. Magnusson and N. S. Elder), pp. 83–98. Erlbaum, Hillsdale, NJ.

Epstein, S. (1979). The stability of behavior: I. On predicting most of the people much of the time. *Journal of Personality and Social Psychology* **37**, 1097–126.

Epstein, S. (1980). The self concept: a review and the proposal of an integrated theory of personality. In *Personality: basic aspects and current research* (ed. E. Starb). Prentice-Hall, Englewood Cliffs, NJ.

Epstein, S. and O'Brien, E. (1985). The person–situation debate in historical and current perspective. *Psychological Bulletin* **98**, 513–37.

Erikson, E. (1950). *Childhood and society*. Norton, New York.

Eysenck, H. (1980). Personality, marital satisfaction, and divorce. *Psychological Report* **47**, 1235–8.

Eysenck, H. and Eysenck, S. (1969). *Personality structure and measurement*. Robert R. Knopp, San Diego.

Eysenck, H. and Wakefield, J. (1981). Psychological factors as predictors of marital satisfaction. *Advances in Behavioral Research and Therapy* **3**, 151–92.

Field, T. (1984). Early interactions between infants and their post-partum depressed mothers. *Infant Behavior and Development* **7**, 517–23.

Field, T., Sandberg, D., Garcia, R., Vega-Lahr, N., Goldstein, S., and Guy, L. (1985). Pregnancy problems, postpartum depression, and early mother-infant interactions. *Developmental Psychology* **21**, 1152–6.

Forehand, R., Lautenschlager, G., Faust, J., and Graziano, W. (1985). Parent perceptions and parent–child interactions in clinic-referred children: a preliminary investigation of the effects of maternal depressive mood. *Behavior Research and Therapy* **14**, 1–3.

Frank, S., Hok, C., Jacobson, S., Justkowski, R., and Huyck, M. (1986). Psychological predictors of parents' sense of confidence and control and self- versus child-focused gratifications. *Developmental Psychology* **22**, 348–55.

Friedrich, W. and Wheeler, K. (1982). The abusing parent revisited: a decade of psychological research. *Journal of Nervous and Mental Diseases* **170**, 577–87.

Gelles, R. (1976). Demythologizing child abuse. *The Family Coordinator* **25**, 135–41.

Glenn, N. and Kramer, K. (1986). The marriages and divorces of the children of divorce. Unpublished manuscript. Department of Sociology, University of Texas.

Glenn, N. D. and Shelton, R. A. (1983). Pre-adult background variables and divorce: a note of caution about overreliance on explained variance. *Journal of Marriage and the Family* **45**, 405–10.

Goodrich, W., Ryder, R., and Rausch, H. (1968). Patterns of newlywed marriage. *Journal of Marriage and the Family* **30**, 383–9.

Heinicke, C. (1985). *Prebirth couple functioning and the quality of the mother-infant relationships in the second half of the first year of life.* Paper presented at the Biennial Meetings of the Society for Research in Child Development, Toronto.

Heinicke, C., Diskin, S., Ramsey-Klee, D., and Given, K. (1983). Prebirth parent characteristics and family development in the first year of life. *Child Development* **54**, 194–208.

Heiss, J. (1972). On the transmission of marital instability in black families. *American Sociological Review* **37**, 82–92.

Herrenkohl, E. C., Herrenkohl, R. C., and Toedter, L. J. (1983). Perspectives on the intergenerational transmission of abuse. In *The dark side of families: current family violence research* (ed. D. Finkelhor). Sage, Beverly Hills.

Hetherington, E., Cox, M., and Cox, R. (1978). The development of children in mother-headed families. In *The American family: dying or developing* (ed. H. Hoffman and D. Reiss). Plenum Press, New York.

Hinde, R. A. and Bateson, P. (1984). Discontinuities versus continuities in behavioral development and the neglect of process. *International Journal of Behavioral Development* **7**, 129–43.

Hunter, R. and Kilstrom, N. (1979). Breaking the cycle in abusive families. *American Journal of Psychiatry* **136**, 1320–2.

Izard, C. E. (1977). *Human emotions.* Plenum Press, New York.

Izard, C. (1984). Emotion-cognition relationships and human development. In *Emotions, cognition and behavior* (ed. C. Izard, J. Kagan, and R. Zajonc), pp. 12–37. Cambridge University Press, New York.

Jacobson, S., Fasman, J., and DiMascio, A. (1975). Deprivation in the childhood of depressed women. *Journal of Nervous and Mental Diseases* **160**, 5–13.

Kalmuss, D. (1984). The intergenerational transmission of marital aggression. *Journal of Marriage and the Family* **46**, 11–19.

Kaufman, J. and Zigler, E. (1986). Do abused children become abusive parents? Unpublished manuscript. Dept of Psychology, Yale University.

Korbin, F. and Waite, L. (1984). Effects of childhood family structure on the transition to marriage. *Journal of Marriage and the Family* **46**, 807–16.

Kulka, R. and Weingarten, N. (1979). The long-term effects of parental divorce in childhood on adult adjustment. *Journal of Social Issues* **32**, 193–207.

Levine, L., Coll, C., and Oh, W. (1984). *Determinants of mother–infant interaction in adolescent mothers*. Paper presented at the International Conference on Infant Studies, New York.

Lewis, M. and Michalson, L. (1985). *Children's emotions and moods*. Plenum, New York.

Lobdell, J. and Perlman, D. (1986). The intergenerational transmission of loneliness: a study of college females and their parents. *Journal of Marriage and the Family* **48**, 589–95.

Longfellow, C., Zelkowitz, P., and Saunders, E. (1982). The quality of mother–child relationships. In *Lives in Stress: women and depression* (ed. D. Belle). Sage, Beverly Hills.

Lyons-Ruth, K., Cornell, D., Gruneboum, M., Botein, M., and Zoll, D. (1984). Maternal family history, maternal caretaking and infant attachment in multiproblem families. *Journal of Preventative Psychiatry* **2**, 403–25.

McCrae, R. (1982). Consensual validation of personality traits: evidence from self reports and ratings. *Journal of Personality and Social Psychology* **43**, 293–303.

McCrae, R. and Costa, P. (1980). Openness to experience and ego level in Loevinger's sentence completion test: dispositional contributions to developmental models of personality. *Journal of Personality and Social Psychology* **39**, 1179–90.

McCrae, R. and Costa, P. (1984). *Emerging lives, enduring disposition: personality in adulthood*. Little and Brown, Boston.

Main, M., Kaplan, N., and Cassidy, J. (1985). Security in infancy, childhood and adulthood: a move to the level of representation. In *Growing points in attachment theory and research* (ed. I. Bretherton and E. Waters). *Monographs for the Society for Research in Child Development*, Serial No. 209, **50**, (1–2), 66–104.

Malatesta, C. (1985). Developmental course of emotion expression in the human infant. In *The development of expressive behavior: biology–environment interactions* (ed. G. Zivin), pp. 183–219. Academic Press, New York.

Malatesta, C. and Haviland, J. (1982). Learning display rules: the socialization of emotion expression in infancy. *Child Development* **53**, 991–1003.

Malatesta, C. and Izard, C. (1984). The ontogenesis of human social signals: from biological imperative to symbol utilization. In *The psychobiology of affective development* (ed. N. Fox and R. Davidson). Erlbaum, Hillsdale, NJ.

Malatesta, C. and Wilson, A. (1986). Emotional cognition interaction in personality development: a discrete emotions functionalist analysis. Unpublished manuscript. New School for Social Research, New York City.

Malatesta, C., Grigonyer, P., Lamb, C., Albin, M., and Culver, C. (1987). Emotion socialization and expressive development in preterm and full term infants. *Child Development* (in press).

Minde, K. (1980). Bonding of parents to premature infants: theory and practice. In *Parent–infant relationships* (ed. P. M. Taylor). Grune and Stratton, New York.

Mischel, W. (1968). *Personality and assessment*. Wiley, New York.

Morris, D. (1980). Infant attachment and problem solving in the toddler: relations to mother's family history. Unpublished doctoral dissertation. University of Minnesota.

Morris, D. (1981). Attachment and intimacy. In *Intimacy* (ed. G. Stricker), pp. 305–23. Plenum Press, New York.

Mott, F. and Moore, S. (1979). The causes of marital disruption among young American woman. *Journal of Marriage and the Family* **41**, 355–65.

Mueller, D. and Cooper, P. (1986). Children of single parent families: how they fare as young adults. *Family Relations* **35**, 169–76.

Mueller, C. and Pope, H. (1977). Marital instability: a study of its transmission between generations. *Journal of Marriage and the Family* **39**, 83–93.

Pagelow, M. (1981). *Children in violent families: direct and indirect victims.* Paper presented at the Research Conference on Young Children and Their Families, Anaheim, Calif.

Parke, R. and Collmer, C. (1975). Child abuse: an interdisciplinary review. In *Review of child development research*, Vol. 5 (ed. E. M. Hetherington). University of Chicago Press.

Pickford, J., Signori, E., and Rempel, H. (1966). Intensity of personality traits in relation to marital happiness. *Journal of Marriage and the Family* **28**, 458–9.

Plomin, R. (1986). *Development, genetics, and psychology.* Erlbaum, Hillsdale, NJ.

Pope, H. and Mueller, C. W. (1976). The intergenerational transmission and marital instability: comparisons by race and sex. *Journal of Social Issues* **32**, 49–66.

Quinton, D. and Rutter, M. (1985). Parenting behavior of mothers raised 'in care'. In *Longitudinal studies in child psychology and psychiatry* (ed. A. Nicol), pp. 157–210. Wiley, London.

Quinton, D., Rutter, M., and Liddle, C. (1984). Institutional rearing, parenting difficulties and marital support. *Psychological Medicine* **14**, 107–24.

Raskin, A., Boothe, H., Reatig, N., and Schulterbrandt, J. (1971). Factor analysis of normal and depressed patients memories of parental behavior. *Psychological Reports* **29**, 871–9.

Ricks, M. (1985). *Origins of individual differences in competence: attachment history and environmental support.* Paper presented at the Biennial Meetings of the Society for Research in Child Development, Toronto.

Roscoe, B. and Benaske, N. (1985). Courtship violence experienced by abused wives: similarities in patterns of abuse. *Family Relations* **34**, 419–24.

Rubenstein, C., Shaver, P., and Peplau, A. (1979). Loneliness. *Human Nature* **2**, 59–65.

Rutter, M. (1982). Protective factors in children's responses to stress on disadvantage. In *Primary prevention of psychopathology*, Vol. 3, *Promoting social competence and coping in children* (ed. M. W. Kent and J. E. Rolf). University Press of New England, Hanover, NH.

Rutter, M. and Quinton, D. (1984). Long-term follow-up of women institutionalized in childhood: factors promoting good functioning in adult life. *British Journal of Developmental Psychology* **2**, 191–204.

Skolnick, A. (1981). Married lives: Longitudinal perspectives on marriage. In *Present and past in middle life* (ed. D. Eichorn, J. Clausen, N. Haan, M. Honzik, and P. Mussen) pp. 243–65. Academic Press, New York.

Snyder, D. (1979). Multidimensional assessment of marital satisfaction. *Journal of Marriage and the Family* **41**, 813–23.

Sroufe, L. A. and Rutter, M. (1984). The domain of developmental psychopathology. *Child Development* **55**, 17.

Sroufe, L. A. and Fleeson, J. (1986). Attachment and the construction of relationships.

In *Relationships and development* (ed. W. Hartup and Z. Rubin). Erlbaum, Hillsdale, NJ.

Steinmetz, S. (1977). The use of force for resolving family conflict: the training ground for abuse. *Family Coordinator* **26**, 19–26.

Stevens, J. (1986). Parenting skill: does social support matter? Unpublished manuscript. Dept of Early Childhood Education, Georgia State University.

Straus, M. (1979). Family patterns and child abuse in a nationally representative sample. *International Journal of Child Abuse and Neglect* **3**, 223–5.

Straus, M. A., Gelles, R. J., and Steinmetz, S. K. (1980). *Behind closed doors: violence in the American family*. Anchor Press, New York.

Tellegan, A. (1982). Brief manual for the Differential Personality Questionnaire. Unpublished manuscript. University of Minnesota, Minneapolis.

Tellegan, A. (1984). Structures of mood and personality and their relevance to assessing anxiety, with an emphasis on self report. In *Anxiety and anxiety disorders* (ed. A. Tuma and J. Moser), pp. 681–706. Erlbaum, Hillsdale, NJ.

Terman, L. (1938). *Psychological factors: in marital happiness*. McGraw-Hill, New York.

Terman, L. and Buttenwieser, P. (1935). Personality factors in marital compatibility. *Journal of Social Psychology* **6**, 143–71.

Tomkins, S. (1962). *Affect, imagery, consciousness*, Vol. 1, *The positive affect*. Springer, New York.

Tomkins, S. (1963). *Affect, imagery, consciousness*, Vol. 2, *The negative affect*. Springer, New York.

Vaillant, G. E. (1974). Natural history of male psychological health: II. *Archives of General Psychiatry* **31**, 15–22.

Vaillant, G. E. and Milofsky, E. (1980). Natural history of male psychological health: XI. Empirical evidence for Erikson's model of the life cycle. *American Journal of Psychiatry* **137**, 1348–59.

Vaillant, G. E. and Vaillant, C. D. (1981). Natural history of male psychological health: X. Work as a predictor of positive mental health. *American Journal of Psychiatry* **138**, 1433–40.

Veit, C. and Ware, J. (1983). The structure of psychological well-being in general populations. *Journal of Consulting and Clinical Psychology* **51**, 730–42.

Watson, D. and Clark, L. (1984). Negative affectivity: the disposition to experience aversive emotional states. *Psychological Bulletin* **96**, 465–90.

Watson, D. and Tellegan, A. (1985). Toward a consensual structure of mood. *Psychological Bulletin* **98**, 219–35.

Watson, D., Clark, C., and Tellegan, A. (1984). Cross-cultural convergence in the structure of mood: a Japanese replication and a comparison with U.S. findings. *Journal of Personality and Social Psychology* **67**, 127–44.

Weissman, M. and Paykel, E. (1974). *The depressed woman*. University of Chicago Press.

Weissman, M., Paykel, E., and Klerman, G. (1972). The depressed woman as a model. *Social Psychiatry* **7**, 98–108.

Zaleski, Z. (1980). Psychoticism and marital satisfaction. *Personality and Individual Differences* **2**, 245–6.

Zaleski, Z. and Galkowska, M. (1978). Neuroticism and marital satisfaction. *Behavior Research and Therapy* **16**, 285–6.

Zaslow, M., Pedersen, F., Cain, R., and Swalsky, J. (1985). Depressed mood in new fathers: associations with parent–infant interaction. Unpublished manuscript. National Institute of Child Health and Human Development, Laboratory of Comparative Ethology, Bethesda.

Zelkowitz, P. (1982). Parenting philosophies and practices. In *Lives in stress: women and depression* (ed. D. Belle). Sage, Beverly Hills.

12

Emergent family patterns: the intergenerational construction of problem behaviour and relationships*
AVSHALOM CASPI and GLEN H. ELDER, Jr.

Social continuity from one generation to the next poses questions regarding the process by which behaviour persists across the generations and over the life span of individuals. The young are influenced by their home environment, but does this influence continue in their lives as they become adults? Are these influences manifest in how they bring up their own children, and, years later, in how this new generation functions as parents for the next generation? How is such continuity achieved and maintained?

In this chapter we summarize our research on such questions by examining the interplay of problem behaviour and family relationships across the life course and across generations of women in the Berkeley Guidance Study, Institute of Human Development, University of California, Berkeley. Launched in 1928 as a longitudinal study of normal children and parents (Macfarlane 1938), the Berkeley study has generated an archive with data on grandparents (birth years before 1890), parents (birth years 1890–1910), children (birth years 1928–29), and grandchildren (birth years after World War II). In this study of individual behaviour and family systems we aim to enhance understanding of the origins, transmission, and sequelae of maladjustment.

Do problems beget problems?

Generations of scholars have argued that people have the tendency to replicate the themes of early life or of previous generations in the context of

*This chapter is based on a programme of research on social change in the family and life course, supported by NIMH Grants MH-34172 and MH-41827 and an NIMH Senior Scientist Award (MH00567) to Glen H. Elder, Jr. We are indebted to the Institute of Human Development, University of California, Berkeley, for permission to use archival data from the Berkeley Guidance Study.

later intimate relationships. We have many reasons to believe that this dynamic is especially true of women's lives.

The female life course has been called 'normal biography', in part because women's lives are highly standardized through familial activities. For example, age at marriage shows less variance for women than for men, and events such as marriage and the birth of the first child have a stronger impact on women's life course than on men's. These events not only determine available lines of action, they also shape the ways in which lives are interpreted. Indeed, evidence on the social construction of the life course suggests that even the mere anticipation of marriage and parenthood leads to changes in real and symbolic participation in non-familial activities on the part of the women (Held 1986).

Socialization into sex-differentiated roles begins in early childhood when boys are provided with incentives for engaging in activities independent of the family while girls are rewarded for helping other family members and are pressured to attend family rituals (e.g. Komarovsky 1950; Parsons 1955). Others have added that such differential socialization practices create a dependency between successive generations of women (Chodorow 1978). While socialization into masculinity involves socialization into separateness outside the home and beyond the family, girls' socialization is embedded in their own ongoing relationships within the family and stresses affective relationships to others. As a result, a woman's efforts to adapt successfully to her role as wife and mother within her own family of procreation are constrained by her family of origin. Although women may attempt to use the instrumental skills they were taught in childhood, the asymmetry of western kinship systems makes it more difficult for women than for men to relinquish their ties to their own parental family (Komarovsky 1950). They are kin keepers in the sense that they are more involved than men in activities that maintain affinal and lineal ties.

Whether or not the nature of women's roles actually encourages a continued dependency and attachment on an anaclitic mode is, of course, an arguable proposition. Less equivocal is the accumulated body of empirical evidence pointing to continuity across successive generations of women. A review of the psychoanalytic literature suggests that a girl's early relationship to her mother is of great importance to her later reproductive adaptation (e.g. Uddenberg 1974). Similarly, research on separation, loss, and disruption points to the enduring consequences of early experiences in the home, and especially in the mother–child relationship, for adaptation to motherhood (Frommer and O'Shea 1973a, 1973b).

The aetiological role of separation *per se* is not unequivocal. Indeed, Hall *et al.* (1979) suggest that what appears to be associated with non-optimal caretaking is not the experience of *short-term separation* as much as the *disruption* of early attachment relationships. This interpretation is buttressed by a series of two-generation studies. Rutter *et al.* (1983) compared the early childhood experiences of parents who had serious family difficulties, defined by having a child in care, with a control group of similar socio–economic status. They report that the multiple problems found in families with children in care were almost always associated with serious childhood adversities in the mothers' family of origin, especially with separation as a result of discord or rejection (see also Chapter 17, this volume).

Intergenerational continuity in the quality of parental behaviour has also been addressed systematically by recent attachment research. In a provocative set of studies, Main (Main *et al.* 1985) and Ricks (1985) have documented significant relations between mothers' retrospective recollections of childhood attachments and their ability to serve as a secure base for their children (see Chapters 2 and 13, this volume).

We have now a corpus of data pointing to intergenerational continuity in the quality of parenting behaviour. In conjunction with other evidence on the intergenerational transmission of marital discord (e.g. Rutter and Madge 1976), as well as on the transmission of problem dispositions (e.g. Huesmann *et al.* 1984; Elder *et al.* 1986), we seem to have corroborated the assertion that, across the life course and across successive generations, problems beget problems.

Several weaknesses in this account should be noted. First, prospective data on multiple generations are still lacking. The evidence briefly reviewed here is compelling, but it is substantiated largely by *retrospective* links. Second, the causal relations among the various personality, marital, and parenting behaviours examined await empirical clarification.

With retrospective and prospective data on personality, marital, and parenting difficulties across four generations of women, we set out in this chapter to examine the intergenerational construction of problem behaviour and relationships.

Relating individual and family development

Guiding hypotheses

Three hypotheses guide our work on the intergenerational construction of problem behaviour and relationships:

1. The *intragenerational* hypothesis concerns the dynamic linking problem behaviour and problem relationships within a generation. As depicted by the 'A' link in Fig. 12.1, the primary flow of influence runs from problematic behaviour to problematic relationships in the family.

2. The *intergenerational* hypothesis views the family environment as a link

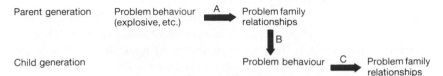

FIG. 12.1   Intra- and intergenerational processes linking problem behaviour and problem family relations. A: the intragenerational hypothesis; A and B: the intergenerational hypothesis; C: the life-course development hypothesis.

between the problem behaviour of parents and the problem behaviour of their offspring in the next generation. This causal pathway combines the 'A' and 'B' linkages in Fig. 12.1.

3. The *life-course development* hypothesis views the problem behaviour of children as one route by which unstable relationships in one generation are replicated in the next—the 'B' and 'C' linkages in Fig. 12.1. Children develop problem dispositions and they carry them into marital and parent–child relationships many years later as adults.

The most satisfactory account of the relation between individual development and emergent family patterns requires that we extend this analysis across two generations or more, since each generation establishes the developmental milieu of the next. This feat is made possible by the resources of the Berkeley Guidance Study.

Sample

The Berkeley Guidance study was initiated in 1928 with every third birth in the city of Berkeley over an 18-month period. The original sample included an intensively studied group of 113 subjects and a less intensively studied group of 101 subjects matched on social and economic characteristics (female N = 112). Most of the Berkeley subjects (G3) were born to white, Protestant, native-born parents (G2). Slightly more than 60 per cent of the parents were positioned in the middle class as of 1929. Although Berkeley is a university town, few fathers were university employees.

Grandparents (G1) were never directly involved in the study, but we are able to learn about their lives through retrospective accounts from Berkeley parents (G2). At the study's inception, during the 1930 interview, parents provided detailed reports of their own childhood and parentage. The Berkeley parents (G2) and their children (G3) were most intensively studied between the years 1930–45. Most of the children (G3) participated in two adult follow-ups (1959–60 and 1969–72) that entailed lengthy interviews and a battery of psychological, medical, and mental tests. Educational, occupational, and family histories were constructed from the interview materials. Of the 214 original subjects, 182 provided information at age 40.

By the 1969–72 follow-up a large majority of Berkeley subjects (G3) had become parents of the G4 generation. The Institute staff at Berkeley attempted to interview all children of the subjects between the ages 14–19. Data on the fourth generation includes information on their own social, personality, and intellectual functioning, as well as their assessments of each parent. A summary of key information on these four generations is contained in Table 12.1.

Multiple problem families

Efforts to understand the interlocking trajectories of individuals and families requires that we first identify key variables that reveal connections between individual development and emergent family patterns across time. This requires an emphasis on the ways individuals learn to deal with the environment.

Over the course of individual lives and across multiple generations we focus on a set of personality, marriage, and parenting variables grouped under the conceptual umbrella of problem behaviour. In doing so, we shall be dealing with what Ackerman (1970) has referred to as 'interlocking pathology' in family relationships, patterns of interaction characterized by a matrix of aversive qualities: unstable behaviours of individuals; marital conflicts and discord; and arbitrary, inconsistent parental practices.

Clues to the origins of problem behaviour and problem relationships may be found in the family patterns of the first Berkeley generation. Information about grandparents (G1) was provided by their adult children—Berkeley parents (G2)—during the 1930 interview. These are retrospective reports and, in all cases, the judgments were based on parents' memories of childhood experiences.

To delineate family systems in the first generation we consider relations between three domains: personality, marriage, and parenting. Central to our investigation is the behavioural disposition we term *instability*. It is indexed by an average of two scores on recall ratings: irritability, with a range from 'extremely even tempered' to 'explosive', and nervous-stability, with a range from 'exceptionally even-keel, even in the face of trying circumstances' to the presence of behaviours 'interfering with social functioning'. The two measures are correlated 0.51. *Marital tension* of grandparents is indexed by a five-point scale with values that indicate a relationship characterized by 'frankness, affection, and agreement' at one extreme, and by 'disruptive conflict' at the other. Parenting quality is indexed by a five-point scale, *hostility toward child*.

This recall rating refers at its low end to a 'friendly, trustful relationship' and at its high end to 'hostility, distrust, and open friction' between parent and child.

The G1 correlations, shown in Table 12.2, describe an aversive system linking unstable people with conflicted marriages and hostile parenting. According to retrospective reports, parental instability, marital tension, and hostility in parental attitudes were linked in the first generation.

Staff assessments of the parents (G2) in 1933–35 include several ratings comparable to the retrospective accounts about the first generation. Each rating on G2 represents an average of an interviewer's judgment and that of a home observer. *Instability* is indexed here by three seven-point scales: irritability, nervous-stability, and tense-worrisome (av. $r = 0.58$). *Marital tension* is indexed by a five-point scale similar to that described for the grandparents. Because hostility toward child was not measured during this assessment period, two other relevant parenting measures are included. Arbitrary behaviour refers at its extreme to inconsistent discipline that expresses parental mood rather than a response to child behaviour: 'the child never knows what to expect'. Extreme discipline refers to a mother who is either unusually punitive or *laissez-faire* and indifferent. These two ratings ($r = 0.68$) are combined into a single index of *arbitrary parenting*. A summary of the key correlations among these indicators of aversive family systems in G2 is shown in Table 12.2.

The correlations among G2 mothers are similar to those observed among G1 grandmothers. Maternal instability was associated with marital tension and the use of extreme and arbitrary discipline with their children. Moreover, these practices were significantly associated with marital tension.

In Table 12.2 we also meet the Berkeley subjects (G3) as adults. A set of items from the California Q-sort (Berkeley follow-up 1970), provides an appropriate measure of *instability* among G3 women (Block 1971). We selected three intercorrelated items that collectively depict an undercontrolled style of behaviour (see Elder et al. 1986): 'self-indulgent' describes an individual's reluctance to deny self-pleasure; 'pushes limits' depicts an individual's efforts to see what she can get away with; 'undercontrolled' refers to impulsive expression of emotions. Marital tension among G3 women is assessed by their spouses' (1970) report of a conflicted marriage. This scale refers at its low end to 'no conflict' and at its high end to 'frequent conflict'. Information on G3 parenting comes from the 1970 interviews with the women's children (G4). From the children's interview an index of ill-tempered parenting was calculated by combining two items: one item summarized the child's perception of the parent's self-control ranging from 'exceptionally good-tempered' to 'usually bad-tempered'. The other 'summarized the child's perception of the parent's self-control, ranging from 'no evidence of parental loss of control' to 'parent shows widespread loss of control—evidence of screaming or crying in front of child, physical abuse'.

Table 12.1 *Four Berkeley generations*

	Grandparents (G1)	Parents (G2)	Children (Ss) (G3)	Grandchildren (G4)
Birth year	Before 1890	1890–1910	1928–29	post-1946
No. of cases*	884	422	182	83
		(211 couples, 1928)	(1928–70)	(age 14–22, 1969–70)
Main source of data	Reports by parents, 1930 interview	Annual and periodic measurements 1928–46; 1969–70	Annual and periodic measurements 1928–46; adult contacts in 1960, 1969–70	Contacted 1969–70: interviews, questionnaires

*This includes males and females.

Table 12.2 *Multiple problem families (Pearson correlation coefficients)*

	Generation 1			Generation 2			Generation 3		
	Personal instability	Marital conflict	Non-optimal parenting	Personal instability	Marital conflict	Non-optimal parenting	Personal instability	Marital conflict	Non-optimal parenting
Personal instability	—	0.48	0.49	—	0.38	0.32	—	0.38	0.42
Marital conflict		—	0.69		—	0.36		—	0.62

The covariation of personality, marital, and parenting difficulties in G3 resembles observations on G1 as well as G2 women. Among G3 women we see, once again, that aversive personalities are associated with marital tension and parenting difficulties, and parenting difficulties are associated also with marital discord. The interlocking pathology of behavioural instability, marital conflict, and non-optimal parenting appears in each generation, with data variously derived from retrospective accounts, observer-based ratings, clinical reports, and interviews with family members.

A formal representation of this observation is provided by a test of the equality of the three correlation matrices. To determine whether the three-dimensional model of interlocking pathology fits the data in each generation, we constructed a measurement model using confirmatory factor analysis in LISREL for G1, G2, and G3 women. The model fits the data at acceptable levels ($\chi^2 = 8.44$, $df = 15$, $p = 0.90$) and supports the conclusion that the empirical relations between the three constructs are invariant across successive generations of women.

In summary, we have three structurally equivalent matrices of multiple problem families; families characterized by the unstable behaviours of individual members, marital conflicts, and parenting difficulties. We are now in a position to evaluate the process by which problem dispositions and problem relationships are transmitted across the generations.

Our examination begins with a test of the dynamic linking problem behaviour and unstable family relationships within a generation (the intragenerational 'A' link in Fig. 12.1). Using simultaneous equations, we investigate the reciprocal influences between individual instability and marital tension. Next we examine the family environment as a link between the problem dispositions of parents and children (the intergenerational 'A' and 'B' linkages in Fig. 12.1) and model this causal pathway across four Berkeley generations. Finally, we examine the processes by which children carry problem dispositions into marital and parent–child relationships many years later as adults (the life-course 'C' linkage in Fig. 12.1).

The construction of problem behaviour and problem relationships

The intragenerational dynamic

Aversive personalities and aversive relationships are often found in the context of a disordered family, and their effects cannot be easily separated from the total pattern. Consider the case of personal instability and marital tension. An interpersonal account views the marital relationship as an evolving dyadic pattern, whereas an intrapersonal account considers problematic relations as a direct extension of individual adjustment problems.

Gottman's (1979) experimental studies exemplify the *interpersonal* emphasis. He suggests that negative interaction patterns are self-perpetuating in the dyadic relationship. Whatever the initial cause, negativity tends to increase in amplitude as husbands react to the negative affect of wives and wives react in kind to their husbands. The *intrapersonal* perspective echoes Waller's (1938) observation that 'the real cause of marriage conflict is always two total personalities in a total situation. Married persons quarrel because, having been born what they were, having been conditioned as they were by their culture, they cannot live in marriage without disagreement.' People who are 'difficult to live with' bring certain liabilities to the marriage relationship.

The correlations in Table 12.2 indicate that personal instability and marital conflicts are moderately related within each generation. The pattern of correlations, however, leaves open the question of reciprocal influences. What is the causal process underlying the correlation between problem dispositions and problem relationships within a generation?

Figure 12.2 presents a formal evaluation of the two-way process of influence among G2 women in 1930 (see Liker and Elder 1983). To estimate reciprocal paths in this non-recursive model, instrumental variables were chosen that met the following requirements: they affected husbands only indirectly through wives, and they affected wives only indirectly through their husbands. Thus, we use indicators of maternal grandparents' (G1) personality (e.g. irritability) as instruments for G2 instability and indicators of her husband's parents' marital tension as an instrument for spouses' reports of marital quality. In doing so, we assume that grandparent (G1) characteristics affect personal instability or the quality of the relationship through socialization experiences occurring prior to their offspring's (G2) marriage. This assumption seems reasonable since the measures of grandparental characteristics refer explicitly to behaviour when the husbands and wives were growing up.

Overall we find that the correlation between unstable behaviour and marital tension is accounted for by the influence of personal instability on marriage; the best estimate of the reverse path is zero (this was not constrained to be zero). Moreover, this pattern of influence is not easily explained by conceptual or measurement deficiencies. Most forms of bias created by inadequate instruments and correlated errors between reports on couples and their parents' qualities would lead to consistently attenuated or inflated reciprocal influences in *both* directions. But the process of influence shown in Fig. 12.2 appears to be unidirectional, from personality to relationship difficulties.

In sum, *within* a generation the causal factor in aversive relationships is primarily attributable to the personality characteristics of the interacting partners. The hypothesized model changes, however, when we examine intergenerational processes. According to the second hypothesis of this study, problematic relationships in the socializing family mediate the influence of parental instability on offspring instability (see Fig. 12.1).

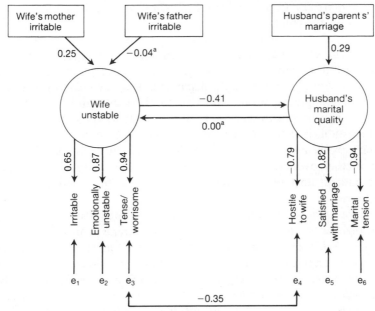

FIG. 12.2   Reciprocal relationship between personal instability and marital conflict within a generation, 1930 data. All measures are based on clinical ratings from transcripts of interviews with each partner separately. Husbands and wives (G2) were interviewed about their parents' (G1) marriage and personality. $\chi^2 = 32.4$, df $= 21$, $p = 0.05$; [a] not significant at 0.05 level.

The intergenerational dynamic

The family produces crescive bonds through social interaction: 'As two or more persons have a succession of shared experiences, they develop a wider and more firmly rooted conception of reality, setting them apart from others who have not been part of the same experience' (Turner 1970). To the extent that shared experiences within the family give rise to similar orientations toward the world, we expect empirical support for the hypothesis that problem behaviours and problem relationships are reproduced across the generations. However, the causal process of intergenerational transmission is not well understood.

Consider the case of marital discord. Numerous studies have identified qualities of parents and their marriage that show modest predictive power in relation to the marital adjustment of their children (e.g. Pope and Mueller 1976). But how is marital discord transmitted? A role model hypothesis represents the most compelling explanation of the transmission process (Heiss 1972). In order to be a successful marriage partner, a child must learn culturally appropriate sex and marital roles. This occurs when two competent parents in marriage are available to teach appropriate behaviour and to serve as models for the child.

An alternative to this 'direct' transmission hypothesis views the empirical relations between marital discord in two generations in terms of a process by which marital tension in the first generation affects certain intervening variables that might, in turn, influence marriage in the second generation. A likely intervening mechanism is defined by the personality make-up of the second generation offspring. Specifically, parents with conflicted marriages tend to establish family environments conducive to the development of children's problem behaviour. These children, in turn, bring such dispositions to bear on their own marriages in adulthood, especially under stress. Unstable people create unstable relationships which in turn produce unstable dispositions.

To address this indirect transmission hypothesis we must first consider how the various factors in aversive family systems combine to affect the behaviour of children. We know that children in disorganized and conflicted families are likely to adopt aggressive and defiant patterns of behaviour, and a substantial body of evidence has been marshalled in support of an association between problematic social development and family characteristics. For example, children of antisocial or disturbed parents have been found to be at high risk for developing antisocial styles of relating to others (Garmezy 1981). Moreover, marital discord is associated with the development of antisocial behaviour and other types of emotional disturbances among children (Emery 1982). Finally, parental practices that are inconsistent and extreme have been repeatedly implicated in the development of aggression and antisocial behaviour (Patterson 1982). Although the need for an integrative approach to understanding these family dynamics is well recognized (e.g. Belsky 1981, 1984; Chapter 11, this volume), little empirical research has detailed the process whereby these factors, in combination, increase the risk of child disturbance.

One possible model is shown in Fig. 12.3 (cf. Elder *et al.* 1986). The model assumes that personality shapes parenting indirectly by influencing the broader relational context (i.e. marital relationship) in which parent-child relationships take place. Moreover, the model assumes that marital problems and interspousal conflicts are linked to children's problem behaviours through the disciplinary strategies adopted by parents. For example, Olweus's (1980) research on the development of aggression suggests that the quality of the emotional relationship between spouses influences mother's negativism toward their children, which itself leads to aggressive, antisocial behaviour. Indeed, studies of different developmental periods provide grounds for inferring a process of influence from marriage to parenting to child development (Crouter *et al.* 1985). A final assumption of the model is that problem behaviours (e.g. irritability, personal instability) established in childhood are relatively stable over the life span.

The findings reported in Fig. 12.3 appear to meet these three assumptions. They are, more importantly, consistent with the second hypothesis of this study. From generation to generation, unstable personalities are reproduced through a socialization environment characterized by marital tension and non-optimal parenting. Unstable adults are significantly more likely to establish a conflicted relational context in which parenting difficulties are likely to result in children's problem behaviours. This process of influence represents a general dynamic that applies equally well to each of the four generations of Berkeley women.

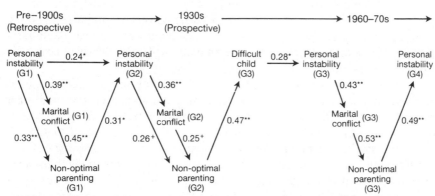

FIG. 12.3   The intergenerational transmission of problem behaviour and problem relationships. OLS estimates; only significant path coefficients are shown. This model was estimated using ordered dyads (G1–G2, G2–G3, G3–G4). A separate model that includes Gn − 1 variables as covariates provided comparable point estimates.

Ordered dyads are the primary domain for the analysis in Fig. 12.3. In the first phase of the model we examine grandparents (G1) and parents (G2). This pattern is replaced by parents (G2) and children (G3) in the second phase. The last part of the picture centres on the grown-up children (G3) and their offspring (G4).

From G1 to G2, unstable personalities are reproduced in part through marital tension and parent hostility. This socialization environment linked unstable grandmothers (G1) to a similar style of behaviour in their middle-aged (G2) daughters. However, these results are based on retrospective accounts, and the uniformly high coefficients are particularly suspect in the present case since G2 women have assumed the roles (i.e. marriage and parenthood) they are describing with respect to their mothers (G1). Many of the recall ratings could involve distortions that provide self-justification for current inadequacies, whether real or fancied. Although we should not assume that a history remembered is not of functional significance to the individual (e.g. Bronson *et al.* 1959; Cohler 1982), retrospective accounts pose numerous interpretative difficulties in accounting for the process of intergenerational transmission (cf. Yarrow *et al.* 1970; Minuchin, Chapter 1, this volume).

Whatever reservations we have about this portion of the analysis, the general process of influence is corroborated by observer-based data on the next ordered-dyad in Fig. 12.3, G2–G3. The G3 measure of interest in this analysis is the difficult child syndrome, a childhood behavioural style that bears on the discussion of the intense, high strung child whom parents find hard to manage (Thomas and Chess 1977). In the Berkeley inventory this syndrome is indexed by an average of three five-point ratings. The *quarrelsome* child had a 'chip on the shoulder' and 'instigates quarrels with no apparent provocation'; the *negativistic* child had a 'compulsive, habitual urge to do the opposite of what is expected'; and the *irritable* child was 'explosive and over-reactive'. Each measure was available annually when the Berkeley girls (G3) were 5–7 years old.

As in the previous generation, Fig. 12.3 shows that unstable mothers (G2) reproduced a similar behavioural style in their daughters (G3) by creating a conflicted family environment characterized by marital tension and non-optimal parenting. This process of influence also repeats itself in the G3 generation during their active years of parenting. As indicated by the stability coefficient in Fig. 12.3, difficult girls were significantly more likely than other girls to become undercontrolled women. In turn, their families of procreation were characterized by marital conflict and parental loss of control; family features that were significantly related to undercontrolled behaviour among fourth generation females. The G4 measure of undercontrolled behaviour includes three California Q-sort items: self-indulgent, pushes limits, and undercontrolled.

The following pattern, then, emerges from our analysis of problem behaviour and problem relationships across four generations of Berkeley women. Born around 1900, women (G2) who reported an unhappy childhood characterized by unstable mothers, marital tensions, and maternal hostility (G1) were especially prone to unstable behaviour and aversive family interactions. Their own behaviour, in turn, predicts arbitrary parenting which finds expression in their daughters' (G3) quarrelsome, irritable, and negativistic tendencies. When we follow these girls (G3) into adulthood we find that they, too, recreate aversive family systems that are moderately predictive of their daughters' (G4) undercontrolled behaviour.

We have assumed in testing this intergenerational model that all childhood family experiences that bear upon undercontrolled behaviour in adulthood are mediated by problem behaviour in childhood. This implies that the long-term influence of growing up in a conflicted family environment is expressed through problematic dispositions in childhood that endure across the adult years. Our findings show that undercontrolled behaviour in adulthood is moderately related to corresponding behaviour in childhood. Is such adult behaviour also *directly* linked to an aversive family experience or upbringing?

We approached this problem by setting up a series of hierarchical regression models in which an index of problem behaviour in childhood (G3 difficult child) was entered first, followed by measures of mothers' (G2) instability and arbitrary parenting. The dependent variable in this analysis is the adulthood (G3) measure of undercontrolled behaviour. The results indicate that parent behaviour (G2) does not add significantly to the prediction of undercontrolled behaviour in adulthood when adjustments are made for problem behaviour in childhood. *Early family experience does not directly predict a generalized pattern of undercontrolled behaviour in adulthood.* Rather, the evidence suggests that childhood problem behaviour *links* an aversive socialization environment with subsequent behavioural difficulties in adulthood.

We are now in a position to examine *how* childhood problem behaviour affects self-other patterns across the life course. In many respects, this is the 'missing link' in studies of intergenerational transmission. How do behavioural patterns in childhood find expression in adult roles? How do individuals recreate their families of origin in their families of procreation? This is our third hypothesis.

Life course dynamics

Theorists have long presumed that social relationships with significant others establish behavioural styles during childhood that become more and more resistant to change with the passage of time. A similar premise guides our research (hypothesis 3): individuals are characterized, in part, by behavioural styles that set broad limits on responses favoured by them in new situations (see Caspi and Elder in press).

We agree with Wachtel (1977)—and others before him (e.g. Sullivan 1953; Cottrell 1969)—who argued that it is not so much a personality trait or a psychoanalytic-like residue of early childhood that is maintained across time, but an interactional style that evokes reciprocal maintaining responses from others. Interactional styles established earlier in the developmental history tend to operate selectively in two ways:

(1) by leading the person to select environments and relationships in which the pattern is readily enacted; and

(2) by being projected on to ambiguous situations that can be structured to permit the pattern to be expressed (see Caspi *et al.* 1987, 1988).

The first process refers to the case in which the individual's dispositions systematically select him or her into particular environments, environments that, in turn, might reinforce and sustain those dispositions (e.g. Scarr and

McCartney 1983). For example, negative self–other patterns established in childhood could increase the risk of marital discord through a process of social selection in which a difficult girl acquires a target for an established negative response. Her maladaptive behaviours increasingly channel or 'select' her into environments and relationships that perpetuate those behaviours. We have called continuity of this kind *cumulative continuity*.

The second process refers to the reciprocal, dynamic transaction between the person and the new environment: the person acts, the environment reacts, and the person reacts in kind. For example, negative self–other patterns established in childhood could increase further the risk of marital discord through projection of a harsh, arbitrary pattern of interaction on to the marriage relationship. Thus, expectations of ill-treatment from the partner could lead to emotional distance and defensive forms of negativity. We have called continuity of this kind *interactional continuity*.

In general, then, we propose that childhood problem behaviours are sustained through the life course by the progressive accumulation of their own consequences (*cumulative continuity*) and by their contemporary consequences in reciprocal social interaction (*interactional continuity*).

This kind of interactional analysis also suggests the kinds of situations in which earlier established relational patterns are likely to be expressed. *A self–other pattern learned in one situation will tend to be evoked in other situations of similar structure*, especially when the respondent occupies one or other of the 'action positions' defined by the earlier established self–other pattern (cf. Cottrell 1969; Wachtel 1977).

Marital and parent–child relationships are two especially relevant settings. As the Berkeley girls (G3) entered adulthood they were called upon to perform roles they had learned in the past by 'taking the action positions' of wives and mothers. In this manner, their marital and parent–child relationships in adulthood may have been subject to the self–other dynamics of their family experiences in childhood.

These two role-relationships are of additional interest because they have a unique effect on the organization of sex roles. For example, Gutmann's (1975) cross-cultural studies suggest that roles such as parenthood structure sex-role performance along highly stereotyped lines. Men become more instrumental as women become more expressive. The result of this parental imperative is that children learn the sex roles of men and women from their parents at a time when 'mothers act most clearly like women' and 'fathers act most clearly like men', thus ensuring further continuity across successive generations.

The adult correlates of difficult child behaviour clearly implicate childhood problem behaviour in aversive self–other dynamics across the life course. An index of undercontrolled behaviour derived from the adult Q-sort ratings, a report on marital dissatisfaction derived from the spouse interviews, and a report on women's ill-tempered parenting derived from the children's interviews are all significantly ($p < 0.05$) correlated with the difficult child syndrome (r's $= 0.28$, 0.31, and 0.56, respectively).

Marital discord in adulthood represents the first relational extension of problem behaviour in childhood. This pattern was earlier identified in our cross-sectional treatment of the personality–marriage link among G2 women (see Fig. 12.2). The present longitudinal analysis on G3 women corroborates our claim that interactional styles established earlier in the developmental history are carried into new situations and are an important causal factor in the quality of subsequent relationships.

Indeed, women who came to marriage with a childhood history of quarrelsome, irritable and negativistic behaviours appear to have done so with a higher risk of marital discord ($r = 0.31$, $p < 0.05$). Although they may have been more difficult to live with, we find no evidence of this in terms of divorce or separation. The cluster of childhood difficult behaviours does not predict marital dissolution by midlife.

Ineffective parenting represents the second relational extension of childhood problem behaviour. Retrospective reports claim that poorly treated children are at risk of becoming adults who relate to their own children as their parents related to them, and it is possible that children so treated will develop sufficient hostility toward the world in general to become the next generation's non-optimal parents (Cicchetti and Rizley 1981). The correlation coefficient provides longitudinal support for this claim as well.

Women with a history of quarrelsome, difficult, and negativistic behaviours were inclined to lose control of their feelings and actions as adults in parental situations ($r = 0.56$, $p < 0.01$). Although several alternative patterns could have been chosen to define their relationships with children, these women were most inclined to project a self–other pattern reminiscent of relationships in their family of creation on to relationships in their family of procreation.

The path model in Fig. 12.4 suggests also that by recreating aversive self–other patterns in their families of procreation, women with a childhood history of difficult behaviour reproduced problem behaviour in the next generation.

But how is consistency in self–other dynamics achieved and maintained? We proposed earlier that continuities in self–other dynamics across the life course may rest upon two mechanisms. A relational pattern established earlier in the developmental history may lead the person to select environments and relationships in which it can be readily enacted, and once enacted in, or projected on to, new situations the relational pattern may elicit responses from others that support and validate it.

These dual processes are nicely illustrated by examining the interactional consequences of mate selection patterns among women with a history of difficult behaviour. What kind of men did difficult girls marry? What kind of relationships did they recreate in their families of procreation?

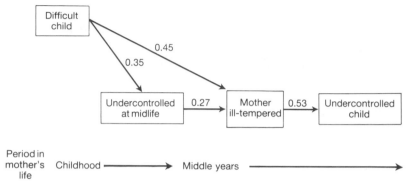

FIG. 12.4   Linking mothers' (G3) behavioural history to undercontrolled offspring (G4). To simplify the diagram only significant ($p < 0.05$) path coefficients are shown.

Correlations between the girls' difficult behaviour scores in late childhood and Q-sort ratings of clinical judges on their husbands in adulthood reveal that difficult girls were significantly more likely to marry non-assertive men. Their husbands in the middle years were more likely than other men to withdraw when frustrated ($r = 0.31$, $p < 0.05$), to complicate simple situations ($r = 0.28$, $p < 0.05$), and to appear less masculine ($r = -0.30$, $p < 0.05$). These attributes are the strongest spouse correlates of girls' difficult behaviour. Whatever the causal mechanism, difficult girls select, or are selected by, marriage partners who would appear to represent a convenient target for the re-enactment of aversive self–other dynamics.

Figure 12.5 provides evidence suggestive of this process. The dependent variable here is women's undercontrolled behaviour at midlife, and the results show a significant interaction effect between girls' difficult behaviour and their spouses' non-assertive behaviour, $F = 8.02$, $p < 0.01$. Women who had a childhood history of difficult behaviour *and* who married non-assertive men were significantly more likely to be undercontrolled at midlife than the remaining three groups. Moreover, regression analyses reveal that the interaction effect remains significant with spouses' occupational status and educational level controlled.

Parallel analyses with marital conflict and ill-tempered parenting as the dependent variables show similar patterns. Women with a childhood history of difficult behaviour who married non-assertive men had more conflicted marriages, as reported by their husbands, than the remaining three groups ($F = 2.67$, $p = 0.11$). These women were also the most ill-tempered mothers, as reported by their children ($F = 8.28$, $p < 0.01$).

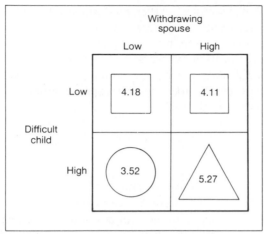

FIG. 12.5   The behavioural consequences of difficult girls' mate-selection patterns. Dependent variable: women's undercontrolled behaviour at midlife (1 = low, 9 = high).

We have neither the data necessary to determine why difficult girls are more likely to enter marriages with non-assertive men nor the fine-grained measurements required to analyse reciprocal interactions within difficult girls' families of procreation. Nevertheless, our relatively crude temporal categories and global measurements suggest that the achievement and maintenance of consistency in self–other patterns across the life course may rest upon two mechanisms: the 'selection' of relationships, and the 'projection' on to these relationships of earlier established relational styles.

Our view of this process can also go a long way toward explaining change. Change may be accounted for by the fact that at times in a person's life an individual emerges or a fortuitous event is encountered that intervenes in the developmental process rather than simply confirms an established mode of relating to others.

Indeed, the most striking—and encouraging—feature of the results in Fig. 12.5 is that difficult girls who managed to escape the 'probabilistic trap' of marrying non-assertive men were the *least* undercontrolled women in adulthood. These women manifest a changed self–other pattern of interaction and appear to have developed a corresponding difference in their family relationships. According to spouse and child reports, these women did *not* differ from the non-difficult group in their level of marital conflict and ill-tempered parenting in adulthood. Interestingly, we can find no variables that effectively discriminate between this group of difficult girls and the group who married non-assertive men. Hence, our phrasing 'managed to escape'.

It is reasonable to suppose that change may occur through corrective experiences in new relationships, perhaps through experiences in relationships and situations that disconfirm earlier established relational styles. Leaving aside the empirical caveats in our data, it is possible that self–other dynamics change when the defining response of a significant other changes. We believe also that the reorganization or change of self–other dynamics across the life course is especially likely during the assumption of new roles, such as marriage, for these events open up wide opportunities for reconstructing definitions of others and the self.

Conclusion

Generations of scholars have written about self and society as two sides of the same coin, from the social genesis of the self to the influence of personalities on the social fabric of groups. Pathological development has social costs, and pathogenic environments leave their mark on the individual. Surprisingly little, however, is known about this dynamic within and across the generations, or within a single life span.

Using data on four generations in the Berkeley Guidance Study, this research has examined three hypothesized dimensions of this dynamic. The first centres on the reciprocal dynamic between problem behaviour and unstable family relations. The second hypothesis focuses on the process by which problem behaviour is transmitted from one generation to another. The third hypothesis examines the problem behaviour of children as one means by which aversive family patterns are reproduced from one generation to the next.

Across the four Berkeley generations, we find substantial documentation of a reinforcing dynamic between problem behaviour and unstable ties in the family. The relationship between unstable, problem behaviour and aversive social interaction is reciprocal in theory. Unstable personalities undermine supportive relationships with others, and weak ties are conducive to the expression of unstable tendencies. In reality, the primary flow of influence *within* a generation moves from problem behaviour to problem relationships. Judging from non-recursive models based on the G2 generation, tense, explosive adults tend to create marital stress and discord. The latter has relatively little influence on problem behaviour within a narrowly defined time period, but we know its effect is stronger when lagged over a number of years (Liker and Elder 1983) and becomes especially noteworthy when viewed across the generations.

Indeed, across the generations unstable personalities are reproduced through unstable family relationships characterized by marital tension and ineffective parenting. This socialization environment linked unstable grandmothers (G1) to a similar style of behaviour in their middle-aged daughters (G2). Likewise, unstable women in the G2 generation markedly increased the difficult behaviour of their daughters (G3) by increasing marital tension and arbitrary parenting. The pattern repeated itself in the G3 generation during their active years of parenting, and their daughters (G4) ranked highest on lack of self control in adolescence. In sum, aversive family patterns mediate the influence of unstable parenting on offspring. This intergenerational cycle of problem behaviour and problem relationships resembles a general dynamic across the four Berkeley generations. This cycle also prompts many questions, including that of the relationship between child and adult tendencies.

Indeed, the missing link in studies of intergenerational transmission concerns the process by which behavioural styles established in childhood are recreated in adulthood. Our longitudinal analysis of self–other dynamics across the life course suggests that relational styles that are learned in one situation are likely to be evoked in other situations of similar structure, especially in relatively ambiguous situations that can be structured to permit the pattern to be expressed. Moreover, when relational patterns are carried into new situations they typically elicit responses from others that support and validate that pattern.

In the life course we do not find situations exactly similar to past situations: we must define every situation as similar to certain past situations in order to apply solutions to new situations and encounters. Indeed, experimental studies suggest that in new situations individuals will work quite hard to ensure the stability of their self conceptions and avoid information that requires accommodation or change (e.g. Secord and Backman 1965; Darley and Fazio 1980; Swann 1983; Snyder 1984). For example, they preferentially search for evidence that confirms propositions they are testing, whether these are about objects, other people, or themselves. Moreover, they act in ways that generate behavioural disconfirmation for hypotheses that challenge or threaten central aspects of their self-concept. And because the strategies people employ in the quest for self-confirming evidence are quite successful, there is often little need to accommodate new experiences. Familiar ways of viewing others and the self will find constant affirmation in a reactive social world, and the tendency to enter new relationships with assumptions from previous relationships is likely to result in the cyclical recreation of interpersonal events and crises.

Though problem behaviour elicits social responses that reinforce such behaviour, turning points do occur in relationships and situations that disconfirm earlier established relational styles. Bandura (1982) has similarly referred to such events in an essay on chance encounters. For example, many experiences channel behaviour into predictable and unprofitable directions, but other experiences may branch people into new life paths. Similarly, many interpersonal encounters confirm expectations and established relational patterns, but some people refuse to be ensnared in social traps. And although our research suggests that continuity in the conduct of individuals and in the quality of relationships across successive generations is the rule, change is no less intrinsic in the intergenerational construction of behaviour and relationships.

References

Ackerman, N. W. (1970). Childhood disorders and interlocking pathology in family relationships. *The international yearbook for child psychiatry and allied disciplines*, Vol. 1, *The child in his family* (ed. E. J. Anthony and C. Koupernick). Wiley, New York.

Bandura, A. (1982). The psychology of chance encounters and life paths. *American Psychologist* **37**, 747–55.

Belsky, J. (1981). Early human experience: a family perspective. *Developmental Psychology* **17**, 3–23.

Belsky, J. (1984). The determinants of parenting: a process model. *Child Development* **55**, 83–96.

Block, J. (1971). *Lives through time*. Bancroft, Berkeley, California.

Bronson, W. C., Katten, E. S., and Livson, N. (1959). Patterns of authority and affection in two generations. *Journal of Abnormal and Social Psychology* **58**, 143–52.

Caspi, A. and Elder, G. H., Jr. (1987). Childhood precursors of the life course: early personality and life disorganization. In *Child development in life-span perspective* (ed. E. M. Hetherington, R. M. Lerner, and M. Perlmutter). Cambridge University Press, New York.

Caspi, A., Elder, G. H., Jr., and Bem, D. J. (1987a). Moving against the world: life-course patterns of explosive children. *Developmental Psychology* (in press).

Caspi. A., Elder, G. H., Jr., and Bem, D. J. (1987b). Moving away from the world: life-course patterns of withdrawn children (in review).

Chodorow, N. (1978). *The reproduction of mothering*. University of California Press, Berkeley, California.

Cicchetti, D. and Rizley, R. (1981). Developmental perspectives on the etiology, intergenerational transmission, and sequelae of child maltreatment. In *New directions for child development: developmental perspectives on child maltreatment* (ed. D. Cicchetti and R. Rizley). Jossey-Bass, San Fransisco.

Cohler, B. J. (1982). Personal narrative and the life course. In *Life span development and behavior*, Vol. 4 (ed. P. B. P. Baltes and O. G. Brim, Jr.). Academic Press, New York.

Cottrell, L. S. (1969). Interpersonal interaction and the development of the self. *In Handbook of socialization theory and research* (ed. D. A. Goslin). Rand McNally, Chicago.

Crouter, A., Belsky, J., and Spanier, G. (1985). The family context of child development. In *Annals of child development*, Vol. 1 (ed. G. Whitehurst). JAI Press, Greenwich, Conn.

Darley, J. and Fazio, R. H. (1980). Expectancy confirmation processes arising in the social interaction sequence. *American Psychologist* **35**, 867–81.

Elder, G. H., jun., Caspi, A., and Downey, G. (1986). Problem behavior and family relationships: life-course and intergenerational themes. In *Human development and the life course: multidisciplinary perspectives* (ed. A. M. Sørensen, F. E. Weinert, and L. R. Sherrod). Erlbaum, Hillsdale, NJ.

Emery, R. (1982). Marital turmoil: interparental conflict and the children of discord and divorce. *Psychological Bulletin* **92**, 310–30.

Frommer, E. and O'Shea, G. (1973a). Antenatal identification of women liable to have problems in managing their infants. *British Journal of Psychiatry* **123**, 149–56.

Frommer, E. and O'Shea, G. (1983b). The importance of childhood experiences in relation to problems of marriage and family building. *British Journal of Psychiatry* **123**, 157–60.

Garmezy, N. (1981). Children born under stress: perspectives on the antecedents and correlates of vulnerability and resistance to psychopathology. In *Further explorations in personality* (ed. A. I. Rabin, J. Aronoff, A. M. Barclay, and R. A. Zucker). Wiley, New York.

Gottman, J. M. (1979). *Marital interaction.* Academic Press, New York.

Gutmann, D. (1975). Parenthood: a key to the comparative study of the life cycle. In *Life span developmental psychology: normative life crises* (ed. N. Datan and L. H. Ginsberg). Academic Press, New York.

Hall, F., Pawlby, S., and Wolkind, S. (1979). Early life experience and later mothering behavior: a study of mothers and their 20-week-old babies. In *The first year of life* (ed. D. Shaffer and J. Dunn). Wiley, New York.

Heiss, J. (1972). On the transmission of marital instability in black families. *American Sociological Review* **37**, 90–126.

Held, T. (1986). Institutionalization and deinstitutionalization of the life course. *Human Development* **29**, 157–62.

Huesmann, L. R., Eron, L. D., Lefkowitz, M. N., and Walder, L. (1984). The stability of aggression over time and generations. *Developmental Psychology* **20**, 1120–34.

Komarovsky, M. (1950). Functional analysis of sex roles. *American Sociological Review* **15**, 508–16.

Liker, J. K. and Elder, G. H., Jr. (1983). Economic hardship and marital relations in the 1930s. *American Sociological Review* **48**, 343–59.

Macfarlane, J. W. (1938). Studies in child guidance, 1: Methodology of data collection and organization. *Monographs of the Society for Research in Child Development* Serial No. 19, **3**.

Main, M., Kaplan, N., and Cassidy, J. (1985). Security in infancy, childhood, and adulthood: a move to the level of representation. In *Growing points of attachment theory and research* (ed. I. Bretherton and E. Waters), *Monographs of the Society for Research in Child Development* Serial No. 209, **50**, (1–2), 66–104.

Olweus, D. (1980). Familial and temperamental determinants of aggressive behavior in adolescent boys: a causal analysis. *Developmental Psychology* **16**, 644–60.

Parsons, T. (1955). Family structure and the socialization of the child. In *Family, socialization, and interaction processes* (ed. T. Parsons and F. Bales). Free Press, New York.

Patterson, G. R. (1982). *Coercive family process.* Castallia, Eugene, Oreg.

Pope, H. and Mueller, C. W. (1976). The intergenerational transmission of marital instability. *Journal of Social Issues* **32**, 49–66.

Ricks, M. (1985). Social transmission of parental behavior. In *Growing points of attachment theory and research* (ed. I. Bretherton and E. Waters), *Monographs of the Society for Research in Child Development* Serial No. 209, **50**, 211–227.

Rutter, M. and Madge, N. (1976). *Cycles of disadvantage: a review of research.* Heinemann, London.

Rutter, M., Quinton, D., and Liddle, C. (1983). Parenting in two generations: looking backwards and looking forwards. In *Families at risk* (ed. N. Madge). Heinemann, London.

Scarr, S. and McCartney, K. (1983). How people make their own environments: a theory of genotype environment correlations. *Child Development* **54**, 424–35.

Secord, P. F. and Backman, W. C. (1965). An interpersonal approach to personality. In *Progress in experimental personality research* (ed. B. Maher). Academic Press, New York.

Snyder, M. (1984). When beliefs create reality. In *Advances in experimental social psychology* (ed. L. Berkowitz). Academic Press, New York.

Sullivan, H. S. (1953). *The interpersonal theory of psychiatry.* Norton, New York.

Swann, W. B., Jr. (1983). Self-verification: bringing social reality into harmony with the self. In *Psychological perspectives on the self*, Vol. 2 (ed. J. Suls and A. G. Greenwald). Erlbaum, Hillsdale, NJ.

Thomas, A. and Chess, S. (1977). *Temperament and development.* Brunner-Mazel, New York.

Turner, R. H. (1970). *Family interaction.* Wiley, New York.

Uddenberg, N. (1974). Reproductive adaptation in mother and daughter. *Acta Psychiatrica Scandinavica*, Supplement 254.

Wachtel, P. L. (1977). *Psychoanalysis and behavior therapy.* Basic Books, New York.

Waller, W. (1938). *The family: a dynamic interpretation* (revised by R. Hill, 1951). Dryden Press, New York.

Yarrow, M. R., Campbell, J. D., and Burton, R. V. (1970). Recollections of childhood: a study of the retrospective method. *Monographs of the Society for Research in Child Development* Serial No. 138, **35**.

13

Maternal attachment representations as related to patterns of infant–mother attachment and maternal care during the first year*

KARIN GROSSMANN, ELISABETH FREMMER-BOMBIK,
JOSEF RUDOLPH, AND KLAUS E. GROSSMANN

The ability to be a successful parent to one's children in influenced by many factors. First, there seems to be an inherent bias towards caregiving, a basic responsiveness to the appearance, communication, and signals of helplessness emitted by infants (Lorenz 1965). Secondly, culture and tradition prescribe specific techniques of infant care. Thirdly, on the individual level, the parent's quality as a teacher of cultural skills is influenced by the parent's own education and socio-economic background (Hess and Shipman 1965; Grossmann 1984). But the quality of the parents' emotional involvement with their child, their willingness to be responsive and giving, is thought to depend on the parents' own experience of being cared for (Bowlby 1973; and Ricks 1985, for a detailed review). Supportive, sensitive parenting seems to allow a child to grow into a parent who is again supportive and sensitive to her or his own children.

Parenting style is influenced by thoughts and by unconscious mental images (Bowlby 1973; Fraiberg *et al.* 1975; Grossmann 1978). Its transmission across the generations does not involve mere imitation, but must be conceptualized as a mental representation of the attachment figures and their expected behaviour to the child. Our understanding of the dynamics of this process must apply not only to those cases in which parental behaviour is similar to the parenting behaviour received in childhood, but also to those not infrequent cases where such continuity does not exist (Ricks 1985).

A parent–child relationship contains many aspects. Bowlby has already pointed out (1982, p. 378) that beside the caregiving/attachment aspect there

*This research was supported by grant Gr299/12 from *Deutsche Forschungsgemeinschaft* to Klaus E. Grossmann.

are other aspects, such as feeding/being fed, being playmates, and that of teacher/learner. The ability to be a good playmate or an effective teacher seems to be independent of the quality of the caregiving/attachment aspect (Grossmann 1984). But for personality development in terms of emotional stability, self-reliance, and supportive parenting the caregiving/attachment aspect of the parent–child relationship seems to be most important.

Within the framework of our two longitudinal studies (Escher-Gräub and Grossmann 1983; Grossmann *et al.* 1985), we related mothers' mental representations of attachment to patterns of infant–mother attachment and, for one sample, to mother–infant behaviour during the first two years.

The two longitudinal studies

The North-German (*Bielefeld*) Study

This sample, originally of 49 families, was recruited shortly before the infants were born. There were about equal numbers of boys and girls and of first- and later-borns. The families were from all social classes (see Grossmann *et al.* 1985, for a fuller description of the sample).

During the first year the following infant and maternal behaviour patterns were assessed: the newborn's interactive capacity on the Brazelton Neonatal Assessment Scale (Grossmann *et al.* 1985; Grossmann and Grossmann, in preparation), maternal sensitivity to and co-operation with her infant, and, at 12 months quality of the infant's attachment to mother (Grossmann *et al.* 1981). At 24 months the emotional atmosphere in the home, mother–child co-operativeness during play (Grossmann 1984), and the mother's child-centredness was observed and rated from interviews (Dorsch 1985).

When the children were 6 years old, 44 mothers and 41 fathers were interviewed (by Theresa Jacobsen) at home about their attachment experiences in childhood, using the interview guidelines of the Adult Attachment Interview (George *et al.* 1985).

The South-German (*Regensburg*) Study

The 51 families of this study were of similar background and composition to the Bielefeld sample (Escher-Gräub and Grossmann 1983). The infants were first seen when they were 12 months old. A free-play situation with either parent in the lab and an empathy assessment situation with a clown was followed after one week by the Strange Situation (Grossmann *et al.* in preparation).

When the children were 5 years old, 45 mothers were interviewed during a home visit about their childhood attachment experiences, using again the translated questions of the Adult Attachment Interview developed by George *et al.* (1985).

Fremmer-Bombik, Rudolph and Veit developed a method of analysis for the Adult Attachment Interview that differs somewhat from that suggested by Main and Goldwyn (1985). The results for 20 Bielefeld mothers will be presented here. The results for the 45 Regensburg mothers will be published (Fremmer-Bombik 1987; Veit 1986). The main findings of their work will be summarized here to confirm the results of the Bielefeld interviews.

The adult attachment interview

This interview probes for descriptions of close relationships, specific supportive memories, contradictory memories, assessments of relationships in childhood, and current evaluations of these childhood experiences and relationships. In this interview the mother (or father) is asked to describe her relationship to both parents, what she did when she was upset in childhood, whether she had ever felt rejected by her parents in childhood, and, if so, why she thought her parents behaved as they did. The mother is also asked whether her parents had ever threatened separation, whether there had been any major changes in her relationships with her parents since childhood, and how she felt about her parents currently. Finally, she is asked how she felt these experiences had influenced her adult personality (Main *et al.* 1985, p. 90).

A highly significant relation between the security of the adult's apparent internal representation of attachment, as assessed by this interview, and her infant's early security of attachment was demonstrated (Main *et al.* 1985).

In both our studies the sequence of questions as listed by George *et al.* (1985) was adhered to. Since this interview is very personal, it was always conducted only after an earlier one about the mother's daily life and about the child. Thus the interviewers were well known to the mothers. The Attachment Interviews took between 25 minutes and two hours.

For the analysis of the Adult Attachment Interviews, several resources were used. The Main and Goldwyn Adult Attachment Classification System (Main and Goldwyn 1985) was available in a preliminary form, but an exchange of interviews for reliability training was not possible because of the language barrier. The second set of resources were the writings of Bowlby (1982, 1973, 1979, 1980), Anna Freud (1936), and Sigmund Freud (1901).

From these writings Fremmer-Bombik (1987), Rudolph (1986), and Veit (1986) selected a number of parameters that were thought to reflect a parent's attachment representation. The parameters were subdivided into quantifiable criteria (see below for definitions and examples). On the basis of these parameters a small number of response patterns could be identified depending on the magnitude of the criteria and the combinations of the parameters (Rudolph 1986; Veit 1986; Fremmer-Bombik 1987). The following account summarizes the criteria, the parameters and the algorithm of their combinations that create the patterns of maternal attachment representations.

Parameters and response patterns

Four main parameters were selected to describe an attachment representation. The parameters with their criteria are as follows:

1. *Presentation of each parent as supportive:*
   the number of times each parent was described as supportive, compared with the number of times each was described as unsupportive.

2. *Focus on the topic of attachment and richness of attachment information:*
   number of attachment-relevant episodes;
   full stories on the topic of attachment;
   noting past versus present;
   parents as a pair or as individuals;
   evaluative statements about the quality of care.

3. *Reflections on early attachment experiences:*
   thoughts on why some encounters had happened/reasons for behaviour;
   comparisons between past and present relationships;
   focus on attachment relationships versus other relationships;
   how attachment history influenced individual personality;
   remembering well versus insisting on not remembering;
   own feelings versus 'objective' facts;
   personal experience versus generalizing.

4. *Defensiveness against the interview and present emotional relationship with parents:*
   short answers or no answers;
   topic changes to non-attachment subjects;
   generalized praise without supportive evidence;
   disparagement of parents;
   angry statements against parents.

Inter-rater reliability for assigning the interview sentences to criteria and counting them ranged from 60 per cent to 99 per cent, with a mean of 87 per cent.

The absolute values of the criteria were transformed into indices according to theoretical considerations, and the whole sample was then rank-ordered on each criterion. Three intervals were defined: high, medium, and low regard for attachment. For instance, many stories without attachment content were taken as indicating low regard for attachment, whereas very few evasions of the questions were taken as indicating high regard. If the majority of the criteria within a parameter were indicating high or low regard for attachment, the whole parameter was considered to reflect respectively a high or low regard for attachment.

Table 13.1 presents the observed patterns of maternal attachment representations as defined by the four parameters. For each observed pattern, Table 13.1 shows the combination of high (+) or low (−) regard for attachment with respect to each parameter. A mother was evaluated as having an attachment representation that values attachment (positive or non-defensive in Table 13.1) if her response pattern to the interview resulted in at least three positive parameters. A response pattern that resulted in at least three negative parameters was considered to be a representation that devalues attachment.

Sixteen possible combinations could emerge from four dichotomous parameters, but only seven combinations or patterns were found. The following descriptions of the empirically found patterns are valid for both samples.

Pattern I: the positive attachment representation

This group of mothers described at least one supportive attachment figure, which was usually the mother. The interview elicited many attachment related stories and statements from childhood. If they had had an unsupportive attachment figure as well, these mothers had reflected a lot about their childhood experiences. Otherwise the number of reflections on their relationships fell into the intermediate interval. Mothers of this group did not say that they couldn't remember, and their memories included their emotions at that time. Some evaded a few questions or volunteered only little, but this was not a predominant response pattern. They neither idealized nor disparaged their parents, and only very few mothers mentioned some anger. All parameters reflected a positive regard for or an attitude of valuing attachment (see Table 13.1).

Pattern II: the non-defensive attachment representation

The major impression of these interviews was the openness of the mothers to the questions and their balanced, thoughtful descriptions of their attachment figures. But none of them described a clearly supportive parent, and for most of them the attachment figures were unsupportive. All had had at least one

Table 13.1 *Parameters and empirically found patterns of mothers' attachment representations*

Parameters	Valuing attachment		Devaluing attachment				
	Positive Pattern I		Non-defensive Pattern II	Idealizing, incoherent intellectualizing Pattern III			Repressive Pattern IV
Presentation of at least one attachment figure as supportive	+	+	—	+	—	—	—
Focus on topic of attachment	+	+	+	—	—	—	—
Reflections on early attachment experiences	+	—	+	—	+	—	—
Low defensiveness against interview and present relations to parents	+	+	+	—	—	+	—

A '+' indicates high regard, and a '—' low regard for attachment relationships. Each of the seven columns represents an observed combination.

rejecting or neglecting parent. Their answers contained at least a moderate number of attachment related statements with a few exceptions. Some mothers remembered little, but reflected intensely upon those experiences or wondered why they couldn't remember much. They often talked about attachment relationships. A few were openly angry at their parents at the present time, but they neither idealized nor disparaged their parents to a large extent. Despite their mostly adverse attachment experiences they valued attachment and regretted the lack of closeness to their parents. Three of the four parameters reflected a positive regard for attachment and thus this representation was also considered to value attachment.

Pattern III: the idealizing, incoherent, or intellectualizing attachment representation

The response pattern of this group of mothers to the interview was very irregular. No coherent picture of their attachment experience emerged. Those that described a supportive parent did not offer enough confirming evidence or they couldn't remember much of their childhood. Some talked about their childhood in a glorious but detached way. Supportive and unsupportive episodes remained unintegrated, since these mothers reflected little upon relationships. Other mothers spent much time explaining their thoughts about themselves, but not about their attachments. Some started to answer the questions but then drifted away from attachment issues. Despite many reported episodes of rejection, all mothers in pattern III idealized their parents in an undifferentiated way, in some cases even while, at the same time, disparaging them. Only one of the four parameters reflected a positive regard for attachment. This representation seems generally to devalue attachment.

Pattern IV: the repressive attachment representation

This group of mothers seemed to dislike, openly or covertly, the whole interview. They made very few attachment relevant statements from their childhood, so that it was difficult to determine their evaluation of their attachment experience. Very little could be learned from their childhood, and some talked more about their present life. Some mothers insisted on not being able to remember, others reported their negative experiences in a detached way. They tended to reflect little upon their childhood experiences. All defended themselves in one way or another against the meaning of the questions answering in one-word sentences, changing the topic, or making generalized statements. They either idealized or disparaged their parents, at least to a moderate extent, and some vented some anger. All four parameters reflected a negative regard for attachment, i.e. a devaluation of attachment.

General responses of the mothers to the adult attachment interview and distribution of the patterns

The interview elicited a great variety of responses. Only half of the mothers in Bielefeld and Regensburg reported a clearly supportive attachment figure: for the other half the available attachment figures were neither supportive nor unsupportive, or predominantly unsupportive. Mothers and fathers were described equally frequently as supportive, and a grandparent was the most supportive attachment figure for six out of the total sample of 65 mothers.

In the Bielefeld subsample the number of attachment relevant statements ranged from 20 to 176. In one interview, one mother repeated 33 times that she remembered well whereas another mother insisted 43 times that she could not remember much at all. Half of the mothers made some devaluing remarks about an attachment figure and all except one idealized a parent somewhat.

The observed distribution of the four patterns is presented in Table 13.2. It was very uneven in the Bielefeld subsample. Only three mothers had a positive attachment representation, and two more were at least non-defensive about the attachment issue. Three mothers were clearly idealizing their attachment figure, but other forms of incoherency were not found in this subsample. The majority of the interviews (12) were considered to reflect a repressive attachment representation. Thus, only five of the 20 interviewed mothers were considered to value attachment, whereas the other 15 showed some form of disregard for attachment. In the Regensburg sample this uneven distribution was counterbalanced. A majority of the Regensburg mothers (58 per cent) showed that they valued attachment and only a minority dismissed its importance (Fremmer-Bombik 1987).

Table 13.2 *Patterns of maternal attachment representations and patterns of infant–mother attachment*

Maternal attachment representations	Patterns of infant–mother attachment				
	Secure	Insecure			
		Avoidant	Ambivalent	No class	*n*
Bielefeld subsample					
I Positive	3	0	0	0	3
II Non-defensive	1	1	0	0	2
III Idealizing/incoherent	1	2	0	0	3
IV Repressive	1	7	3	1	12
Subtotal	6	10	3	1	20
Regensburg sample					
I Positive	10	2	0	0	12
II Non-defensive	11	1	1	1	14
III Idealizing/incoherent	3	7	1	1	12
IV Repressive	2	4	0	1	7
Subtotal	26	14	2	3	45
Total	32	24	5	4	65

Patterns of maternal attachment representations and patterns of infant–mother attachment

The cross-tabulation of the three patterns of infant–mother attachment and the four maternal response patterns is shown in Table 13.2 for the Bielefeld subsample and for the Regensburg sample. A 'positive' maternal attachment representation (pattern I) corresponded to an infant's secure attachment to her with all three Bielefeld mothers and with 10 of the 12 Regensburg mothers. The Strange Situations were done five years earlier in Bielefeld and four years earlier in Regensburg.

The opposite attachment representation (pattern IV), the 'repressive' one, was closely related to an insecure attachment pattern in the infant. Eleven of the 12 Bielefeld mothers of pattern IV had infants judged to be insecurely attached to them (including an unclassifiable attachment). All three insecurely-ambivalently attached infants had mothers in this group and also the only one in this subsample that was unclassifiable. In the Regensburg sample, five of the seven mothers with this kind of attachment representation had infants who were insecurely attached to them.

The relation between pattern II, the 'non-defensive' representation, and infant security of attachment remained unclear in the Bielefeld subsample, with one infant securely attached and one infant insecurely attached. But in the Regensburg sample pattern II was found to be typical of mothers of securely attached infants (11 out of 14). Therefore the non-defensive attachment representation could be empirically associated with the positive representation in terms of infant attachment pattern.

Pattern III, the 'incoherent' attachment representation, was found for two Bielefeld mothers of insecurely and for one mother of a securely attached infant. This tendency was supported by the results of the Regensburg sample: among the 12 mothers responding according to this pattern III, nine (75 per cent) had infants who were insecurely attached to them.

The results of both samples support the notion that two major maternal attachment representations exist: one that values attachment and regards it as important, evidenced by a readiness to relate positive and negative attachment experiences in the interview, and one that devalues attachment either by detachment from the experience or by treating the issue as closed.

The correspondence between the two types of maternal attachment representations and the two major patterns of infant attachment was highly significant in both samples. In the Bielefeld subsample, an attachment-valuing representation was associated with a secure infant attachment in four of the five cases, an attachment-devaluing representation with an insecure infant attachment in 13 of the 15 cases (Fisher's Exact Probability, $p = 0.01$). This produces concordance for 17 of the 20 pairs (85 per cent). For the Regensburg sample concordance was found for 35 of the 45 pairs (78 per cent, see Table

13.2). Pooling the two samples, infant–mother attachment corresponds to maternal attachment representation in 80 per cent of the cases.

Criteria and parameters of maternal attachment representations and patterns of infant–mother attachment

Some of the criteria on which the parameters depended by themselves differentiated between mothers of infants with differing attachment qualities. For the Bielefeld sample Table 13.3 shows the significant and marginally significant findings of a non-parametric analysis of variance between the three infant attachment patterns. Two criteria and the parameter 'defensiveness' differentiated significantly ($p \leqslant 0.05$) between the three attachment qualities, and four criteria showed a tendency ($p < 0.18$). (In all, 20 criteria and the parameter defensiveness were tested.)

Table 13.3 *Criteria and parameters of maternal attachment representations and patterns of infant–mother attachment*

| | Infant–mother attachment patterns | | | |
| | Secure | Insecure | | |
Criteria and parameter	$(n=6)$	Avoidant $(n=10)$	Ambivalent $(n=3)$	Significance level
Attachment-relevant contents	12.6*	10.0	4.8	0.14
Stories about parents and self in childhood	14.0	9.9	2.5	0.02
Reflections on attachment experiences	14.7	8.7	5.0	0.03
Claims to remember	12.5	10.0	5.0	0.17
Recall of feelings	12.1	10.7	3.7	0.09
Low defensiveness**	14.3	9.2	4.2	0.03
Low disparagement of parent	12.8	7.9	11.3	0.18

* Means of rank positions within the groups.
** Defensiveness is a parameter, i.e. a composite score of five criteria.

Mothers of infants who had been securely attached to them five years earlier related more stories about their parents in relation to themselves than mothers of insecurely attached infants. This was especially true for mothers of infants who had been ambivalently attached. Mothers of securely attached infants reflected more on attachment issues, i.e. they looked for reasons for someone's behaviour, compared behaviours and motives of themselves and their attachment figures, and saw the influence of their attachment experiences on their personality. They were much less defensive about the interview topic and readily recalled their feelings then and currently. They tended not to idealize or disparage their parents. They emphasized their good memory, and they provided answers with more attachment information than the other mothers.

In the Bielefeld subsample as well as in the Regensburg sample there were few insecure-ambivalently attached infants. Although all mothers of the three Bielefeld infants having an insecure-ambivalent attachment were found to have a repressive attachment representation (pattern IV), the mothers of the two Regensburg infants with C-type attachments were assigned to patterns II and III (see Table 13.2). With respect to the values of the criteria, the three Bielefeld mothers of the ambivalently attached infants were consistently low ranking except for disparagement of parents.

The relations between the rank positions of the mothers on the criteria and their infants' secure or insecure attachment status were largely confirmed by the analysis of the Regensburg interviews (Fremmer-Bombik 1987). In both samples, the parameter 'defensiveness' differentiated most significantly between mothers of securely versus all insecurely attached infants.

Valuing and devaluing attachment and mother–infant behaviour

In the Bielefeld subsample of 20 mothers, five were found to value attachment, 15 seemed to devalue attachment. Comparisons between the two groups on maternal and child variables assessed five years earlier yielded significant differences. The mothers who valued attachment were more sensitive toward their infants during the first year ($p < 0.05$, U-Test) than the mothers who devalued attachment. The attachment-valuing mothers tended to be more accepting of the individuality of their infants, as judged from the three interviews with them during the first year ($p = 0.12$). The difference was significant for the 10-month home visit ($p < 0.02$). In addition, at the 24-month home visit they showed more understanding for the developmental problems and individuality of their toddlers ($p < 0.02$). They also reported themselves as more willing to adjust the family routine to the special needs of the 2-year-old ($p < 0.03$).

It was reported (Grossmann et al. 1985) that in the Bielefeld sample newborn orientation was as highly related to the infant's attachment quality as was maternal sensitivity. This was interpreted as the infant's contribution to the developing relationship since orienting ability was unrelated to maternal sensitivity. In keeping with this view, newborn orienting ability was not related to the patterns of maternal attachment representation nor to any of the criteria that contributed to them.

Criteria and parameters of maternal attachment representations and mother–infant interactions

Correlations between the values on the criteria of maternal attachment representations and the behaviour of a mother toward her infant and her acceptance of her infant during the first two years yielded a number of significant findings (Table 13.4). Mothers who had been interacting sensitively and co-operatively with their infants during the first year remembered five years later, in response to the questions of the interviewer, many episodes and stories that were relevant to their own attachment experiences as a child. They presented a vivid recollection of their parents and seemed to enjoy remembering, since they often said that they could remember well. Emotions of themselves and their attachment figures played an important role in their memories. Sensitive mothers were much less defensive than insensitive mothers, and co-operative mothers seemed to regard their parents highly instead of disparaging them, as was more common for unco-operative mothers. The relations between maternal sensitivity and the three criteria 'attachment-relevant contents', 'stories about parents in childhood', and 'claims to remember' were so strong that we found significant correlations between the values of these criteria and each of the three sensitivity assessments when the infants were 2, 6 and 10 months old. Maternal acceptance of her infant, as rated from interviews with the mother always correlated positively with the criteria of the maternal attachment representations but not as strongly as maternal sensitivity and co-operative behaviour toward her infant.

A somewhat different picture emerged from the home visits around the second birthday of the Bielefeld children. Now the quality of their joint play in terms of how effectively they co-operated and talked to each other during a 10-minute play observation (Grossmann, 1984) was unrelated to the criteria of maternal attachment representations. But the way a mother talked about her toddler in the lengthy interview compared well to the way she talked about her own childhood in the Adult Attachment Interview. A mother who showed more acceptance of her child in the sense of being able to describe the positive and negative aspects and emotions of her toddler and still accept him as a lovable person, who showed a good understanding of the special problems and developmental tasks of her 2-year-old, and who was willing to structure the family life around the special needs of her child, remembered better and more vividly her own attachment experiences.

On the other hand, a total of 20 criteria were examined here, and 13 were not

Table 13.4 *Criteria and parameter of maternal attachment representations and mother–infant behaviour in the first two years*

Criteria and parameter	Mother–infant behaviour					
	Over the first year				At 24 months	
	Sensitivity[1]	Cooperation[1]	Acceptance[2]	Quality of joint play[1]	Understanding[2]	Child-centredness[2]
Attachment-relevant contents	0.60***	0.37(*)	0.27	−0.16	0.37*	0.45*
Attachment stories	0.52**	0.44*	0.16	−0.08	0.38*	0.47*
Stories about parents in childhood	0.76***	0.72***	0.47*	0.22	0.40*	0.44*
Reflections on attachment experiences	0.33(*)	0.24	0.24	−0.18	0.56**	0.64***
Claims to remember	0.63***	0.52***	0.31(*)	−0.08	0.45*	0.44*
Recall of feelings	0.43*	0.39*	0.31(*)	0.06	0.31(*)	0.38*
Low defensiveness[3]	0.43*	0.17	0.32(*)	0.18	0.47*	0.58**
Low disparagement of parents	0.25	0.40*	0.10	0.14	0.52**	0.52**

Spearman $r(n=20)$, two-tailed: (*) $p \leqslant 0.10$; * $p \leqslant 0.05$; ** $p \leqslant 0.01$; *** $p \leqslant 0.001$. [1] Behavioural observations. [2] Ratings from interviews. [3] Parameter, see Table 13.3.

related to the quality of maternal behaviour or attitude toward her infant. It made no difference whether the mothers evaluated their attachment experiences on second thoughts or just reported them, or whether they often said they supposed something had happened instead of 'really' remembering the episode. It did not matter either whether they used the more direct form, saying 'I' instead of the more indirect form, saying 'you'.

No special form of defense was associated with a lack of sensitivity. Some insensitive mothers evaded the theme, some blocked off the question by giving no or sparse answers. Neither idealization nor present anger was a major issue in itself. Only the value of the total parameter 'defensiveness', i.e. the sum of all defenses, was strongly related to maternal sensitivity towards her baby.

On the other hand, maternal co-operation was related more strongly to special defenses than to total defensiveness. Mothers who had been less co-operative during the first year were more disparaging of their parents (Table 13.4). At the child's age of 2 years, mothers who did not succeed in playing co-operatively with their toddler used the defense of blocking off the questions more than other kinds of defenses (Spearman $r = -0.48$, $p = 0.02$).

Discussion

The findings reported here for the subsample of 20 Bielefeld mothers, supported by the findings of the Regensburg sample of 45 mothers (Fremmer-Bombik 1987), show strong relations between the mother's attachment representation and her behaviour toward her infant as well as her infant's pattern of attachment to her, 4–5 years earlier. This corroborates the findings of Main et al. (1985).

For the appropriate interpretation of the findings, a number of factors surrounding the quantitatively defined variables should be kept in mind.

1. The responses of the mothers to the Adult Attachment Interview have to be seen in the light of a relative stranger asking about very personal experiences. It needs very tactful interviewers to ensure that an accepting, positive, and trusting atmosphere prevails. For many parents it was a strange and often painful journey into the past. Many had not thought about their childhood for a long time and were caught by surprise by the questions. Some parents cried silently while remembering their sad and distressing childhood experiences, while others put on a stiff upper lip while either trying to present a wonderful childhood or claiming that distressing experiences had not harmed them in any way.

2. The three home visits during the infant's first year were somewhat comparable to the Adult Attachment Interview situation. The spontaneous tender, playful, and caretaking behaviours of the mothers often had a childish

emotional or intimate quality. But, of course, there were differences among the mothers in how much they were willing to loosen their control. As in the interview, some parents tried to present the image of a happy family, or at least to play the role of a 'good parent'. But since the baby's reactions gave us a clue as to how usual or unusual the mother's behaviour was to the infant, we could observe the degree of idealization in the presentation of happiness.

3. In the Strange Situation pretence was difficult, too, since the mothers were given little influence over the baby's behaviour. If the infant did not miss her while she was gone, and did not greet her upon her return, the mothers often either expressed their disappointment about the impolite behaviour of their infants or they excused it by claiming the infant was ill, tired, or too busy playing. If the infant cried during her absence most mothers were empathic and felt guilty at having caused unnecessary distress to their infants. But some mothers also showed satisfaction with an undercurrent of revenge, when they saw how much their babies missed them.

The reported relations between the maternal response patterns to the Adult Attachment Interview, maternal sensitivity to and acceptance of her infant, and the infant's attachment pattern in the Strange Situation, suggest that we are dealing with an underlying organization of thoughts and behaviour. The maternal sensitivity rating scale depends largely upon the mother's *responses* to her infant's signals and much less upon her *actions* toward her baby. It is not the number of tender kisses, loving words or seconds of bodily contact that are important (see also Tracy and Ainsworth 1981), but whether and how these behaviours were appropriate to the infant's communications. Correspondingly, in the analysis of the Adult Attachment Interview, the attachment representation is inferred from comparing and integrating all answers and not from the number of times a mother said her parents loved her.

We now know a little more about the dynamics of transmission of parental behaviour across generations, and about stability and change. Mothers who have a lively and rich memory of their parents, of themselves as a child, and of their experiences or the wished-for responses of their parents when they were distressed, were more sensitive to and accepting of their infants even if their attachment figures had been unsupportive (pattern II). Being more sensitive means that these mothers had open ears and eyes for the signals of their infants, tried to understand their messages, interpreted them correctly, and responded to them promptly (Ainsworth *et al.* 1974).

It has been suggested by Bowlby (1979), Fraiberg (Fraiberg *et al.* 1975), and Main (Main *et al.* 1985, p. 100) that attachment-relevant signals of the infant activate subconsciously attachment-relevant memories of the mother. The response comes in correspondence with her internal working model of attachment. Our results can illuminate this process a little. It appears that a mother who remembers well how she felt when something bad had happened to her and how her parents responded or *should have* responded to comfort her, will listen empathically to her own infant's distress signals. Being able to identify with her infant, she interprets them correctly and responds to them in the interest of the infant. A mother who cannot remember much of her childhood distress, or remembers only in a distorted form, seems less able to listen openly and feel sympathetic with her infant. She may push aside memories of her own former distress by ignoring her infant's distress.

This notion of the dynamics underlying the mental attachment representation of the mother and her behaviour toward her infant is supported by several of our findings. First, mothers of pattern II did not report a supportive attachment figure but reflected upon their attachment experience and were not defensive toward the intention of the interview. Over both samples, 16 mothers were assigned to this group and 12 of them had securely attached infants. Thus, a large majority of these mothers had been at least sufficiently sensitive to their infants to foster a secure attachment. Ricks (1985) reports similar findings: mothers of infants seen as anxious were more defensive and more likely to idealize their parents than were mothers of infants seen as secure.

The other evidence comes from the high correlation between some of the criteria of the attachment representation and maternal sensitivity. For instance, a mother was given a high rank position on the criterion 'attachment-relevant contents' if her answers were full of attachment information. It did not matter whether she reported happy or unhappy, supportive or unsupportive episodes, it only mattered whether they were relevant to attachment. A lively image of how the mother wished her parents had treated her seems to be almost as effective in permitting open and sympathetic feelings towards her infant, and in acting sensitively toward him, as a memory of actual experience of tender parenting.

The attachment-relevant effects of a mother's sympathetic responses to her infant are seen at the end of the first year, when the distressed infant turns to her trustingly. Maternal sensitivity was, in turn, related to more non-distress vocalizations during the second half of the infant's first year (Grossmann and Grossmann 1984), and securely attached infants communicated more openly with their mothers in the Strange Situation (Grossmann et al. 1986). Thus, an easy access to attachment-related memories and feelings in the mother, whether happy or unhappy, seemed to promote her appropriate responsiveness and understanding of her infant, which in turn enhanced the infant's communicative skills and readiness to turn to the mother for support when distressed.

We can now identify mothers (12 out of 65 in both samples) who were able to break the cycle of unsupportive parenting by their willingness to be open and constructively regretful of their unhappy attachment experiences. As Main and Goldwyn (1985) and Ricks (1985) have found, many of these mothers have forgiven their parents, made peace with them and their relationships are now better. But the Adult Attachment Interview gave us only very few indications of the circumstances in the development of these mothers who resisted transmitting poor parenting patterns. One reported a very stormy adolescence in which she broke completely with her parents, but later became reconciled. For some their husbands and his family helped them to see their childhood and their parents in a different light and be more accepting of their own needs. A similar finding is reported by Ricks (1985). Three mothers had lost a close person since their youth and were still preoccupied with this loss, at least during the interview. Their infants were classified as securely attached in 1982 (Escher-Gräub and Grossmann 1983) but a re-analysis showed (Wartner and Grossmann, in preparation) that they fell into the newly established class of infants whose attachment pattern is disorganized (Main and Solomon 1986). But for many we do not know what made them more empathetic and responsive to their infant's distress than their own mothers had been to their distress.

Correspondingly, we do not as yet have any explanations why some mothers who were found to have positive or non-defensive attachment representations had infants who were insecurely attached to them. The infants' attachment classification had been very difficult in some cases, and in one case it was a repeated interview. But these explanations are not exhaustive.

We do have evidence for the transmission of empathy. In the Regensburg study, one week prior to the Strange Situation, another standardized session with a stranger playing a clown was conducted to assess the infant's empathy with the clown's changing emotions. As Fremmer-Bombik et al. (in prep.) will report, infants of mothers who remembered their attachment experiences well and vividly showed more signs of empathy with the crying clown than infants of defensive mothers.

The transmission of a mother's attachment relationship to her parents to her attachment-promoting behaviour towards her infant has to pass through the organization of a mental representation of attachment. If the mother has had supportive parents and nothing traumatic had happened to their relationships, she can imitate fairly unthinkingly this good model of parenting. We found this for mothers of securely attached infants who have had at least one convincingly supportive attachment figure. But in the case of mothers who had had unhappy attachment experiences we found different kinds of influences on her functioning as an attachment figure, depending on her attitude towards those unhappy experiences. Some felt deeply sorry for what had happened, some still idealized their parents, and some did not want to talk about it. An unsupportive parenting pattern experienced by a mother was predictive of an unsupportive mothering pattern toward her infant only if she showed a strong defensiveness against the attachment topic as presented in the Adult Attachment Interview.

Summary

The relations between a mother's descriptions of her attachment experiences as a child with her parents and her maternal behaviour toward her infant relevant to attachment were investigated. Twenty mothers of the Bielefeld longitudinal study and 45 mothers of the Regensburg longitudinal study responded to the Adult Attachment Interview. Patterns of maternal attachment representations were determined from 20 criteria which were condensed to four parameters. Four patterns consisting of different combinations of the four parameters were found. The maternal patterns corresponded closely (80 per cent) to their infants' patterns of attachment to them. Twenty-five of the 31 mothers with positive or non-defensive patterns of attachment representations had securely attached infants. Twenty-seven of the 34 mothers with inconsistent or repressive patterns of attachment representation had infants who had been insecurely attached to them 4–5 years earlier.

Maternal sensitivity and acceptance of her infant during the first year of the infant's life, and her acceptance of the individuality of her toddler, correlated significantly with the amount of attachment-relevant contents and stories during the interview, with the mother's readiness to recall childhood experiences including her feelings as a child, and with the mother's lack of defensiveness.

The transmission of attachment-relevant parenting patterns seems to go through a mental representation of the attachment experiences. Generally, the mothers of this and other studies passed on their own attachment experiences to the next generation. But an unsupportive parenting pattern, as reported in the Adult Attachment Interview, was passed on to the next generation only if the mother showed a strong defensiveness against the interview and had not shown any substantial reflections on her experiences as a child.

References

Ainsworth, M. D. S., Bell, S. M., and Stayton, D. J. (1974). Infant–mother attachment and social development: socialisation as a product of reciprocal responsiveness to signals. In *The integration of a child into a social world* (ed. M. P. M. Richards). Cambridge University Press.

Bowlby, J. (1973). *Attachment and loss*, Vol. 2, *Separation: anxiety and anger*. Basic Books, New York.

Bowlby, J. (1979). On knowing what you are not supposed to know and feeling what you are not supposed to feel. *Canadian Journal of Psychiatry* **24**, 403–8.

Bowlby, J. (1980). *Attachment and loss*, Vol. 3, *Loss*. Basic Books, New York.

Bowlby, J. (1982). *Attachment and loss*, Vol. 1, *Attachment*, (2nd edn). Basic Books, New York.

Dorsch, K. (1985). *Analyse von Interviews mit Müttern über die Beziehung zu ihren 2-jährigen Kindern.* Universität Regensburg, Diplomarbeit.

Escher-Gräub, D. and Grossmann, K. E. (1983). Bindungssicherheit im zweiten Lebensjahr—die Regensburger Querschnittuntersuchung. Research Report. Unpublished manuscript. Psychological Institute, University of Regensburg.

Fraiberg, S., Adelson, E., and Shapiro, V. (1975). Ghosts in the nursery: a psychoanalytic approach to the problems of impaired infant–mother relationships. *Journal of the American Academy of Child Psychiatry* **14**, 387–421.

Fremmer-Bombik, E. (1987). Beobachtungen zur Beziehungsqualität im zweiten Lebensjahr und ihre Bedeutung im Lichte mütterlicher Kindheitserinnerungen. Dissertation. Universität Regensburg.

Fremmer-Bombik, E., Grossmann, K., Veit, B., and Grossmann, K. E. (in preparation). The transmission of attachment: maternal attachment representations as related to infant–mother attachment and infant's ability to show empathy.

Freud, A. (1936). *Das Ich und die Abwehrmechanismen.* Internationaler psychoanalytischer Verlag, Wien. (*The ego and the mechanismus of defence,* International University Press, New York, 1971.)

Freud, S. (1901). *Zur Psychopathologie des Alltagslebens.* Fischer, Frankfurt. (*The psychopathology of everyday life.* In The Standard Edition of the *Complete Psychological Works of Sigmund Freud,* Vol. 6. Hogarth Press, London, 1960.)

George, C., Kaplan, N., and Main, M. (1985). Adult Attachment Interview. Privileged Communication. Department of Psychology, University of Berkeley, California.

Grossmann, K. (1978). Die Wirkung des Augenöffnens von Neugeborenen auf das Verhalten ihren Mütter. *Geburtshilfe und Frauenheilkunde* **38**, 629–35. (The effect of the newborn's eye opening on the behaviour of their mothers.)

Grossmann, K. (1984). Zweijährige Kinder im Zusammenspiel mit ihren Müttern, Vätern, einer fremden Erwachsenen und in einer Überraschungssituation: Beobachtungen aus bindungs -und kompetenztheoretischer Sicht. Dissertation. Universität Regensburg.

Grossmann, K. and Grossmann, K. E. (in preparation). Newborn behaviour, early parenting quality and later toddler–parent relationships in a group of German infants. In *The cultural context of infancy,* Vol. II (ed. J. K. Nugent, B. M. Lester, and T. B. Brazelton). Ablex, Norwood, N.J.

Grossmann, K., Grossmann, K. E., Spangler, G., Suess, G., and Unzner, L. (1985). Maternal sensitivity and newborn's orientation responses as related to quality of attachment in northern Germany. In *Growing points in attachment theory and research,* (ed. I. Bretherton and E. Waters). *Monographs of the Society for Research in Child Development,* Serial No. 209, **50**, (1–2) 233–256.

Grossmann, K. E. and Grossmann, K. (1984). Die Entwicklung von Konversationsstilen im ersten Lebensjahr und ihr Zusammenhang mit der mütterlichen Feinfühligkeit und der Beziehungsqualität zwischen Mutter und Kind. In *Bericht über den 34. Kongress der Deutschen Gesellschaft für Psychologie,* Wien (ed. D. Albert (Hogrefe, Göttingen.)).

Grossmann, K. E., Grossmann, K., Huber, F., and Wartner, U. (1981). German children's behaviour towards their mothers at 12 months and their fathers at 18 months in Ainsworth's Strange Situation. *International Journal of Behavioural Development* **4**, 157–81.

Grossmann, K. E., Grossmann, K., and Schwan, A. (1986). Infant's communications after brief separation: a reanalysis of Ainsworth's Strange Situation. In *Measuring Emotions in Infants and Children*, Vol. 2, (ed. P. Read and C. E. Izard), 124–71. Cambridge University Press.

Grossmann, K. E., Fremmer-Bombik, E., and Escher-Gräub, D. (in preparation). Toddlers' responses to displays of sadness as related to the qualities of the attachments to their mothers and fathers: cross-cultural implications.

Hess, R. D. and Shipman, V. C. (1965). Early experience and the socialisation of cognitive modes in children. *Child Development* **36**, 869–86.

Lorenz, K. (1965). Ganzheit und Teil in der tierischen und menschlichen Gemein-schaft. In *Über tierisches und menschliches Verhalten*. Gesammelte Abhandlungen, Band II. Piper, München.

Main, M. and Goldwyn, R. (1985). An adult attachment classification and rating system. Unpublished manuscript, University of California, Berkeley.

Main, M. and Solomon, J. (1986). Discovery of an insecure disorganized/disoriented attachment pattern: procedure, findings and implications for the classification of behaviour. In *Affective development in infancy* (ed. T. B. Brazelton and M. Yogman). Ablex, Norwood, NJ.

Main, M., Kaplan, N., and Cassidy, J. (1985). Security in infancy, childhood and adulthood: A move to the level of representation. In *Growing points of attachment theory and research*, (ed. I. Bretherton and E. Waters), *Monographs of the Society for Research in Child Development* Serial No. 209, **50**, (1–2), 66–104.

Ricks, M. (1985). The social transmission of parental behaviour: attachment across generations. In *Growing points of attachment theory and research*, (ed. I. Bretherton and E. Waters), *Monographs of the Society for Research in Child Development* Serial No. 209, **50**, (1–2), 211–227.

Rudolph, J. (1986). *Befragung von Müttern aus Bielefeld über ihre Kindheitserlebnisse: Zusammenhänge zwischen ihren Erinnerungen an die Elternbeziehungen und der Beziehungsqualität zum eigenen Kind*. Diplomarbeit, Universität Regensburg.

Tracy, R. L. and Ainsworth, M. D. S. (1981). Maternal affectionate behaviour and infant–mother attachment patterns. *Child Development* **47**, 571–8.

Veit, B. (1986). *Befragung von Müttern über ihre Kindheitserlebnisse: Zusammenhänge zwischen ihren Erinnerungen an die Elternbeziehungen und Beziehungsqualität zum eigenen Kind*. Diplomarbeit, Universität Regensburg.

Wartner, U. and Grossmann, K. (in preparation). Stability of attachment patterns and their disorganizations from infancy to age six in South Germany.

V

Families in distress

14

Conflict and alliance in distressed and non-distressed families*
ANDREW CHRISTENSEN AND GAYLA MARGOLIN

'. . . whenever you have a disturbed child, you have a disturbed marriage.' Framo 1975, p. 22

A common notion in scholarly as well as lay theories of the family proposes that marital discord creates child problem behaviour. While few would state the relationship as strongly as Framo, many assume a causal connection between marital and child functioning. In fact, a considerable body of empirical work has documented an association between marital conflict and child problems, particularly child conduct problems (for reviews see Margolin 1981; Emery 1982). In this paper, we try to extend this body of work by examining the mechanisms involved.

How does marital discord affect child behaviour? First and most obviously, marital discord prevents the spouses from establishing the unified alliance necessary for parental leadership. The functioning of the executive system of the home is weakened by internal division; the two most experienced and capable members may be unable to work together to solve the problems of family life. Specifically, the parents may be unable to join together to provide consistent direction, guidance, and discipline for the children.

Secondly, marital discord may lead to dysfunctional parent–child alliances. Haley (1963, 1967) was perhaps the first to implicate such cross-generational alliances in the aetiology of child disturbance and family dysfunction (Hoffman 1976). In his classic paper on pathological systems, Haley (1967) describes his concept of 'perverse triangle', in which one person forms a covert coalition against a peer by uniting with another person from a different generation (or order of power hierarchy). In Haley's view, classic problematic situations in business organizations, marital relationships, and family interaction illustrate perverse triangles. The manager who 'plays favourites',

*The project reported here was supported by a grant from the National Institute of Mental Health, 1 RO1 32616. The authors wish to thank Rachel Simon for her assistance in collecting the telephone data and Richard S. John for his assistance with data analysis.

the employee who 'goes over the head' of his superior, the spouse who takes on a lover, and the parent who engages in an incestuous relationship with a child are forming covert coalitions across different orders of the existing hierarchy. Pertinent to the current paper, Haley argues that '. . . the ways parents form coalitions with the child against one another appear "causal" to the disturbance in the child' (Haley 1967, p. 104).

How do covert cross-generational alliances create disturbance in the child? Minuchin (1974) and others have suggested specific effects of extreme parent–child alliances.

1. These alliances may create anxiety in children by forcing them to side with one parent against the other. To get close to one parent means betraying the other.

2. The alliances may create conflict and confusion in children by placing them in undesirable positions of power relative to the non-aligned parent. Although this parent may at times treat them as if they were of lower rank, the other parent empowers them with higher authority.

3. The alliances may inhibit children's social development with peers in that the parent–child over-involvement creates little time for the development of peer relationships. Both the child and the aligned parent obtain gratifications from each other which should be obtained from peers.

4. Finally, and most importantly for conduct problems, the cross-generational alliance precludes the strong parental alliance necessary to establish discipline for the child. The parents can not maintain authority over the child since the child has too much authority of his or her own and any attempt to diminish this authority would disrupt the cross-generational alliance.

A third reason for the association between marital discord and child problems concerns the transmission of conflict across family subsystems, particularly between the marital and parent–child subsystems. A common notion is that conflict can be resolved best if it is first contained. The more a conflict spreads across different participants and issues, the less likely it can be speedily resolved. However, in families with discordant marriages, conflict is likely to spread beyond the marital dyad to include others, particularly children. Because of the intensity of their conflict, their inability to deal with it, and its threat to their relationship, parents may 'detour' their conflict onto the child (Minuchin 1974; Minuchin *et al.* 1978). In a scapegoating process (Vogel and Bell 1960), they may unite in attack against the child, who is viewed as bad, or they may unite in concern and over-protection for a child who is viewed as sick (Minuchin *et al.* 1978). The child may also participate in this process by initiating or escalating problem behaviour to redirect parents away from the threatening marital conflicts.

Conflict may also spread in the opposite direction, from other family subsystems into the marital system. When one parent and child are in conflict, the other parent may enter the conflict to protect the child or criticize the parent, thus turning a parent–child conflict into a marital conflict or a full family conflict.

Margolin (1981) has noted that social learning theory, as well as systems theory, would predict a transmission of conflict across family subsystems. Through mechanisms of modelling and imitation, we would expect hostility and aggression in parents to be reflected in their children. Furthermore, the coercive skills that parents have learned with each other might naturally generalize to their dealings with their children (see also Chapter 15, this volume).

In this paper we will examine data relevant to three ideas: that weak marital alliances, strong cross-generational alliances, and transmission of conflict across family subsystems are associated with child disturbance. In so far as possible, we will examine these ideas with different types of data: observational, monitoring, and questionnaire measures. But first we must explain the overall project which generated the data.

The University Family Studies Project

The University Family Studies Project was a collaborative study conducted jointly at the University of California, Los Angeles under Christensen and at the University of Southern California under Margolin. The project sought a sample of distressed families who were experiencing both marital discord and child conduct problems, and a sample of non-distressed families who were relatively free of both marital discord and child disorders. The former were recruited through clinic referrals, public service announcements, and advertisements for a comprehensive treatment programme of marital and family therapy. The latter were recruited through public service announcements and advertisements for a research project. To participate, all families had to have both parents living in the home and at least one child between the ages of 3 and 13.

Strict screening criteria, involving questionnaire cut-off scores and interviewer judgements, were established for both samples. The Dyadic Adjustment Scale (Spanier 1976), which assesses marital satisfaction, and the Areas of Change Questionnaire (Weiss and Perry 1979), which assesses desired changes in a marital partner, were used to assess marital discord. Cut-off scores indicating marital distress were set at one standard deviation away from the mean in the direction of maladjustment: total couple score on the

Areas of Change Questionnaire > 14; spousal mean score on the Dyadic Adjustment Scale < 97. Two parent questionnaires were used to assess child conduct problems: the Child Behavior Checklist (Achenbach 1978; Achenbach and Edelbrock 1979), which assesses a wide variety of symptomatic behaviour in children, and the Becker Bipolar Adjective Checklist (Becker 1960), which has parents rate their children on a variety of polar adjectives. The cut-off score for child conduct problems was set at one standard deviation in the direction of disorder for the Child Behavior Checklist: parental mean on the externalizing dimension > 60. The cut-off score for child conduct problems on the Becker Bipolar Adjective Checklist, which was slightly greater than one standard deviation, was set at the point of best discrimination between referred and non-referred child for conduct problems (Lobitz and Johnson 1975): parental mean on the sum of Factors $1 + 3 + 5 > 20$. Interview criteria for distress and non-distress consisted of the consensus between two interviewers about the presence or absence of moderate to severe marital and child conduct problems.

To qualify as distressed, families had to score in the distressed range on at least two questionnaire measures and be judged by the interviewers as having both marital discord and child conduct problems. In addition, family members had to desire treatment for their difficulties and be appropriate for a six-month marital and family therapy programme. To qualify as non-distressed, families had to score out of the distressed range on all four questionnaires and the interviewers had to judge them free of marital discord and child disorders. Furthermore, all children assessed (those between 3 and 13) had to meet these criteria and no family member could be currently in psychotherapy.

Out of a much larger number of families who applied for the study, 40 families met the criteria for distressed and 41 met the criteria for non-distressed. However, two distressed families and six non-distressed families did not complete the assessment procedures, leaving a final sample of 38 distressed families and 35 non-distressed families.

The two samples of families were similar on demographic variables. A series of t-tests indicated non-significant differences between distressed and non-distressed families on the parent variables: number of previous marriages ($M = 0.6$ versus 0.4), years of education ($M = 14.6$ versus 15.2), yearly income ($M = \$31\,200$ versus $\$36\,600$), and family socio-economic status (Hollingshead 1975; $M = 47.1$ versus 49.5); and on the child variables: number of children living at home ($M = 2.4$ versus 2.4), and age of target child ($M = 8.3$ versus 8.1). The only group difference discovered was for number of years married, which was lower for distressed ($M = 9.8$, $SD = 5.1$) than for non-distressed families ($M = 12.4$, $SD = 5.4$), $t(69) = 4.05$, $p = 0.048$. Chi square analyses on ethnic and religious composition of the two groups also proved insignificant.

To assist in the comparisons between distressed and non-distressed families, a 'target' child was identified in each family as the child who scored the poorest on conduct problems on the two child questionnaires. Not surprisingly, in distressed families, the child identified in this manner also was identified by parents as the focus of treatment. In non-distressed families, the 'target' child fell within normal range on both questionnaires but did not score as well as his or her sibling(s).

All distressed and non-distressed families participated in an assessment period which lasted about two weeks and consisted of home observations, laboratory observations, self-report questionnaires, and monitoring data collected through daily telephone calls. Distressed families were paid $25 to participate in the pre-treatment assessment but then could earn up to $200 more over the next two years in post-treatment and follow-up assessments. Non-distressed families were paid $50 to participate in a one-shot assessment.

The data described below come from papers completed at different points during the course of the project. Therefore, some of the papers describe a smaller N than that discussed above and include only the earlier families recruited into the research. Also, some papers focus on particular subsamples of families. When comparisons were made between subsamples of distressed and non-distressed families, the families were demographically similar to each other.

Observational data

Procedures

We conducted a detailed observational analysis comparing 12 distressed and 12 non-distressed families who all had at least one school-age child (5–13) living at home (Gilbert et al. 1984). These families completed two 10-minute structured interaction tasks: a problem-solving task and a negotiation skills interaction. In the first, family members selected a current, salient problem from a standard list of family problems (e.g. problems involving teasing, chores, bedtime) and discussed this problem with the goal of understanding it and moving toward resolution. In the second task, a negotiation skills interaction borrowed from the Minuchin research group because of its putative relevance for assessing family alliances, family members negotiated a mutually agreeable dinner menu.

Audiotapes of these interactions were coded with the Family Alliances Coding System (Gilbert et al. 1981). This system consists of six content codes indicating positive alliance (e.g. affection, defend/protect), eight content codes indicating negative alliance (e.g. attack, disaffiliation), as well as codes of positive and negative affect. To use this coding system, verbatim transcripts which indicate the speaker and content of each statement of the interaction are first made. Then the observers code each speech event, defined by a change in speakers, by listening to the raw interaction and studying the transcript. For each event, the observer marks the appropriate content and affect code and indicates to whom the statement was addressed and, if relevant, about whom the statement was referring.

We assigned weightings ranging from -10 to $+10$ to each content and affect code depending on the degree to which the code indicated a positive or negative alliance. We obtained these weightings by having 20 advanced graduate students in clinical psychology read descriptions of each code and rate them according to their positive or negative alliance value. The average rating of the 20 graduate students on a particular code determined the weighting of that code. For example, defend/protect earned an average rating of $+5$ while attack earned a rating of -9.

Alliance scores were computed for each event by assigning these code weights to each dyad implicated in the event. For example, if father makes a statement that attacks mother and defends daughter, the father–mother dyad would receive a score of -9 while the father–daughter dyad would receive a score of $+5$. By averaging these dyad scores across all events (about 200) in the entire interaction, we obtained a set of 'total alliance scores' which reflected the alliance patterns in the family. Figure 14.1 depicts these alliance scores for a distressed family of four. As can be seen in the diagram, each dyad has two scores, one reflecting the interaction of person A toward person B and the other reflecting the reverse. The family in Fig. 14.1 has a weak marital alliance and discrepant parent–child alliances with the target child but not the non-target child.

Inter-observer agreement was determined by consensus agreement (see Cohen and Christensen 1980). After participating in a six-week training programme on the Family Alliances Coding System, observers independently coded each transcript, with three observers per transcript. We computed the percentage of consensus (at least two of the three coders agree) on all possible coding decisions (i.e. content, affect, to whom, about whom, about whom content). Across all families and coding decisions, consensus agreement was 97 per cent.

Observers were uninformed concerning treatment status of the families, the numerical value of the codes, and the specific purposes of the investigation.

Results

To examine the hypothesis about weakness in the marital alliance of distressed families, we converted the marital alliance scores into alliance rates by adjusting for differences in family size and amount of speech. A two-way analysis of variance examining treatment status (distressed versus non-distressed) by situation (problem-solving versus negotiation task) revealed a

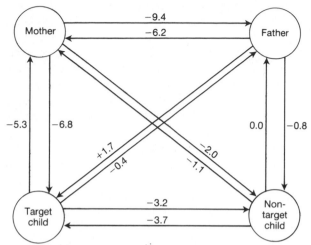

F_{IG}. 14.1   An alliance diagram of a distressed family of four, obtained from the problem-solving task (reprinted with permission from Gilbert *et al.* 1984).

significant main effect of treatment status, indicating that the marital alliance in distressed families was indeed weaker. Additional analyses confirmed that all dyadic alliances in the distressed families, except the father–target alliance and the sibling alliance, were significantly weaker in distressed than in non-distressed families. A number of significant interactions between treatment status and situation indicated that the problem-solving task produced more negative alliance rates than the negotiation skills task.

While the finding on the marital dyad is consistent with our hypothesis, it merely provides confirmation, through observational data, of our selection procedures. We had selected families with marital discord so it is hardly surprising that their data indicate a weak marital alliance. To provide a non-tautological analysis of our hypothesis, we examined the *relative* strength of the marital dyad in comparison with other family dyads. Our data indicated that our distressed families had weak alliances throughout the system, but would the marital alliance be in a weaker position compared with other family dyads? To examine the relative strength of the marital alliance, we converted the alliance rate data into rank data, by ordering the dyads in the family according to strength of alliance. A two-way analysis of variance revealed no main effects but a significant interaction, such that marital rank was lower in distressed families in the problem-solving situation but not in the negotiation skills task. Thus, the marital alliance in distressed families was weaker relative to other family dyads than in non-distressed families, but this relative weakness only appeared in a stressful problem-solving task and not in the more innocuous negotiation task for a dinner menu.

To examine the hypothesis about cross-generational alliances, we created discrepancy scores between mother–child and father–child alliance rates. Like the rank data, these data are independent of the overall strength of the alliance. One could have a discrepancy between two positive alliances or between two negative alliances. Separate, two-way analyses of variance were conducted for the target child and non-target child data. No main effects were apparent, but there was a significant interaction for target child scores. Scheffe *post hoc* comparisons (Scheffe 1959) indicated that distressed compared with non-distressed families had significantly greater discrepancies in the parent–target child alliance rates but only in the problem-solving interaction. The difference in rates of support to the target child by the mother and father was more than twice as great for distressed as compared with non-distressed families. Inspection of the data indicated that the discrepancy in distressed families was due to greater negativity in the mother–target child relationship rather than to maternal support.

Monitoring data

During the two-week assessment period, we monitored a variety of daily marital and child behaviours in our participating families by using the Daily Behavior Report (DBR, Christensen and Margolin 1978). Christensen and Margolin (1981) compared a matched sample of 20 non-distressed with 20 distressed families on aspects of these data; Margolin and Christensen (under review) compared the entire sample of distressed and non-distressed families on these data.

Procedures

The DBR was designed to assess marital and family behaviour through daily telephone interviews of the parent who had most contact with the children. The DBR consists of four sections which measure tension events, target behaviours in marital and child areas, time together with each family member, and satisfaction with each family member.

At a home visit at the beginning of the two-week assessment period, a staff member met with the family to explain the DBR. First, the staff member assisted the family in operationally defining tension events, which were described as occasions in which one member of the family expressed tension or conflict toward another. Typically, the behaviours involved in tension events consisted of emotional expressions (e.g. yelling, cursing) or withdrawal (e.g. refusal to talk, leaving the room). Then the staff member assisted the parents in defining 2–3 marital behaviours (e.g. criticisms) and 2–3 child behaviours (e.g. doing chores) which they would like to see increased or decreased. Finally, the staff member instructed the parents in the use of a nine-point scale for rating satisfaction with spouse and each child, and in the estimation of time together with spouse and each child. This initial visit included practice in reporting these measures. The definitions and procedures were reviewed one week later when the family came into the laboratory for an observational assessment.

During the two-week assessment, a staff member called the primary caretaker, usually the mother, to gather information on the previous day's events. The interviewer first asked about tension events, recording the active participants in these events as well as the uninvolved observers. Information about tension events was recorded as occurring in one of three time blocks: morning, afternoon, or evening. Next the interviewer obtained a frequency count of each marital and child target behaviour (which may have been involved in a tension event). Finally, the interviewer obtained ratings of satisfaction and estimates of time together. During these phone calls, the interviewer reviewed the definitions of tensions and important behaviours as necessary.

Approximately once a week, the interviewer collected data independently from both the primary observer and his or her partner, focusing only on the period of time during the previous day when both spouses were together. Each partner was asked identical questions in order to estimate the reliability of the primary observer.

Results

Reliability.   To examine the three hypotheses proposed in this paper, we focused only on the tension event data and the satisfaction ratings. We first classified the tension events according to family subsystem involvement: marital tension (husband and wife only), parent–child tension (one parent and one or more children), sibling tension (two or more children), and family tension (both parents and one or more children). Then we examined the reliability of these data in several ways. Exploring the stability of the data through traditional odd-even and split-half approaches, we found no significant effects for even versus odd days but a significant main effect for week 1 versus week 2. The total of all tension events declined from week 1 to week 2, but this decline occurred for both distressed and non-distressed families and across all four types of tension events. Exploring the inter-parent agreement on tension events, we conducted Pearson product–moment correlations between husband and wife across those days when both reported independently. We found moderate agreement for total tension events ($r = 0.56$) but considerable variability for individual tension events, due in part to the frequency of these events: 0.76 for the high-frequency parent-child tension events, 0.10 for the low-frequency family tensions, and 0.42 and 0.46 for the intermediate-frequency marital and sibling tension events respectively.

A finer-grained analysis, using Cohen's (1960) Kappa to examine inter-parent agreement within specific time blocks (e.g. morning, afternoon, or evening), found Kappas of 0.50 for parent-child tensions, 0.42 for sibling tensions, 0.29 for marital tensions, and 0.27 for family tensions. While these data indicate statistically significant agreement between parents, they reveal considerable disagreement between their reports. However, our data may be more reliable than these results indicate. First, the low range of some tension events limit the correlation coefficient as well as Kappa. Secondly, the reliability observer, usually the father, was not as familiar with the procedures or typically as interested in them as the mother, and may have been less accurate. Finally, the necessity of reporting on a selected time block when husband and wife were together made the reliability observation a more difficult task than the standard daily observation.

Although one can not speak of the reliability of subjective ratings, in the sense of inter-observer agreement, we examined the correlations between mother's and father's satisfaction ratings as an indication of the extent to which their subjective feelings were shared. Husband's and wife's ratings of spouse satisfaction were correlated 0.52 while their ratings of satisfaction with a selected child were correlated 0.45.

Tension event data.   To investigate our first hypothesis of weak marital alliances in distressed families, we examined the frequency of the four types of tension events in distressed versus non-distressed families using a 2 × 4 mixed-design ANOVA. Table 14.1 presents mean daily rates for these tension events. Not surprisingly, distressed families experienced significantly more tension events than non-distressed families (about twice as many per day). Also, different types of tension events occurred with significantly different frequencies, the most common being parent–child tensions. However, a significant interaction between family status and type of tension event indicated different distributions for tension events in distressed versus non-distressed families. Although marital tensions were the least frequent tension event in non-distressed families, they were the second most frequent tension event in distressed families. Thus, we see that marital conflict is not only more frequent in distressed families, as we would expect from our selection procedures, but, in harmony with the observational data, marital conflict is also *relatively* more frequent than other family conflicts in distressed families.

To examine the hypothesis about the transmission of conflict across family subsystems, we conducted sequential analyses on the tension event data. These analyses examined the transition probabilities that a particular conflict in one time interval (e.g. the morning) would lead to another conflict at another time interval (e.g. the evening). Transition probabilities had to be specified for each lag (i.e. for each period between intervals). In our data, lag 0 referred to the transition between different conflict events that occurred in the same interval; lag 1 referred to the transition from morning to afternoon, from

Table 14.1   *Daily rates of tension events for distressed and non-distressed families: means and standard deviations*

Type of tension	Distressed ($n = 38$)	Non-distressed ($n = 35$)
Marital	0.62 (0.52)	0.12 (0.15)
Parent–child	1.86 (2.10)	0.95 (0.86)
Sibling	0.41 (0.56)	0.27 (0.40)
Family	0.24 (0.21)	0.14 (0.19)

A two-way analysis of variance yielded significant main effects for type of family ($p < 0.01$) and type of tension ($p < 0.001$) and a significant interaction ($p < 0.01$).

afternoon to evening, or from evening to the next morning; lag 2 referred to a transition across two intervals (e.g. from morning to evening); and lag 3 referred to a transition three periods later (i.e. the same time period the next day).

Sequential analyses, as applied to our data, examined whether the occurrence of an antecedent conflict changed the probability of a consequent conflict. For example, did the occurrence of a marital conflict increase the probability of a parent–child conflict at a particular lag? To conduct these analyses, the conditional probability of a consequent conflict given the antecedent conflict was compared with the unconditional (or base-rate) probability of the consequent conflict. For example, the conditional probability of a parent–child conflict given a marital conflict at a particular lag was compared with the unconditional probability of a parent–child conflict. The Z-score test was used to make these comparisons between conditional and unconditional probabilities. According to Gottman *et al.* (1977), the Z-score must be greater than 1.96 to conclude that a difference exists between the two probabilities and that a sequence has thus been discovered. For example, in our distressed families the unconditional probability of a parent–child conflict was 0.32. However, the probability of a parent–child conflict at lag 1 given a marital conflict was 0.39. The Z-score for this difference was 2.30, indicating that in these families marital conflict did lead to parent–child conflict at lag 1.

In our analyses, unconditional or base-rate probabilities were based on rate per interval, regardless of how many times a particular type of conflict appeared in a given interval. Thus, the base-rate probability of 0.32 for parent–child conflicts in our distressed families means that at least one parent–child conflict appeared in about one-third of all reported intervals. Because sequential analyses require long chains of interaction, we aggregated data across all distressed families and all non-distressed families. This aggregation precludes inferential statistics comparing the two types of families (which would require the unit of analysis to be each family). However, with this qualification in mind, it is none the less interesting to compare the sequences that appear in the two types of families. Table 14.2 lists the number of significant sequences ($Z > 1.96$) that were obtained for distressed and non-distressed families when the four types of tension events were examined across the four possible lags. For any particular case of one type of conflict leading to another type of conflict, a maximum of four significant sequences are possible (at lags 0, 1, 2, and 3).

Table 14.2 *Number of significant sequences (lags) between family conflicts across distressed and non-distressed families*

		Subsequent conflict			
Initial conflict	Type of family	Marital conflict	Family conflict	Parent–child conflict	Sibling conflict
Marital conflict	Distressed	—	0	2	1
	Non-distressed	—	0	0	0
Family conflict	Distressed	1	—	1	2
	Non-distressed	0	—	0	1
Parent–child conflict	Distressed	0	2	—	4
	Non-distressed	0	1	—	4
Sibling conflict	Distressed	1	2	4	—
	Non-distressed	0	0	3	—

Significant lags were defined as $Z > 1.96$. Four possible lags were investigated (lags 0–3). All significant lags had positive Z scores. Only sequences involving different types of conflict were investigated here, so the above cells which indicate repetition of a conflict have no data in them.

Looking first at the spread of conflict *from* the marital subsystem, we see that in distressed families marital conflict increased the probability of parent–child conflict and sibling conflict, while in non-distressed families marital conflict did not change the probabilities of any other conflict. Looking at the spread of conflict *to* the marital subsystem, we see that sibling conflict and family conflict increased the probability of marital conflict in distressed families, but that no other type of conflict led to marital conflict in non-distressed families.

Looking next at the spread of conflict *from* the family system, which involves both parents and at least one child, we see that family conflict increased the probability of marital, parent–child, and sibling conflicts in distressed families, but only increased the probability of sibling conflict in non-distressed families. Looking at the spread of conflict *to* the family system, we see that parent–child and sibling conflict led to family conflict in distressed families, but only parent–child conflict led to family conflict in non-distressed families.

Looking next at the spread of conflict *from* the parent–child subsystem, we see that parent–child conflict increased the probability of sibling and family conflict in both types of families. However, marital conflict, sibling conflict, and family conflict led to parent–child conflict in distressed families, while only sibling conflict led to parent–child conflict in non-distressed families.

Before looking at the sibling subsystem, we should note that the spread of conflict *from* the siblings is often functional for the family. For example, parents often intervene appropriately in sibling conflict to resolve that conflict, but in so doing, create a temporary parent–child or family conflict. Also, the spread of conflict *to* siblings may be minimally dysfunctional in that the major forces in the family, the parents, are not involved. With these qualifications in mind, we see from Table 14.2 that sibling conflict led to marital, parent–child, and family conflict in distressed families, but only to parent–child conflict in non–distressed families. Looking at the spread of conflict *to* the sibling subsystem, we see that marital conflict, parent–child conflict, and family conflict led to sibling conflict in distressed families, but only parent–child conflict and family conflict led to sibling conflict in non–distressed families.

One additional feature of these comparisons should be noted. When conflict spread similarly in both types of families, the number of lags indicating such a spread in distressed families was, in all cases but one, greater than the number of lags indicating such a spread in non-distressed families. In this one case, involving the spread of parent–child conflict to sibling conflict, the number of lags for distressed and non–distressed families were equal.

Satisfaction data.   We also used the satisfaction ratings to examine, indirectly, the spread of conflict across family subsystems. We reasoned that a correlation across days between satisfaction with spouse and satisfaction with child might indicated linkages between conflict in the marital and parent–child area. For example, the parent gets angry with the spouse, draws in the child, gets in conflict with the child, and gives both a low rating. However, a plausible alternative hypothesis would be that a correlation exists between spouse and child satisfaction ratings only because of response sets and a natural interdependence between family events (e.g. on good days the parent is satisfied with everyone; on bad days, the parent is satisfied with no one). We thought we could tease out these two hypotheses by

(1)   examining the relative association between spouse and child ratings in distressed and non-distressed families; and

(2)   comparing the associations between spouse and target-child ratings with spouse and non-target-child ratings across both types of families.

If there is greater spread of conflict between marital and parent–child subsystems (or in general greater involvement of the child in the marriage) in distressed families, then distressed families should evidence

(1)   stronger correlations between spouse and child satisfaction ratings; and

(2)   greater discrepancies between target-child and non-target-child associations with spouse satisfaction (with the target-child associations being stronger).

For each family, we computed product–moment correlations between spouse and child satisfaction ratings across the entire two-week assessment period. For families with more than one child, separate correlations were computed for each child aged between 3 and 13, and a mean correlation was obtained. Across the total sample of families, the mean of these correlations between spouse satisfaction and child satisfaction ($M = 0.45$, $SD = 0.31$) was significantly greater than zero. However, a comparison of these correlations between distressed and non-distressed families revealed no significant differences.

In families with more than one child, the correlation between spouse satisfaction and child satisfaction for the target child were compared with the mean correlation between spouse satisfaction and child satisfaction for all other children aged between 3 and 13. Across distressed families, the correlations for the target child ($M = 0.52$) were greater than the correlations for the non-target child/children ($M = 0.33$), while in non-distressed families the correlations for the target child ($M = 0.53$) were less than the correlations for the non-target child/children ($M = 0.60$). The difference between the target and non-target child correlations were then compared across distressed and non-distressed families. Distressed families showed a significantly greater difference in the predicted direction (i.e. target child satisfaction had a higher correlation with spouse satisfaction than did non-target child satisfaction). Thus, in distressed families there may be a 'spill over' of feelings between the target child and the spouse, possibly mediated by a spread of conflict between the marital and parent–child system.

Questionnaire data

We had parents and children in both samples of families complete a variety of questionnaires. Some of these questionnaires allowed us to assess indirectly the hypothesis about cross-generational alliances in distressed families. Hazzard *et al.* (1983) examined questionnaire data from 75 children aged between 5 and 13; Christensen *et al.* (in preparation) examined questionnaire data from distressed and non-distressed families with at least two children aged between 3 and 13.

Child data

Hazzard and Christensen (Hazzard *et al.* 1983) developed the Parent Perception Inventory (PPI) to assess children's perceptions of 18 classes of parent behaviour. The PPI assesses nine positive behaviour classes (e.g. positive reinforcement, allowing independence, and non-verbal affection) and nine negative behaviour classes (e.g. physical punishment, criticism, and yelling). The PPI is administered verbally to the child by reading descriptions and exemplars of each behaviour class until the child understands the concept. The child responds by circling a phrase on a five-point scale (never, a little, sometimes, pretty much, a lot). The 18 behaviour classes are assessed for mother and then for father.

We hypothesized that children in distressed families would see their parents as less positive and more negative than children in non-distressed families. Means for all four measures derived from the PPI (mother positive, mother negative, father positive, and father negative) were in the predicted direction, but only mother negative behaviour reached statistical significance. However, this analysis merely provided indirect confirmation of our selection procedures. Since we selected families with conduct disordered children, it is not surprising that the parents in these families may have behaved less positively and more negatively than parents in non-distressed families, and that the children perceived them as such.

However, we also hypothesized that non-distressed children, apart from any difference in overall negativity or positivity, would perceive their mother and father more similarly than children in distressed families. If distressed families experience discrepant cross-generational alliances, in which one parent has a markedly different alliance with the child than the other parent, then the children in these distressed families should see their mother and father as behaving more differently toward them than children in non-distressed families. To test this notion, we created a perceived parent similarity index for each child by correlating his or her ratings of mother and father across all 18 items. The correlation coefficients for children in non-distressed families ($M = 0.71$) were significantly greater than the correlation coefficients for children in distressed families ($M = 0.47$).

Parent data

All parents completed the Child Behavior Checklist (Achenbach 1978; Achenbach and Edelbrock 1979) for each child aged between 3 and 13. This questionnaire produces scores on two major dimensions of problem behaviours: an externalizing score (disruptive behaviours such as physical aggression, stealing, truancy) and an internalizing score (withdrawn reactions and subjective experiences such as anxiety and guilt). A deviancy cut-off score (one standard deviation from the mean in the direction of deviancy) on the externalizing dimension was used as a criterion for classifying families as distressed or non-distressed.

Consistent with the notion of discrepant cross-generational alliances in distressed families, we hypothesized greater differences between distressed parents' perceptions of their children, particularly their target child, as compared with parent perceptions in non-distressed families. If parents in distressed families have markedly different alliances with their child, then they might indicate different levels of symptomatology on a diagnostic measure such as the Child Behavior Checklist. Using the difference between parent's scores as the dependent variable, we conducted a 2×2 analysis of variance (distressed versus non-distressed family and target versus non-target child) on both the externalizing and internalizing scores. The predicted interaction effect did not occur with the externalizing dimension but showed the appropriate trend ($p < 0.1$) with the internalizing dimension. It should be noted that the externalizing score reflects observable behaviours and produces higher inter-parent agreement than the internalizing score, which reflects less observable phenomena. Thus, the parent's own feelings about the child can be better reflected in the internalizing scores. In the present data, parents in distressed families tended to perceive their target child but not their non-target child more differently than non-distressed families on this internalizing dimension.

We also investigated the direction of parental disagreements on the Child Behavior Checklist. Across all families, mothers saw their children more negatively than fathers, but this difference reached statistical significance only on the internalizing scores ($p < 0.05$).

Discussion

In this paper, we examined data relevant to three hypotheses about conflict and alliance in distressed and non-distressed families. The first hypothesis, that weak marital alliances would characterize distressed families, was strongly supported by both observational and monitoring data. Compared with non-distressed families, distressed families evidenced less positive and more negative alliances in an observational situation and evidenced more daily marital conflicts over the two-week assessment situation. However, these findings were somewhat tautological, in that we had selected distressed families with marital discord, albeit on questionnaire and interview measures. The observational and monitoring data merely provided convergent valida-tion of our selection procedures. A more rigorous test of our first hypothesis was provided by a comparison between distressed and non-distressed families on the relative strength of the marital alliance and by the relative frequency of marital conflict. The data indicated that most of the dyads in distressed families were weaker than the comparable dyads in non-distressed families, but that the marital dyad in distressed families occupied a *relatively* weaker position than other family dyads. Likewise, the monitoring data indicated not only that conflict was more frequent in distressed families but that marital conflict was *relatively* more frequent in these families.

The second hypothesis, which concerned discrepant cross-generational alliances, was examined with both observational and questionnaire data. On the observational data, mothers and fathers in distressed families evidenced markedly different alliances with the target but not the non-target child; in contrast, the parents in non-distressed families evidenced greater similarity in their dealings with the target as well as the non-target child. On questionnaire data, children in distressed families reported greater differences in the way their parents treated them than did children in non-distressed families. Parents' questionnaire data about their children's symptoms showed some evidence of greater disagreement in distressed versus non-distressed families, but only for the target child and only for the internalizing symptom score.

These data are consistent with notions about cross-generational alliances in distressed families. The theory in this area often suggests that the mother is the parent who is over-involved with the child in an intense alliance that provides her gratifications not available from her husband (Hoffman 1976; Leibman *et al*. 1976). However, our observational data, as well as the questionnaire data from children, indicate that the mother is more negative while the father is more neutral towards the child. While the mother may be intensely over-involved with the child, this involvement produces conflict rather than an over-protective supportiveness. It is doubtful the mother finds this relationship gratifying! We should remember the nature of the child problems in interpreting these findings. Problems of over-control in children may be associated with maternal over-protectiveness but problems of undercontrol in children, such as in our sample, may be associated with maternal negativity and punitiveness.

We examined the third hypothesis, which concerned conflict containment, with monitoring and satisfaction rating data. Our sequential analysis indicated more frequent movement of conflict across family subsystems in distressed than in non-distressed families. The findings were particularly striking for the transmission of conflict into and out of the marital subsystem. Although non-distressed and distressed families experience conflicts in all possible family subsystems, the non-distressed families are better able to contain these conflicts within the system in which they originate.

Our findings with the satisfaction rating data provided indirect evidence that the target child in distressed families was involved in marital conflict. In distressed families only, ratings of satisfaction with the target child correlated more strongly with ratings of satisfaction with spouse than did the ratings of satisfaction with the non-target child. In non-distressed families the ratings of target and non-target child showed similar correlations with ratings of spouse satisfaction. Perhaps conflict in distressed families often includes both the marital and parent–target-child subsystems, so that satisfaction with spouse and target child are correlated. This interpretation is clearly speculative and must be qualified by the fact that correlations between spouse satisfaction and child satisfaction in non-distressed families were as high as those in distressed families, although the non-distressed families did not show significant difference between target child and non-target child correlations.

We freely acknowledge the limitations of our study and thus the data that support our hypotheses. The nature of our sample, our measures, our design, and our analyses limit the interpretations that can be made. For example, I think our criterion measures selected very happy, non-distressed families who were possibly more problem free than most families. Our monitoring data, like much other monitoring data (e.g. Christensen *et al.* 1983), was part objective recording and part subjective reaction. Our design permitted only interpretations of association, not causation. And finally, because our sequential analyses were done on the aggregate data from distressed and non-distressed families, they do not permit inferential statistics comparing the two samples.

With these limits in mind, we can none the less assert that the data are consistent with a number of notions from structural family systems theory (Haley 1967; Minuchin 1974; Minuchin *et al.* 1978), namely, that distressed families with problem children are characterized by weak marital alliances, discrepant cross-generational alliances, and spread of conflict between family subsystems, particularly the marital and parent–child subsystems. These notions help us understand the empirical data demonstrating a relation between marital discord and child problem behaviour. If parents cannot act jointly to guide and discipline their children, if they have markedly different views about their children, if they involve their children in their own conflicts, or if they interfere in each other's efforts to deal with their children, then it is hardly surprising that these parents may create, or at least facilitate, the development of problematic children.

Summary

Family systems theories implicate weak marital alliances, inappropriate cross-generational alliances, and the transmission of conflict across family subsystems as causative factors in the aetiology of child disorder. Using observational, monitoring, and questionnaire data obtained from samples of distressed and non-distressed families, the present study provided evidence for the association of child conduct problems with each of these three factors.

References

Achenbach, T. M. (1978). The child behavior profile: I Boys aged 6–11. *Journal of Consulting and Clinical Psychology* **46**, 478–88.

Achenbach, T. M. and Edelbrock, C. S. (1979). The Child Behavior Profile: II. Boys aged 12–16. *Journal of Consulting and Clinical Psychology* **47**, 223–33.

Becker, W. C. (1960). The relationship of factors in parental ratings of self and each other to the behavior of kindergarten children as rated by mothers, fathers, and teachers. *Journal of Consulting Psychology* **24**, 507–27.

Christensen, A. and Margolin, G. (1978). Investigation and treatment of multiproblem families. National Institute of Mental Health. Grant No. RO1 MH32616.

Christensen, A. and Margolin, G. (1981). *Correlational and sequential analyses of marital and child problems*. Paper presented at the annual convention of the American Psychological Association, Los Angeles, Calif.

Christensen, A., Sullaway, M., and King, C. E. (1983). Systematic error in behavioral reports of dyadic interaction: egocentric bias and content effects. *Behavioral Assessment* **5**, 131–42.

Christensen, A., Margolin, G., and Sullaway, M. (in preparation). Parental agreement on the Child Behavior Checklist.

Cohen, F. A. (1960). A coefficient of agreement for nominal scales. *Educational and Psychological Measurement* **20**, 37–46.

Cohen, R. S. and Christensen, A. (1980). Further examination of demand characteristics in marital interaction. *Journal of Consulting and Clinical Psychology* **48**, 121–3.

Emery, R. E. (1982). Interparental conflict and the children of discord and divorce. *Psychological Bulletin* **92**, (2), 310–30.

Framo, J. L. (1975). Personal reflections of a family therapist. *Journal of Marriage and Family Counseling* **1**, 15–28.

Gilbert, R., Christensen, A., and Margolin, G. (1984). Patterns of alliance in nondistressed and multiproblem families. *Family Process* **23**, 75–87.

Gilbert, R., Saltar, K., Deskin, J., Karagozian, A., Severance, G., and Christensen, A. (1981). The family alliances coding system (FACS) manual. Unpublished manuscript University of California, Los Angeles.

Gottman, J., Markman, H., and Notarius, C. (1977). The topography of marital conflict: a sequential analysis of verbal and nonverbal behavior. *Journal of Marriage and the Family* **39**, 461–77.

Haley, J. (1963). Strategic therapy when a child is presented as the problem. *The Journal of the American Academy of Child Pschiatry* **12**, 641–59.

Haley, J. (1967). Towards a theory of pathological systems. In *Family therapy and disturbed families* (ed. G. Zuk and I. Nagy). Science and Behavior Books, Palo Alto.

Hazzard, A., Christensen, A., and Margolin, G. (1983). Children's perceptions of parental behaviors. *Journal of Abnormal Child Psychology* **11**, 49–59.

Hoffman, L. (1976). Breaking the homeostatic cycle. In *Family therapy: theory and practice* (ed. P. Guerin, Jr.). Gardner Press, New York.

Hollingshead, A. B. (1975). *Two-factor index of social status*. Privately published. Yale University.

Leibman, R., Honig, P., and Berger, H. (1976). The role of the family in the treatment of chronic asthma. In *Family therapy: theory and practice* (ed. P. J. Guerin, Jr.). Gardner Press, New York.

Lobitz, G. K. and Johnson, S. M. (1975). Normal versus deviant children: a multi-method comparison. *Journal of Abnormal Child Psychology* **3,** 353–74.

Margolin, G. (1981). Behavior exchange in distressed and nondistressed marriages: a family cycle perspective. *Behavior Therapy* **12,** 329–43.

Margolin, G. and Christensen, A. (under review). Everyday conflict in distressed and nondistressed families.

Minuchin, S. (1974). *Families and family therapy.* Harvard University Press, Cambridge, Mass.

Minuchin, S., Rosman, B. L., and Baker, L. (1978). *Psychomatic families: anorexia nervosa in context.* Harvard University Press, Cambridge, Mass.

Scheffe, H. (1959). *The analysis of variance.* Wiley, New York.

Spanier, G. B. (1976). Measuring dyadic adjustment: new scales for assessing the quality of marriage and similar dyads. *Journal of Marriage and the Family* **38,** 15–28.

Vogel, E. F. and Bell, N. W. (1960). The emotionally disturbed child as a family scapegoat. In *A modern introduction to the family* (ed. N. W. Bell and E. F. Vogel). The Free Press, New York.

Weiss, R. L. and Perry, B. A. (1979). *Assessment and treatment of marital dysfunction.* University of Oregon Marital Studies Program, Eugene, Oregon.

15

Multilevel family process models: traits, interactions, and relationships
G. R. PATTERSON AND T. J. DISHION

Hinde (1979) and Hinde and Stevenson-Hinde(1987) describe the complex matrix in which family relationships are embedded: 'Social scientists . . . come to terms with a series of dialectics between successive levels of complexity—the behaviour of individuals, interactions, relationships, social structure, socio-cultural structure, and intergroup relationships. At the same time they must remember that each level represents not an entity but a process in continuous creation through the agency of the dialectics' (Hinde and Stevenson-Hinde, 1987, p. 3). The present report represents an effort to examine empirically models relating multiple descriptive levels of family adaptation within a theoretical context. First, what is the relation between parents' antisocial personality traits and their interactional style in the home with the child? Secondly, what is the impact of the parent–child interaction upon the development of the child's antisocial trait? Thirdly, what is the impact of early experiences and stressful events from within and from outside the family on the interaction sequences; how does this interact with parental personality traits in affecting the child's behaviour? Fourthly, how do family interaction patterns and child behavioural dispositions affect molar perceptions of the parent–child relationship across time?

The data set for these analyses was provided from an ongoing longitudinal study (the Oregon Youth Study). The sampling and data collection procedures, as well as the findings from the first data collection wave, are reported by Patterson *et al.* (in press). Two cohorts, each of roughly 100 families with fourth-grade boys, were recruited from the metropolitan area's highest crime neighbourhoods. The families of these fourth-grade boys participated in over 20 hours of assessment, including observations in the home, interviews, videotaped family interactions and daily telephone interviews, and filled out numerous questionnaires. Partial data sets consisting of very brief interviews and a few questionnaires were also collected at grade five. At the time of writing, a full assessment has also been obtained for Cohort 1 when the boys were in the sixth grade.

Both the longitudinal design and the assessment battery were tailored to provide an empirical base for devising a process model of how families change over time. The social interactional perspective it reflects lends itself nicely to the questions framed by Hinde and Stevenson-Hinde (1987). The focus on social *process* involves problem solving and a theoretical framework. The problem-solving emphasis requires two stages in approaching a research agenda. The first stage concerns the conceptualization and operationalization of theoretical constructs that have some applied significance with respect to defining social processes amenable to change (Patterson and Reid 1984). This process of definition, empirical validation, and re-definition is assumed to be iterative because empirical findings and further understanding of the phenomena often lead to re-conceptualization of the problem. The second stage focuses on confined temporal units of interpersonal interchange, typically measured by direct observation. This moment-by-moment focus is theoretical because these processes are thought to be the primary mechanisms accounting for substantial portions of the variance in generalized indices of adjustment. This social interactional model has been labelled as a third generation learning paradigm (Cairns 1979), distinguished from earlier learning models by the inclusion of affective, cognitive and physiological processes in the effort to better understand behaviour. For example, in the effort to understand antisocial behaviour in boys, Patterson *et al.* (in press) developed models of emotional and cognitive variables as outcomes of reasonably stable social processes. To date, these hypotheses await further testing with longitudinal data. In the sections that follow, we will apply our data to each of these questions in turn.

From parental traits to interaction patterns

The term *trait* is being used as a level of description in behaviour that reflects an individual's generalized disposition. Trait constructs are to be defined on the basis of an aggregation of information summarizing the individual's behaviour across settings and from the viewpoint of different reporting agents (Epstein 1979; Buss and Craik 1983). It is assumed that certain parental personality traits place them at risk for irritable-explosive exchanges with their children. The coercion model suggests that both antisocial and depressed parents may be at risk for increased irritability in their interactions with their children (Patterson 1982).

In the current study, the parent irritable discipline construct is designed to assess these explosive exchanges. The assumption is that the parent is most at risk to display irritable behaviour during discipline confrontations. There are three indicators that define the parental irritable discipline construct. All of them are based on information collected during three home observation sessions: the likelihood of the parent nagging, given that she/he is interacting with the child; the likelihood of the parent threatening or hitting, given that the child is deviant; and the observer's global ratings of consistency in discipline confrontations.

An empirical bridge between molecular observations of parental interaction sequences and more molar measures of parental traits or dispositions is required for a test of the hypothesis.

The parental antisocial trait and discipline confrontations

The analyses of follow-up data by Caspi *et al.* (1986) showed that, when antisocial children later became parents, they tended to be ill-tempered in child-rearing. For women, there was a direct path between their own temper tantrums during childhood and their children and spouses reporting ill-tempered and inadequate parenting.

The analyses by Patterson *et al.* (in press) combined the data from intact, single-parent, and stepparent families, as well as for mothers and fathers. In keeping with the hypothesis, the Parent Antisocial construction co-varied significantly with the measure of parental irritable discipline (-0.26). The analyses in the current study disaggregate both the dependent and independent variables and should thus provide a more revealing picture of the relation between parental traits and discipline practices. The parental antisocial trait is defined by three indicators: state records of arrests (excluding traffic violations), records of driving violations from the Motor Vehicle Department, and the MMPI scales for psychopathic deviance and hypomania (4–9 profile).

Parental depression and discipline confrontations

The hypothesis is that irritability is often a concomitant of depression. The accompanying hypothesis is that depressed parents are more irritable in their discipline confrontations. In effect, the relation between parental depression and child antisocial behaviour is mediated by disruptions in discipline.

There is now a set of empirical findings that relates parental depression to a spectrum of child problem behaviours (Bone 1977; Billings and Moos 1983; Radke-Yarrow *et al.* 1985). The present writers assume that some, but not all, depressed parents become more irritable in their interactions with their children. Presumably, it is the depressed, irritable parent that is most likely to produce an antisocial problem child.

In a follow-up study of separated families, Forgatch (1987) showed that, for single mothers, irritability was a frequent accompaniment of maternal depression. She found significant correlations between self-report measures of depression and observed irritable behaviour, both with family members in the home and during family problem-solving exchanges. During six telephone interviews, 22 per cent of the single mothers reported feeling only sad, while another 42 per cent reported feeling both sad and irritable. She also found a high degree of stability for observed maternal irritability over a six-month interval.

In keeping with the hypothesis, the findings from intensive observations in the homes of depressed and non-depressed mothers by Hops *et al.* (1987) showed that children of aggressive mothers were significantly more aggressive. The trait for parental depression was measured by the CES-D and the Lubin self-report scales. The natural question raised by these data is to what extent is the mother's depression a product of raising a difficult child or children (e.g. Brown and Harris 1978)?

Social disadvantage and discipline confrontations

Our clinical experience in treating several hundred families referred because of antisocial children suggested that many of the parents were extremely irritable in their interactions with each other and with the therapists as well (Patterson 1985; Patterson and Chamberlain, in press). Observations in the homes of problem and non-problem children showed that parents of problem children were much more irritable in their reactions to family members (Patterson 1982). For mothers of problem children, 6.5 per cent of their interactions were irritable, as compared to 4.9 per cent for mothers of non-problem children. The comparable values for fathers were 6.8 per cent and 3.3 per cent, respectively. Many of these families were socially disadvantaged in respect to education, income, and employment. Perhaps a majority of them had been reared by ineffective parents. It seemed that there was a pervasive lack of social skills that affected many areas of their lives, as reflected both in their chaotic employment records and their histories of disrupted marriages. The implication is that effective parenting skills may be a subset of a larger set of social skills. As an example, Scarr (1985) used both observation and interview measures to define discipline practices. The mothers' vocabulary scores, and to a lesser extent educational levels, correlated significantly with their discipline effectiveness. Scarr also points out that such correlations may reflect an interweaving of genetic with parent–child effects. In the present context, the findings emphasize that socially advantaged parents might be more effective in their discipline practices.

The clinical speculations led us to attempt a definition of a construct for social disadvantage. As it now stands, it is comprised of three indicators: occupational level (Hollingshead 1975), educational level, and interviewer's ratings of social skills. The convergence among the three indicators is moderate, as shown by the range of correlations from 0.21 to 0.35. A socially disadvantaged parent is one who is poorly educated, unemployed, and observed to be socially unskilled. As we proceed further with this concept, it may become necessary to break it down into some general measure of social skills (if indeed there is such a measure) on the one hand, and socio-economic status on the other. For the moment, there seems to be much to gain by combining the two threads into a single construct.

Empirical findings

The data in Tables 15.1 and 15.2 summarize the interrelations among various indicators measuring parental traits and parental irritable discipline. It can be seen that there is moderately good co-variation between some of the measures of the parental antisocial trait and some of the observation measures of social interaction in the home. It should also be kept in mind that, while the data for the two constructs were collected during the same three-week period, they are not necessarily concurrent measures; presumably, most of the parental arrests and traffic violations occurred prior to the measures of discipline confrontation with the child.

Table 15.1   *Bivariate co-variation of parental distress and irritable discipline practices*

Parental traits	Co-variation with discipline	
	Maternal ($n=70$)	Paternal ($n=64$)
Antisocial trait	−0.51*	−0.40*
Social disadvantage	0.10	0.49*
Drug use	−0.07	−0.08
Depression	−0.11	−0.04

   * $p < 0.01$

The maternal irritable discipline score was regressed on the constructs measuring maternal depression and the maternal trait for antisocial behaviour. The multiple correlation of 0.43 ($R^2 = 0.18$) showed that a moderate amount of the variance in discipline practices is accounted for by the measures of maternal traits. Of the three traits, the standard partial betas reflected significant effects for the antisocial trait (0.29) and social disadvantage (0.17), but a non-significant effect for maternal depression. The more antisocial and socially disadvantaged mothers showed greater disruptions in their discipline practices.

The paternal irritable discipline scores were regressed against the measures for paternal depression and antisocial traits. The multiple correlation value of

Table 15.2   *Parental irritable discipline regressed against parental traits*

Parental traits	Standardized partial betas	Multiple correlation	F value
Paternal			
Antisocial trait	−0.24**		
Social disadvantage	0.40***		
Depression	−0.05		
		0.50	13.93***
Maternal			
Antisocial trait	−0.29***		
Social disadvantage	0.17*		
Depression	−0.15		
		0.43	9.51***

* $p < 0.05$; ** $p < 0.01$; *** $p < 0.001$.

0.50 ($R^2 = 0.25$) reflects a similar story. Paternal antisocial behaviour and social disadvantage both made statistically significant contributions.

When the relation between the parental trait for antisocial behaviour and observed irritable discipline practices in the home are examined in a structural modelling context, the outcome is in close accord with that obtained for the multiple regression analyses. As shown in Fig. 15.1, the paternal antisocial construct is significantly related to the paternal irritable discipline construct, as shown by the path coefficient of 0.36. However, only 13 per cent of the variance in the parental irritable discipline construct is accounted for by this variable. Similarly for the mother, the path coefficient value is significant (0.27), but only 7 per cent of the variance is accounted for by indicators occurring long before the observers went to the home to observe the family interaction (see Fig. 15.2).

Summary

The findings reviewed in this section are compatible with the idea that parental irritable discipline interactions correlate with measures of the antisocial child trait. The findings are also compatible with the idea that there are empirical linkages between molecular and molar levels of data describing family members.

According to the coercion model, it is the disruption at the level of social interaction exchanges that may set a pathological process in motion. As described in Patterson *et al.* (in press), there are many outcomes that may follow if the disturbance in social exchanges continues long enough. The most

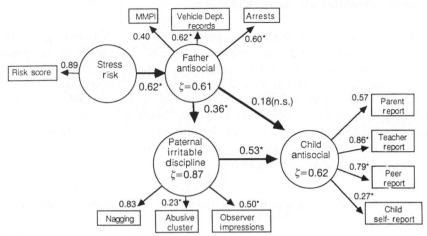

FIG. 15.1   Paternal irritable discipline as mediator for child antisocial traits. $\chi^2 = 5.301$, $p = 0.082$; $n = 127$; * $p < 0.05$.

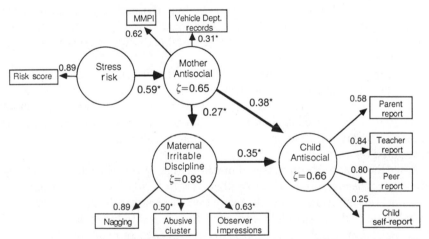

FIG. 15.2   Maternal irritable discipline as mediator for child antisocial traits. $\chi^2 = 42.89$, $p = 0.076$; $n = 127$; * $p < 0.05$.

immediate outcome for disruptions during discipline confrontations would presumably be an increase in antisocial behaviour. Other outcomes for the child include increased depressed mood and school failure (Capaldi and Patterson 1987) and for the mother, rising levels of stress and accompanying depressed mood (Forgatch 1987).

From disrupted interactions to child trait

The following section traces the empirical linkage between disrupted interactions (during discipline confrontations) and the impact on the child. There are two hypotheses to be examined. Do irritable-explosive discipline interactions from either mothers or fathers have similar co-variations with measures of the antisocial child trait? Previous studies examined only the relation between the combined parental irritable discipline practices and the child trait. The second hypothesis is that the relation between parental and child antisocial traits are mediated by the measure of irritable–explosive interactions during discipline confrontations.

Co-variation of maternal and paternal irritable discipline with child antisocial behaviour

It is assumed that antisocial child behaviour reflects equally the maternal and paternal discipline practices. This means that the measures of maternal and paternal irritable discipline practices should both co-vary significantly with the measures of child antisocial behaviour. A stronger test of the hypothesis requires that the magnitude of the correlations be equal.

Data presented in Fig. 15.1 support the hypothesis that paternal irritable discipline practices are significantly related to child antisocial behaviour. The path coefficient (0.53) from the paternal irritable discipline construct to the child antisocial construct was significant.

The comparable data for mothers of intact families are summarized in Fig. 15.2. The data presented are in keeping with the hypothesis that maternal irritable discipline co-varies significantly with measures of antisocial child behaviour. The path coefficient (0.35) from the maternal irritable discipline construct to the child antisocial construct was significant, but the variance accounted for was low.

Since the maternal and paternal matrices differ, there is no way of directly comparing the magnitude of one coefficient with another. It would be possible to model this question directly by using the two separate discipline constructs to calculate paths to the child antisocial construct. However, for the sake of expediency, a multiple regression analysis was used to examine the relative contribution of the two parents' discipline practices to child antisocial behaviour. The child antisocial construct score was regressed against each of the observation-based measures of irritable (likelihood of aversive reaction, given interacting with child) and explosive (likelihood of threaten or hit, given child deviant) reactions. The regression analyses showed that the contributions of the measures of irritable discipline were of borderline significance, so these variables were dropped. It was interesting to note, however, that the standard partial beta coefficients for this variable suggested that fathers contributed about twice as much as did the mothers. The analysis was re-run using just the nagging measure. The multiple correlation value was 0.49 ($p < 0.001$). The contributions of both the mother and the father were significant; however, the standard partial beta for fathers was 0.37 and for mothers, 0.19. It should be kept in mind, however, that there is a great deal of similarity between maternal and paternal nagging. The correlation of 0.42 ($p < 0.001$) between the two scores suggests that it is something analogous to a shared parental trait.

The results were something of a surprise to us. A decade of home observation studies had consistently shown that, in clinical samples, maternal rates of coercive behaviours were significantly higher than those for fathers when interacting with the problem child (Patterson 1982; Patterson et al., in press). It had been assumed from this that the interaction with the mothers might carry more weight in determining pathologic outcomes. However, it seems from the present analyses that fathers more than carry their own weight in determining outcomes. Fathers may nag, threaten, and explode at somewhat lower rates than their spouses, but this nevertheless makes a strong contribution to the children's problem behaviour.

At one level, the findings fit neatly into those reported earlier by Elder et al. (1985a). They found that, while irritability in both fathers and mothers was associated with disrupted discipline practices, it was the paternal irritable discipline that co-varied significantly with child antisocial behaviour. It might also be noted, however, that Elder and his colleagues failed to find a significant correlation between measures of maternal and paternal irritability.

The correlation data presented here could equally well be interpreted to mean that antisocial children cause their parents to be both irritable and antisocial. Indeed, the analyses of bidirectional effects for the observation data suggest that there is some merit to this idea (Patterson 1982). The possibility remains that increases in child antisocial behaviour further exacerbate parental use of ineffective and irritable discipline. However, teaching the parents to use more effective discipline is associated with reductions in both irritable parental behaviour and in antisocial child behaviour. In the one pre- and post-treatment comparison study done thus far, mothers self-reported significant improvements on four of the MMPI scales (Patterson 1980), but their reports of antisocial behaviour (psychopathic deviant and hypomanic scales) were not reduced. Actually, there was a non-significant increase in both scales. What is required is a series of treatment manipulation studies that demonstrate

(1)   parents' improvement in discipline produces reduced rates of child antisocial behaviour; and

(2)   parent training does not substantially alter levels of parental antisocial behaviour found before treatment.

The latter finding would be consistent with the idea that improved discipline practices do not alter the parents' more general antisocial disposition.

The findings support the Hinde and Stevenson-Hinde (1987) assumption that the interactional levels must co-vary in some fashion with individual traits (see also Chapter 4, this volume). At this point, the data presented here suggest that the dispositions brought by the adult to the family co-vary with the (irritable–explosive) quality of the interaction they have with their children. Secondly, the data also show that irritable parental interactions may actually produce a matching trait in the child.

Relation of parental to child trait mediated by interactional style

The behavioural genetics hypothesis. There are data consistent with the hypothesis that across-generational stabilities in antisocial behaviour reflect heritability components. Reviews by Plomin (1986) and others generally show positive correlations of about 0.20 or less between personality traits for parents and their children. In these reviews, the correlations among siblings are of about the same order. The study by Elder *et al.* (1985*b*) showed that parents' retrospective reports of grandparental irritability co-varied 0.34 with maternal irritability and 0.36 with paternal irritability. The behavioural geneticists conclude that much of the variance in measures of personality traits do not simply reflect experiences that are shared among family members.

Spouse homogeneity hypothesis. It is assumed that antisocial men and women are likely to select each other as mates: presumably living together will further buttress the strength of this trait. For example, the studies cited by Robins and Earls (1986) showed that antisocial persons tend to marry one another. Since antisocial personalities are more common in men than women, most antisocial women are married to antisocial men, while most antisocial men are *not* married to antisocial women.

In that most of the studies reviewed by behavioural geneticists rely upon self-report questionnaires, it was of some interest to examine the relation between parental and child antisocial personality traits when using more generalized construct scores. The correlation between maternal and child antisocial traits was 0.34 ($p < 0.001$) and between father and child 0.24 ($p < 0.002$). The correlation between maternal and paternal traits of 0.39 ($p < 0.001$) confirms that antisocial men and women may either select each other as mates or that they train each other in antisocial behaviours.

It was of some interest to examine parent MMPI scales to determine the degree to which they might co-vary on scales relating to antisocial behaviour. The psychopathic deviant score has been shown to differentiate delinquent from non-delinquent individuals; as noted earlier, it is also one of the indicators used to define parental antisocial traits. The correlation between maternal and paternal scores was 0.34 ($p < 0.001$). Other than that, the five highest paternal scores correlating with maternal psychopathic deviate scores were father psychathenic (0.36), paranoid (0.30), schizophrenic (0.30), the F scale (0.30) and depression (0.28). Given the paternal psychopathic deviant scores, the five highest correlations with mothers' scales were paranoid (0.34), the F scale (0.28), schizophrenic (0.27), depression (0.26) and hypochondriasis (0.23).

It is obvious that both the construct scores and the parental self-reports reflect a surprising degree of mutuality. Given the present data set, it is not possible to disentangle selection from mutual training processes. The least that can be said is that antisocial people tend to live together.

The trait-interactional style hypothesis. It is assumed that these cross-generational trait correlations for antisocial behaviour occur because the trait places the individual at risk for predictable disruptions in social interaction with family members, as well as fellow workers, supervisors, and casual acquaintances. In the present context, having one or more parents who are themselves antisocial implies that they are likely to be irritable and explosive in their discipline confrontations with the child. This, in turn, places the child at risk of becoming antisocial. In this sense, then, the effect of the parents' trait upon the child is mediated by the interactional style (parental irritable discipline construct).

The longitudinal findings provided by Huesmann *et al.* (1983) provide data that make the connection between parenting practices and next generation personality traits a plausible one. They studied a large sample of families living in semi-rural New York. The subjects and their families were repeatedly assessed over a 22-year period. The data showed significant correlations between first generation parental punitiveness and aggressivity and the grandchildren's antisocial behaviour.

To examine these ideas further, two hypotheses will be compared. The first is the non-mediational hypothesis. The parental antisocial trait contributes *directly* to the son's antisocial trait. The hypothesis could rest on the assumption that parents directly contribute to the heritability of child antisocial behaviour. It should be noted that the reviews of the twin studies on the heritability of delinquency (in children and adolescents) do *not* strongly support this hypothesis, in that the concordance rates are about the same for twins and siblings (Rowe and Plomin 1981; Cloninger and Gottsman, in press). Both the twin and the adoption studies show a consistent effect of heritability for *adult* crimes (Pollock *et al.* 1987). Other analyses have suggested the heritability effect may be stronger for adult crimes against property than for violent crimes against persons. Our own position is that those children with an early onset of antisocial behaviour may be most at risk for later adolescent chronic offending and for the involvement of heritable factors.

The second hypothesis is that the effect of parental antisocial trait on child antisocial trait is mediated by measures of irritable interaction styles (discipline). The mediational model examines the possibility that the impact of the parental trait on the child trait is primarily mediated by the disruption in discipline in the form of maladaptive reinforcement schedules (Patterson 1982) and in modelling irritable and antisocial behaviour (Bandura 1973). It is hypothesized that the mediational model will provide the better fit to the data.

The data in Fig. 15.1 summarize the findings for a sample of 127 fathers from intact families; these include both biological and stepparents. These are families of fourth-grade boys living in high-crime areas of a moderate size metropolitan area (Patterson *et al.*, in press). The demographic data for the sample suggest an over-sampling of working class and unemployed parents.

Each of the four latent constructs were defined by multi-agent and multimethod indicators. The details for building constructs are described in Patterson and Bank (1986, in press) and in Patterson *et al.* (in press). In the case of the antisocial child construct, the indicators were designed to sample both home and school settings and both overt and clandestine forms of antisocial behaviour. Structural equation modelling was used to define both the factor structure for the latent constructs and the magnitude of the relation between them (Bentler 1980; Jöreskog and Sörbom 1983).

Only one part of this model is of concern in the present discussion. The direct effects hypothesis would require that the path between the parental antisocial and the child antisocial trait would be significant. The mediational hypothesis would require that the path from parent antisocial to irritable discipline as well as the path from parental irritable discipline to child antisocial be significant. It can be seen that the data support the mediational but not the direct path hypothesis: the path coefficients for the mediational were 0.36 ($p < 0.05$) and 0.53 ($p < 0.05$), and for the direct path hypothesis 0.18 (ns).

There are several other features of the data that are of interest. Notice that the paternal trait accounts for a significant but modest amount (13 per cent) of the variance in the paternal irritable discipline construct, and that the model accounts for about 38 per cent of the variance in the measure of child antisocial behaviour. This is roughly equivalent to the findings from prior studies where the irritable discipline construct was a composite from both parents (Patterson *et al.* 1984; Patterson 1986).

Figure 15.2 summarizes the comparable data for mothers. There are striking differences between parents in the findings for the critical path coefficients. As shown in the figure, the mothers' path coefficients provide support for both the direct and the mediational hypotheses. Maternal antisocial trait was defined somewhat differently than paternal antisocial trait because so few of the mothers had arrest records that that indicator was dropped. (This shift in definition may account for the difference, but the writers think not.) Maternal antisocial trait is shown to relate both directly and indirectly to their sons' antisocial behaviour. The maternal trait accounts for only a modest amount of variance (7 per cent) in their interaction styles with their sons. Therefore, we need to reconsider the model we have been using. Are there some variables that might mediate further between mother and son traits (e.g. antisocial attitudes, monitoring, modelling)? We examined the possibility that the impact of the maternal antisocial trait upon the child trait might be mediated by parental monitoring (i.e. that this alternative path would be different for mothers and fathers). The data did not support this assumption.

Again, it is of some interest to note that the maternal model accounts for roughly the same amount of variance (34 per cent) in the child trait as did the paternal model. Knowing that the estimates of their discipline practices tend to be intercorrelated implies a shared style in their discipline confrontations.

Discipline as a mediator for antisocial traits across generations

A growing body of evidence supports the hypothesis that individual differences in some social behaviour may be, in part, passed from one generation to another. What is not clear is the means by which such cross-generational transfer might occur. The present report examines two possibilities. On the one hand, it is conceivable that the transmission of the antisocial trait is very direct, involving a complex genetic mechanism that produces a general social disposition. The direct transmission model would be more likely to place parenting skills as the products of the parents' traits, rather than key determinants, in the transmission of antisocial behaviour. The alternative view, entertained by the present authors, is that the child-rearing skills practiced by one generation are related to the development of stable personality traits for the mothers and fathers of the next generation. These traits are, in turn, reliably correlated with parenting practices that reproduce the same personality traits for the next generation. The hypothesis is that there is significant stability across generations for the antisocial trait. The corollary hypothesis is that the effect of the antisocial trait for one generation on that of the following generation is mediated by disrupted discipline procedures. In effect, parental traits disrupt parent–child interaction processes; when the disruption occurs during discipline confrontations, the effect is to produce an antisocial child (especially in boys).

Implicating parenting practices as the mediating factor for cross-generational transmission of some personality traits is consistent with the position taken by Belsky (this volume) and with the longitudinal findings of Huesmann et al. (1983).

The data presented in this section provide only a weak test for part of these hypotheses. Parental retrospective ratings of the child-rearing practices of the grandparents are correlated with the antisocial traits of the parents.

To become an effective parent, it seems one must have first passed successfully through the socialization process. The analogous studies of primates reared in isolation offer some support for this (Suomi and Harlow 1972). But at present, we do not understand what the necessary components of the socialization experience are that produce effective parents. Is it that an adequate socialization experience provides models of effective family management skills? Or is it that an inadequate socialization experience produces socially unskilled and antisocial personality traits that, in turn, lead to the development of ineffective family management practices?

Our best guess is that about two-thirds of referrals to the Oregon Social Learning Center for treatment of antisocial children represent families in which the parents simply did not have effective role models. In these families, one or both parents seem woefully ignorant of even the simplest family- or relationship-management skills. A rapidly expanding body of research shows that disruptions in the socialization process are related to later difficulties in parenting. Quinton and Rutter (1983; Rutter, Chapter 17, this volume) carried out a retrospective study of girls who had been admitted into a children's home when quite young. As young adults, they were interviewed about their experiences. Quinton and Rutter found that, of the 48 women who had become inept parents, 59 per cent reported themselves as having experienced multiple separations due to parental discord, persistent family discord, or disruption of long-term care prior to 2 years of age. Their studies included a comparison group comprised of many parents who had experienced severe early disruptions in socialization. They went on to point out that the co-variation between early socialization disruptions and later disruption in parental skills is far from perfect.

Knutson and his colleagues (Knutson et al. 1985) developed a pool of items sampling adults' recollections about the home environment they had experienced. Among other things, the items were designed to sample a wide spectrum of abusive parenting practices. To develop the six different subscales, they collected data from a sample of families applying for services at a child psychiatry clinic. They found that when both mothers and fathers of children referred for psychiatric diagnosis had experienced punitive parenting and/or acrimonious family interactions as children, the likelihood of the child being diagnosed as antisocial was 81 per cent. Given that only the mother had experienced punitive or acrimonious parents, the comparable figure was 50 per cent. For fathers only, it was 63 per cent. The findings are also consistent with a study of Black families by Robins et al. (1975). They found that 31.4 per cent were characterized by one or both paternal grandparents being antisocial. Of the delinquent sample, 53 per cent were so characterized.

 The findings are consistent with the hypothesis that negatively-toned, punitive early socialization experiences are associated with the development of antisocial traits in the next generation.

The specific hypothesis we tested was that subscales measuring parental retrospective accounts of the irritable, punitive behaviours of the grand-parents would co-vary significantly with the parental antisocial trait. The Knutson *et al.* (1985) Assessing Environments questionnaire was adminis-tered to mothers and fathers. Six of the subscales (physical punishment, perception of discipline, family violence, negative family atmosphere, positive parent contact, and community involvement) were correlated with the measures of parental traits.

The analyses showed that only two of the scales seemed to make a significant contribution; these were the parents' recollection of physical punishment and perception of discipline. Regressing the construct score for paternal antisocial trait on these two variables produced a multiple correlation of 0.37 ($p < 0.001$). It was the paternal recollection of perceived (negative) discipline that made the most significant contribution in accounting for variance. The comparable analyses for the mothers showed a multiple correlation value of 0.21 ($p < 0.05$); again, it was the maternal ratings on the perception of discipline variable that accounted for most of the variance in their antisocial trait score.

In general, the more punishing, distant, and negative the home environment recalled by the mother and the father, the more likely they were to be antisocial in terms of their self-report and arrest records. The findings are consistent with comparable data from the study by Elder *et al.* (1985*b*). In that study, the parents' ratings of their parents' irritable behaviour and arbitrary discipline correlated significantly with their own irritable behaviour.

In passing, it might be noted that similar analyses revealed very little correlation between recollection of the grandparental home environment and parental traits for depression and drug use, or for the measure of social competence, marital conflict, and stress.

Stress as an amplifier for the parental antisocial trait

This section examines the findings relevant to Elder's stress-amplification hypothesis (Elder *et al.* in press). The simplest and most general statement of the hypothesis would be that stress tends to amplify the impact of the parents' most dominant negative trait. In their modelling of the data from the Berkeley longitudinal studies, Elder and his colleagues found such an effect for fathers, but not for mothers. In their analyses, the prolonged major economic stressor (the Great Depression of the 1930s) was associated with increases in irritable discipline for the father. This, in turn, was related to higher scores for antisocial child behaviour.

The actual findings require several qualifications. First, the data showed an amplifier effect only for those fathers previously identified (before the Great Depression) as irritable. In our own efforts to use parental self-reported irritability, we found that, while it was moderately related to the stress risk construct $(0.29, p < 0.05)$, the correlation with the irritable discipline construct score was non-significant. One alternative would be to proceed to use the data from family interaction to develop a more powerful measure of irritability (we plan to do this). A second alternative was to expand the definition of the paternal trait from irritability to antisocial. In our own work, we tend to view irritability as one subset of the larger antisocial set. It was also decided to extend the Elder model to mothers.

Aldwin and Revenson (1986) used longitudinal data to examine the hypothesis of a reciprocal relation between individual traits and economic stress. For example, individuals experiencing relatively more psychological distress prior to an economic stressor would be more likely to suffer more symptomatology following the stressor. Relying on survey questionnaires, these investigators found support for this hypothesis. In an hierarchical regression analysis, it was found that both economic stress and psychological symptoms at t_1 accounted for significant portions of variance when examining economic stress at t_2. Similarly, when psychological symptoms at t_2 were examined as the dependent variable, both psychological symptoms and economic stress at t_1 accounted for significant portions of variance. The authors concluded that these data supported a reciprocal process linking stress and psychological adaptation. Individuals with lower adaptive skills are more vulnerable to the pressure of stress, which in turn may exacerbate their long-term level of functioning.

Stress

The inclusion of diverse indicators of both stress and parental adjustment in structural equation models may provide a means of disentangling the construct variance from measurement variance. This problem can be particularly severe, as evidenced by the research reported by Forgatch et al. (in press). In that study, single maternal reports were used to build multiple indicators (from a single agent) for irritability, depression, and stress constructs. A confirmatory factor analysis revealed that these were not three, but rather one, construct. This finding emphasizes the need to introduce different modes of assessment, other than self-report, when examining the relationship of stress to other family-related constructs. One of the strategies developed, and used in the present study, is to permit self-report indicators only as major definitions for one construct (Bank et al. in press). Additional methodological studies show that while it is possible to obtain a coherent structural equation model based on report data from a single agent, such models tend to be of very limited generality (Reid *et al.* 1987).

Under the rubric of stress, we included measures of daily hassles, major life events (Holmes and Rahe 1967), medical problems, unemployment, the number of children, and the family's adjusted income. We are sensitive to the issue raised by stress researchers on the confound between personal distress and the report of stress on self-report measures (Gersten *et al.* 1977; Depue and Monroe 1986).

The factor loadings for the stress indicators have been shown to be satisfactorily robust across the two cohorts for the longitudinal studies as well as for a sample of single-parent families (Patterson *et al.* in press). However, our experience in actually using the construct suggests that the general, rather low, level of convergence among indicators can pose serious problems. Some of the indicators demonstrate very high correlations with indicators in other constructs, but these correlations do not seem due to problems of shared methods (cf., attached convergent and discriminant matrix). For this reason, we frequently collapse the indicators into a single risk score in order to keep the model from exploding. See the description of this procedure in Bank *et al.* (in press).

We have been moderately successful in using the construct in two earlier modelling studies. Both showed that the effect of stress on child behaviour was mediated by its apparent effect on parental discipline practices (Viken 1987; Forgatch *et al.*, in press).

Reciprocal effects of stressors and traits

It was assumed that the relation between stressors and traits may be bidirectional. This would imply that when the antisocial parents are stressed, they are more likely to behave in such a way as to increase the stressors impinging on their families (e.g. have a blowup with the boss and lose their job; quarrel with neighbours, friends, and colleagues; get into fights; have traffic accidents). On the other hand, it is also assumed that the antisocial individual is likely to increase both irritable and assaultive behaviour when under stress. A model based on the cross-sectional data from Cohort 1 showed that the impact of the antisocial trait for fathers on stress was so slight that it has been dropped from our current studies.

It seems reasonable, however, to re-examine the bidirectional issue using longitudinal data.

Empirical findings

There are two sets of findings that relate to our revised Elder amplification model. The first requirement would be that the path coefficient that describes the relation between the stress risk construct and the parental antisocial construct be significant. The second requirement would be an overall fit of the data to the Elder model. A general model would also require that the data fit mothers and fathers about equally well.

As shown in Figs 15.1 and 15.2, the path coefficients from stress risk to parental antisocial constructs were significant for both parents: higher stress risk is associated with higher scores on the parental antisocial trait.

To provide a more precise test for the Elder amplification model (Fig. 15.3), the direct path from parental to child antisocial construct was dropped from the models presented in Figs 15.1 and 15.2. Notice that the parental antisocial construct came before the irritable discipline construct. The resulting χ^2 value for fathers was 54.84 with the resulting probability value of 0.073. The comparable analysis for mothers' data produced a χ^2 value of 50.62 with a probability value of 0.019 (remember, one indicator for antisocial was dropped). The Elder amplification model provides a better fit for the data from the fathers than mothers; this also replicates his earlier finding.

The findings are consistent with the Elder amplification model. In that the data from the Elder et al. (1985a) study had early estimates of paternal antisocial trait followed by the advent of the economic stressor, followed in turn by the impact on discipline encounters, their longitudinal design provides the more powerful support for the hypothesis. It is reassuring, however, to see the effect reproduced in cross-sectional data. It seems that the amplification effect may be a frequently occurring one, as suggested by the re-analysis of the Berkeley growth sample that included an interview of the males who had been in combat during World War II, Korea, and Vietnam. The data showed that, if as adolescents they tended to be sombre, introspective, and self-preoccupied, they were more likely to show a post-combat stress syndrome (Elder and Clipp, in press). This suggests that it might be worthwhile searching for an interactive model where certain kinds of stress serve as multipliers for certain kinds of pre-stress adjustment patterns. The longitudinal study by Block et al. (1986) showed that boys from subsequently divorced families tended to be more aggressive, labile, and physically active. This suggests that the effect of divorce might be to increase the aggressivity of boys who tended to aggressivity prior to the divorce.

Effects of other disruptors on the parent antisocial trait

It is conceivable that other types of disrupting variables, such as marital conflict, might co-vary with the antisocial trait. This, in turn, would suggest a further extension of the amplification model. The maternal antisocial score was regressed against both the marital conflict and the stress risk construct scores. The multiple correlation value was 0.20 ($p=0.013$). Of the two variables, the standard partial beta for stress (0.18) was significant, while that

Fathers

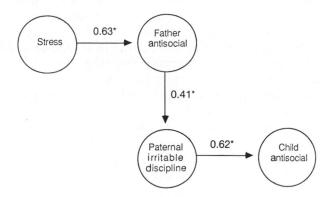

Mothers

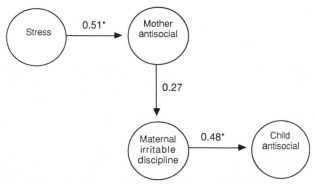

Fig. 15.3   Replication for Elder's stress amplification model. Fathers: $\chi^2 = 54.84$, $p = 0.073$; mothers: $\chi^2 = 50.62$, $p = 0.014$; both: * $p < 0.05$.

for marital conflict (0.14) was not. The comparable analyses for paternal data showed a multiple correlation value of 0.41 ($p < 0.001$); again, only the beta for the stress risk score was significant.

It is noteworthy that we also examined the correlation matrices that would define an amplifier effect for parental depression interacting with both stress and marital conflict. The data did not support this alternative model for the Elder amplification effect; however, it did support a model for a direct path from marital conflict to discipline.

An examination of the data for intact families quickly demonstrated that, for this sample, there was no link between measures of disruptors and irritable discipline. In a multiple regression analysis of the mothers' data, both the marital adjustment and stressor measures were entered as independent variables. A multiple correlation value of 0.10 (n.s.) showed that these two variables were not significantly related to maternal irritable discipline practices. The comparable value of 0.22 (n.s.) for the paternal data bore a similar result (the beta for the stress variable was of borderline significance).

Future modelling studies might consider the interesting relation between parental antisocial and depression traits. Mothers who were antisocial also tended to report themselves as being depressed. This is of interest because it supports the findings from the longitudinal study reported by Robins (1984), who found that antisocial girls were at significant risk for adult depression. For the fathers, however, the variables that contributed significantly to self-reported depression scores were social competence and antisocial behaviour. Of the two variables, the former made a much more substantial contribution. It was decided that little would be gained by analysing the alternative model. These findings also imply that the direct effects (stress risk to irritable discipline) models described earlier may be limited to single-parent families, and perhaps to step-families.

Familial relationships and interactions

As discussed throughout this volume, an important issue for understanding familial adaptive processes is the affective tone of the relationships. Affect in relationships can be studied on a molecular level as specific emotional responses to interpersonal exchanges (Gottman and Levenson 1984; Radke-Yarrow *et al.*, Chapter 3, this volume). These affective reactions can be seen from the points of view of all participants in the dyad or triad. In the context of relationships, participants tend to summarize the history of the partnership in respect of their past and projected needs, yielding a global judgement of relationship satisfaction and acceptance of the dyadic or triadic partner. In the study and treatment of marital distress, the general dependent variable becomes marital satisfaction, a combined assessment of the husband's and wife's satisfaction with each other as marital partners. This can be thought of as the general affective tone of the relationship, and tends to be stable across time (Spanier 1976). Studies of marital interaction and treatment indicate that social interaction patterns reliably differentiate distressed from non-distressed relationships in terms of social reinforcement practices (Birchler *et al.* 1975) and reactivity to positive and negative behaviour (Jacobsen *et al.* 1982). We think a similar process unfolds for the parent–child dyad or triad, where both the parents and child become dissatisfied with their family counterpart.

Consistent with the position developed earlier by Patterson (1986), the affective outcome of the relationship is seen as generated by maladaptive social exchanges within the family. From developmental studies, it is impossible to test whether the parent–child relationship determines the microsocial process, or the reverse. However, from a clinical standpoint, the problem becomes more practical. Behavioural approaches to treatment of distressed families document improvements in relationship satisfaction as a consequence of improved communication skills, reinforcement skills, and conflict resolution skills (Patterson *et al.* 1975; Jacobson 1984). Consistent with the dialectical paradigm discussed by Hinde and Stevenson-Hinde (1987), most behaviour-ally-oriented clinicians will testify that the hard work of change becomes insurmountable given a certain level of relationship dissatisfaction, both in behavioural parent training and in marital therapy. In fact, occasionally the best advice for a distressed couple is to separate, as relationship satisfaction for the couple is unpredictable given their current dissatisfaction, expectations, history, competencies, and social context. Such decisions are much more difficult when it comes to distressed parent–child relationships, where the responsibility for change more clearly rests on the shoulders of the parent.

Empirical findings

We have addressed the empirical question of the role of relationships in the progression of the child's antisocial behaviour from age 10 to age 12, again using the data from OYS boys and families in Cohort 1 (Cohort 2 is not yet available for these ages). A structural equation modelling format was again used to test two basic alternative developmental models. The first model, consistent with the social interactional perspective, depicts the parents' acceptance of the child as a product of the child's problem behaviour (*Product Model*; Fig. 15.4). Parental irritable discipline is placed as the primary determinant of a child's antisocial trait, and this dispositional characteristic of the child leads to low parental acceptance.

The alternative model, the *Co-determinant* Model (see Fig. 15.4), places parental acceptance as an additional determinant of the child's antisocial behaviour, as might be seen from the dynamic of an attachment perspective (Bowlby 1969, 1973; Ainsworth *et al.* 1974; Sroufe and Fleeson 1986). A basic assumption in attachment theory is that social behaviour is, in part, a product of the underlying affective bond between the parent and child (see Chapters 2 and 13, this volume).

Our empirical definition of parental acceptance has shifted, and is now based on parental report of satisfaction with the child and the interviewer's perception of parental acceptance of the child. We have found measures of the parent–child relationship based on home observers' impressions of parental acceptance to be highly correlated with their perception of parental discipline. Thus, parents who use harsh, irritable, or explosive discipline are seen by observers as being rejecting towards the child. This is related to the problem of method variance in the definition and confirmatory testing of the identities of

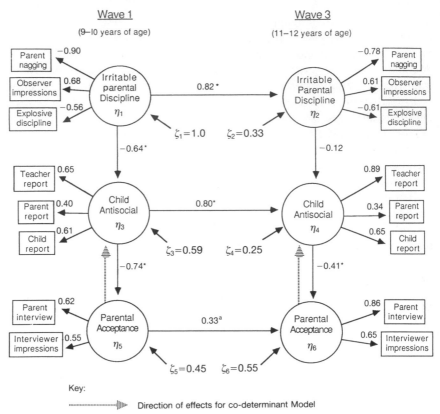

Key:

•••••••••••••••••••••••||||▶   Direction of effects for co-determinant Model

FIG. 15.4   Product Model; [a] $p < 0.10$; * $p < 0.05$.

constructs discussed by Bank *et al.* (in press). The solution we have adopted in this model is to define parental acceptance on the basis of parental report of the boy being:

(1) pleasant to raise;

(2) difficult to be patient with;

(3) whether the son tries to please others (has good intentions); and

(4) parental report of how well each gets along with the son.

The second indicator for parental acceptance is based on the interviewer's global impression of whether each parent 'seemed generally accepting of the son'.

   Contrasting the Product Model with the Co-determinant Model proved to be an instructive enterprise. In examining the overall goodness-of-fit index, the Product Model gave a slightly better fit ($\chi^2 = 106.9$, $df = 89$, $p = 0.10$)

compared with the Co-determinant Model, which is also shown in Fig. 15.4, with parent acceptance having a direct effect on Child Antisocial Behaviour ($\chi^2 = 110.04$, $df = 89$, $p = 0.07$). Because the two models do not afford any difference in degrees of freedom, it is difficult to compare them formally (Bentler and Bonnett 1980). However, a conservative test would be to examine the difference in χ^2 tests using one degree of freedom. In examining these two models, the difference in χ^2 values is 3.17, which is marginally significant when using one degree of freedom ($p < 0.10$). In addition, both longitudinal models adequately fit the observed correlations. Although the Product Model seemed to provide the most parsimonious fit, the patterns of findings in the Co-determinant Model have led us to consider more seriously the possibility of parental acceptance of the child as providing a context that may contribute to reducing antisocial behaviour. That is, in some sense, there may be some truth to both theoretical models in that the effect of parental acceptance may be bidirectional.

Implications

Following Hinde and Stevenson-Hinde (1987), the above analyses developed and tested theoretical hypotheses concerning the interrelation between multiple descriptive levels of family process from a social interactional theoretical framework. The data are consistent with the idea that disruptions in parental discipline may be the mechanism that is associated with antisocial behaviour in children. Parents who are irritable and explosive have been shown to be ineffective in changing antisocial child behaviour (Patterson 1982). On the other hand, training parents to back up threats and commands with effective discipline, such as work chores, time out, and point loss, have been shown to reduce significantly antisocial behaviour.

The data from the current study, as well as from the longitudinal study by Eron and his group, provided modest support for the idea that disrupted discipline by grandparents is correlated with antisocial behaviour in the following generation. However, the crucial data that would directly test for the correlation between disrupted discipline and antisocial behaviours across more than two generations are missing. The data assessing grandparental discipline practices employed in both our own studies and the studies by Elder and his group reply on retrospective reports by the persons being disciplined. The findings from both studies are consistent with the hypothesis, grandparents described as explosive and negative in their discipline practices produced children who were manifestly antisocial as adults. The best that can be said is that the data from all three studies are consistent with the idea that disrupted parental discipline in the first and second generation seems to be associated with antisocial traits in the second and third generations.

The data for the intact families studied here showed that the simple direct effects model for stress risk on parental irritable discipline did not fit. It seemed that stress risk was more relevant when considering paternal than maternal irritable discipline practices. Antisocial mothers tended to be more disrupted in their discipline practices, and stress risk was related only minimally to their antisocial trait and not at all to their irritable discipline practices or to their children's antisocial behaviour. For fathers, the data supported the hypothesis that current stressors may amplify current levels of antisocial behaviour in such a manner as to disrupt discipline practices further.

The analyses of the parent's acceptance of the child as a product of disrupted family interaction processes was generally supported by these data. However, the alternative hypothesis that low parental acceptance was a co-determinant of the child's antisocial behaviour was also marginally supported. To this extent, at the level of these data, the Product Model and Co-determinant Model are only marginally differentiated empirically. Perhaps a research design focusing on the parent–child relationship in more confined temporal units, such as moment-by-moment affective interchanges, or even on a month-by-month basis, might yield data describing the interrelation between the parent–child relationship and socialization practices. At this point, it seems reasonable to conclude a bidirectional effect between these two levels of description, consistent with the model provided by Hinde and Stevenson-Hinde (1987).

Acknowledgements

The writers gratefully acknowledge the support provided by the National Institute of Mental Health, section of Studies in Antisocial and Violent Behavior for grant MH 37940; and the National Institute of Alcohol Abuse, Family Mental Health and Policy Research Branch for grant MH 38318.

References

Ainsworth, M. D. S., Bell, S. M., and Stayton, D. J. (1974). Infant–mother attachment and social development: socialization as a product of reciprocal responsiveness to signals. In *The integration of the child into a social world* (ed. M. P. M. Richards). Cambridge University Press, London.

Aldwin, C. and Revenson, T. (1986). Vulnerability to economic stress. *American Journal of Community Psychology* **14,** (2), 161–75.

Bandura, A. (1973). *Aggression: a social learning analysis.* Prentice Hall, Engelwood Cliffs, NJ.

Bank, L., Dishion, T. J., Patterson, G. R., and Skinner, M. (in press). The glop problem in structural equation modeling. In *Family social interaction* (ed. G. R. Patterson). Erlbaum, Hillsdale, NJ.

Bentler, P. M. (1980). Multivariate analysis with latent variables: causal modeling. *Annual Review of Psychology* **31**, 419–55.

Bentler, P. M. and Bonnett, D. G. (1980). Significance tests and goodness of fit in the analysis of covariance structures. *Psychological Bulletin* **88**, 588–606.

Billings, A. G. and Moos, R. H. (1983). Comparisons of children of depressed and nondepressed parents: a social environmental perspective. *Journal of Abnormal Child Psychology* **11**, 463–86.

Birchler, G. R., Weiss, R. L., and Vincent, J. P. (1975). Multi-method analysis of social reinforcement exchange between marital distressed and nondistressed spouse and stranger dyads. *Journal of Personality and Social Psychology* **31**, (2), 349–60.

Block, J. H., Block, J., and Gjerde, T. F. (1986). The personality of children prior to divorce: a prospective study. *Child Development* **57**, 827–40.

Bone, M. (1977). *Preschool children and the need for day care: a survey carried out on behalf of the Department of Health and Social Security, Office of Population Census and Surveys, Social Survey Division.* Her Majesty's Stationery Office, London.

Bowlby, J. (1969). *Attachment and loss*, Vol. 1, *Attachment.* Hogarth Press, London.

Bowlby, J. (1973). *Attachment and loss*, Vol. 2, *Separation.* Hogarth Press, London.

Brown, G. R. and Harris, T. (1978). *Social origins of depression.* Tavistock, London.

Buss, D. M. and Craik, K. H. (1983). The act frequency approach to personality. *Psychological Review* **40**, (2), 105–26.

Cairns, R. B. (ed.) (1979). *The analysis of social interaction: methods, issues, and illustrations.* Erlbaum, Hillsdale, NJ.

Capaldi, D. and Patterson, G. R. (1987). Multiple comparisons of intact, stepfather, and single-mother families in family management practices and parent and child behaviors. Manuscript in preparation.

Caspi, A., Elder, G., and Bem, D. (1986). Moving against the world: life patterns of explosive children. Unpublished manuscript. (Available from G. Elder, Department of Psychology, University Square East, 300A, University of North Carolina, Chapel Hill, NC 27514.)

Cloninger, C. R. and Gottesman, I. I. (in press). Genetic and environmental factors in antisocial behavior disorders. In *Biosocial bases of antisocial behavior* (ed. S. Mednick, T. Moffitt, and D. Z. Lack). Cambridge University Press.

Depue, R. and Monroe, S. (1986). Conceptualization and measurement of human disorder in life stress research: the problem of chronic disturbance. *Psychological Bulletin* **99**, (1), 36–51.

Elder, G. H. and Clipp, E. C. (in press). Combat experience, comradeship, and psychological health. In *Human adaptation to extreme stress: from the holocaust to Vietnam* (ed. C. Figler). Brunner/Mazel, New York.

Elder, G., Van Nguyen, T., and Caspi, A. (1985a). Linking family hardship to children's lives. *Child Development* **56**, 361–75.

Elder, G. H., Caspi, A., and Downey, G. (1985b). Problem behavior and family relationships: a multigenerational analysis. In *Human development and the live course: multidisciplinary perspectives* (ed. A. Sorenson, F. Weinert, and L. Sherrod). Erlbaum, Hillsdale, NJ.

Elder, G., Caspi, A., and Van Nguyen, T. (in press). Resourceful and vulnerable children: family influences in hard times. In *Development in context: integrative perspectives on youth development* (ed. R. Silbereisen and K. Eyferth). Springer, NY.

Epstein, S. (1979). The stability of behavior: I. On predicting most of the people much of the time. *Journal of Personality and Social Psychology* **37**, (7), 1097–127.

Forgatch, M. S. (1987). A family process model for depression in mothers. NIMH proposal, submitted March 31, 1987. Oregon Social Learning Center, Eugene, Oreg.

Forgatch, M. S., Patterson, G. R., and Skinner, M. (in press). A mediational model for the effect of divorce on antisocial behavior in boys. *Impact of divorce, single parenting, and step-parenting on children* (ed. E. M. Hetherington and J. D. Arestah).

Gersten, J. C., Langner, T. S., Eisenberg, J. G., and Simcha-Fagan, O. (1977). An evaluation of the etiologic role of stressful life-change events in psychological disorders. *Journal of Health and Social Behavior* **18**, 228–44.

Gottman, J. M. and Levenson, R. W. (1984). Why marriages fail: affective and physiological patterns in marital interaction. In *Boundary areas in social and developmental psychology* (ed. J. C. Masters and K. Yarkin-Levin). pp. 67–106. Academic Press, New York.

Hinde, R. A. (1979). *Toward understanding relationships*. Academic Press, Ontario.

Hinde, R. A. and Stevenson-Hinde, J. (1987). Interpersonal relationships and child development. *Developmental Review* **7**, 1–21.

Hollingshead, A. B. (1975). Four factor index of social status. Unpublished manuscript. (Available from the author, Department of ' Sociology, Yale University, New Haven, Conn.)

Holmes, T. H. and Rahe, R. H. (1967). The social readjustment rating scale. *Journal of Psychosomatic Research* **11**, 213.

Hops, H., Biglan, A., Sherman, L., Arthur, J., Friedman, L., and Osteen, V. (1987). Home observations of family interactions of depressed women. *Journal of Consulting and Clinical Psychology* (in press).

Huesmann, L. R., Eron, L. D., Lefkowitz, M. N., and Walder, L. O. (1983). *The stability of aggression over time and generations*. Paper presented at the meeting of the Society for Research in Child Development, Detroit, Mich.

Jacobson, N. (1984). A component analysis of behavioral marital therapy: the relative effectiveness of behavior exchange and communication/problem–solving training. *Journal of Consulting and Clinical Psychology* **52**, (2), 295–305.

Jacobson, N. S., Follette, W. C., and McDonald, D. W. (1982). Reactivity of positive and negative behavior in distressed and nondistressed married couples. *Journal of Consulting and Clinical Psychology* **50**, 706–14.

Jöreskog, K. G., and Sörbom, D. (1983). *LISREL: analysis of linear structural relationships by the method of maximum likelihood* (2nd edn. Versions V and VI). International Education Services, Chicago.

Knutson, J. F., Mehm, J. G., and Berger, A. M. (1985). Is violence in the family passed from generation to generation? Manuscript in preparation. (Available from the first author, Department of Psychology, University of Iowa, Iowa City.)

Patterson, G. R. (1980). Mothers: the unacknowledged victims. *Monographs of the Society for Research in Child Development Monographs,* **45,** (5, Serial No. 186).

Patterson, G. R. (1982). *A social learning approach: 3. Coercive family process.* Castalia Publishing, Eugene, Oreg.

Patterson, G. R. (1985). Beyond technology: the next stage in developing an empirical base for parent training. In *The handbook of family psychology and therapy* (ed. L. L'Abate), pp. 1344–79. The Dorsey Press, Homewood, Ill.

Patterson, G. R. (1986). Performance models for antisocial boys. *American Psychologist* **41,** 432–44.

Patterson, G. R. and Bank, L. (1986). Bootstrapping your way in the nomological thicket. *Behavior Assessment* **8,** 49–73.

Patterson, G. R. and Bank, L. (in press). When is a nomological network a construct? In *Assessment for decision: psychology in action* (ed. D. R. Peterson and D. B. Fishman). Rutgers University Press, New Brunswick, NJ.

Patterson, G. R. and Chamberlain, P. (in press). Treatment process: a problem at three levels. In *State of the art in therapy research: controversies and recommendations* (ed. L. Wynn).

Patterson, G. R. and Reid, J. B. (1984). Social interactional processes within the family: the study of moment-by-moment family transactions in which human social development is embedded. *Journal of Applied Developmental Psychology* **5,** 237–62.

Patterson, G. R., Hops, H., and Weiss, R. L. (1975). Interpersonal skills training for couples in early stages of conflict. *Journal of Marriage and the Family* **37,** 295–303.

Patterson, G. R., Dishion, T. J., and Bank, L. (1984). Family interaction: a process model of deviance training. *Aggressive Behavior* **10,** (special edn. ed. L. Eron), 253–67.

Patterson, G. R., Reid, J. B., and Dishion, T. J. (in press). *A social learning approach: 4. Antisocial boys.* Castalia Publishing, Eugene, Oreg.

Plomin, R. (1986). *Genetics, development and psychology.* Erlbaum, Hillsdale, NJ.

Pollock, V., Mednick, S., and Gabrielli, W. (1987). Crime causation: biological theories, In *The encyclopedia of crime and justice.* Macmillan and the Free Press, New York.

Quinton, D. and Rutter, M. (1983). Parenting behaviour of mothers raised 'in care'. In *Practical lessons from longitudinal studies* (ed. R. Nicol). Wiley, Chichester, England.

Radke-Yarrow, M., Cummings, E. M., Kuczynski, L., and Chapman, M. (1985). Patterns of attachment in two and three year olds in normal families and families with parental depression. *Child Development* **56,** 884–93.

Reid, J. B., Bank, L., and Patterson, G. R. (1987). *Models of the mind.* Paper presented at the biennial meeting of the Society for Research in Child Development, Baltimore, Md.

Robins, L. N., (1984). Conduct disorders in adult psychiatric diagnosis. Unpublished manuscript. (Available from the author, Department of Psychiatry, School of Medicine, Washington University, St. Louis, MO 63130).

Robins, L. N. and Earls, F. (1986). A program for preventing antisocial behavior for high risk infants and preschoolers: a research perspective. In *Psychiatric epidemiology and prevention: the possibilities* (ed. R. Hough, P. Gongola, V. Brown, and S. Goldston). Neuropsychiatric Institute, UCLA, Los Angeles.

Robins, L. N., West, P. A., and Herjanc, B. L. (1975). Arrests and delinquency in two generations: a study of black urban families and their children. *Journal of Child Psychology and Psychiatry* **16**, 125–40.

Rowe, D. C. and Plomin, R. (1981). The importance of nonshared environmental influences on behavioral development. *Developmental Psychology* **17**, 317–31.

Scarr, S. (1985). Constructing psychology: making facts and fables for our times. *American Psychologist* **40**, 499–512.

Spanier, G. B. (1976). Measuring dyadic adjustment: new scales for assessing the quality of marriage and similar dyads. *Journal of Marriage and the Family* **38**, 15–28.

Sroufe, L. A. and Fleeson, J. (1986). Attachment and the construction of relationships. In *Relationships and development* (ed. W. Hartup and Z. Rubin), pp. 51–72. Erlbaum, Hillsdale, NJ.

Suomi, S. J. and Harlow, H. F. (1972). Social rehabilitation of isolate rearing monkeys. *Developmental Psychology* **6**, 487–96.

Viken, R. (1987). Stress, family process, and child antisocial behaviour. Manuscript in preparation. (Available from the author, Department of Psychology, Indiana University, Bloomington, IN 47405.)

16

Parents, children, and siblings: six years after divorce
E. MAVIS HETHERINGTON

In the past 15 years an accumulating body of relatively well-designed research has focused on the impact of divorce on the adjustment of parents and children and on the role of changing life experiences and family relationships that mediate positive or negative outcomes (Hetherington *et al.* 1982; Forgatch 1987; Hetherington 1987, in press). In the period immediately surrounding separation and divorce, most family members experience emotional distress and disrupted functioning. However, if the aftermath of divorce is not compounded by continued or additional stressors, both parents and children are able to adapt to their new life situation within 2–3 years following divorce. The adverse effects of divorce are more intense and enduring for boys than for girls, although there have been some reports of delayed effects in the form of rebellious behaviour, depression, and disruptions in heterosexual relations emerging in adolescent girls (Hetherington 1972; Wallerstein 1987). Moreover, when differences between children in divorced and non-divorced families are found, they are most likely to be obtained in externalizing disorders involving poor impulse control, aggression, and non-compliance and in achievement deficits rather than in internalizing disorders or disruptions in self-esteem. Finally, when such behaviours occur they tend to be found not only in the home but also in the school and in peer relationships, and are correlated with inept parenting on the part of the custodial parent (Hetherington *et al.* 1982; Forgatch 1987). It should be kept in mind that most studies of divorce involve mother custody homes, and it has been found that elementary-school-aged children manifest fewer behaviour problems when they are in the custody of a parent of the same sex (Warshak and Santrock 1983; Peterson and Zill 1986).

In contrast to the substantial research literature on divorce, there is a paucity of studies on remarriage. The available research indicates that although the behaviour of both boys and girls may be disrupted initially by the addition of a stepparent to the family, boys often benefit from the presence of a stepfather. However, girls appear to have more long-term difficulty adjusting to either a stepfather or stepmother than do boys, and show more behaviour problems than do girls in non-divorced families (Hetherington *et al.* 1985; Brand *et al.* 1987; Bray 1986). Furthermore, younger children or older adolescents and young adults more readily accept and benefit from a stepparent than do early adolescents. The age period from 9 to 15 seems to be a particularly difficult one in which to gain acceptance of a remarriage and stepparent by children (Hetherington *et al.* in press). Finally, the relationships and behaviour within the family that mediate positive or negative outcomes for children are sometimes found to differ between non-divorced and remarried families.

Although we have some information about relationships among family members and within family subsystems, such as the husband–wife dyad or the parent–child dyad, in divorced and remarried families, little is known about sibling relationships. Moreover, the few reports available present contradictory findings. Some clinical studies report enhanced sibling relationships (Bank and Kahn 1982*a*, *b*; Wallerstein 1987) and other studies find few differences between sibling relationships in divorced and non-divorced families (Anderson 1986). These studies have usually involved assessments of siblings beyond the crisis period in the first few years of divorce. It seems likely that siblings will adjust to marital transitions over time. In contrast to the findings on divorce, a recent study found that biological siblings in stepfamilies were less mutually involved and empathic, more avoidant and aggressive, and showed more rivalry than siblings with non-divorced parents (Anderson 1986). This was particularly marked when one of the siblings involved was a boy. It should be noted that these data refer to the first seven months following remarriage and involved early adolescents: such reponses may well vary with the age of the child. Thus it has been suggested that, even in non-divorced families, middle childhood and early adolescence are periods in which sibling relationships are characterized by high ambivalence involving both sibling facilitation and interference (Bryant 1982).

This paper presents part of the findings from a longitudinal study of divorce. Children, who initially resided in mother-custody households, and their divorced parents were studied at two months, one year, two years and six years following divorce. In this paper we will examine family functioning and family relationships at six years following divorce in an expanded sample of 180 families, including 124 of the families from the original 144 who began in the study. A summary of the results of the first two years of the project are reported in Hetherington *et al.* (1982). A more detailed report on the marital relationship, parent–child relationships, and child outcomes six years following divorce can be found in Hetherington (1987, in press) and Hetherington *et al.* (1985).

It was found that during the first two years following divorce most children and many parents experienced emotional distress, psychological and behavioural problems, disruptions in family functioning, and problems in adjusting to the new roles, relationships, and life changes associated with their altered family situation. However, as reported in other studies, by two years following divorce the majority of parents and children were adapting reasonably well and certainly were showing great improvement since the time of the divorce. In the two-year assessment period in this study some continuing problems were found in the adjustment of boys and in the relationships between divorced custodial mothers and their sons. In comparison with boys in non-divorced families, these boys from divorced families showed more antisocial, acting out, coercive, and non-compliant behaviours in the home and in the school, and exhibited difficulties in peer relationships and school achievement. By contrast, girls from divorced families were functioning well and had positive relationships with their custodial mothers.

In considering these results two things must be kept in mind. First, this study involves mother-custody families, and there is some evidence that children may adjust better in the custody of a parent of the same sex (Warshak and Santrock 1983; Santrock and Warshak 1986). Secondly, age of the child may be an important factor in sex differences in children's responses to divorce. In this study, children were an average age of 4 years at the beginning of the study, 6 at the two-year assessment, and 10 at the time of the six-year assessment, with an approximate range of a year at each assessment point. Reports of more severe and long-lasting disruption of behaviour in boys than girls following their parents' divorce have tended to come from studies of pre-adolescent children. However, our children were just entering adolescence at the time of the six-year follow-up and, as mentioned earlier, this is a time when behaviour problems in girls and in parent–child relations in divorced mother-custody families may emerge (Hetherington 1972; Wallerstein 1987).

Attempts to assess the long-term effects of divorce on parents and children, and the factors that mediate these outcomes, face the difficulty that family members encounter widely varying sequences of family reorganizations and family experiences following divorce. For most parents and children divorce is only one in a series of family transitions that follow separation. Life in a single-parent household following divorce is usually a temporary condition since 80 per cent of men and 75 per cent of women will remarry. About 30 per cent of American children will spend some time in a stepparent family before they are young adults. Moreover, since the divorce rate is higher in remarriages than in first marriages, some parents and children encounter a series of divorces, periods in a one-parent household, and remarriages. These shifts in marital arrangements were a problem encountered in the six-year follow-up in this study.

Method

Subjects

The original sample was composed of 144 middle-class White children and their parents. Half of the children were from divorced, mother-custody families, and the other half were from non-divorced families. Within each group, half were boys and half were girls. All were first- or second-born children.

In the six-year follow-up the subjects included residential parents and children in 124 of the original families who were available and willing to continue to participate in the study. In the 60 available originally divorced families, 42 of the custodial mothers had remarried; and of the 64 originally non-divorced families, only 53 were still married (see Hetherington 1987 for more details on the composition of this sample).

To these participating original families on whom there was complete data (except for non-custodial father measures) were added other families, in order to expand the size of the groups to 30 sons and 30 daughters in each of three groups—a remarried mother/stepfather group, a non-remarried mother-custody group, and a non-divorced group—for a total of 180 families. For some analyses, the remarried group was broken down into those remarried less than two years and those remarried longer than two years. The additional subjects were matched with the original subjects on age, education, income, religion, length of marriage and, when appropriate, length of time since divorce and time of remarriage.

For the sibling comparisons in this study, the sibling closest in age to the target child was selected, and only siblings less than three years apart in age were used. The average age separation was 22 months. This resulted in 166 biological sibling pairs approximately equally distributed across same sex male and female sibling pairs, opposite sexed pairs, and across family types.

The cross-sectional analyses of child and parent adjustment and of the relations among family interaction, child adjustment, parent adjustment, and marital adjustment in this paper utilize the expanded sample. Inconsistencies between the six-year follow-up data reported in Hetherington et al. (1982) and in this paper occur because the first paper used only the original sample and this paper uses the expanded sample.

Procedure and analysis

Data on parent–child relationships reported in this paper were based on interviews of the mother, father, target child, and sibling, and in direct observations in the home of the family, of free interactions, and of structured family-problem-solving tasks involving various dyadic, triadic, and tetradic combinations of family members. In addition, on 10 different occasions residential parents and children were asked to record and report in a telephone interview whether certain events had occurred in the past 24 hours. The 24-hour behaviour checklist was designed to assess problem behaviour and desirable behaviour in the child, conflict and conflict resolution, parental discipline, warmth/involvement and monitoring, and positive and negative behaviour with siblings. More details on these measures and parent–child relationships are available in Hetherington (1987, in press). In addition, both spouses took the Dyadic Adjustment Scale (Spanier 1976) which yields an overall measure of marital satisfaction and subscales assessing satisfaction, consensus, cohesiveness, and expressiveness.

A Sibling Relations Inventory was developed using five-point Likert scales and was completed by parents and siblings. The Cronbach alphas for the internal consistency of seven inventory scales ranged from 0.72 to 0.89. Test/re-test reliabilities for the inventory administered one month apart averaged 0.79 for parents and 0.66 for children in the age range of this study. The scales on the inventory are similar to some of those developed by Furman (Furman *et al.*, in press) and by Schaefer and Edgerton (1981). These are involvement, warmth/empathy, rivalry, conflict/aggression, avoidance, coercive power/control, positive power/control.

First- and second-order factor analyses with oblique rotation and internal consistency analysis involving interview, 24-hour-behaviour checklist, observational measures, observer impressions, and test measures were used to develop subscales of parenting behaviour, husband–wife relationships, and the child's relationships to parents and siblings. Separate analyses were performed for each set of measures and for fathers', mothers', and children's reports. Finally, factor analyses involving multiple data sources were done on the standardized scores from the factors on the first set of analyses.

The composite sibling relationship dimensions across multiple measures were involvement, warmth/empathy, avoidance, rivalry, aggression/coercion, power/control, communicates/facilitates.

The children's interactions with their parents yielded somewhat different factors. These were aggression/coercion, warmth/involvement, power, disengaged/withdrawn, prosocial behaviour, and negative mood.

The parenting dimensions were warmth/responsiveness, including expressive affection, social involvement, and instrumental involvement; control, including rule setting, firmness, and power; monitoring, including monitoring strategies and successful monitoring; conflict/irritability, including coercion, punitiveness, negative mood, conflict over parental authority, conflict over household and personal issues, and conflict over character development; and, finally, maturity demands, involving both maturity expectations and maturity enforcement. These factors resemble, but are not identical to, those found in another ongoing longitudinal study of remarriage and divorce (Hetherington and Clingempeel 1986).

Multivariate analyses, followed by univariate analyses of significant multivariate effects with sex of the child and family type as the independent measures, were performed on the individual and composite indices of parent and child behaviour. In addition, analyses were performed for factors derived separately from mothers', fathers', and children's reports. It was thought to be important to examine reports from individual family members as well as the composite measures, since differences between the perceptions of family members are often important indicators of family dynamics and discrepant perceptions have been found to be related to family conflict (Hagan 1986) and marital distress (Gottman 1979).

Parent–child relationships

How do non-divorced, divorced non-remarried, and remarried mothers behave with their early adolescent children? The findings of our study suggest that mother–son relationships were problematic in the divorced non-remarried families as were those between parents and children in the early stage of remarriage, particularly those involving stepdaughters. It is important to note that these divorced non-remarried families were what we might call stabilized divorced families. The parents had been divorced for six years and the families were well beyond the two- or three-year crisis period following divorce. However, six years after divorce, divorced non-remarried mothers were continuing to exhibit with their sons many of the behaviours that were seen two years after divorce. Although interview and observational measures suggest that there were few differences among the three groups of mothers in the physical and verbal affection they directed toward their children, divorced mothers with sons tended to spend less time with their sons and reported feeling less rapport or closeness to them. In addition, mothers in all three family types showed more expressive affection toward girls than toward boys.

It was more differences in control attempts and in punitive, coercive behaviours than in warmth and affection that distinguished divorced non-remarried mothers from mothers in the other family types. These divorced mothers were ineffectual in their control attempts and gave many instructions with little follow-through. They tended to nag, natter, and complain to their sons. Although these divorced mothers were as physically and verbally affectionate with their children as were mothers in the other family groups, they more often got involved with their sons in angry, escalating coercive cycles. Spontaneous negative start-ups, that is negative behaviour initiated following neutral or positive behaviour by the other person, were twice as likely to occur with mothers and sons in divorced families as with those in non-divorced families. Moreover, once these negative interchanges between divorced non-remarried mothers and sons occurred they were likely to continue significantly longer than in any other dyad in any family type. The probability of continuance of a negative response was higher in the divorced non-remarried mother–son dyad than in any other parent–child dyad, with the exception of daughters' behaviour toward stepfathers in the early stage of remarriage. It should be noted that the sons of divorced non-remarried women recognize their own aggressive, non-compliant behaviours and reported that their mothers had little control over their behaviour; however, they also reported and exhibited reasonably high levels of warmth toward their mothers. It might be best to view this relationship between divorced non-remarried mothers and sons as intense and ambivalent rather than as purely hostile and rejecting.

Both sons and daughters in divorced non-remarried families were allowed more responsibility, independence, and power in decision making than were children in non-divorced families. They successfully interrupted their divorced mothers, and their mothers yielded to their demands more often than in the other family types. In some cases this greater power and independence resulted in an egalitarian mutually supportive relationship. In other cases, where the emotional demands or responsibilities required by the mother were inappropriate, were beyond the capabilities of the child, or interfered with normal activities of the child, such as in peer relationship or school activities, resentment, rebellion, or psychological disturbance might follow.

Finally, divorced non-remarried mothers monitored their children's behaviour less closely than did mothers in non-divorced families. They knew less about where their children were, who they were with, and what they were doing than did mothers in two-parent households. Boys in these divorced families on their 24-hour behaviour checklists reported being involved in more antisocial behaviour that the mother did not know about than did children in any other group, although this discrepancy was also high in the mother–daughter reports in the stepfamily groups. In addition, children in the one-parent households were less likely than those in the two-parent households to have adult supervision in their parent's absence. Both Robert Weiss (1975) and Wallerstein and Kelly (1980) report that one way that children may cope with their parents' divorce is by becoming disengaged from the family. In this study, boys from divorced non-remarried families were spending significantly less time in the home with their parents or other adults and more time alone or with peers than were any of the other groups of children. In addition, stepsons also were significantly more disengaged than were sons in non-divorced families.

In contrast to divorced non-remarried mothers and sons, there were few differences between the relationships of divorced non-remarried mothers with their daughters and those of mothers and daughters in non-divorced families. However, girls in divorced one-parent households did have more power and were assigned more responsibilities. They did, in the words of Robert Weiss

(1975), 'grow up faster'. Mothers and daughters in mother-headed families six years after divorce expressed considerable satisfaction with their relationship. However, there was an exception to this happy picture. Interview measures of pubescent status had been obtained from the parents and their children, and interviewers had made ratings of pubescent status. As might be expected, few children had entered puberty by this time since they were only aged 10; however, 26 of our 90 girls were early maturers, and showed some signs of impending puberty. In all three family types, family conflict was higher for these early-maturing girls than for late-maturing girls, and was most marked betwen mothers and daughters in the single-parent households. Early maturity in girls was associated with a premature weakening of the mother–child bonds. These early-maturing girls, especially in the mother-headed families, were alienated and disengaged from their families, talked less to their mothers but interrupted them more and became involved in activities with older peers. Past research suggests that divorced mothers and daughters may experience problems as daughters become pubescent and involved in heterosexual activities (Hetherington 1972). The difficulties in interactions between these early-maturing girls and their divorced non-remarried mothers may be precursors of more intense problems yet to come.

In looking at stepfamilies it is important to distinguish between those families in the early stages of remarriage, when they are still adapting to their new situation, and those in the later stages of remarriage, when family roles and relationships should have been worked through and established. In some ways the early stage of remarriage may be a honeymoon period when the parents, if not the children, want to make the family relationships successful. In discussing stepfamilies it becomes particularly important to identify which family member's perspective is being discussed, since these may vary widely. Family members agreed that mothers in remarried families were as warm to their children as were mothers in other types of families. However, such mothers saw themselves as having more control over their children's behaviour than they were seen as having by either the children or stepfathers. Both interview and observational data indicated that they had greater control over their sons than was found in the one-parent households, but less than that found in non-divorced families. Moreover, they had less control over their daughters than was found in mothers in either of the other two family types. Control over both sons and daughters was greater for mothers who had been remarried more than two years. In the first two years following remarriage, conflict betwen mothers and daughters was high. In addition, these daughters were more demanding, hostile, coercive, and less warm toward both parents than girls in mother-only or non-divorced families. Their behaviour improved over the course of remarriage, however, even two years after remarriage these girls were still more antagonistic and disruptive with their parents than were girls in the other two family types. This greater negativity in the behaviour of stepdaughters was supported by the report of both parents and children and by the observational measures.

In contrast to biological fathers, stepfathers were more likely to be disengaged and less likely to have an authoritative parenting style involving warm, responsive but firm discipline and good communication. Disengaged parents were characterized by low involvement, warmth, monitoring, control, and maturity demands, and by high hostility when children were persistent in their needs. They were adult-oriented parents who wanted to minimize the amount of time, effort, and interference with their needs that child-rearing entails.

Although authoritative parenting by stepfathers increased over time for boys, authoritative behaviour by stepfathers with daughters decreased and disengagement doubled as the remarriage continued. In addition, even for boys after two years of remarriage, disengagement remained the predominant parenting style of stepfathers. Even when the remarriage was longer than two years many stepfathers did not mention their stepchildren when asked to identify the members of their families.

During the first two years following remarriage stepfathers reported themselves to be low on felt or expressed affection for their stepchildren, although they spent time with them attempting to establish a relationship. They expressed less strong positive affect and showed fewer negative, critical responses than did the non-divorced fathers. Biological fathers were freer both in expressing affection and in criticizing their children for poor personal grooming, for not doing their homework, not cleaning up their rooms, or for fighting with their siblings. However, they also were more involved and interested in the activities of their children. Initially, stepfathers were far less supportive to stepsons than to stepdaughters. In the interactions during the first two years of the remarriage the stepfather's interaction was almost that of a stranger who was attempting to be ingratiating, was seeking information, and was polite but emotionally disengaged. During this stage of the remarriage stepfathers remained relatively pleasant in spite of the aversive behaviour they encountered from their stepdaughters. By two years after remarriage they were more impatient. Athough they tried to remain disengaged, they occasionally got into extremely angry interchanges with their stepdaughters. These conflicts tended to focus on issues of parental authority and respect for the mother. Stepdaughters viewed their stepfathers as hostile, punitive, and unreasonable on matters of discipline. The interchanges between stepfathers and stepdaughters and the conflicts between divorced non-remarried mothers and sons and early-maturing daughters were rated as the highest on hostility of any dyad. Stepfathers made significantly fewer control attempts and were less successful in gaining control with both sons and daughters than were non-divorced fathers. Their control of stepsons, but not of stepdaughters, was better in longer remarriages.

In contrast to the effects of parenting styles of non-divorced fathers, both authoritative and authoritarian parenting involving hostile, rigid control by stepfathers was related to high rates of behaviour problems in both stepdaughters and in stepsons in the first two years of remarriage. After two years, authoritative parenting by stepfathers was related to fewer behaviour problems and greater acceptance of the stepfather by stepsons, but was not, at this time, significantly related to stepdaughters' behaviour. In general, the best strategy of a stepfather to gain acceptance by stepchildren seems to be one where there is no initial active attempt to take over and/or actively to control the child's behaviour, either through authoritarian or the more desirable authoritative techniques. Instead, the new father should first work at establishing a relationship with the child and support the mother in her parenting. This period can be effectively followed later by more active authoritative parenting, which leads to constructive outcomes, at least for boys.

The outcomes for stepsons were very different from those for stepdaughters. Although mothers and stepfathers viewed sons as initially being extremely difficult, their behaviour improved over time. In the families who had been remarried for over two years, these boys were showing no more aggressive, non-compliant behaviour in the home or problem behaviours, as measured on tests such as the Children's Behavior Checklist, than were boys in non-divorced families (see Hetherington et al. 1985 for more details on the adjustment of children). However, mothers, sons, and teachers reported these boys more positively than did stepfathers. Although stepfathers continued to view stepchildren, especially stepdaughters, as having many more problems than nondivorced fathers see their children as having, they reported improvement in their stepchildren's behaviour. Some of the stepsons in the longer-remarried families reported being close to their stepfathers, enjoying their company and seeking their advice and support. As was found in divorced non-remarried families, monitoring of children's behaviour was often not effective in stepfamilies. It should be noted that this salutary long-term effect of remarriage on boys may be confined to pre-adolescent boys. In a study of early adolescents, both boys and girls in stepfather families were exhibiting excessively high rates of behavioural disorders (Hetherington and Clingem-peel 1986).

Marital relationships and parent–child relationships

It has been proposed that the marital relationship may affect the parents' well-being, their relationships with their children, and consequently their children's adjustment (Belsky 1984; for more details on these relationships see Hetherington 1987, in press). The marital relationships in first marriages and in remarriages were more notable for their similarities than for their differences, especially with couples who had been remarried for more than two years. Two important exceptions to this occurred. The first was that on the Dyadic Adjustment Scale parents in remarried families reported their relationships to be less cohesive. The second was that there was more conflict about children and about financial matters relating to children in stepfamilies than in non-divorced families.

In addition, different correlations between closeness and satisfaction in marital relationships and children's responses were found in non-divorced and in remarried families. For non-divorced couples, a close marital relationship and support by the spouse in child-rearing were related to parental warmth and involvement and low parental–child conflict. However, in the stepfamilies there occurred what might appear to be an anomalous finding. In contrast to non-divorced families, a close marital relationship and active involvement in parenting by the stepfather were associated with high levels of parent–child conflict involving both mothers and stepfathers, especially when the stepchild was a girl. For sons this relation was significant in the early but not later stages of remarriage. How can we explain these unexpected results? It seems likely that in the early stages of remarriage the new stepfather is viewed as an intruder or a competitor for the mother's affection. Since boys in divorced families often have been involved in coercive or ambivalent relationships with their mothers, in the long run they may have little to lose and something to gain from the remarriage. In contrast, daughters in one-parent families have played more responsible, powerful roles than girls in non-divorced families and have had more positive relationships with their divorced non-remarried mothers than have sons. They may see both their independence and their relationship with the mother threatened by the introduction of the stepfather and therefore resent the mother for remarrying. Evidence for this was found in the very high correlation between closeness to the mother before the remarriage and subsequent conflict with the mother ($r = 0.65$, $p < 0.001$) and stepfather ($r = 0.71$, $p < 0.001$). This was reflected in resistant, ignoring, critical behaviour by the daughter toward her remarried mother. In addition, it was reflected in the sulky, negativistic, hostile behaviour observed in step-daughters with their stepfathers and in the girls' own reports of their negative, rejecting attitudes toward the stepfathers. It was notable that the positive behaviour of the stepfathers toward stepdaughters did not correlate with daughters' acceptance of stepfathers in the early stages of remarriage. No matter now hard the stepfathers tried, the daughters rejected them.

Finally, let us turn to the relation between the marital relationship, spousal support and children's adjustment. In non-divorced families, marital satisfaction, active involvement of the father in child-rearing, and the father's support of the mother in her child-rearing role were related to less externalizing behaviour in boys and greater social competence in both boys and girls. In these families active involvement of the mother in child-rearing and her support of the father in child-rearing also were related to lower externalizing in boys. No other relations between maternal support of the father and child outcomes were found. In the longer-remarried families, support of the mother in her child-rearing role and participation in child-rearing, not mainly as a disciplinarian but in the role of a friend and confidant, by the stepfather also led to less externalizing behaviour in boys. Boys from the small group of authoritative stepfathers in the longer-remarried group had fewer total behaviour problems than did boys with stepfathers having other parenting styles. In contrast, active participation in child-rearing by the stepfather and a close marital relationship actually led to an increase in acting out behaviour and in depression in stepdaughters.

Sibling relationships

So far we have focused on the marital relationships and parent–child relationships. We turn now to sibling relationships in non-divorced, divorced non-remarried, and remarried families.

Two alternative hypotheses might be offered about siblings' experiences of their parents' marital transitions. One would be that siblings will become increasingly hostile and show more rivalry as they compete for scarce resources of parental love and attention following their parents' divorce or remarriage. Many investigators have commented on the period of diminished parenting, characterized by decreased involvement and affection and increased irritability and punitive behaviours by custodial mothers, that follows shortly after separation and divorce (Wallerstein and Kelly 1980; Hetherington et al. 1982). Similarly, children may perceive less availability and affection of the custodial mother and loss of personal power and independence with the introduction of a stepfather.

An alternative hypothesis would be that siblings in families that have gone through marital transitions will view relationships with adults as unstable, untrustworthy, and painful and will turn to each other for sources of solace, support, and alliances. Bank and Kahn (1982a, b) have suggested that under highly specific conditions involving an early harmonious family relationship and a close relationship with one parent, parental loss can result in intense sibling loyalties.

Preliminary analyses indicated that whether the target sibling was older or younger contributed significantly only to differences in power. Positive power or status which involved such things as teaching, being imitated by the sibling, and admiration by the sibling was higher for both older sisters and brothers. Not surprisingly, first-born children saw themselves, and were seen by their parents, as having more positive power. Negative power which involves gaining control through coercion, being bossy, nagging, and physical power was higher for older brothers than older sisters. This was because older brothers were likely to use highly salient types of physical power such as chasing, hitting, and wrestling. Since no other differences related to birth order were found, in all further analyses older and younger target siblings were combined.

Four main findings were apparent. First, siblings in stepfamilies exhibited and were viewed as having more problematic relationships than siblings in non-divorced or divorced families. Second, stepfathers tended to rate sibling relationships between their stepchildren more negatively than did other family members, and mothers tended to rate boys' problems with siblings as more severe than those of girls. Third, any sibling dyad involving a boy was reported and observed to be more troubled than those involving only girls. Not only were boys seen as exhibiting more aversive behaviours than girls, but girls behaved in a less congenial fashion when interacting with brothers than sisters. Finally, as can be seen in Table 16.1, there were fairly consistent relations among the negative behaviours of siblings, few relations among positive behaviours, and few significant correlations between negative and positive behaviours.

Fewer positive behaviours and more negative behaviours were found in sibling interactions in stepfamilies than in non-divorced families. Reports on the Siblings Relations Inventory indicated that all family members perceived siblings in non-divorced families to exhibit more positive power, involvement, and warmth than those in stepfamilies. However, mothers and children reported stepsons to be significantly lower than stepdaughters on these attributes, whereas stepfathers saw no differences between stepsons and stepdaughters. In the stepfamilies, the lowest levels of positive power, warmth, and involvement and the highest in aggression, coercive power, and avoidance were reported when the sibling was a brother. Stepfathers and stepchildren saw sibling relationships as more rivalrous, aggressive, and avoidant than those in non-divorced families. Mothers in stepfamilies saw these character-istics as being greater only in sons. Children and stepfathers saw stepdaughters as more avoidant than stepsons in their relationships with siblings.

Stepchildren also were observed to be less warm, more aggressive and competitive, and more avoidant than siblings in other groups, with the one exception that sons in divorced families were more aggressive and coercive than any other group of children. In addition, boys in divorced families showed more rivalry than those in non-divorced families. Negative start-ups, reciprocated aggression, and long chains of aggressive coercive behaviour with siblings were more common in stepchildren than in children in non-divorced families, and were most frequently found in sons in divorced families. Again, such behaviour was higher if the target child was interacting with a male sibling.

Table 16.1 *Significant relations between target child and sibling behaviours*

	Target child						
Sibling	Involvement	Warmth/ empathy	Communicates/ facilitates	Power/ control	Avoidance	Rivalry	Aggression/ coercion
Involvement					−0.32*		
Warmth/empathy		0.32*					
Communicates/facilitates				−0.28*			
Power/control			−0.31*	−0.68*			
Avoidance	−0.35*				0.41**	0.38**	0.46**
Rivalry					0.47**	0.52**	0.49**
Aggression/coercion					0.55**	0.46**	0.65**

Pearson coefficients: * $p < 0.01$ two-tailed; ** $p < 0.001$ two-tailed. ($n = 166$).

Stepdaughters spent less time in active interaction with their siblings than did other children. They were observed to be less likely to initiate conversation or activities and more likely to refuse or ignore overtures on the part of the sibling, especially if it was a boy. Both children and stepfathers also reported that stepdaughters were more avoidant than stepsons in their relationships with siblings. In contrast, daughters in divorced non-remarried families were more involved in teaching and play activities with their female siblings than were other daughters. However, they also were seen to communicate less well with their brothers.

In summary, in the observational measures, inventory measures, and 24-hour checklists there was a marked pattern occurring across family types, but particularly in stepfamilies and divorced non-remarried families, for interactions with male siblings to be more agonistic, rivalrous, and less supportive. In addition, an interesting pattern emerged for siblings in divorced non-remarried families. In spite of the greater aggression found in boys in these families, both boys and girls in divorced non-remarried families were warmer, more involved, and less avoidant of their siblings than were children in stepfamilies. In addition, girls in divorced non-remarried families were observed to be more involved with their female siblings but to communicate less positively with their brothers than did children in non-divorced families.

Earlier it was speculated that time since a marital transition has occurred may be a critical factor in family relationships. In this study it was found to be important in both marital relationships and parent–child relationships. How might it be related to sibling interactions? Analyses involving sex of child and family type, with stepfamilies split into those in the first two years of remarriage and those married longer, were done separately for the target child and the sibling. It was found in the longer-remarried families that aggression in siblings had decreased to the level of that found in nuclear families. However, although rivalry also had significantly decreased, it remained higher than that in nuclear families, and stepdaughters remained more avoidant and disengaged from their siblings, especially if the sibling was a brother. Thus, although sibling relationships in stepfamilies were more disturbed in the period immediately following remarriage and improved, especially for boys, as the children adjusted to their new life situation, they remained more disrupted than those in non-divorced families.

No systematic sibling data had been collected in the first three waves of this project. However, as part of a class project, ratings of sibling relationships had been made one year after divorce. At that time both male and female siblings, but especially boys in divorced non-remarried families, were seen as less affectionate, more rivalrous, and more aggressive than those in nuclear families. Daughters of divorced mothers who did not remarry certainly had improved in their sibling relationships, whereas less improvement was found in the sibling relationships of sons.

Typologies of sibling relationships

A cluster analysis to identify styles of sibling relationships was performed on inventory, observer impressions, molecular observation measures, 24-hour checklists, and selected interview measures. Four clusters emerged. The first was a small cluster which included less than 10 per cent of our children and which was characterized by very high warmth, involvement, and communication, and very low rivalry and aggression. These children spent little time playing with other children, most of their time with each other, were interdependent and asked each other's advice on most issues, and were fiercely protective of each other. Although they were nurturant and empathetic with each other, they often showed little sensitivity or concern with the feelings of adults or peers. They scored moderately high on internalizing and were often in the neglected but not rejected group on peer nominations. Although, this might seem to be Bank and Kahn's intense loyalty cluster, we called it an *enmeshed* relationship since it seemed to be a pathologically intense, symbiotic, and restrictive relationship. Moreover, it did not occur under the conditions of an early close parental relationship proposed by Bank and Kahn. These enmeshed siblings were most likely to be girls, and to be found in divorced non-remarried or remarried families and in families where the child had no regular contact or involvement with an affectionate involved adult. This enmeshment, then, tends to occur under stressful life conditions without available adult support.

The second cluster, labelled *companionate-caring*, was related to moderate involvement and high warmth and empathy, open communication and moderately low aggression and rivalry, and included about 33 per cent of our siblings. This was found most often in non-divorced families, and in families with authoritative biological parents. In addition, more girls than boys in divorced families were found in this group. It was associated with positive peer relationships, high academic achievement, positive self-concepts, and low rates of externalizing and total behaviour problems on Achenbach's Children's Behavior Checklist.

The third cluster, labelled *ambivalent*, was characterized by high rivalry and aggression, and moderately high warmth and involvement. Although these siblings were competitive and coercive with each other, they were loyal and protective against adverse outside forces, whether adults or peers. On the ratings by observers of the most extreme behaviour that occurred during the observational session they were rated as extremely high on both warmth and on aggression. They would show intermittent flashes of intense concern, sensitivity, and caring but could also go on coercive rampages. This sibling relationship was found in sons in divorced non-remarried families, and in families where one parent was authoritarian or authoritative and the other was disengaged or permissive. They were equally likely to occur for boys or girls in stepfamilies and non-divorced families. These children tended to be scored by parents, but not by teachers, as above average on externalizing, and sometimes to have problems in achievement but to have reasonably good peer relationships. It should be noted that this is a very common sibling interaction pattern involving about 35 per cent of our siblings, substantiating Bryant's (1982) observation that early adolescence is characterized by both sibling facilitation and interference. Thus, ambivalent and companionate-caring sibling relationships occurred approximately equally often.

Finally, the fourth cluster, the *hostile alienated* sibling relationship, included about 22 per cent of our siblings and was characterized by low involvement, communication, warmth or empathy, and high coercion and aggression. These siblings avoided each other's company as much as possible and were cold or actively complaining, critical, and aggressive when they did interact. They were found most often with boys in divorced non-remarried families with a disengaged mother, and in girls in remarried families. They also were most likely to occur in families where both parents were disengaged, or one was disengaged and one authoritarian. Such a sibling interaction pattern was associated with high externalizing and high rates of total behaviour problems on the Children's Behavior Checklist, low achievement, and difficulties in the school and in the peer group.

The relation between parent–child interactions and sibling relationships

The pattern of correlations between parents' behaviour toward the child and the child's behaviour with the sibling were similar for the target child and the target sibling. In general, families in which parents were punitive, unaffectionate, and unresponsive to children's needs but erratic in the enforcement of discipline had higher levels of hostile, rivalrous, unaffectionate sibling interactions. However, although there were many significant correlations between various dimensions of parental behaviour and sibling relationships, the largest findings were obtained when the differential treatment of the siblings by parents was examined. If one sibling in comparison to the other was treated by parents with less warmth and affection, and more coercion, punitiveness, irritability, and restrictiveness, that sibling was more likely to behave in an aggressive, rivalrous, avoidant, unaffectionate manner toward his or her sibling. It was the disparity in treatment rather than the absolute levels of parental behaviour that had the most profound effects on sibling relationships (see also Dunn, Chapter 9 this volume). Perhaps more surprising is the finding that if there was a disparity in treatment, the more advantageously treated sibling also showed more aggression, avoidant, unaffectionate behaviour toward the less well-treated sibling than was found in families with egalitarian treatment. In addition, negative shifts in parental behaviour, such as increased ignoring, punitiveness, and direct or indirect negative comparative evaluations, and decreases in warmth, from when the child was interacting with the parents in the absence of the sibling to those situations in which the sibling was present, were strongly correlated with aversive sibling relations. The most positive sibling interactions were found when both siblings were well treated by the parents. These relations were similar for boys and for girls, and for mothers in the three family types, although a few more significant and somewhat larger correlations between the differential treatment of siblings and the sibling relationship were found for divorced mothers. When there was preferential treatment of children by stepfathers this led to even more dissention and avoidance than was found with preferential treatment by biological fathers in non-divorced families. Moreover, these effects were most marked when both siblings were girls.

Finally, when preferential treatment occurred, rivalry, aggression, and avoidance were more intense if both parents favoured the same child than if the mother and father favoured different siblings. In such a situation, being the child favoured by the biological father was associated with decreased aggression and sibling rivalry in the favoured son.

Conclusion and summary

The effects of divorce and remarriage on family relationships were pervasive and affected not only relationships within the marital dyad, parent–child dyad, and sibling dyad but among these family subsystems. These relationships differed for non-divorced, divorced, and remarried families.

Divorced non-remarried mothers and their sons continued to have problems even six years after divorce and these problems were reflected in disrupted sibling relationships. In contrast, the close relationship between divorced non-remarried mothers and their daughters was often extended to congenial relationships between female siblings.

The pattern of relationships found in remarried families differed from divorced non-remarried or non-divorced families. One notable finding was that whereas marital satisfaction was related to positive family relationships in non-divorced families, in the remarried families it was related to increased family conflict and behaviour problems, especially in stepdaughters. Although boys in divorced non-remarried families had more problems inside and outside of the home, they gradually adapted to and benefited from contact with a supportive stepfather. Stepdaughters also gradually adapted to the remarriage, but they continued to have more problems in family relationships and adjustment than did girls in non-divorced families or in families with custodial mothers who had been divorced for six years and who had not remarried.

Furthermore, although authoritative parenting was related to fewer behaviour problems in children in homes with divorced non-remarried custodial mothers than in non-divorced families, in stepfamilies a different pattern occurred. Attempts by the stepfather directly to exert control, even authoritative control, over the child's behaviour or disengagement early in the remarriage were associated with rejection of the stepfather by the children, and with children's problem behaviour. A stepfather who first established a warm relationship with the stepson and supported the mother's parenting, and later moved into an authoritative role, had the greatest probability of gaining acceptance and facilitating the adjustment of stepsons. In contrast, even when the stepfather was supportive and appropriate in responding to stepdaughters, her acceptance was difficult to gain. A troubling finding in this study was that disengaged parenting was the most common parenting style of stepfathers, and disengagement with stepdaughters increased over time.

More problems in sibling relationships also were found in stepfamilies and families with a divorced non-remarried custodial mother than in non-divorced families. However, differential treatment of children by parents intensified aversive sibling relations in all three family types.

A concluding word of caution must be offered to these findings. The children in this study were 4 years old at the beginning of this study and 10 years old at its conclusion, and some of the findings may be specific to the age of the children involved. In a study by Hetherington and Clingempeel (1986) of children who were aged between 9 and 13 at the time of remarriage, both boys and girls showed marked behaviour problems and difficulties in parent–child relationships after remarriage, and these did not moderate greatly in the following two years. Moreover, these older children more often disengaged themselves from the families and became involved in the peer group at school and activities outside of the home. Furthermore, although sibling relationships were conflictual and non-supportive in the period immediately following remarriage when the children were entering adolescence, female sibling relationships were improved in divorced non-remarried and remarried families two and a half years later. The timing of marital rearrangements in the developmental course of children's and parents' lives may greatly modify their effects.

References

Anderson, E. (1986). *Sibling relationships during remarriage*. Paper presented at the Southeastern Regional Meeting of the Society for Research in Child Development, Nashville, Tennessee.

Bank, S. and Kahn, M. (1982a). Intense sibling loyalties. In *Sibling relationships* (ed. M. E. Lamb and B. Sutton-Smith). Erlbaum, NJ.

Bank, S. and Kahn, M. (1982*b*). *The sibling bond*. Basic Books, New York.

Belsky, J. (1984). The determinants of parenting: a process model. *Child Development* **55**, 83–96.

Brand, E., Clingempeel, G. W., and Woodward, K. (1987). Family relationships and children's psychological adjustment in stepmother and stepfather families. In *The image of divorce, single parenting and step-parenting on children* (ed. E. M. Hetherington and J. Arasteh), in press.

Bray, J. H. (1986). The effects of early remarriage on children's development: preliminary analyses of the developmental issues in stepfamilies. In *The impact of divorce, single parenting and step-parenting on children* (ed. E. M. Hetherington and J. Arasteh), in press.

Bryant, B. K. (1982). Sibling relationships in middle childhood. In *Sibling relationships* (ed. M. E. Lamb and B. Sutton-Smith), pp. 87–121. Erlbaum, NJ.

Forgatch, M. (1986). A trait process model for family stress. Chapter to appear in *The impact of divorce, single parenting and step-parenting on children* (ed. E. M. Hetherington and J. Arasteh), in press.

Furman, W., Jones, L., Buhrmester, D., and Adler, T. (in press). Childrens', parents' and observers' perspectives on sibling relationships. In *Sibling interaction across culture* (ed. P. G. Zukow). Springer-Verlag, New York.

Gottman, J. M. (1979). *Marital interaction: experimental investigations*. Academic Press, New York.

Hagan, M. S. (1986). *The effect of discrepant perceptions and conflict on marital satisfaction and child adjustment in remarried versus nondivorced families*. Paper presented at the Southeastern Regional Meeting of the Society for Research in Child Development, Nashville, Tennessee.

Hetherington, E. M. (1972). Effects of father absence on personality development in adolescent daughters. *Developmental Psychology* **7**, 313–26.

Hetherington, E. M. (in press). Family relations six years after divorce. In *Remarriage and stepparenting today* (ed. K. Pasley and M. Ihinger-Tollman). Guilford Press, New York.

Hetherington, E. M. and Clingempeel, G. (1986). *The adjustment of parents and children to divorce and remarriage*. Symposium presented at the Southeastern Regional Meeting of the Society for Research in Child Development, Nashville, Tennessee.

Hetherington, E. M., Cox, M., and Cox, R. (1982). Effects of divorce on parents and children. In *Nontraditional families: parenting and child development* (ed. M. E. Lamb), pp. 233–88. Erlbaum, Hillsdale, NJ.

Hetherington, E. M., Cox, M., and Cox, R. (1985). Long-term effects of divorce and remarriage on the adjustment of children. *Journal of the American Academy of Psychology* **24**, (5), 518–30.

Hetherington, E. M. Arnett, J., and Hollier, A. (in press). The effects of remarriage on children and families. In *Family transition* (ed. P. Karoly and S. Wolchik). Garland Press, New York.

Peterson, J. L. and Zill, Z. (1986). Marital disruption, parent–child relationships and behavior problems in children. *Journal of Marriage and the Family* **48**, 295–307.

Santrock, J. W. and Warshak, R. A. (1986). Developmental relationships and legal/clinical considerations in father-custody families. In *The father's role: applied perspectives* (ed. M. E. Lamb), pp. 135–63. Wiley, San Francisco.

Schaefer, E. and Edgerton, M. (1981). Short description of the Sibling Inventory of behavior. Unpublished manuscript.

Spanier, G. B. (1976). Measuring dyadic adjustment. *Journal of Marriage and the Family* **1**, 13–26.

Wallerstein, J. S. (1987). Children of divorce: a ten-year study. In *The impact of divorce, single parenting and step-parenting on children* (ed. E. M. Hetherington and J. Arasteh), in press.

Wallerstein, J. S. and Kelly, J. B. (1980). *Surviving the breakup: how children and parents cope with divorce*. Basic Books, New York.

Warshak, R. A. and Santrock, J. W. (1983). The impact of divorce in father-custody and mother-custody homes: the child's perspective. In *Children and divorce* (ed. L. A. Kurdek), pp. 29–46. Jossey-Boss, San Francisco.

Weiss, R. (1975). *Marital separation*. Basic Books, New York.

17

Functions and consequences of relationships: some psychopathological considerations

MICHAEL RUTTER

In the field of psychopathology, two main themes have dominated concepts of how one relationship may affect another. First, there is the notion that the presence of one supportive relationship serves contemporaneously to increase the likelihood that the individual will maintain good relationships with other people (Rutter, in press *a*). For example, several studies have shown that parenting of children tends to be less adequate when the mother's marital relationship is discordant and disharmonious or when she lacks the support of the spouse (Hetherington *et al.* 1982; Wallerstein 1983; Quinton and Rutter 1984*a*, 1984*b*; Rutter and Quinton 1984*a*). Similarly, there is evidence that parenting tends to be influenced by the presence or absence of effective social supports outside the marital relationship, perhaps especially at times of stress or when dealing with a difficult child (Cochran and Brassard 1979; Crockenberg 1981; Werner and Smith 1982; Crnic *et al.* 1983; Belsky 1984). Also, cross-cultural data (Rohner 1975; Werner 1979) suggest that socially isolated mothers who carry the entire burden of shared responsibility are more likely to become rejecting of their children. This set of findings concerns the possible effect of one relationship on another at a single point of time.

The second theme concerns effects that extend over time to later relationships (Rutter 1987*a*). Thus, Freud (1938) maintained that the mother–infant relationship constituted the prototype of all future love relationships. In the same vein, attachment theory suggests that infants' selective attachments with their parents provide the basis for later relationships involving mutual commitment (Bowlby 1969/82, 1973, 1980; Bretherton and Waters 1985). It is argued that there is a sensitive phase in early life during which infants have the capacity to make secure discriminating attachment relationships and that, if such selective attachments are not formed then, there is likely to be a persistently impaired capacity to make committed relationships in later life. The proposition in this case is that the experience of one sort of relationship has a relatively enduring impact on the person's social capacities. The possible mechanisms that are likely to be involved in these two rather different sorts of effects are not the same.

Possible mechanisms mediating the effects of relationships on other relationships

An understanding of the mechanisms involved in these effects is crucial to the determination of therapeutic strategies in clinical work. In recent years, the concept of contemporaneous influences of relationships upon relationships has been reflected in the various different varieties of systems theories. These have made a major impact on clinical work through the development of conjoint family therapies to alleviate children's psychiatric problems (Barnes 1985; Dare 1985). The basic concept of systems approaches is that the family constitutes a social group in which the functioning of the whole is qualitatively different from the sum of its parts. This arises because the properties of the family as a whole derive from the properties of the relationships between the individuals in the family, and not just from the characteristics of the individuals as separate persons (Hinde 1980). Emphasis is placed on the boundaries of systems, on feedback loops, and on the tendency of systems to exhibit homeostasis and resistance to change (see also Chapter 1, this volume).

The developmental perspective, by which early relationships are thought to influence later relationships, has had an impact on clinical practice through the application of dynamic concepts deriving from attachment theory (Heard and Lake 1986); through internal working models of relationships (Bowlby 1969/82; Bretherton and Waters 1985; Sroufe and Fleeson, this volume) as applied to the development as self concepts (Harter 1983, 1986); and through the application of cognitive features such as learned helplessness, thought to derive from adverse relationship experiences in childhood, to vulnerability to stress and hence to liability to depressive disorders in adult life (Brown and Harris 1978; Brewin 1985). These various concepts have made certain assumptions about the mode of action of relationships in affecting other relationships and it is necessary to consider the alternative possibilities that require to be tested.

Effects on other relationships in the same time period

The first possibility that always needs to be considered in the explanation of a statistical association between two variables is that the association is an artefact of some kind deriving from the effect of some third variable. Thus, for example, it is possible that the association between marital support and good parenting might be explicable in terms of both being a consequence of some personality attribute of the individual rather than anything to do with the relationship.

Secondly, it could be that a dyadic relationship simply operates as part of the general environment without there being any features that are different by virtue of its being a relationship. For instance, parenting seems to be impeded not only by marital discord but also by seriously adverse living conditions. It could be that both constitute environmental stressors in which the relationship aspect is significant only in so far as it is part of the person's environment.

Thirdly, the mediation could lie in the generalization of the person's reputation for social behaviour. Dodge (1980, 1983) showed that children tended to respond to the reputation of others in their peer group, as determined by their past behaviour, as well as to their behaviour of the moment. Similarly, Brunk and Henggeler (1984) in an experimental study showed that adults, too, responded to children on the basis of past as well as current behaviour. Perhaps children's behaviour leads to adverse parenting because the children are responding to their parents on the basis of expectations based on their being witness to, or part of, earlier quarrels between parents.

Fourthly, one relationship may have an effect through altering the meaning of other relationships. As Parke and his colleagues (1979) noted, this process may operate both in the here and now (i.e. the dyadic interaction is altered only when the person is physically present in the social environment) and more enduringly when the existence of one dyadic relationship alters the qualities in another dyad even when no one else is present (i.e., there are effects on the relationship that are enduring both over time and over space).

Perhaps an example of the first is provided by the effect of fathers' presence on reducing the amount of interaction between mothers and children (Clarke-Stewart, 1978) and the differences between adult–child interactions under dyadic and polyadic conditions (Schaffer and Liddell 1984). Examples of enduring effects are provided by the sibling rivalry or jealousy phenomenon whereby children with particularly warm close relationships with their mothers are more likely to develop negative reactions with younger siblings (Dunn and Kendrick 1982), or the sibling de-identification phenomenon by which children in the same family react in ways to emphasize differences from their siblings (Schachter et al. 1978). Both types of effects indicate the relevance of Bronfenbrenner's (1979) concern that both child development and personal functioning more generally be viewed in an ecological perspective.

The ecological perspective is also applicable to the fifth mechanism, namely that stemming from the function of the social group as a group. It is a general characteristic of social groups, for example, that they tend to throw up leaders (Kelvin 1969) and that in-group preferences and stereotyping tend to lead to conflicts with other social groups (Sherif et al. 1961; Brown 1986). When the leader leaves a social group, another individual tends to assume the leadership role. This general concept, that social groups need to have people fulfilling particular roles in order to maintain their cohesion, has led family therapists to argue that the sick role of one child in the family may have a function in providing family unity. If that child leaves the family or ceases to be sick, another child will take over the sick role. This extrapolation lacks adequate empirical support but it could operate in some circumstances.

Finally, it is possible that the relevant process resides in changes within the individual. For example, Hay (1984) found that among pre-school children, the loser of a dispute between peers was more likely than the winner to initiate the next conflict. It appears that a child's feelings or thoughts about a past experience (perhaps resentment in that example) may determine future actions.

Enduring developmental effects

Somewhat similar considerations apply to the possible mechanisms to be considered for effects that endure over time. Again, it is necessary to start with the possibility that the associations may reflect an artefact of association with some third variable. For example, Kagan (1982) has argued that insecurity of attachment in infants may be largely a function of temperamental qualities. Accordingly, the association between insecure attachment and later social behaviour (Bretherton and Waters 1985) could stem from persistence of temperamental features that affect both types of relationships. Alternatively, because it has been shown that the qualities of children's attachments alter according to changing family circumstances (Thompson *et al.* 1983; Egeland and Farber 1984), it might be suggested that the linkages between early and late relationships simply reflect continuities in environmental influences.

In turning to the possible processes by which there may be a true causal effect on later relationships stemming from earlier ones, the basic question concerns how the qualities of a dyadic *relationship* become transformed into some aspect of *individual* functioning. One possibility is that children who have suffered from insecure discordant relationships with their parents develop styles of social behaviour that predispose to further maladaptive social interactions. Children with 'difficult' temperamental features have been shown to elicit more negative responses from their parents (Rutter 1978; Lee and Bates 1985). Similarly, unpopular boys' aggressive social approaches tend to bring about rebuffs from their peers (Dodge 1983). A related possibility is that the children develop expectations about relationships that stem from earlier experiences and which serve to influence their response to later social overtures. For example, aggressive boys are more likely than other boys to attribute hostile intentions to others; as a result, they elicit as well as initiate more negative interactions (Dodge 1980). People interpret experiences according to their attribution of the intention of others (Parke and Slaby 1983). Another possibility is that children learn social skills from social interactions. If their earlier relationships are maladaptive and unsatisfactory, they may lack the skills to make the most of later social opportunities. Thus, there is evidence that socially rejected children tend to be maladroit in the ways they interact with their peers (Hartup 1983). It is these considerations that have led to the current interest in the potential value of training children with social difficulties to improve their interpersonal cognitive problem solving strategies (Pellegrini 1985).

A fourth alternative, which incorporates many of the elements in the preceding three, emphasizes an internal organization of needs, attitudes, beliefs, and styles of coping that amount to an overall coherence of personality functioning (Rutter 1987*b*). A particular example of this view is provided by the concept of internal working models of both external attachment figures and of the self (Bowlby 1969/82, 1973, 1980; Bretherton and Waters 1985). Such models are both affective and cognitive, incorporating the people's beliefs about themselves (e.g. as a lovable person or as someone who is incapable of eliciting affection or commitment from others) and also about how other people respond to them. Bowlby has argued that a single individual may actually operate two or more incompatible working models and that defensive processes are used to allow the incongruity between models, or with reality, to persist. It is supposed that the internal models are revised in the light of later relationships, but also that they tend to be somewhat resistant to marked change because new information is assimilated to the existing models.

Finally, there is the notion, stemming from Bowlby's (1951) review of maternal deprivation, that the child's capacity to form selective attachments is dependent upon having first formed such attachments during a sensitive phase in the first few years of life. It is not clear quite what mechanisms are supposed to underlie the acquisition of this social capacity, but Bowlby (1969/82) has suggested that it constitutes a form of imprinting. That suggestion does not, however, identify the internal processes involved. Of course, there is nothing very particular about the uncertainty regarding internal mechanisms, as that applies to the mode of operation of most human experiences (Rutter 1984). There are, however, several examples of sensitive period effects that have the properties attributed in the social capacity acquisition hypothesis. Perhaps the best known is the acquisition of binocular vision. If children do not gain binocular vision during the early years of life (as, for example, through their having a strabismus) it is unlikely that normal binocular vision will be acquired later. It is presumed that some sort of effect on neural organization is involved.

The pros and cons of these various postulated mechanisms for contemporaneous and developmental effects as applied to the functions and consequences of relationships in general will not be discussed, as there is no reason to suppose that all effects are mediated by the same mechanism. Rather, attention will be focused on the evidence applicable to the two psychopathological examples already noted—namely the effects of marital support or conflict on parenting and of a lack of adequate early child–parent attachments on later relationships.

Marital support and quality of parenting

The effects of marital support on the quality of parenting were examined in our follow-up study into early adult life on women who had received much of their upbringing in residential institutions, as a result of a breakdown in their own parenting (Quinton *et al.* 1984*a*; Rutter and Quinton 1984*a*; Quinton and Rutter, in press). In brief, the girls had been admitted to institutional care because their parents could not cope with their rearing, rather than because of any type of disturbed behaviour shown by the children themselves. The sample of 94 girls was followed up in their mid-twenties and compared systematically with a quasi-random general population sample of 51 women of the same age from the same general area in Inner London. In both cases, the girls had had their behaviour assessed at school by means of a teacher questionnaire. The follow-up assessment in adult life included a detailed interview using well-tested standardized methods, together with systematic direct observations of mother–child interaction in the home.

Not surprisingly, the institution-reared women were more likely to show serious difficulties in parenting at the time of follow-up. This was evident in terms of overt parenting breakdown (with children being removed compulsorily or voluntarily from the mother's care), in interview assessments of parenting qualities, and in observational measures. However, the findings showed that the parenting outcome in the ex-institutional group was massively affected by whether or not the women had a supportive spouse. In the absence of marital support, none of the women showed good parenting but, of those who had such support, about half were parenting well. The difference according to the presence or absence of marital support went in the same direction in the comparison group, but the effects were much less marked. Again, about half were parenting well in the presence of support but nearly one-third of those without support also showed good parenting (Rutter, in press *b*).

Artefact or true protective effect?

The question of whether this surprisingly strong association was an artefact was tackled in several different ways. The most obvious possibility was that the girls who were non-deviant themselves during childhood and adolescence might be the ones who chose better functioning supportive men to marry or live with. In fact, the findings showed that this was not the case to any significant extent. Behavioural disturbance in childhood and adolescence *was* quite strongly associated with parenting outcome (only 4 per cent of those with behavioural deviance or delinquency showed good parenting at follow-up), but it was not associated with choice of spouse.

Although the choice of spouse was not a function of behavioural deviance in childhood or adolescence, it was related to other aspects of the girl's functioning. In particular, it was found that girls who showed evidence of 'planning' in their choice of spouse (meaning only that they had known their future spouse for six months or more and that the reasons for living together were positive and not a response to outside pressures) were more likely to marry non-deviant men who later provided a supportive marital relationship. The girls who showed 'planning' in their choice of spouse were also likely to exhibit 'planning' in other aspects of their lives, such as work and careers. Again, it was necessary to tackle the possibility that the better social functioning in adult life was a consequence of these planning characteristics rather than marital support. Linear logistic modelling showed that, although there was an association between planning and social outcome, the effects of marital support were stronger and held even after controlling for the effects of planning. Thus, in so far as we could examine the matter, the data were consistent in showing a significant and substantial effect of marital support even after taking into account measures of the women's prior emotional and behavioural disturbance.

A rather different sort of artefact concerned the possibility that the apparent effect of marital support was a consequence of the effect of the women on their husbands, rather than the other way round. Of course, the strong likelihood was that the effects were two-way. However, it was possible, at least in part, to test the possibility that the effects were entirely from wife to husband. This possibility arose because it had been found that the 'protective' effect of marital support was mirrored by the effects of having a non-deviant spouse (the two measures overlapped to a major extent). Accordingly, an analysis was undertaken to determine if there was an association between the spouses' teenage deviance (i.e. that present before meeting their wives and hence not due to the wives influence) on the women's current social functioning.* The findings indicated that the women who had married men showing deviant behaviour in their teens were more likely to have poor social functioning at follow-up. It was concluded that the effects of marital support were unlikely to be an artefact due to the associations being entirely a consequence of women's influences on their husbands.

Is the effect on parenting specific?

The association between marital support and quality of parenting was considered because it concerned the possible influence of one relationship on

---

*In several of the analyses it was necessary to use a broader measure of social functioning as the dependent variable because the number of women with children was too small for more detailed statistical analysis of parenting. As reported more fully in the references cited, where parallel analyses could be undertaken, the results for social functioning were closely comparable to those for parenting as such.

another. However, in seeking to understand the mechanisms involved, it is necessary to ask whether the effect was in any way specific to dependent variables concerned with relationships. The evidence is clearcut in showing that the findings were far from confined to parenting. Indeed, the effects of marital support were broadly similar for all our measures of functioning in adult life. For example, it applied to an overall measure of psychosocial outcome that took into account criminality and psychiatric disorder as well as marriage and social relationships; it also applied to a measure of personality disorder (meaning persistently abnormal interpersonal relationships associated with definitely impaired social functioning). Of course, it is the case that all these measures relied, in part, on the women's ability to make and maintain harmonious relationships, albeit not just with their children. However, that is a consequence of the fact that most measures of adult functioning are in some way connected with people's social abilities. Thus, depressive disorders in adult life are quite strongly associated with marital discord, as well as with other social problems (Rutter and Quinton 1984b). Evidence from numerous other studies is consistent in showing that the protective effects of marital support extend very widely (Cohen and Syme 1985). There is no reason to suppose that the effects are necessarily mediated through the consequences of one relationship for another, although this is likely to be part of the story. This is an issue to which I shall return.

What is entailed in marital support?

Comparable questions arise with respect to the nature of marital support. In our own study we sought to differentiate between relationship functions as such and qualities of the spouse as an individual. Our relationship measure was based on the presence of a warm harmonious marital relationship that included definite confiding by the wife in her husband. The individual measure was concerned solely with the presence of psychosocial problems in the spouse, as defined in terms of psychiatric disorder, criminality, a drink or drug problem, or long-standing difficulties in personal relationships. The findings showed that the protective effect was of roughly comparable strength with the two measures. There was too much overlap between them to assess their independent effects but, so far as could be determined, both were comparably effective. The nature of the factors providing support could be looked at another way by asking whether similar protective effects were found for variables outside the marriage. It was found that poor parenting was substantially more likely to occur when the women were living in poor social circumstances (operationally defined in terms of variables such as the children sharing a bed, a lack of washing machine or telephone, and the presence of housing defects such as severe damp). This effect was of roughly similar degree in both the institution and comparison groups. It may be concluded that protective and vulnerability mechanisms with respect to parenting derive from a wide range of variables that are not necessarily concerned with relationships. However, it remains to be considered whether or not the mechanisms involved are the same in all cases.

That issue has been widely discussed in attempts to specify the relevant elements of support (Cohen and Syme 1985). Thus, Wills (1985) has discussed support in terms of emotional aspects (feeling accepted and valued), status (as through marriage or position in a social organization), information (in terms of advice, decision making, etc.), instrumental features (i.e. tangible help with child rearing, shopping, etc.), social companionship (as through the rewards of friendships and leisure activities), and motivational features (encouragement and the like). Wills concluded that each of these aspects served an important role but that, possibly, emotional support was most infl ential in terms of mental health (see also Chapter 5 this volume).

Main effect or buffering function?

There has been much debate in the literature on supportive relationships as to whether the influence constituted a main effect or whether, rather, support acts only as a buffer or moderating influence in the presence of stress or other risk factors. The arguments have been inconclusive, both because the empirical findings are somewhat contradictory but also because 'buffering' or 'protection' have been conceptualized in terms of variables rather than mechanisms (Rutter, in press b). It is clear, that in different circumstances, relationship variables can have both main effects and buffering functions. Nevertheless, it has been striking that in many cases the effects of support have been substantially more marked in the presence of other adversities or stressors. As already noted, that was so in our study of institution-reared women, where the benefits of marital support were much less marked in the comparison group. In somewhat similar fashion, Crockenberg (1981; Crockenberg and McCluskey 1986) found that the effects of social support were most evident with mothers who had irritable babies. It is necessary to consider the mechanisms that may be involved in buffering effects as well as in direct influences.

Possible mechanisms of support

The data are not available to enable any decision on the precise means by which marital support aids parental functioning. However, there are several possibilities that warrant attention. Perhaps the first question is whether supportive relationships function in comparable ways at all age periods (Wolkind and Rutter 1985). It is well established that attachment relationships in infancy have a powerful anxiety-reducing function (Bowlby 1969/82; Rutter 1981). Young children are more ready to explore their environment in the presence of an attachment figure and they seek proximity to such figures when faced with stressful circumstances. Does the protective effect of a warm confiding marital relationship work in the same fashion? Of course, a marital relationship differs from an infant's attachment to a parent in many different ways. Obviously, it includes many elements that could not possibly be encompassed by the concept of attachment, but it could still be that attachment components constitute the crucial elements in the provision of support. It seems from the studies in adult life that confiding is an essential part of a supportive relationship. Does this mean that the emotional and informational exchanges that constitute confiding are a necessary ingredient in the provision of support, or is it simply that in adult life confiding serves as an index of a secure attachment? Adequate answers to these questions are not as yet available. It is clear that at all ages from infancy onwards human beings develop committed relationships that share many similar qualities. The loss of a love relationship is a stressful event at all ages and the presence of a loved one is supportive throughout the life span. But, are the mechanisms the same throughout and what concepts are most useful in defining qualities of such relationships? It is only in recent years that attempts have been made to extend concepts and measures of security of attachment to older age groups beyond infancy (Bretherton and Waters 1985).

It might be suggested that it is not so much the presence of support that is protective but rather that the presence of discordant and disharmonious relationships is stressful. Doubtless that is the case to some extent, but our findings (based on very small numbers) that women without a spouse function somewhat similarly to those with a non-supportive spouse suggests that there is a need to consider support separately from stressful relationships. The same conclusion derives also from the evidence that non-marital confiding relationships seem to exert a similar (although lesser) protective function for parenting and for other aspects of adult functioning (Cohen and Syme 1985).

While it seems likely that, to an important extent, the effects of support operate through effects on the individual, the effects may also operate through a reduction in task demands. For example, do the benefits of having a supportive spouse derive from the fact that the care of the children is divided or that the burden of housework is shared; or from the opportunity of sharing decision making in discipline and child-care decisions, or through the backing up of one another when faced with conflict with the children; or, indeed is it just that when the mother is stressed or under pressure her spouse is able to take over the difficult aspects of parenting? While the data are not adequate to provide an answer to these questions, it seems unlikely that the whole explanation lies simply in a diminution of task demands or a dilution of stress because such evidence as there is suggests that supported mothers interact more harmoniously and effectively with their children than do unsupported mothers. But that raises another possibility, namely, that some of the benefits may derive from stressed mothers having a model of good parenting provided by their supportive spouses. The fact that the benefits on parenting from having a non-deviant spouse seem broadly comparable to those from a supportive spouse suggest that there may be something in that suggestion (as well as in the suggestion that part of the benefits derive from a lack of stressful interactions).

Perhaps the last point to make in this connection is that the evidence suggests that protection does not lie in the availability of potentially supportive relationships but rather in the use that people make of the relationships that are available (Quinton 1980; Henderson *et al.* 1981; Cohen and Syme 1985). That finding has been interpreted as meaning that the protective effect comes from qualities in the individual's own personality that enable them to develop and make use of supportive relationships (Henderson *et al.* 1981), but equally it could be argued that the necessary quality lies in the dyadic nature of the relationship rather than in the external provision of a supportive prop. In so far as that might be the case, it brings us back to the notion that one relationship may influence another one. There is still a great deal to learn on how such mechanisms may operate in reducing the risk of psychopathology.

Early attachment relationships and social relationships in adolescence and adult life

Institutional-rearing and later parenting qualities

In the last few years there has been an increasing interest in the possibility of intergenerational continuities in serious parenting difficulties (Rutter, in press *a*), and in particular to the suggestion that there may be links between security of attachment in infancy and qualities of parenting in adult life (Main *et al.* 1985; Ricks 1985; Grossmann *et al.* Chapter 13 this volume). The possibility was examined in the follow-up of institution-reared women that has already been mentioned. Serious breakdowns in parenting were evident only in the institutional group: one-third had experienced temporary or permanent breakdown in parenting, compared with none in the comparison group. These findings, of course, might be a function of the institution-reared women's willingness to give up their children or the inclination of authorities to intervene, as well as a reflection of parenting qualities *per se*. However, currently poor parenting at the time of the follow-up was also much more frequent in the institution-reared group—40 per cent versus 11 per cent. The findings indicated quite strong continuities between an institutional upbringing and later difficulties in parenting. Even so, it was notable that there was marked heterogeneity in outcome with nearly one-third of the institution-reared women exhibiting good parenting.

The institution-reared women had experienced a wide range of adversities of different kinds, any or all of which might have played a part in the predisposition to parenting difficulties. In an attempt to tie down more closely the relevant risk factors, we subdivided the group according to a range of possible risk factors. One of the most important predictors proved to be whether or not the girls had experienced disruptive parenting during the first four years of life, defined in terms of short-term admissions into institutional care, multiple separations through parental discord or disorder, persistent family discord, or admission into long-term institutional care before the age of two years. The long-term effects associated with disrupted early parenting were most evident in the association with personality disorder in adult life (this was present in 32 per cent of those experiencing disruptive parenting compared with 5 per cent in the remainder). The proportion with poor parenting was also higher (59 per cent versus 29 per cent) in the disrupted parenting subgroup, although the difference was not as great as found with personality disorder. The implication is that early disruption of parenting may be particularly damaging to the development of those aspects of personality concerned with social relationships; such damage may include ill effects on parenting but parenting difficulties may arise in other ways as well.

Possible mechanisms involved

Further questions arise in relation to these findings. First, it was necessary to consider whether the apparent effects of early disrupted parenting might constitute an artefact deriving from genetic influences. This possibility arose because disrupted parenting had so frequently occurred because the parents were suffering from psychiatric disorder or persistent criminality. However, linear logistic analyses showed that there was still a major effect of disrupted parenting after account had been taken of parental deviance. Hence, in so far as parental deviance can be taken as a proxy for genetic risk, the inference is that the main risk was experientially mediated and not genetically determined. The circumstantial evidence suggested that there were some genetic effects with respect to personality disorder but not for psychosocial functioning more generally or for parenting.

The second question concerns the possibility that it was not so much the experiences of infancy that were important but rather that such experiences served as an index for continuing adversities that persist throughout the growing years. The findings indicated that there was substance in that suggestion. There were important associations between infancy experiences and the girl's circumstances on leaving the institution in late adolescence. Whereas some of the girls who had experienced disrupted parenting during the first few years were able to leave the institution to return to a non-discordant family, this applied to scarcely any of those who had experienced disrupted parenting in infancy. The early disruption was not only an adverse experience in its own right, but also it was an index of a severely troubled family that continued to have major problems throughout the girls' growing years.

Most of the early disruptions of parenting involved a complex mixture of adverse experiences. For example, on the one hand there was the range of stressful and unpleasant happenings associated with severe and chronic family discord; on the other, there was the lack of continuity in parenting that provided the opportunity for the development of secure selective attachments. In other words, it was necessary to consider the alternatives of whether the damage arose from adverse family experiences or from the lack of adequate attachment opportunities. In an attempt to answer that question, we focused on the subgroup of girls who had been admitted to the institutions under the age of two years and who had remained there throughout childhood. This was the group that had suffered the shortest period of family discord (the institutions had been studied in detail at the time that the girls were there and were known to be generally harmonious places). However, as in most institutions of that era, there was very considerable turnover in parent-figures and it is likely that the marked discontinuity in personal caregiving would have meant a considerably reduced opportunity for the acquisition of persistent selective attachments. Most of the women in the study looked back on their period in the children's home as a period that lacked personal meaning or affection, and only a minority reported any strong personal attachments to members of staff.

There were only 10 girls who fell into the subgroup who had been admitted in infancy and who remained in the institution throughout their upbringing, but it was striking that they included the highest proportion of all (80 per cent) with poor parenting. The finding is particularly noteworthy because the parenting outcome was better for girls admitted before 2 years of age who returned to their families, where most of them experienced both social disadvantage and severe family discord. It may be inferred that it was likely that the risks for parenting, and for later social relationships more generally, stemmed in part from the lack of attachment opportunities in infancy. However, the nature of our sample made it difficult to disentangle the effects of early and late childhood experiences. For that purpose, it is necessary to turn to prospective studies of children whose parenting broke down but who varied markedly in their later experiences. Two studies provide data of this sort.

Institutional rearing in infancy and later peer relationships

The first by Roy (1983) compared family-fostered and institution-reared primary school children who had been removed from their biological families because of a breakdown in parenting in infancy. Both groups differed from the controls in showing a higher rate of inattentive, poorly modulated social behaviour and task performance, but all these features were much more marked in the institutional group than in the family-fostered group. The between-group difference was not explicable in terms of family background, which was similar and extremely disturbed in both cases. It appeared that the institutional upbringing (in conjunction with a deviant family background) had led to an increased rate of social difficulties.

The second study by Tizard and Hodges (1978; Hodges and Tizard, in press *a*, *b*) also started with a group of children admitted to a residential nursery, but it differs both in its inclusion of a late adopted subgroup and also in the follow-up to 16 years of age. The findings at 8 years were closely comparable to those of Roy (1983) but the data on 16-year-olds add an important new dimension. The main interest lies in the comparison between the children who had been adopted and those who had returned to their biological families. Both had experienced institutional upbringing for the first 4 years or so but they differed markedly in their later childhood experiences. The adoptive families were, as might be expected, socially advantaged compared with the general population, and most provided an harmonious, well-functioning setting. In sharp contrast, the children who had been restored to their biological parents were mostly in socially disadvantaged, discordant, and troubled families.

The difference in current circumstances between the adopted and restored children was reflected in various aspects of their behaviour. For example, most of the restored adolescents had been in trouble with the police and/or had been referred for psychiatric treatment, whereas that was so for only a minority of the adoptees. The restored children's high level of behavioural disturbance was in keeping with their markedly poor psychosocial circumstances. Conversely, the adoptees were somewhat more likely to differ from their matched controls in being unhappy, or fearful, or having tics and mannerisms. These emotional differences had not been apparent at age 8 and are perhaps a reflection of the concerns over identity that some adopted adolescents experience.

What is remarkable about the findings is that the ex-institutional adolescents differed markedly from their controls in their pattern of social relationships outside the home, and that the pattern was closely similar for the adopted and restored subgroups. In particular, the ex-institutional adolescents were less likely to confide in peers, more likely to have difficulty in peer relationships, were less likely to have a definite special friend, and were more likely to be indiscriminately friendly to any peer. There was some tendency for these social qualities at 16 years to be associated with an earlier lack of close attachment to the mother, and with over-friendly relationships with adults at age 8. Nevertheless, it was evident that the close similarity between the adopted and restored groups with respect to peer relationships was *not* accompanied by comparable similarities in their family relationships. The great majority of the adopted mothers felt that their child was deeply attached to them, whereas this was less often the case in the restored group. Furthermore, the restored group got on particularly badly with their siblings, whereas this was less often the case with the adoptees. At 8 years of age the adopted children had been strikingly affectionate and cuddly, and the restored children the least cuddly. As they grew older the adoptees had become rather less demonstrative as a group but the restored group was strikingly less demonstrative than both the adoptees and their own matched controls.

Disparity between peer relationships and other measures

The paradox is posed by the disparity between the pattern of peer relationships and almost all other measures. Most aspects of the psychosocial function of the 16-year-olds could be seen as an expected response to their social environment at the time and in the recent past. This included their relationships with their immediate families. In contrast, the peer relationships seemed relatively unaffected by present social circumstances and, instead, appeared to be a function of the early years in the institution (because the restored and adopted children were similar in ways that differentiated both of them from their matched controls). The question is why this should be so.

There are now quite a number of studies that have shown significant associations between early insecurity of attachment and social relationships a few years later (Bretherton and Waters 1985; Lutkenhaus et al. 1985; Jacobson and Wille 1986; Sroufe and Fleeson, Chapter 2 this volume). Though there are differences in emphasis between studies, the general finding seems reasonably solid. It poses the query, however, as to why a dyadic measure in infancy should predict to later social relationships of a different kind, when it does not predict to comparable dyadic relationships at the same time (Bretherton and Waters 1985). The existing data do not provide an entirely satisfactory answer to that question. However, it may be supposed that, although the dyadic parent–child attachment relationship is sensitive to both dyadic features and also broader family circumstances, if the relationship is maintained over a sufficient length of time it may come to have consequent effects upon personal functioning. If so, one would expect to find that the predictions to later social functioning should be stronger when the quality of the child's dyadic relationship with both parents is similar and where the quality remains the same over time. It is not yet known whether in fact that is the case although the available data are consistent with that possibility (Rutter 1987a).

The next query concerns the conceptualization and measurement of qualities of attachment. Most studies have relied on the traditional classification of children's responses to the Ainsworth Strange Situation Procedure. This has worked well in practice but findings over the last few years have suggested that the traditional measures do not adequately encompass the more unusual responses from children that may be seen with more extreme patterns of rearing, as with abusing or seriously depressed parents (Crittenden 1985; Main and George 1985; Radke-Yarrow *et al.* 1985). Although not tested by the strange situation procedure, it is also likely that the institution-reared children studied by Roy, Tizard and Hodges, and ourselves differed from both normal and abused children. Their early behaviour was characterized by indiscriminately friendly responses towards adults rather than by the features usually associated with secure or insecure patterns. The evidence from the Tizard and Hodges' data strongly suggests that many of the children had failed to develop any persisting selective attachments. Much further work is required in order to make the most effective discriminations between these different varieties of attachment pattern. At present, we just do not know whether the developmental consequences of the different types of amodal patterns are the same or different. However, it is probable that they are different, and the persisting consequences seen in the institution-reared groups may well not be paralleled with the less extreme insecurely attached children in other studies.

Mechanisms involved in developmental continuities

The next issue is what mechanisms underlie the continuities between the early lack of attachment and the later pattern of peer relationships in the institution-reared children. It does not seem likely that the continuity is provided by consistency in temperamental functioning because the children's behaviour in the adopted and restored groups was so dissimilar in other respects. It may well be that temperamental features play some part in the quality of children's responses to their caregivers, but it does not seem likely that the qualities of attachment are largely explicable in these terms, if only because the qualities of one dyadic attachment relationship do not predict the qualities of another dyadic relationship (Sroufe 1985). Equally, it does not seem likely that the continuity is provided by the consistencies in environmental experiences, because the experiences of the adopted and restored groups were so markedly different. The explanation that a failure to develop attachments in infancy necessarily prevents the development of later selective attachments also cannot be supported. The great majority of the children adopted after the age of 4 years in the Tizard and Hodges study *did* develop close attachments with their adoptive mothers. A few did not, and they did particularly badly in the years that followed, but that does not account for the findings in the group as a whole. The suggestion that the early pattern of parent–child relationships provides the basis for the child's internal working model of relationships, which in turn affects his later social functioning, also does not seem to provide an adequate fit for the data. The problem is posed by the finding that the relationships in the adoptive family did change from those in the institution but that, in spite of that, the relationships with peers did not. It is not immediately apparent why the strongest effects should be found outside the family when the close intimate relationships that had suffered most initially from the institutional rearing had modified greatly.

In my view, the data do not as yet have an adequate explanation. Of course, the data are based on relatively few studies but the findings are remarkably consistent across the investigations that have been carried out. That applies both to the studies in childhood that have been mentioned and also to the intergenerational investigations that seek to link childhood experiences with later parenting behaviour (see Rutter, in press *a*). Any hypothesized explanation that postulates a fixity of social functioning deriving from infantile experiences cannot account for the powerful modifying effect of experiences in later life, as for example from marital support in the early years of adulthood. Equally, any explanation that postulates that relationships simply reflect current social circumstances fails to account for the apparent persistence to 16 years of age of effects deriving from experiences during the first 4 years. There is, of course, an abundance of evidence pointing to a complex mesh of indirect developmental connections providing for both continuities and discontinuities in development (Rutter 1987*a*). That general view of a developmental progression that represents both coherence and change is well supported. However, it does not account for the rather different pattern of findings with respect to peer relationships compared to other aspects of children's functioning. That there are effects deriving from early relationships that serve to influence later relationships can scarcely be doubted. However, it seems that we are still rather a long way from understanding precisely how the developmental processes operate.

Conclusions

Studies of abnormal groups can often throw light on normal developmental processes through their focus on examples of extremes that provide contrasts with respect to factors postulated as playing a key role in the hypothesized mechanisms. Nevertheless, there should be no necessary assumption that the processes involved in normal and abnormal development are the same. Rather the comparison between the two is used to test for continuities and discontinuities across the span of behavioural variation (Rutter and Garmezy 1983; Sroufe and Rutter 1984; Rutter and Sandberg 1985; Rutter 1986). That general principle applies to the specific issue considered here; namely, the contemporaneous and long-term developmental effects of one relationship on other relationships. The psychopathological data are clearcut in their demonstration of statistical associations that reflect such effects. Unfortunately, they are not yet as decisive in their delineation of the mechanisms involved. It is apparent that marital support predisposes to more effective parenting. In part, this association seems to represent a set of direct effects that parallel those found with a range of environmental variables not necessarily involving relationships. But, also in part, there seem to be buffering effects by which marital support modifies the parental response to other life hazards in the past or present. The mechanisms involved in such protective processes remain uncertain and require further study (Rutter, in press *b*). The long-term effects of relationships upon relationships is seen most strikingly in the sequelae of an institutional rearing. These involve both subtle (but important) differences in the quality of peer relationships in adolescence and also difficulties in parenting. The findings indicate a tantalizing mixture of relationship effects that persist over time in spite of a radical change in environment, combined with a continuing responsivity to environmental effects. Any hypothesis on the processes involved must take account of both the continuities *and* discontinuities.

References

Barnes, G. G. (1985). Systems theory and family theory. In *Child and adolescent psychiatry: modern approaches* (2nd edn.) (ed. M. Rutter and L. Hersov), pp. 216–19. Blackwell Scientific, Oxford.

Belsky, J. (1984). The determinants of parenting: process model. *Child Development* **55**, 83–96.

Bowlby, J. (1951). *Maternal care and mental health*. World Health Organization, Geneva.

Bowlby, J. (1969). *Attachment and loss*, Vol. 1, *Attachment*. London: Hogarth Press (1982, 2nd edn. Hogarth Press, London).

Bowlby, J. (1973). *Attachment and Loss*, Vol. 2, *Separation, anxiety and anger*. Hogarth Press, London.

Bowlby, J. (1980). *Attachment and Loss*, Vol. 3, *Loss, sadness and depression*. Hogarth Press, London.

Bretherton, I. and Waters, E. (ed.) (1985). Growing points of attachment and research. *Monographs for the Society for Research in Child Development* Serial No. 209, **50**, (1–2).

Brewin, C. (1985). Depression and causal attributions: what is their relation? *Psychological Bulletin* **9**, 297–309.

Bronfenbrenner, U. (1979). *The ecology of human development: experiments by nature and design*. Harvard University Press, Cambridge Mass.

Brown, G. W. and Harris, T. O. (1978). *Social origins of depression: a study of psychiatric disorders in women*. Tavistock, London.

Brown, R. (1986). *Social Psychology* (2nd edn.). Free Press, New York.

Brunk, M. A. and Henggeler, S. W. (1984). Child influences on adult controls. An experimental investigation. *Developmental Psychology* **20**, 1074–81.

Clarke-Stewart, K. A. (1978). And Daddy makes three. The father's impact on mother and young child. *Child Development* **49**, 466–78.

Cochran, M. M. and Brassard, J. A. (1979). Child development and personal social networks. *Child Development* **50**, 601–16.

Cohen, S. and Syme, S. L. (ed.) (1985) *Social support and health*. Academic Press, New York.

Crittenden, P. M. (1985). Maltreated infants: vulnerability and resilience. *Journal of Child Psychology and Psychiatry* **26**, 85–96.

Crnic, K. A., Greenberg, M. T., Ragozin, A. S., Robinson, R. N. M., and Basham, R. B. (1983). Effects of stress and social support on mothers and premature and full term infants. *Child Development* **54**, 209–17.

Crockenberg, S. (1981). Infant irritability, mother responsiveness and social support influences on the security of infant–mother attachment. *Child Development* **52**, 857–65.

Crockenberg, S. and McCluskey, K. (1986). Change in maternal behavior during the baby's first year of life. *Child Development* **57**, 746–53.

Dare, C. (1985). Family therapy. In *Child and adolescent psychiatry: modern approaches* (2nd edn.) (ed. M. Rutter and L. Hersov), pp. 809–25. Blackwell Scientific, Oxford.

Dodge, K. A. (1980). Social cognition and children's aggressive behaviour. *Child Development* **51**, 162–72.

Dodge, K. A. (1983). Behavioural antecedents of peer social status. *Child Development* **54**, 1386–99.

Dunn, J. and Kendrick, C. (1982). *Siblings: love, envy and understanding*. Grant McIntyre, London.

Egeland, B. and Farber, E. A. (1984). Infant–mother attachment: factors related to its development and changes over time. *Child Development* **55**, 735–77.

Freud, S. (1938). *An outline of psychonanalysis*. Hogarth Press, London.

Harter, S. (1983). Developmental perspectives on the self-system. In *Handbook of child psychology*, Vol. 4, *Socialization, personality and social development* (ed. E. M. Hetherington, Series ed. P. H. Mussen), pp. 275–385. Wiley, New York.

Harter, S. (1986). Processes underlying the construction, maintainènce and enhancement of the self concept in children. In *Psychological perspectives on the self*, Vol. 3 (ed. J. Suls and A. Greenwald). Erlbaum, New York.

Hartup, W. W. (1983). Peer relations. In *Handbook of child psychology*, Vol. 3, *Socialization, personality and social development* (ed. E. M. Hetherington, Series ed. P. H. Mussen), pp. 103–96. Wiley, New York.

Hay, D. (1984). Social conflict in early childhood. In. *Annals of Child Development*, Vol. 1 (ed. G. J. Whitehurst), pp. 1–44. JAI Press, Greenwich Conn.

Heard, D. H. and Lake, B. (1986). The attachment dynamic in adult life. *British Journal of Psychiatry* **149**, 430–8.

Henderson, S., Byrne, D. G., and Duncan-Jones, P. (1981). *Neurosis and the social environment*. Academic Press, Sydney.

Hetherington, E. M., Cox, M., and Cox, R. (1982). Effects of divorce on parents and children. In *Non-traditional families* (ed. M. E. Lamb), pp. 233–88. Erlbaum, Hillsdale, NJ.

Hinde, R. A. (1980). Family influences. In *Scientific foundations of development psychiatry* (ed. M. Rutter), pp. 47–66. Heinemann Medical, London.

Hodges, J. and Tizard, B. (in press *a*). IQ and behavioural adjustment of ex-institutional adolescents. *Journal of Child Psychology and Psychiatry.*

Hodges, J. and Tizard, B. (in press *b*). Social and family relationships of ex-institutional adolescents. *Journal of Child Psychology and Psychiatry.*

Jacobson, J. L. and Wille, D. E. (1986). The influence of attachment pattern on developmental changes in peer interaction from the toddler to the pre-school period. *Child Development* **57**, 338–47.

Kagan, J. (1982). *Psychological research on the human infant: an evaluative summary.* WD Grant Foundation, New York.

Kelvin, P. (1969). *The bases of social behaviour: an approach in terms of order and value.* Holt, Rinehart and Winston, New York.

Lee, C. I. and Bates, J. E. (1985). Mother–child interaction at age two years and perceived difficult temperament. *Child Development* **56**, 1314–25.

Lutkenhaus, P., Grossmann, K. E., and Grossmann, K. (1985). Infant–mother attachment at 12 months and style of interaction with a stranger at the age of 3 years. *Child Development* **56**, 1538–42.

Main, M. and George, C. (1985). Responses of abused and disadvantaged toddlers to distress in age mates: a study in the day care setting. *Developmental Psychology* **21**, 407–12.

Main, M., Kaplan, N., and Cassidy, J. (1985). Security in infancy, childhood and adulthood. In *Growing points of attachment theory and research* (ed. I. Bretherton and E. Waters). *Monographs for the Society for Research in Child Development* Serial No. 209, **50**, (1–2), 66–104.

Parke, R. D. and Slaby, R. G. (1983). The development of aggression. In *Handbook of child psychology*, Vol. 4, *Socialization, personality and social development* (4th edn.) (ed. E. M. Hetherington, series ed. P. H. Mussen), pp. 547–641. Wiley, New York.

Parke, R. D., Powers, T. G., and Gottman, J. M. (1979). Conceptualizing and quantifying influence patterns in the family triad. In *Social interaction analysis: methodological issues* (ed. M. E. Lamb, S. J. Suomi and G. R. Stephenson), pp. 231–52. University of Wisconsin Press, Madison.

Pellegrini, D. S. (1985). Training in social problem-solving. In *Child and adolescent psychiatry: modern approaches* (2nd edn.) (ed. M. Rutter and L. Hersov), pp. 839–50. Blackwell Scientific, Oxford.

Quinton, D. (1980). Cultural and community influences. In *Scientific foundations of developmental psychiatry* (ed. M. Rutter), pp. 77–91, Heinemann Medical, London.

Quinton, D. and Rutter, M. (1984*a*). Parents with children in care: I. Current circumstances and parenting. *Journal of Child Psychology and Psychiatry* **25**, 211–29.

Quinton, D. and Rutter, M. (1984*b*). Parents with children in care: II. Intergenerational continuities. *Journal of Child Psychology and Psychiatry* **25**, 231–50.

Quinton, D. and Rutter, M. (in press). *Parental breakdown: the making and breaking of intergenerational links.* Gower Publishing, Aldershot, Hants.

Quinton, D., Rutter, M., and Liddle, C. (1984). Institutional rearing, parenting difficulties and marital support. *Psychological Medicine* **14**, 107–24.

Radke-Yarrow, M., Cummings, E. M., Kuczynski, L., and Chapman, M. (1985). Patterns of attachment in two and three year olds in normal families and families with parental depression. *Child Development* **56**, 884–93.

Ricks, M. (1985). The social transmission of parental behavior: attachment across generations. In *Growing points of attachment theory and research* (ed. I. Bretherton and E. Waters), *Monographs for the Society for Research in Child Development* Serial No. 209, **50**, (1–2). 211–227.

Rohner, R. P. C. (1975). *They love me, they love me not: a worldwide study of the effects of parental acceptance and rejection.* HRAF Press, New Haven, Conn.

Roy, P. (1983). *Is continuity enough? Substitute care and socialization.* Paper presented at the Spring Scientific Meeting, Child and Adolescent Psychiatry Specialist Section, Royal College of Psychiatrists, London.

Rutter, M. (1978). Early sources of security and competence. In *Human Growth and Development* (ed. J. S. Bruner and A. Garton), pp. 33–61. Oxford University Press.

Rutter, M. (1981). *Maternal deprivation reassessed* (2nd edn.). Penguin Books, Harmondsworth, Middx.

Rutter, M. (1984). Psychopathology and development. II. Childhood experiences and personality development. *Australian and New Zealand Journal of Psychiatry* **18**, 314–27.

Rutter, M. (1986). Child Psychiatry: the interface between clinical and developmental research. *Psychological Medicine* **16**, 151–60.

Rutter, M. (1987a). Continuities and discontinuities from infancy. In *Handbook of infant development* (2nd edn.) (ed. J. Osofsky). Wiley, New York.

Rutter, M. (1987b). Temperament, personality and personality disorder. *British Journal of Psychiatry* **150**, 443–58.

Rutter, M. (in press a). Intergenerational continuities and discontinuities in serious parenting difficulties. In *Research on the consequences of child maltreatment* (ed. D. Cicchetti and V. Carlson). Cambridge University Press, New York.

Rutter, M. (in press b). Psychosocial resilience and protective mechanisms. In *Risk and protective factors in the development of psychopathology* (ed. J. Rolf, A. Masten, D. Cicchetti, K. Nuechterlein, and S. Weintraub) Cambridge University Press, New York.

Rutter, M. and Garmezy, N. (1983). Developmental psychopathology. In *Handbook of Child Psychology, Vol. 4. Socialization, personality and social development* (ed. E. M. Hetherington, Series ed. P. H. Mussen), pp. 775–911. Wiley, New York.

Rutter, M. and Quinton, D. (1984a). Long-term follow-up of women institutionalized in childhood: factors promoting good functioning in adult life. *British Journal of Developmental Psychology* **2**, 191–204.

Rutter, M. and Quinton, D. (1984b). Parental psychiatric disorder: effects on children. *Psychological Medicine* **14**, 853–80.

Rutter, M. and Sandberg, S. (1985). Epidemiology of child psychiatric disorder: methodological issues and some substantive findings. *Child Psychology and Human Development* **15**, 209–233.

Schacter, F. F., Gilutz, G., Shore, E., and Avler, M. (1978). Sibling de-identification judged by mothers. *Child Development* **49**, 543–46.

Schaffer, H. R. and Liddell, C. (1984). Adult–child interaction under dyadic and polyadic conditions. *British Journal of Developmental Psychology* **2**, 33–42.

Sherif, M., Harvey, O. J., White, B. J., Hood, W. R., and Sherif, C. W. (1961). *Intergroup conflict and cooperation: the robber's cave experiment.* University of Oklahoma Press, Norman, Oklahoma.

Sroufe, L. A. (1985). Attachment classification from the perspective of infant–caregiver relationships and infant temperament. *Child Development* **56**, 1–14.

Sroufe, L. A. and Rutter, M. (1984). The domain of developmental psychopathology. *Child Development* **55**, 17–29.

Thompson, R. A., Lamb, M. E., and Estes, D. (1983). Harmonizing discordant notes: a reply to Waters. *Child Development* **54**, 521–4.

Tizard, B. and Hodges, J. (1978). The effect of early institutional rearing on the development of eight-year old children. *Journal of Child Psychology and Psychiatry* **19**, 99–118.

Wallerstein, J. S. (1983). Children of divorce: stress and developmental tasks. In *Stress, Coping and Development in Children* (ed. N. Garmezy and M. Rutter), pp. 265–302. McGraw-Hill, New York.

Werner, E. E. (1979). *Cross-cultural child development: a view from the planet Earth.* Brooks/Cole, Monterey Calif.

Werner, E. E. and Smith, R. S. (1982). *Vulnerable but invincible: a longitudinal study of resilient children and youth.* McGraw-Hill, New York.

Wills, T. A. (1985). Supportive functions of interpersonal relationships. In *Social support and health* (ed. S. Cohen and S. L. Syme). Academic Press, New York.

Wolkind, S. and Rutter, M. (1985). Separation, loss and family relationships. In *Child and adolescent psychiatry: modern approaches* (2nd edn.) (ed. M. Rutter and L. Hersov), pp. 82–100. Blackwell Scientific, Oxford.

18

The effect of relationships on relationships: a developmental approach to clinical intervention

ROBERT N. EMDE*

Discussion in this chapter will take a seemingly new direction, but one implied by the preceding chapters. In involves the role of a third relationship—the 'Interventionist Relationship'—in influencing the effects of relationships on relationships within families. In understanding this influence, primary attention must be given to meaning—in the sense of individual representations and affective themes, in the sense of shared values and expectations, and in the sense of particular developmental contexts and particular social contexts. Attention to meaning may require the use of atypical research approaches. Discussion of these matters will include some examples from recent research which raise new opportunities for future work, and will emphasize a number of cross-cutting themes that arise elsewhere in this volume.

Cross-generational effects of parenting on parenting

There is a clinical adage: 'Care for your children as you wish them to care for your grandchildren' (Solnit and Provence 1979, p. 800). The chapters of Sroufe and Fleeson, Grossmann *et al.*, Caspi and Elder, and Belsky and Pensky (all this volume) review evidence for cross-generational patterns of continuity with respect to insecure attachment and adverse child-rearing experiences. But such maladaptive patterns of cross-generational continuity have interesting exceptions. As Belsky and Pensky (this volume) have reminded us, these can be regarded as 'lawful discontinuities'. Prominent in the studies of Sroufe and colleagues (Sroufe and Fleeson, this volume), the Grossmanns and colleagues (Grossmann *et al.* this volume), and Main and

*Dr Emde is supported by the National Institute of Mental Health project grant No. MH22803, Research Scientist Award No. 5 KO2 MH36808, and the John D. and Catherine T. MacArthur Foundation Network on the Transition from Infancy to Early Childhood.

colleagues (Main *et al.* 1985) are some patterns of discontinuity associated with a special quality in the mother's account of her early child-rearing experiences. Unlike the usual cross-generational pattern, these mothers recount the facts of early adverse circumstances of child-rearing but have become reflective. They have objectified the early experience so that they can talk about its having been adverse. These mothers do not idealize their parents in the face of specific memories of adversity and maltreatment; furthermore, in contrast to the maladaptive continuity group, they do not ward off or defend themselves against painful affects. How has this come about? Grossmann *et al.* (this volume) and Sroufe and Fleeson (this volume) give us the common denominator. A third relationship has intervened between the early parenting relationship and the later parenting relationship in the next generation. This has included either an alternative parenting relationship in childhood or a psychotherapeutic guidance relationship. Furthermore, in most cases, it has also been associated with a concurrent supportive spousal relationship (Rutter, this volume).

Before pursuing the question of these interventionist relationships, it is necessary to consider another theme that cuts across the chapters of this volume, namely that of individual meaning. In our observations of *interactionally-based relationships*, we must attend to the processes whereby they become transformed into *represented relationships*—in other words, we must understand how repeated interactions influence the formation of represented relationships according to cognitive schemes, affective themes, and social values. A similar point is emphasized in the chapter by Radke-Yarrow *et al.* (this volume), in which the need to understand intrapsychic affective themes becomes prominent in studies of families with cross-relationship influences involving a depressed parent and two children.

This theme of meaning has a corollary. We need better methods for capturing ipsative or idiographic data sets, for tracking both individual relationships and relationships within individuals over time. A number of chapters in this volume (for example the configurational patterns of Kreppner, the case-intensive studies of Radke-Yarrow, and the communication patterns of Barrett and Hinde) are a promising start. Is it possible that we might be able to describe changing patterns over time in the coherence of separate structures within relationship systems? Is it possible that relationship systems may become more or less loosely coupled with other systems—more or less rigid or stereotypic in their environmental transactions? As Patterson reminds us in his studies of developing antisocial behaviour (Patterson and Dishion, this volume), at some point the child's system of relationships becomes relatively inflexible and self-perpetuating. It is as if an ipsative pattern becomes established and stands out for the researcher in the midst of group data. In Patterson's view, further sequential-analytic and structural equation approaches may soon address this problem in a systematic manner.

Subgrouping within populations may also be helpful in the researcher's approach to the problems of meaning. This is a time-honoured strategy for clinical research, especially epidemiology (Rutter, this volume), and it has also been used by many others for non-clinical populations (see Sroufe and Fleeson; Stevenson-Hinde, this volume, for subgrouping that uncovers influences within pre-school relationships; and see Hetherington, this volume, for subgrouping that uncovers influences among family relationships following divorce).

It is also necessary to specify multiple aspects of context in order to establish meaning. Thus, Radke-Yarrow reminds us in her studies that anger has a different signal value in low SES families from that which it has in middle-class families. Case-intensive review may yield a great deal of knowledge about context, as the work of Caspi and Elder (this volume) shows, using data from the Berkeley Guidance Study. The context for meaning, however, involves not just social context but also the physiological context for the individuals involved. This topic has not been included in this volume. Research with marital couples provides a dramatic example of how physiological variables can help the researcher to understand the meaning of the behaviour of individuals within relationships. Gottman and Levenson (1986) describe a behavioural response phenomenon called 'stonewalling'. This occurs when, in a marital conflict, one partner attacks the other and the individual being complained about does not give an obvious emotional reaction or a 'counter-complaint'. But it turns out that 'stonewalling' can have two very different meanings. In Gottman's laboratory individuals were monitored with respect to autonomic nervous system measures during a marital conflict resolution task in the laboratory. Some individuals were found to have an autonomic arousal pattern (for example with cardiac acceleration) while engaged in 'stonewalling' while other individuals were not. In subsequent interviews, when they were viewing videotapes of their interactions and reliving the laboratory experience, it became clear that those with the autonomic arousal pattern were feeling distress and had the idea they were being attacked unfairly; in marked contrast, those 'stonewallers' who were not aroused were feeling empathic with the spouse's complaint during such incidents.

Most of us use a multimethod/multimeasure approach to establish meaning with respect to our constructs of interest. It is also important, as mentioned elsewhere in this volume, to take multiple approaches to looking at our data once they are collected. Thus, Kreppner (this volume) talks about his 'hermeneutic' approach to immersion in data analysis and in viewing videotapes before embarking on a final strategy for looking at configurations. Some of the most interesting associations between variables concern non-linear effects; hence, even though we use correlations for much of our work, we must always look at scattergrams for unusual distributions. Not only can we avoid interpretative errors in this way, but we can also entertain the possibility of separate analyses for different parts of a given distribution. We may also consider approaches wherein we categorize individuals as an alternative to linear analysis (see Hinde and Dennis 1986).

In any discussion of meaning, it is also necessary to stress the importance of rare events. A lesson from the field of artifical intelligence is that the finding of a positive instance is of enormous value in human problem-solving, outweighing by far strategies involving systematic surveys of negative instances. Thus, in diagnosis, the experienced clinician proceeds from the positive instance of the patient's chief complaint and its associated symptoms without necessarily going through a systematic detailed review of systems. Patterson and Dishion (this volume) remind us that the unusual event of a father intervening when mother and child were arguing was found to be associated with a good outcome for children at risk for antisocial behaviour. Thus, unusual events are often determinative in human affairs and we need ways of data collection and analysis that will capture them. It is no small challenge to capture such events among individuals who are embedded in sets of relationships which are influencing one another.

This digression on the importance of meaning can be concluded by reminding ourselves that man is a symbolic animal and that our evolutionary biology has arranged man's complexity so that the experience of no two individuals can be the same (see Platt 1966). From the point of view of relationships, we therefore need ipsative methods which encompass man's complex representational world of shared meaning and intersubjectivity. Such a concern occupies one of the frontiers of developmental research and thinking (see Trevarthen 1979; Kaye 1982; Bretherton 1985; Stern 1985).

Now to return to the main theme of this discussion—the interventionist relationship and our need to conceptualize how it influences the effects of relationships on relationships.

Interventionist relationships on parent–child relationships

To examine effects of interventionist relationships on relationships within the family, I shall refer to three studies of at-risk parents and offspring. They all involve varying degrees of assistance for parents: practical parenting guidance, providing support, assisting in contingency awareness in relation to infant needs, and facilitating play. One study involves a risk population of teenage mothers and their infants, and is being conducted by Joy Osofsky. Another study involves infants and mothers at risk because of prematurity and low SES, and is being conducted by Leila Beckwith, Arthur Parmelee, and colleagues. The third study, by Kathryn Barnard and colleagues, involves mothers and infants who are at risk because of poverty and socially defined multiple risk factors. Each of these studies is still in progress, but preliminary assessments have been made with infants well into their second year. Two points came out of their work at a recent symposium presentation (Barnard 1986; Beckwith 1986; Osofsky 1986). First, all the above-named investigators have concluded that, to a large extent, intervention effects depend upon the quality of the interventionist–subject relationship. To understand salutary intervention effects one must establish an 'effective dose' of this kind of intervention. In other words, one must subgroup interventions according to the qualities of such relationships, as determined from such measures as interviews with participants in the relationship, the number of appointments kept, and completion of required tasks. In future intervention studies, more attention must be given to the quality, affective characteristics, and nature of the interventionist–subject relationship (in addition to the general strategy of the intervention manipulation itself). The second point from these studies is that the investigators have found no effects of their interventions on the security of attachment when assessed at one year. In other words, interventions aimed at influencing the parenting relationship in a salutary manner, did not produce a greater incidence of security of attachment than occured in the non-intervention groups. How can we understand this finding?

The above question introduces another theme that cuts through the chapters in this book. It is important to understand the meaning of the attachment construction itself in the context of a relationship. From the infant's point of view, attachment is only one aspect of the early caregiving relationship. Other aspects include those having to do with:

(1)   physiological need satisfaction;

(2)   protection/vigilance;

(3)   play;

(4)   teaching/learning; and

(5)   control/autonomy.

These aspects are obviously overlapping and interdependent, but they are conceptually and empirically separable as subsystems having different set-goals (see also Grossmann et al., this volume). Thus, with interventions largely directed to these other aspects of parenting, primary or differential influences on the attachment/security system are not necessarily to be expected.

Another aspect of meaning which these intervention studies bring to our attention concerns the interpretation of the Strange Situation at age 1 year from the infant's point of view. Recently, studies of Japanese infants in the Strange Situation have resulted in an unusually high proportion of infants being classified as 'resistant' or in the 'Type C Attachment Pattern'. Such findings are probably best understood in terms of the high amount of stress Japanese infants experience in this situation against a background of their relative unfamiliarity with strangers and their not having been previously separated from their mothers (Miyake *et al.* 1985). In the above-mentioned intervention studies, many of the high-risk parenting relationships may have been under particular kinds of intense environmental stress; this could have led to different background experiences for infants in the Strange Situation as compared with the normative samples originally standardized by Ainsworth and her colleagues (Ainsworth *et al.* 1978).

Adult psychotherapy and psychoanalysis

The centrality of the therapeutic relationship has long been considered axiomatic across a range of psychotherapies. Still, there is much remaining to be understood. A basic question is: 'When psychotherapy works, how can we understand the influence of the therapeutic relationship in disentangling the untoward influences of representations of past relationships on current life relationships?' In a recent review of brief psychotherapies, Ursano and Hales (1986) document that dynamic, cognitive, and interpersonal approaches all acknowledge the initial working alliance as perceived by patient and therapist as being a major determinant of success; indeed, the selection of cases for brief psychotherapy usually involves taking those who can form an initial working alliance. The review of these authors also indicates a remarkable agreement across the range of brief psychotherapies concerning the length of recom-mended treatment, namely, from 10–20 sessions. After such a time, the therapist–patient relationship changes rather dramatically: it is as if there is a turning point following which qualitatively different relationship phenomena appear. These are variously referred to as regressive, dependent, unfocused, or unnecessarily complicated. It is well known in clinical circles that after this time, the therapist ceases to be seen as part of the solution and instead increasingly becomes part of the problem, although psychodynamic clinicians generally conceptualize such phenomena as opportunities for further reorganization and growth (usually described in terms of transference regressions and transference defences). In spite of this, such a commonly observed transformation in the nature of the therapeutic relationship, as a function of time, has not received systematic empirical research. It is as if the effect of the therapeutic relationship on other represented relationships undergoes a major shift.

Also relevant is the recent research of Luborsky and colleagues (Luborsky *et al.* 1985). Reviewing numerous studies of psychotherapy, these investigators accumulated evidence that the way the therapist and patient relate to one another early in treatment is an important predictor of therapeutic outcome. In a carefully controlled study involving cognitive and brief dynamic psychotherapy with random assignment of patients to therapists and to type of treatment, they found that an early in-treatment measure of the patient–therapist relationship was a more meaningful predictor of outcome than were measures of therapist characteristics, patient characteristics, or treatment orientation. All of this work is quite promising. We seem to be at a time when psychotherapy research may be able to elucidate what contributes to relationship matches and mismatches and, furthermore, what facilitates adult development in a relationship context.

In studies of long-term psychotherapy and psychoanalysis, research recordings and transcripts of the discourse between therapist (or analyst) and patient are now being used to study repetitive themes of conflict and symptomatic behaviour. Episodes of what have been termed 'core conflictual relationship themes' and 'role relationship conflicts' are being studied by major programmatic research teams and subjected to hypothesis testing, systematic formulations, and interdisciplinary scrutiny using a variety of methods (Horowitz et al. 1984; Luborsky et al. 1985). In these approaches, schemas involving relationships experienced in the past are seen to influence unduly (and maladaptively) current relationships, including the therapeutic relationship. Horowitz and his colleagues have used what they call 'configuration analysis' to assess the complex and changing influences of representative relationships on other relationships. As with brief psychotherapy, one gains a sense there is increasing appreciation of the relationship context as being salient when conflicts are repeated in neurotic behaviour; there is also a need to study what makes for 'matches' and mismatches' in therapeutic relationships at different phases of such work.

Infant psychiatry—a special psychotherapeutic intervention

A relatively recent form of psychotherapeutic intervention that is increasingly used is of considerable interest from the point of view of influencing relationships and their representation. In this form of intervention, psychotherapy takes place with a parent, usually the mother, with the additional presence of a baby who, quite naturally, develops and grows over the course of the sessions. Therapy addresses a focal parenting conflict, which is seen by the therapist as an edition of a past conflict, such as between mother and grandmother. In other words, the represented conflict from the past is relived in the present and 'opened', as it were, by the experience of parenting the baby. The psychotherapeutic relationship with the baby present is seen as a special opportunity—a 'new beginning' for the individual parent, just as infancy in general is seen as a 'new beginning' for generational and cultural renewal.

The model for this kind of treatment derives from the pioneering studies of Selma Fraiberg. Fraiberg used the haunting metaphor of 'ghosts in the nursery' to refer to the unpleasant and warded-off influences of past caregiving relationships on the current caregiving experience. Fraiberg discovered the special opportunities for therapeutic change and for development when a mother and her baby could be assisted by a therapist. Because of the baby's developmental thrust in the context of the parenting relationship, Fraiberg once remarked that from the therapist's view, 'it's a little bit like having God on your side' (Fraiberg *et al.* 1975). The Fraiberg model of psychotherapy of the parent with the baby present is now being used not only in the US but also in France and Switzerland (Cramer and Stern 1986; Lebovici 1986).

Family therapy

I would like to propose a heuristic proposition about family therapy which is based on our current knowledge and should therefore exist until disproven. The proposition is as follows: the major working area of all forms of family therapy involves the effects of relationships on relationships. An immediate objection to this proposition will be raised from a systems point of view. It will be argued that the proposition simply cannot be true because there is another emergent level of family phenomena in which the whole is greater than the sum of the parts: configurations of relationships can only be understood in a dynamic (or homeostatic) sense if we go beyond the effects of relationships on relationships. Still, I maintain this proposition remains to be proven wrong with empirical research. Alternative hypotheses can then be developed as necessary. What we seem to be working with now are the effects of relationships on other relationships. Such a view has been stated in a prior communication by Hinde (in press).

   Aside from its heuristic value, the above proposition is given impetus by recent evocative findings from behavioural genetics (summarized in recent reviews: Plomin 1986; Plomin and Daniels 1987). Both with respect to temperamental traits and to psychopathology, evidence involving family pedigree studies, adoption studies, and twin studies leads to the coherent conclusion that it is the non-shared family environment, not the shared family environment, that determines non-genetic influences on individual differences. Such a point of view is also fully consistent with Dunn's formulations from her studies of siblings observed in the home environment (this volume). There are many interpretations as to what is involved in the non-shared family environment, but for me it implies that specific relationships are important to study as opposed to the family as a whole.

   Overall, I believe it is incumbent upon us to specify the family and the life course context of meaning for the effect of relationships on other relationships. We also need to specify when therapeutic change (that is, a third interventionist relationship influencing the effect of relationships on relationships is possible. In concluding, I would like to advance two more points.

First, we may be able to mobilize strong developmental functions in the process of forming relationships. As with a new child, there may be other opportunities in the life cycle for capitalizing on a developmental thrust involving new relationships. There also may be key times in the midst of therapeutic relationships when such opportunities arise or do not arise. Secondly, I would remind us that *all research* is an intervention involving the relationship of the researcher to one or more human subjects. There will necessarily be uncertainty and influence with respect to our relationships with others whom we have in scientific focus. I think it would be valuable, therefore, if we study the researcher–subject relationship more than we have. What is certain is that multiple perspectives are needed.

Summary

All clinical intervention involves the influence of a new relationship on a pre-existing set of problematic relationships. In understanding this influence, primary attention must be given to meaning—in the sense of individual representations and affective themes, in the sense of shared values and expectations, and in the sense of particular developmental contexts and particular social contexts. Attention to meaning may require the use of atypical research approaches. These include ipsative methods, ways of accounting for non-linear and unusual events, and ways of specifying what matters most for individuals coping within a relationship context. A crucial research strategy involves assessing the match between interventionist and subject. These principles are illustrated by a discussion of several kinds of interventionist relationships. Among these are:

(1)   cross-generational effects on parenting;

(2)   parent–child relationships;

(3)   adult psychotherapy;

(4)   infant psychiatry; and

(5)   family therapy.

References

Ainsworth, M. D. S., Blehar, M., Waters, E., and Wall, S. (1978). *Patterns of attachment*. Erlbaum, Hillsdale, NJ.
Barnard, K. (1986). *Intervention with high social risk mothers and their infants*. Presented at the Annual Scientific Meeting of the National Center for Clinical Infant Programs, Washington, DC.

Beckwith, L. (1986). *Intervention with disadvantaged parents of sick preterm infants.* Presented at the Annual Scientific Meeting of the National Center for Clinical Infant Programs, Washington, DC.

Bretherton, I. (1985). Attachment theory: retrospect and prospect. In *Growing points of attachment theory and research* (ed. I. Bretherton and E. Waters). *Monographs of the Society for Research in Child Development* Serial No. 209, **50**, (1–2), 3–35.

Cramer, B. and Stern, D. (1986). *Mother–infant psychotherapy: objective and subjective changes.* Plenary presented at the Third World Congress of Infant Psychiatry and Allied Disciplines, Stockholm, Sweden.

Fraiberg, S., Adelson, E., and Shapiro, V. (1975). Ghosts in the nursery: a psychoanalytic approach to the problems of impaired infant-mother relationships. *Journal of the American Academy of Child Psychiatry* **14**, 387–421.

Gottman, J. M. and Levenson, R. W. (1986). Assessing the role of emotion in marriage. *Behavioral Assessment* **8**, 31–48.

Hinde, R. A. (in press). Reconciling the family systems and the relationships approaches to child development. In *Family systems and life-span development* (ed. K. Kreppner and R. M. Lerner). Erlbaum, Hillsdale, NJ.

Hinde, R. A. and Dennis, A. (1986). Categorizing individuals: an alternative to linear analysis. *International Journal of Behavioral Development* **9**, 105–19.

Horowitz, M., Marmar, C., Krupnick, J., Wilner, N., Kaltreider, N., and Wallerstein, R. (1984). *Personality styles and brief psychotherapy.* Basic Books, New York.

Kaye, K. (1982). *The mental and social life of babies.* The University of Chicago Press.

Lebovici, S. (1986). *Fantasied interaction and intergenerational transmission.* Plenary presented at the Third World Congress of Infant Psychiatry and Allied Disciplines, Stockholm, Sweden.

Luborsky, L., McLellan, A. T., Woody, G. E., O'Brien, C. P., and Auerbach, A. (1985). Therapist success and its determinants. *Archives of General Psychiatry* **42**, 602–11.

Main, M., Kaplan, N., and Cassidy, J. (1985). Security in infancy, childhood, and adulthood: a move to the level of representation. In *Growing points of attachment theory and research* (ed. I. Bretherton and E. Waters). *Monographs of the Society for Research in Child Development* Serial No. 209, **50**, (1–2), 66–104.

Miyake, K., Chen, S., and Campos, J. J. (1985). Infant temperament, mother's mode of interaction, and attachment in Japan: an interim report. In *Growing points of attachment theory and research* (ed. I. Bretherton and E. Waters). *Monographs of the Society for Research in Child Development* Serial No. 209, **50**, (1–2), 276–97.

Osofsky, J. D. (1986). *Intervention challenges with adolescent mothers and their infants.* Presented at the Annual Scientific Meeting of the National Center for Clinical Infant Programs, Washington, DC.

Platt, J. R. (1966). *The step to man.* Wiley, New York.

Plomin, R. (1986). *Development, genetics, and psychology.* Erlbaum, Hillsdale, NJ.

Plomin, R. and Daniels, D. (1987). Why are children in the same family so different from one another? *Behavioral and Brain Sciences* **10**, 1–59.

Solnit, A. J. and Provence, S. (1979). Vulnerability and risk in early childhood. In *Handbook of infant development* (ed. J. D. Osofsky). Wiley, New York.

Stern, D. N. (1985). *The interpersonal world of the infant.* Basic Books, New York.

Trevarthen, C. (1979). Communication and cooperation in early infancy: a description of primary intersubjectivity. In *Before speech: the beginning of interpersonal communication* (ed. M. Bullowa), pp. 321–47. Cambridge University Press.

Ursano, R. J. and Hales, R. E. (1986). A review of brief individual psychotherapies. *American Journal of Psychiatry* **143,** 1507–17.

Epilogue

ROBERT A. HINDE AND JOAN STEVENSON-HINDE

In this final chapter, we attempt to draw together some of the issues arising in the earlier chapters. As might be expected, on some of them there is no general agreement. Over some of these we have exerted the editorial privilege of stating our own views, and in doing so we should emphasize that the other contributors to this volume may not share them and have had no chance to comment.

Family systems vs. relationships vs. interactions vs. individuals

The contributors differed dramatically in the level of analysis that they considered appropriate. Some focused on the family as a system, emphasizing that the whole is more than the sum of its parts, that any change in the family involves all its members, and that causal sequences are liable to be circular and reverberating (e.g. Kreppner*; Minuchin). Others, by contrast, focused on individuals and their relationships, implying that the behaviour of individuals depends on the interaction or relationship in which they are involved, but that change must ultimately involve changes in individuals (e.g. Belsky and Pensky; Caspi and Elder; Patterson and Dishion; Sroufe and Fleeson; Stevenson-Hinde). However, nearly every contribution involves the integration of data from several levels: for instance, Sroufe and Fleeson also use concepts from family systems theory, and Radke-Yarrow, Richters, and Wilson relate properties of the family as a whole (stable vs. chaotic) both to the behaviour of individuals and to the properties of relationships.

In a similar way, some contributors drew conclusions about individuals from studies of relationships or families, while others described relationships or families from studies of individuals. Such extrapolations are inevitable. On the one hand, individuals cannot be studied in isolation from their relationships, and on the other, relationships or families can be studied over only a limited time span, so that the memories of individuals are the most fruitful source of information on many of their properties. At the same time, it is important to recognize the dangers in such procedures. As we have seen, the properties of each interaction or relationship are influenced by both

*Here, chapters are referred to by authors' names only.

individuals, and the properties of any family by every one of its constituent relationships. Furthermore, each level of social complexity has properties not relevant to that below. For such reasons, attempts to reconstruct patterns of dyadic interaction from independent reports by the two individuals miss the processes of feedback and adjustment that characterize individuals in interaction with each other (Minuchin), while attempts to characterize an individual from behaviour in one social context may lead to erroneous predictions about his/her behaviour in another.

Recognition of the dangers of arguing from one level to another does not imply that any one procedure is wrong, but it does underline the value of multimethod approaches. If family members are seen or interviewed both as individuals and in the context of relationships or groups, a much clearer picture is likely to emerge. Our own view (Hinde and Stevenson-Hinde 1987a), shared by Emde, is that the level of dyadic relationships merits special attention, though it is of course essential to go beyond the dyad, recognizing that how two individuals behave may be influenced by the presence of a third (e.g. Christensen and Margolin; Dunn; Barrett and Hinde; Kreppner; Minuchin; Radke-Yarrow et al.). The crucial issue must be a readiness to cross and re-cross the dialectics between the levels of social complexity.

There is, however, one point that needs to be made. We suggested in the Introduction that relationships, groups, and socio-cultural structure were to be seen from two points of view—the objective reality of the outside observer, and the subjective reality of the participants. This distinction is especially important for the socio-cultural structure. 'Family tasks' may be apparent to the outside observer, and he/she may record 'family myths', but such concepts influence process only in so far as they are inside the heads of the individual participants. For that reason, we feel that great care is needed with discussion that involves imputing an 'internal working model' to the family as a whole (Kreppner). A similar issue arises with the distinction between 'family style', concerned with behavioral interactions and supported by rules that organize the family's behaviour, and 'family world view' which concerns the family's self-perceptions (Minuchin). With regard to the former, it is necessary to distinguish between regularities as perceived by an outside observer and rules that operate within the heads of family members to guide their behaviour. And with regard to the 'family world view', although much may be shared (see also, e.g. Christensen and Margolin; Radke-Yarrow et al.), there may be marked differences between family members in the way they perceive the family.

We also feel that, if it is emphasized that families are 'organized' and all relationships within the family are constrained by that organization—especially if that organization is linked to an evolutionary argument about the functions the family must fulfil (Sroufe and Fleeson)—it is important to emphasize that the effects are two-way, and that also the organization is affected by the relationships. Since those relationships involve individuals and the goals of individuals may conflict, there may be argument between family members over many aspects of the family's 'organization'.

These issues are discussed further in an important paper by Minuchin (1985) which brings together the family systems approach with that of the developmental psychologist. While agreeing with her point of view on most issues, we would put the emphasis differently in some (Hinde, in press; see also Keller *et al.* 1987).

Methodology

The contributors to this volume have used diverse methods to attack problems of family dynamics. Here we summarize some of the issues that arise.

The problem of the selection of variables

What people say happens is not always the same as what actually happens. What people believe to have happened or want to happen may be as important as what actually transpires. Thus interview, questionnaire, and observational approaches all have their place, and indeed they may complement each other. Our own inclination is to emphasize the dividends that accrue from comparing data obtained by diverse techniques. Several of the contributors to this volume raise the question of the difficulty of getting at the meaning behind behaviour, and of understanding the real bases of expressed affect or attitudes. One route to this end involves the comparison of observational, questionnaire, interview, and test data. Radke-Yarrow and colleagues emphasize the potential of interviews even with 6-year-olds.

Where observational studies are used, a number of decisions about technique and about level are necessary. The former are to a large extent specific to the particular study, but the latter have general implications. The majority of observational studies of child development concern particular types of interaction. For example mother–infant feeding or play may be observed in a number of dyads, with generalizations based on means or medians across dyads. But within any one relationship, interactions of different types may affect each other: difficulties over feeding may carry over into the play situation. Thus, the study of relationships demands that we study each dyad in a number of behavioural contexts. That, however, poses a problem, for measures of different types of interaction of the same dyad lie along different dimensions, and any attempts to reduce them to a single scale would involve possibly unjustified assumptions. As a matter of fact, the same problem arises with interactions or individual behaviour, but is often overlooked: the several measures that might be taken, such as latency or intensity, usually show only low inter-correlations, so that the choice of which to measure is arbitrary, and the different measures cannot be reduced to a common scale.

Several solutions to this dilemma are put forward in this volume. Dunn suggests that one type of interaction may serve as an index of the whole relationship; clearly the success of this approach depends upon judicious choice of the type of interaction. Kreppner uses the time that particular dyads or triads spend in interaction—an approach that provides some insight into family dynamics, but postpones issues of content and quality. Radke-Yarrow and colleagues neglected content in favour of *quality*, using an affect measure which reflected the quality of diverse types of interaction (see also Easterbrooks and Emde). We suggest that the latter approach holds much promise for many problems, but that analyses of the relations between different types of interaction will still be necessary for an understanding of process.

It is in this context that Emde's emphasis on the importance of selecting measures relevant to relationships has a special importance. It is one thing to count (from observational or interview data) how often certain events occur, but frequency may not be the most meaningful measure: ratio measures, indicating, for instance, the proportion of the child's cries to which the mother responded, may be more meaningful than, or may provide an insight different from, the absolute frequency of responses (Hinde and Herrmann 1977). Such ratio measures are relevant to 'maternal sensitivity', a dimension that has proved meaningful in understanding the development of attachment relationships (e.g. Grossmann *et al*.): a similar point arises from discussions of 'goodness of fit' between the family and the child's temperament (Lerner, in press).

Another meaningful dimension is 'commitment'. This is especially relevant where there is a possibility of terminating the relationship, as in marital relationships, foster families, and therapeutic relationships (Emde). Commitment to a relationship is not easy to assess. There is evidence that it is better predicted by the sacrifices made for the relationship or family, including what the individual forgoes doing in order to make a contribution, than by what they appear to get out of it (Lund 1985). Again, how individuals perceive each other may in the long term be more important for some issues than how they behave to each other, but is again not easy to measure. These and a number of related issues are discussed by Hinde (1979).

Some points about observational studies

The research worker needs above all to know what goes on in real life, and it might seem that observational techniques are an obvious choice. However, apart from the difficulties of their necessarily involving some degree of artificiality, the limited time span that can be covered, and the problems of analysis posed by the data, some other limitations emphasized in the contributions to this volume may be noted. One concerns the importance of sequential analysis (Minuchin). Although analytic techniques are well established (Bakeman 1978), conclusions about sequential dependencies require very large data sets, which may be impossible to obtain in the changing dynamics of normal family life. Christensen and Margolin adopt a coarser-grained but useful approach to this problem.

Secondly, although techniques for coding the behaviour of dyads in interaction are well developed (e.g. Caldwell 1969), coding triadic interactions tends to be cumbersome (Barrett and Hinde).

A third issue is that of context. Observational studies may be conducted in a structured situation in the laboratory, or in a semi-structured situation in the home, or they may attempt to get at the normal course of family life in an unstructured way. The Ainsworth Strange Situation (Ainsworth *et al.* 1978), which is designed to measure a specific aspect of the mother–child relationship, is an example of the former, while Kreppner's study of parents with two children approaches the latter. It is important to remember that no method is perfect: for instance, observation of mother and child alone neglects the important influence that the father may have, while inclusion of the father may involve a situation that occurs for only a small proportion of the time in real life.

While we have mentioned some of their difficulties, we would emphasize that observational methods, especially when employing video techniques that permit the detailed analysis of expressive sequences, provide data obtainable in no other way.

Specification of the questions

Minuchin makes the important point that the mere presence of a third individual may affect the course of interaction in a dyad. Her discussion raises an important point about studies of development. She was referring to the work of Grotevant and Cooper (1985) who had found that the communication patterns of daughters in a variety of intrafamilial interactions were associated with identity exploration, whereas with sons 'only father–son interactions were related to exploration ratings. These differences suggest that sources of family influence on identity exploration may be more diverse for female adolescents than for males' (p. 425). Perhaps a more accurate statement would be that *differences* in the communication patterns in several relationships are related to *differences* in identity exploration for daughters, but *differences* in communication patterns only in father–son interaction to *differences* in exploration in sons. In other words, the data address questions of sources of differences, not the absolute importance of a given source of influence (for further discussion see Hinde 1979).

Use of extreme, pathological, or high-risk groups vs. unselected samples

Extreme groups demand study in their own right. Furthermore, it is sometimes possible to expose family processes more readily by studying extreme groups. By exaggerating differences, they can provide principles which would be more difficult to detect in a more homogeneous normal sample. For example, Christensen and Margolin compared distressed with smoothly running families, and were thus able to throw light on some of the properties operating in both (see also Easterbrooks and Emde). Usually, data from extreme groups can be generalized to more normal families: thus Belsky and Pensky reviewed evidence that cross-generational transmission of the quality of parent–child relationships and of marital relationships occurs both in extreme and in 'normal' families. But, of course, this does not *necessarily* mean that the psychological processes operating are the same: indeed Rutter emphasizes that different principles may apply in extreme or pathological families from those that apply elsewhere. For example, Radke-Yarrow *et al.* found that the nature and effectiveness of maternal control techniques differed between chaotic and stable families. Some such differences might be predicted on biological grounds: in the course of evolution individuals have become adapted to cope with a range of relationships and of social situations, but the principles that applied then may not be appropriate to all circumstances in modern societies.

Small vs. large sample sizes

Case studies of individual families, large-scale surveys, and many inter-mediates are all cited in this book. Each has its advantages. Small samples can be useful for demonstrating the importance of particular variables, and for throwing light on process. Large samples are necessary for demonstrating interactions between variables, and are essential for proving the generality of principles. They also permit the isolation of subsamples for the examination of particular effects. But large samples also carry dangers. For example, logistic considerations may constrain the degree of detail in the data, and this in turn may handicap the understanding of process. And, of course, with a large sample effects may be significant statistically and yet account for little of the variance. Furthermore, important differences, such as those between chaotic and stable families (Radke-Yarrow *et al.*), may be overlooked. Without wishing to impugn the value of other approaches, our own bias is in favour of moderate sample sizes which permit moderately detailed data collection and a degree of insight into the affairs of individual families, the latter being an important source of ideas for the interpretation of data and for guiding new studies. Radke-Yarrow and colleagues advocate a rather similar approach, and emphasize the value of identifying within the sample small groups which have some significant characteristics, and of a subsequent search for significant issues in their development: this provides the basis for new hypotheses that can be tested (cf. Magnusson 1987).

Retrospective data

Relationships are extended in time, and what happens today may be affected by what happened a day, a week, a month, or years previously. For that reason, important insights may come from retrospective material about the past experiences of the individuals concerned. Indeed, the foundations of attachment theory came with Bowlby's (1944) observation that a number of juvenile delinquents shared a common type of early experience. In the present volume, Caspi and Elder were able to achieve a four-generational study by using retrospective data on their G1 generation provided by individuals who were adult when the study started.

There are, however, obvious problems with retrospective data. Minuchin argues that recall of the past is essentially a current construction, and thus cannot be used to indicate a clear cause–effect relation between past and present (see Bartlett 1932). Radke-Yarrow and her colleagues and Meyer make a similar point. Grossmann et al. go further, showing that retrospection can be used as an index of current state: aspects of the mother–child relationship are related less to the mother's own childhood experiences than to her current recollection of and attitudes to them (see also Main et al. 1985).

When retrospective data are used as a key to the past, two important issues arise. One concerns their potential unreliability. As emphasized by Meyer, a number of affective and cognitive processes are involved in self-descriptions, and especially in descriptions of the past. More importantly, the finding that all individuals with characteristic 'Y' formerly had experience 'X' is not evidence that all individuals having experience 'X' will develop characteristic 'Y'. The connections between 'X' and 'Y' may be devious, and a variety of protective and vulnerability factors may affect the prognosis of individuals who have experienced 'X' (e.g. Belsky and Pensky; Rutter). For such reasons, prospective studies can be of crucial importance.

The use of transitions

A number of contributions stress that transition periods in the development of a family may be especially revealing of its dynamics. Thus Dunn, and Kreppner, used the arrival of a second child; Minuchin discusses the consequences of severe illness in a family member, and Hetherington's contribution centres round divorce. The changes that occur after such events may provide important insights into processes operative throughout the family life span.

Problems with correlational methods

Many of these studies involve analyses which depend ultimately on correlational techniques. Although the difficulties that can arise are well known, a few points especially pertinent to this volume may be noted.

1. Ubiquitous effects. Absence of a significant correlation does not imply no influence: individuals may still be affected by a relationship, even if there is no correlation between measures of the relationship and measures of their behaviour.

2. Means and correlations. In longitudinal studies, the mean of a given dependent variable may change when the inter-individual correlation is high, or vice versa.

3. Linearity. Most correlational techniques assume linearity. Many data are not linear. In such cases categorization of subjects may be a fruitful alternative (e.g. Hetherington; Radke-Yarrow *et al.*; Sroufe and Fleeson; Stevenson-Hinde; see also Hinde and Dennis 1986).

4. Direction of effects. Correlations cannot by themselves indicate the direction of effects. Several of the contributors to this volume use structural models and forms of path analysis to surmount this problem (Caspi and Elder; Engfer; Meyer; Patterson and Dishion). The value of this approach is evident, but the robustness of the conclusions that can be drawn has been the subject of some discussion (see Rutter 1987).

Limitations on generalizations

Research attempts to establish principles with a degree of generality. However, family processes are influenced by diverse factors, and the effect of any one may be influenced by the presence of others. Four issues important in a number of the contributions are summarized briefly here.

Values, norms, and the socio-cultural structure

Most family studies take place within a given culture, and attitudes towards parenting, norms and values are taken as given. However, influences may be important even though ubiquitous, and ubiquitous influences may act differently on different segments of the population. Concepts of child difficultness, marital quality, and so on all imply a social norm, and comparisons between perceptions of the current situation and perceptions of norms (or of what can reasonably be expected) play a crucial part in family dynamics. Furthermore, differences in social-contextual factors may be associated with marked differences in familial relationships (Radke-Yarrow *et al.*). Again, the consequences of divorce depend critically on prevailing social attitudes, and the difficulties that adults experience in forming relationships with stepchildren (Hetherington) must depend, in part, on differences between children's expectations concerning behaviour that is appropriate for a parent and for a stepparent.

Gender

A crucial issue here is child gender. Although differences between the behaviour of girls and boys must ultimately have biological determinants, differential adult treatment of, and expectations for, boys and girls play a crucial role. Radke-Yarrow *et al.* discuss three types of boy–girl differences: differences in the associations between aggressiveness and maternal affect; between shyness, other child characteristics, and mother–child interaction; and between maternal mood and her expressions of physical affection to the child. We have obtained strikingly similar data with British 4-year-olds (Hinde and Stevenson-Hinde 1987*b*; Simpson and Stevenson-Hinde 1985). Radke-Yarrow and colleagues ascribe the gender differences to differences between the behavioural correlates of aggression and shyness in boys and girls, the mothers responding to the patterns of interrelated behaviour of which aggression and shyness are a part. In no way contradictory to this view, we have ascribed a basic importance to differences between maternal norms about behaviour that are appropriate for (or to) little girls and little boys. Thus, we have suggested that maternal control (and perhaps anger) over boys tends to be found primarily in relationships that are generally tensionful, but to be more evenly distributed across mother–daughter relationships; that shyness in daughters is regarded as an asset, but shyness in boys is evaluated negatively; and that it is alright to cuddle a little girl but not a little boy (or that girls allow themselves to be cuddled more than do boys). We take the view that gender differences depend on a dialectical interplay between biological propensities and social forces, the latter mediated by relationships but derived from gender stereotypes in the socio-cultural structure that themselves depend on the exaggeration of biological propensities (Hinde 1987). It thus remains a formidable task to disentangle the developmental processes involved, and to reach understanding of why (for instance) marital conflict tends to lead to undercontrolled behaviour in boys and over-controlled in girls (Easterbrooks and Emde), or of the many gender differences in relationships between parents and stepchildren described by Hetherington (see also Dunn).

A number of other contributions report marked differences between father–child and mother–child relationships, with differential impact on child personality development. Again, the precise role of social factors remains to be explored: Caspi and Elder argue that the socialization of women renders them more likely than men to be the vehicles of cross-generational transmission; and Sroufe and Fleeson ascribe the differences between male and female teachers as partly due to their own choice of roles with which they are compatable.

Developmental stages

Age of child is another important constraint on generalizations. For example, Dunn suggests that the relative importance of several processes in the mother–first child–second child triad may change with age of child. Using a dimension of 'perceived' child difficultness, Engfer emphasizes that the behavioral characteristics conducive to difficulty change with age. Easterbrooks and Emde review evidence that marital support is especially important during the transition to parenthood, and that the influence of marital quality on a child changes with developmental stage. Rutter points out that disruption of parenting is especially likely to be important if it occurs before the age of 4 years. Hetherington, concerned with the consequences of divorce and remarriage, provides numerous examples of the ways in which time since divorce and time since remarriage, as well as age of child, are important variables.

Type of relationships or family

A fourth limitation on generalizations about the effects of relationships on relationships concerns the nature of the relationships in question. For instance, Dunn suggests that some of the associations between mother–first-born and sibling relationships that she found were a consequence of the degree of emotional dependency characterizing the former. Again, Radke-Yarrow et al. demonstrate that the relation between child compliance and the quality of the mother–child relationship was different between stable and chaotic families, and Hetherington's data showed that the influence of the parent–child relationship on the sibling relationship may vary with the nature and quality of the former. We have argued elsewhere that progress in the understanding of such issues demands adequate methods for describing and categorizing relationships and families (Hinde 1979).

General

It is, of course, easy to assemble examples demonstrating that life is complicated, and that the influence of many factors may obstruct the generality of the principles for which we seek. However, as we shall see in the next section, the processes by which relationships affect relationships are diverse. The everyday issues of cultural norms, gender, stage, and the nature of the relationships, as well as the effects of extreme conditions discussed earlier, must be taken into account in understanding which processes are important.

How do relationships affect relationships?

To the simple question of whether relationships affect relationships within the family, the contributions to this volume supply an unequivocal positive answer, and go a considerable way towards indicating where the more important effects lie. They also contain much evidence about the processes involved. However, unequivocal evidence about how relationships affect relationships is not easy to obtain, for a number of reasons. One of the most important is that diverse simultaneous processes may be involved, so that it is difficult to demonstrate clearly the operation of any one. Another is that influences between relationships are often mutual and circular. Yet another reason is that a given process may act in some circumstances and not others—circumstances here referring not only to the nature of the relationships and the age and sex of the participants, but also to the presence of 'protective' or 'risk' factors that ameliorate, add to, or exacerbate its effects. And, of course, it is essential always to bear in mind that the effects implied by correlational methods are not necessarily the ones that really matter in terms of psychologically important processes.

In what follows we are not concerned with the possibility that correlated characteristics of, or changes in, two relationships may be due to a third factor, rather than to a causal influence between the two relationships (Rutter) except in the case of individual characteristics of a participant. We may also note that two issues, scarcely discussed in this volume, could merit further consideration.

First, members of a family are genetically similar, so that similarities in relationships within a family (or cross-generational effects) could be mediated by similarities in the genetic constitutions of the participants—either directly, or through some form of gene–environment interaction (Jaspars and Leeuw 1980; Scarr and Kidd 1983; Plomin 1986). However, none of the chapters in this volume contain evidence that this is an important issue (cf. Patterson and Dishion; Rutter). Recent studies show the heritability of personality traits not to be high, and conclude that most of the variance in personality traits reflects experiential factors not shared amongst family members (Rowe and Plomin 1981).

Secondly, we shall also not be concerned with contextual factors, important as they may be in contributing to the 'cycle of deprivation'. Radke-Yarrow and colleagues suggest that contextual factors may affect the entire pattern of relationships throughout a family. They may also affect continuities or discontinuities in individuals, relationships, or family structure over time (Rutter).

In the following sections we list a number of ways in which relationships affect relationships, most of which are considered by one or more contributors to this volume. It is necessary to say at once that it is not obvious how to classify satisfactorily the processes whereby relationships affect relationships, and we fully acknowledge overlap and interrelations between the categories we have used. It is convenient to consider first contemporaneous effects and then effects persisting over a part or most of a lifetime which may form the basis of transgenerational transmission.

Contemporaneous influences

(1) *Time and energy.*   Interactions consume time and energy. 'A''s relationship with 'B' may reduce the time or energy that 'A' has for interactions with 'C': such a mechanism undoubtedly contributes to the effect of the mother–second-born relationship on that between mother and first-born, where the first-born may feel an emotional need consequent upon displacement by the new baby (Dunn). The negative effect of a difficult child on the marriage (Engfer) may be mediated in part at this level. Alternatively, if 'B' helps 'A' with necessary tasks, this may increase the time 'A' has for 'C': thus a co-operative marital relationship can augment the mother–child relationship (Engfer; Rutter).

(2) *Psychological support.*   Even more important than practical support may be psychological support. Engfer refers to the supportive effect of a warm marital relationship on the mother–child relationship as 'spill-over', and Easterbrooks and Emde describe a positive marital relationship as fuelling the parents for the task of sensitive parenting. Amongst their findings was an interesting difference between mothers and fathers: fathers who perceived their marriages as happy were warmer to and less aggravated by their children than other fathers: no such effect was found amongst mothers. Easterbrooks and Emde suggest that mothers may be more effectively buffered against variations in the caregiving environment. Rutter and Garmezy (1983) emphasize the valuable effects of other positive relationships on children after divorce (see also Hetherington), and in this volume Rutter refers to the ameliorating influence of a good marital relationship on the consequences of institutional upbringing.

However, as over so many issues, generalizations about the effects of relationships on relationships must be hedged about with reservations. Hetherington describes how support of a mother and active participation in child-rearing by a stepfather led to less externalizing behaviour in their stepsons but to an increase in acting-out behaviour and depression in their stepdaughters.

(3) *Deficient support.*   Changes or deficiencies in relationships may involve needs in individuals, whose relationships with others are affected in consequence. In a sense this is the opposite side of the coin to the issues

mentioned in the previous paragraph. For example, siblings may need mutual support from each other more if maternal warmth is lacking (Dunn) or after divorce (Hetherington); women in poor marriages may become intensely involved with their children, and mothers with difficult children may make extra demands on their marriage (Engfer; Easterbrooks and Emde). However, in families suffering both marital discord and child conduct problems, Christensen and Margolin found that mothers were more negative and fathers more neutral to the child: they comment that maternal over-involvement with undercontrolled children tends to produce conflict rather than supportiveness, and is unlikely to be gratifying to the mother.

(4) *Competition.* Competition between two individuals may affect their relationship with a third. Thus Dunn described how first-borns who had a close relationship with their mothers tended to have a poor relationship with a new sibling whom they could perceive as displacing them, and to be sensitive to differences between maternal responsiveness to them and the new sibling (cf. (3) above). Hetherington cites evidence that siblings, deprived of parental affection after divorce, compete more. She also provides evidence for a positive correlation between divorced mother–daughter closeness before remarriage and subsequent conflict with mother and stepfather, and shows that preferential treatment by stepfathers was especially likely to lead to sibling disharmony. Barrett and Hinde's data also demonstrate competition between siblings for maternal attention. Such competition between siblings may lead to parental intervention (Kreppner; Barrett and Hinde). Christensen and Margolin show that conflict may spread from one relationship to another. As Rutter points out, this may be mediated by the general emotional climate or by relationships.

Competition may occur not only between siblings, but also between spouse and child. Easterbrooks and Emde suggest that, with a positive marriage, parents see children as less of an interference in their own lives as well as less difficult temperamentally.

(5) *Spread of affect.* A harmonious/disharmonious relationship may affect the general atmosphere in the family, and thus other relationships. The study by Radke-Yarrow and colleagues demonstrates concordance in affect in different relationships within the family, and more negative affect in 'chaotic' as compared with 'stable' homes. Dunn suggests that changes in a first-born's general emotional well-being after the arrival of a new baby may affect his/her other relationships in the family. Spread of positive affect between parents and children is associated with parental agreement (Easterbrooks and Emde).

While a high marital quality may have a positive effect on the mother–child relationship, low marital quality may have a reverse effect. Furthermore, the effects may be interactive: spousal criticism of the mother consequent upon a poor mother–child relationship may affect the mother's self-esteem and reflect back on the marital relationship (see also Patterson and Dishion). Such effective interrelations presumably have physiological concomitants, though Emde emphasizes their relative neglect by the authors in this volume.

Christensen and Margolin discuss three ways in which marital discord may affect child development—by disrupting discipline procedures and other parental functions; by causing dysfunctional parent–child alliances which affect the child's development in a number of ways; and by spread of conflict across issues and across relationships (see also Easterbrooks and Emde; Patterson and Dishion). Of course, it is not implied that the direction of causation is necessarily from the marital relationship to the child: a difficult child may produce or exacerbate difficulties in the marriage (Easterbrooks and Emde; Engfer).

Competition and conflict do not necessarily have negative outcomes. In this volume, Hetherington records that the daughters of divorced unremarried mothers may grow up faster—though this may lead to problems later.

(6) *Influences on perceptions of others.*   How individuals perceive others and the relationships within the family are as important as what actually happens. Thus Engfer's data indicate that a mother's perceptions of infant difficultness may be associated more with her own characteristics than with those of the child, but may have long-lasting repercussions by creating real difficulties. Other contributors mentioned a number of other not easily classifiable issues that involve changes in the perceived meaning of relationships. Dunn found that discussion between mother and first-born about the new baby was associated with a more positive sibling relationship. There are a number of possible mechanisms here—for instance, the discussion could affect the first-born's perception of the baby, or of himself (i.e. the big one). She also provides evidence indicating that a first-born may show focused hostility as a result of observing affection between mother and second-born, or may be sensitive to the difference between his or her own relationship with the mother and that of the new baby (see (4) above). As another example, it has been suggested that a child's problems may lead to a refocusing of the family's attention, and thereby relieve marital discord (Christensen and Margolin; Easterbrooks and Emde; Minuchin *et al.* 1978). Perhaps also to be included here are differences between adult–child or child–child interactions between dyadic and polyadic situations (Barrett and Hinde), and the jealousy induced between siblings (Dunn; other examples are given by Rutter).

Of special interest, and perhaps related to the spread of affect between relationships, is Easterbrooks and Emde's concept of a 'perceptual bias screen', such that marital and parent–child relationships tend to be seen in a similar (favourable or unfavourable) light.

(7) *Social learning.*   A number of contributors mention the possible importance of social learning or modelling (e.g. Belsky and Pensky; Caspi and Elder; Easterbrooks and Emde; Patterson and Dishion; Stevenson-Hinde), and cite supportive data from other studies. Easterbrooks and Emde suggest

that their data are compatible with an influence of observational learning, and point out that its influence is likely to change with age. On the whole, we feel the importance of modelling may have been underestimated in this volume.

(8) *Monitoring.*   Parental monitoring of children may show strong associations with child behaviour and relationships (Hetherington).

(9) *Properties of groups.*   Those who draw on systems theory tend to refer to properties of the family as a unit influencing the properties of its constituent relationships: sometimes such influences are said to act in the direction of homeostasis, and sometimes to produce change (Kreppner; Minuchin; Sroufe and Fleeson). While we believe in the crucial importance of incorporating many principles from systems theory into developmental psychology, we suggest that principles of homeostasis and of change are valuable in the description of family dynamics, but we would prefer to seek for the processes underlying consistency or change in the component relationships or individuals (Hinde, in press).

In addition, Rutter refers to a number of general properties of groups that may operate within families. For instance groups tend to throw up leaders: the absence or illness of the leader may shift this reponsibility (Minuchin).

(10) *Personality.*   Finally, similarities between relationships or influences of one relationship on another can often be seen as mediated by personality characteristics of the participants. This is discussed in the next section.

Longer term effects

We shall now focus on factors within the individual that could have medium to long-term sequelae for relationships. Influences of individual characteristics on the parent–child relationship, or of the latter on child characteristics, are discussed by many of the contributors. The focus is on characteristics that are consistent across contexts or across time (Stevenson-Hinde) but there is no general consensus as to which are important. Some of the apparent discrepancies stem from mere differences in nomenclature. Nevertheless the variables used appear to fall into seven groups:

(1) *Dimensions of temperament and personality.*   Stevenson-Hinde discusses ways in which childhood temperament may be influenced by the mother–child relationship. Belsky and Pensky stress the need for a framework that includes a 'dynamic self system'. While referring to the 'internal working model' of attachment theory, they place their main emphasis on dimensions taken from personality theory; neuroticism/negative affectivity and extraversion/positive affectivity.

(2) *Affect.*   Easterbrooks and Emde cite previous studies indicating that the strongest associations between parenting and child development involve the affective dimensions. Their own data support this view. Such a conclusion would also be fully in accord with the data of Radke-Yarrow *et al.*, and the

emphasis placed on affect by other contributors (e.g. Dunn; Grossmann *et al.*; Sroufe and Fleeson).

(3) *Aspects of 'negative emotionality'*.   This category, clearly closely related to the last, includes a number of dimensions. Meyer is primarily concerned with two personality traits, negative emotionality and activity–achievement. Activity–achievement predicted marital quality, but had opposite relations with reported satisfaction and observed quality of interaction: it was also related to mother–child interaction. Maternal emotionality was predictive of mother–child interaction, but not marital quality. Engfer found wives' self-descriptions as depressed, moody, irritable, and unstable to be related to aspects both of marital quality and of mother–child interaction. Patterson and Dishion's data indicate that parents who are irritable and explosive provide ineffective discipline, leading to antisocial behaviour in their children.

(4) *Interactional style*.   Caspi and Elder suggest that continuity depends 'not so much on a personality trait or a psychoanalytic-like residue of early childhood', but on an interactional style. They propose two processes whereby childhood problem behaviour is sustained into adulthood. The first, 'cumulative continuity', refers to a continuing tendency to be involved in negative environments and situations, including discordant marriages. The second, 'interactional continuity', involves the evocation in new situations of self–other patterns learned earlier in life. Thus difficult girls tend to marry non-assertive men, have more conflictful marriages, and tend to be ill-tempered with their children (Belsky and Pensky; Engfer; Rutter).

(5) *Child-related attitudes, feelings and behaviour*.   Meyer distinguishes relatively stable personality traits from child-related attitudes and feelings, particularly those related to the parent's competence in child-rearing, though in his own data the latter was not significantly related to the quality of mother–child interaction. Patterson and Dishion keep 'parental traits' as a different set of variables from 'parental acceptance of the child'. Engfer, likewise, distinguishes between maternal personality characteristics and maternal sensitivity. Sensitive mothering plays a crucial part in the theoretical approach of both Grossmann and colleagues and of Sroufe and Fleeson, as discussed in the next section.

(6) *Attachment*.   A basic tenet of attachment theory is that attachment relationships formed in childhood will set a pattern for relationships in adulthood (Ainsworth *et al.* 1978; Bowlby 1982). This paradigm is drawn on by a number of authors, including Belsky and Pensky; Emde; Grossmann *et al.*; and Sroufe and Fleeson. As Grossmann *et al.* emphasize, attachment is but one aspect of the parent–child relationship, but it is believed to play a crucial role in mediating 'felt security' in other relationships.

Bowlby pictured this role of early attachment as involving the formation by the child of a working model of his/her relationships with his/her parents, which subsequently affected behaviour in relationships with others. More recently, Sroufe and Fleeson (1986) have suggested that the child can act out either side of this internalized 'working model' of relationships: thus a child who behaved in a submissive way to a dominating parent might subsequently show either dominating or submissive characteristics in other relationships. Thus an important aspect of this way of thinking is that it allows for the facts that individuals may behave differently in different relationships, that the behaviour shown in an interaction depends on both participants, and that the behaviour of an individual over time may not show continuity, as earlier trait theories suggested, but 'coherence' (see Bretherton 1985, 1987).

The comprehensive explanatory power of the concept of an internal working model is mentioned by Rutter, who uses it to exemplify explanations of continuity in terms of 'an internal organization of needs, attitudes, beliefs, and styles of coping that amount to an overall coherence of personality functioning' (see also Belsky and Pensky; Stevenson-Hinde). But therein lies a danger that it will lose its explanatory power because it could too easily be used to explain anything. So long as it is used heuristically, it has great value in most contexts (e.g. Sroufe and Fleeson). But one of us (Hinde, in press) feels that, so far as explanation is concerned, it can perhaps best be used as a guide towards discussion in terms of better known psychological processes. This could lead to an integration with work which has used other concepts, such as the learning of social skills (Patterson and Dishion), the development of expectations about relationships (Caspi and Elder), or learned helplessness (Rutter), to a better understanding of the role of protective factors and the capacity to use them (Belsky and Pensky; Rutter), and to an explanation of the differential effects of institutional upbringing on relationships with peers and adoptive parents (Rutter; Tizard and Hodges 1978).

(7) *Coming to terms with childhood experiences.* Grossmann *et al.*'s chapter takes the use of attachment theory one stage further. Their data show that maternal sensitivity does indeed lead to secure attachment, and secure attachment to sensitive mothering. However, sensitive mothering is linked retrospectively to the extent to which mothers *remembered* their own attachment experiences and valued their positive qualities, rather than on the actual extent to which their own parents were, in fact, supportive. Grossmann suggests that a mother who can remember her own childhood experiences, whether positive or negative, can empathize with her own infant. The cycle of unsupportive parenting can thus be broken by a willingness 'to be open and constructively regretful of their unhappy attachment experiences'. Grossmann thus goes farther than other contributors in suggesting that women may not merely re-enact the parent–child relationship they have experienced, but reflect upon and profit from its dynamics.

General points. Finally, a number of general points about explanations of long-term effects in terms of such individual characteristics may be made.

1. Influences on individual characteristics may, in some cases, produce long-term sequelae not because of continuity in those characteristics, but because of their indirect consequences. Thus, Quinton *et al.* (1984) argue that the adverse effects of institutional upbringing on a woman's maternal behaviour are largely mediated by an influence of institutional upbringing on choice of spouse (Rutter).

2. Trans-generational effects often involve two parents. We can regard the nature of each parent–child relationship as depending in part on parental characteristics, and in part on the relationship between the two parents. Patterson and Dishion give evidence that antisocial people tend to live together, and there is some evidence that similarity is a fairly general principle in human mate selection, though also some evidence against it (Hinde 1979; Rushton *et al.* 1985). In either case, the relations between parental personality and the parent–child relationship are likely to be complicated by the spousal relationship in ways not easily revealed by statistical analysis.

3. Whether or not the spouses act similarly, a number of contributors refer to differences between the determinants and sequelae of mother–child and father–child relationships (Easterbrooks and Emde; Hetherington; Patterson and Dishion).

4. In any case, parenting practices do not have invariant sequelae. Other factors may exacerbate, ameliorate, or sum with them (Rutter). Amongst the most important issues here are alternative parental figures, a supportive relationship in adulthood (perhaps depending on a planned marriage, sometimes on a chance encounter), and psychotherapy. As we have seen, the beneficial effects of some or all of these may be mediated by an increased capacity to come to terms with the childhood environment (Belsky and Pensky; Caspi and Elder; Easterbrooks and Emde; Emde; Grossmann *et al.*; Hetherington; Rutter).

5. It is always tempting to associate 'bad' antecedants with 'bad' outcomes and 'good' with 'good'. Life is more complicated than that. For example, in a study of the associations between the home environment and behaviour in pre-school, the best predictor of negative behaviour to peers in the pre-school was not the frequency of 'negative' mother–child interactions at home, but rather a low level of positive ones (Stevenson-Hinde *et al.* 1986).

6. Finally, to repeat a caveat mentioned already, statistical associations do not necessarily point directly to the psychological mechanisms actually involved.

Thus, as we move towards more precise formulations about the effects of relationships on relationships, it will be necessary to incorporate conditional elements specifying at the least the types of relationships and the personalities involved and their histories. No one of the current theoretical approaches is likely to prove adequate, and several of the contributions to this volume illustrate the current value of theoretical eclecticism. A multimethod approach, with measures, including 'outcome' measures relevant to the problem at hand, should lead to a more complete understanding than any single line of attack. It is hoped that the present volume shows what different lines of attack have achieved, and indicates what may be achieve with further integration.

References

Ainsworth, M. D. S., Blehar, M. C., Waters, E., and Wall, S. (1978). *Patterns of attachment.* Erlbaum, Hillsdale, NJ.

Bakeman, R. (1978). Untangling streams of behavior: sequential analyses of observation data. In *Observing behavior, II* (ed. G. P. Sackett). University Park Press.

Bartlett, F. C. (1932). *Remembering.* Cambridge University Press.

Bowlby, J. (1944). Forty-four juvenile thieves: their characters and home life. *International Journal of Psychoanalysis* **5**, 19–52 and 107–27.

Bowlby, J. (1982). *Attachment and loss*, vol. 1, *Attachment* (2nd edn.). Hogarth, London.

Bretherton, I. (1985). Attachment theory: retrospect and prospect. In *Growing points of attachment theory and research* (ed. I. Bretherton and E. Waters). *Monographs of the Society for Research in Child Development* Series No. 209 **50**, (1–2), 3–35.

Bretherton, I. (1987). New perspectives on attachment relations: security, communication and internal working models. In *Handbook of infant development* (2nd edn.) (ed. J. D. Osofsky). Wiley, New York.

Caldwell, B. M. (1969). A new 'approach' to behavioral ecology. In *Minnesota symposia on child psychology* (ed. J. P. Hill) **2**, 74–109. University of Minnesota Press, Minnesota.

Grotevant, H. D. and Cooper, C. R. (1985). Patterns of interaction in family relationships and the development of identity exploration in adolescence. *Child Development* **56**, 415–48.

Hinde, R. A. (1979). *Towards understanding relationships.* Academic Press, London.

Hinde, R. A. (1987). *Individuals, relationships and culture: links between ethology and the social sciences.* Cambridge University Press.

Hinde, R. A. (in press). Reconciling the family systems and the relationships approaches to child development. In *Family systems and life-span development* (ed. K. Kreppner and R. M. Lerner). Erlbaum, Hillsdale, NJ.

Hinde, R. A. and Dennis, A. (1986). Categorizing individuals: an alternative to linear analysis. *International Journal of Behavioural Development* **9**, 105–19.

Hinde, R. A. and Herrmann, J. (1977). Frequencies, durations, derived measures and their correlations in studying dyadic and triadic relationships. In *Studies in mother–infant interaction* (ed. H. R. Schaffer) Academic Press, London.

Hinde, R. A. and Stevenson-Hinde, J. (1987*a*). Interpersonal relationships and child development. *Developmental Review* **7**, 1–21.

Hinde, R. A. and Stevenson-Hinde, J. (1987*b*). Implications of a relationships approach for the study of gender differences. *Infant Mental Health Journal* (in press).

Jaspers, J. M. F. and Leeuw, J. A. de (1980). Genetic–environment covariation in human behaviour genetics. In *Psychometrics for educational debate* (ed. L. J. T. van der Kamp *et al.*). Wiley, Chichester.

Keller, H., Wolk, G., Gauda, G., and Scholmerich, A. (1987). System und Person: Einige entwicklungspsychologische Uberlegungen. In *Gemeinsames–Kontroverses* (eds. J. Kriz and A. v. Schlipps). Bericht des ersten Weiheimer Symposiums in Osnabruck 1986. Verlag Mona Bogner-Kaufmann.

Lerner, R. M. (in press). Individual development and the family systems: a life-span perspective. In *Family systems and life-span development* (ed. K. Kreppner and R. M. Lerner). Erlbaum, Hillsdale, NJ.

Lund, M. (1985). The development of investment and commitment scales for predicting continuity of personal relationships. *Journal of Social and Personal Relationships*, **2**, 3–23.

Magnusson, D. (1987). Longitudinal studies: individual and variable based approaches. In *Risk and protective factors in psychosocial development* (ed. M. Rutter). Cambridge University Press.

Main, M., Kaplan, N., and Cassidy, J. (1985). Security in infancy, childhood, and adulthood: a move to the level of representation. In *Growing points of attachment theory and research* (ed. I. Bretherton and E. Waters). *Monographs of the Society for Research in Child Development* Serial No. 209, **50**, (1–2), 66–104.

Minuchin, P. (1985). Families and individual development: provocations from the field of family therapy. *Child Development* **56**, 289–302.

Minuchin, S., Rosman, B., and Baker, L. (1978). *Psychosomatic families*. Harvard University Press, Cambridge, Mass.

Plomin, R. (1986) *Development, genetics and psychology*. Erlbaum, Hillsdale, NJ.

Quinton, D., Rutter, M., and Liddle, C. (1984). Institutional rearing, parenting difficulties and marital support. *Psychological Medicine* **14**, 107–24.

Rowe, D. C. and Plomin, R. (1981). The importance of nonshared environmental influences in behavioral development. *Developmental Psychology* **17**, 517–31.

Rushton, J. P., Russell, R. J. H., and Wells, P. A. (1985). Personality and genetic similarity theory. *Journal of Social Biological Structure* **8**, 63–86.

Rutter, M. (1987). Longitudinal data: their use and pitfalls in tackling causal questions. In *Risk and protective factors in psychosocial development* (ed. M. Rutter). Cambridge University Press.

Rutter, M. and Garmezy, N. (1983). Developmental psychopathology. In *Handbook of child psychology*, Vol. 4 (ed. P. H. Mussen). Wiley, New York.

Scarr, S. and Kidd, K. K. (1983). Developmental behaviour genetics. In *Handbook of child psychology*, Vol. 2 (ed. P. H. Mussen). Wiley, New York.

Simpson, A. E. and Stevenson-Hinde, J. (1985). Temperamental characteristics of three- and four-year-old boys and girls and child-family interactions. *Journal of Child Psychology and Psychiatry* **26**, (1), 43–53.

Sroufe, L. A. and Fleeson, J. (1986). Attachment and the construction of relationships. In *Relationships and development* (ed. W. W. Hartup and Z. Rubin). Erlbaum, Hillsdale, NJ.

Stevenson-Hinde, J. and Hinde, R. A. (1986). Changes in associations between characteristics and interactions. In *The study of temperament: changes, continuities and challenges* (ed. R. Plomin and J. Dunn). Erlbaum, NJ.

Stevenson-Hinde, J., Hinde, R. A., and Simpson, A. E. (1986). Behavior at home and friendly or hostile behavior in preschool. In *Development of antisocial and prosocial behavior* (ed. D. Olwens, J. Block and M. Radke-Yarrow). Academic Press, New York.

Tizard, B. and Hodges, J. (1978). The effect of early institutional rearing on the development of eight-year-old children. *Journal of Child Psychology and Psychiatry* **19**, 99–118.

Author index

Abraham, M. 203
Abramovitch, R. 143, 181
Achenbach, T. M. 58, 266, 277
Ackerman, N. W. 220
Adelson, E. 241, 255, 361
Ainsworth, M. D. S. 31, 70, 71, 121, 132, 255, 303, 359, 369, 380
Alder, 5. 315
Aldous, J. 144
Aldwin, C. 298
Anderson, B. 83, 84, 85, 89
Anderson, E. 312
Arend, R. A. 28, 60
Arnett, J. 312
Arthur, J. 286
Ash, P. M. 87
Asher, S. J. 84
Auerbach, A. 359, 360
Auslander, N. 203
Ayler, M. 334

Backman, W. C. 237
Baerends, G. P. 70
Bakeman, R. 369
Baker, L. 18, 84, 85, 264, 280, 378
Banaske, N. 194
Bandura, A. 28, 29, 237, 294
Bank, L., 294, 298, 299, 304
Bank, S. 312, 322
Barnard, K. 357, 358
Barnes, G. G. 333
Barnes, H. 17, 18, 143, 147
Barnett, C. R. 88
Barrett, J. 366, 369, 378, 379
Bartlett, F. C. 371
Basham, R. B. 121, 332
Bates, J. E. 119, 122, 124, 125, 134, 335
Bateson, G. 162
Bateson, P. P. G. 206
Baumrind, D. 89
Bayles, K. 122, 134
Beavers, W. 17, 18
Becker, W. C. 85, 266
Beckwith, L. 357
Bell, N. W. 264
Bell, R. Q. 143
Bell, S. M. 255, 303
Belmont, B. 51, 52, 59, 63, 64

Belsky, J. 10–12, 31, 75, 76, 83, 84, 86, 88, 104, 119, 120, 143, 168, 181, 194, 228, 320, 332, 365, 371 378, 380
Bem, D. 28, 285
Benn, R. 210
Bentler, P. M. 202, 294, 305
Berger, A. M. 296, 297
Berger, H. 279
Biglan, A. 286
Billings, A. G. 89, 285
Birchler, G. R. 302
Blatt, S. J.. 202, 203
Blechman, E. 18
Blehar, M. C. 31, 70, 71, 121, 359, 369, 380
Block, J. 39, 85, 87, 95, 97, 199, 223, 300
Block, J. H. 39, 85, 87, 95, 97, 199, 300
Bloom, B. L. 84
Bloxom, B. 92
Bone, M. 285
Bonnett, D. G. 305
Boothe, H. 203
Botein, M. 203
Bottomly, L. 51, 52, 59, 63, 64
Bowlby, J. 29, 31, 32, 74, 76, 78, 79, 144, 198, 241, 255, 303, 332, 333, 336, 340
Brand, E. 312
Brassard, J. A. 332
Bray, J. H. 312
Brennan, T. 203
Bretherton, I. 70, 71, 72, 198, 357, 358, 381
Brewin, C. 333
Breznitz, Z. 64
Broderick, J. W. 88
Brody, G. H. 83, 84, 173
Bronfenbrenner, U. 49, 83, 334
Bronson, G. W. 70
Bronson, W. C. 230
Brooks, J. 205
Broussard, E. R. 109
Brown, G. W. 86, 286, 333
Brown, R. 334
Brüderl, L. 105
Brunck, M. A. 334
Bryant, B. 173
Bryant, B. K. 312, 327
Buhrmester, D. 315
Bumpass, L. 195
Burgess, R. J. 194, 197
Burton, R. V. 230

Buss, A. H.   69, 73, 124, 125
Buss, D. M.   284
Buston, B. G.   104
Buttenveiser, R.   201
Butterfield, P. M.   97
Byrne, D. G.   342

Cain, R.   83, 84, 85, 89, 200
Cairns, R. B.   11, 284
Caldwell, B. M.   182, 369
Calladine, A.   169
Calladine, C.   169
Camara, K. A.   85, 87
Campbell, J. D.   230
Campos, J. J.   69, 73, 359
Capaldi, D.   89
Carey, W. B.   70
Carlson, E.   207
Carroll, J.   208
Caspi, A.   28, 75, 76, 116, 120, 205, 208, 210,
    228, 231, 285, 291, 292, 297, 300, 371, 372,
    378, 380
Cassidy, J.   72, 86, 88, 121, 133, 144, 198,
    220, 243, 244, 255, 342, 354
Chamberlain, P.   286
Chapman, M.   285, 302, 347
Chen, S.   359
Chess, S.   8, 69, 73, 74, 122, 230
Chevron, E.   202, 203
Chodorow, N.   219, 267, 268, 269, 270, 276,
    277, 280
Chrichton, L.   134
Christensen, A.   16, 88, 116, 134, 366, 369,
    370, 377, 378
Cicchetti, D.   195, 233
Clark, L.   199, 201
Clarke, M. C.   121
Clarke-Stewart, K. A.   143, 334
Clingempeel, G. W.   312, 316, 329
Cloninger, C. R.   293
Cochran, M. M.   332
Codreanu, N.   108
Cohen, F. A.   272
Cohen, R. S.   268
Cohen, S. E.   50
Cohen, S.   339–342
Cohler, B. J.   230
Coll, C.   201
Colletta, N.   200
Collmer, C   194
Conger, R.   200
Conley, J. J.   200
Constantine, L.   17
Cooper, C.   12–14, 18, 369
Cooper, P.   116, 195

Corder, C   143, 181
Cornell, D.   203
Corry, T.   92
Corter, C.   181
Costa, P.   199, 200, 202
Cottrell, L. S.   27, 231, 232
Cowan, C. P.   104, 105, 143, 202
Cowan, P. A.   143, 202
Cox, M.   85, 87, 207, 311, 312, 314, 320,
    322, 332
Cox, R.   85, 87, 207, 311, 312, 314, 320, 322,
    332
Cox, M. J.   104, 105, 196, 200
Craik, K. H.   284
Cramer, B.   361
Crittenden, P. M.   347
Crnic, K. A.   121, 200, 332
Crockenberg, S.   92, 131, 173, 208, 209, 332,
    340
Crook, C. K.   122, 126
Cross, C. E.   116
Crouter, A.   104, 228
Cummings, E.   197, 198, 285, 302, 347
Cutrona, L. E.   122, 133
Cytryn, L.   59

Daniels, D.   72, 174, 361
Dare, C.   333
Darley, J.   237
Datta, S.   182
Dean, D. G.   212
Deane, K. E.   74
DeAngelo, E.   28, 38, 44, 121
Defries, J.   174
Deinard, A.   122
DeLeeuw, J. A.   375
Dennis, A.   71, 372
Depue, R.   299
Deskin, J.   267
DiMascio, A.   203
Dishion, T. J.   75, 76, 283, 285, 291, 294,
    298, 299, 304
Diskin, S.   196, 201
Ditto, W. B.   72
Dix, T.   144
Dodge, K. A.   334, 335
Domittner, G.   124, 125
Dorsch, K.   242
Dougherty, F.   92
Dowdney, L.68, 206
Downey, G.   205, 228, 292, 297, 300
Duncan, B.   195
Duncan, O.   195
Duncan, S. W.   104, 116
Duncan-Jones, P.   342

Dunn, J.   15–17, 143, 170, 172, 173, 174, 175, 176, 181, 334, 366, 373, 377, 378, 380
Duvall, E.   143, 144

Earls, F.   292
Easterbrooks, M. A.   73, 83, 84, 85, 86, 88, 91, 92, 98, 104, 105, 107, 115, 120, 122, 123, 124, 125, 168, 368, 370, 373, 377–9, 382
Easton, D.   182
Edelbrock, C. S.   266, 277
Egeland, B.   29, 31, 122, 134, 194, 207, 209, 335
Eisenberg, J. G.   299
Elder, G. H.   28, 75, 76, 116, 120, 205, 208, 210, 226, 227, 228, 231, 285, 291, 292, 297, 300, 305, 371, 372, 378, 380
Emde, R.   73, 77, 85, 92, 97, 98, 105, 107, 115, 120, 122, 123, 366, 368, 370, 377–9, 382
Emery, R. E.   85, 87, 228, 263
Engfer, A.   63, 108, 109, 111, 113, 120, 121, 124, 125, 372, 377, 380
Epstein, S.   27, 28, 199, 284
Erickson, M.   31
Erikson, E.   204
Eron, L. D.   220, 293, 295
Escher-Gräub, C. D.   242, 257
Estes, D.   335
Eysenck, E.   202
Eysenck, H.   196, 199
Eysenck, S.   199

Fahrenberg, J.   108, 124, 132
Farber, E. A.   335
Fasman, J.   203
Faust, J.   200
Fazio, R. H.   237
Featherman, D. L.   145
Feldman, S. S.   84
Ferreira, A.   17
Field, T.   121, 200
Fitch, P.   59
Fleeson, J.   27–29, 31, 39, 40, 76, 99, 168, 208, 303, 365, 366, 372, 379, 380, 381
Follette, W. C.   302
Ford, M. E.   144
Forehand, R.   200
Forgatch, M. S.   285, 289, 298, 299, 311
Forstrom, A.   92
Fraiberg, S.   241, 255, 361
Framo, J. L.   263
Frank, S.   202
Frankel, K. A.   122
Freedie, R.   143

Fremmer-Bombik, E.,   243, 244, 251, 254, 257
Freud, S.   332
Friedman, L.   286
Friedrich, W.   194
Frodi, A. M.   92
Frodi, M.   92
Frommer, E.   219
Furman, W.,   315
Furstenburg, F. F.   174

Gabrielli, W.   293
Galkowska, M.   202
Garcia, R.   121, 200
Garcia Coll, C.   99
Garmezy, N.   228, 348, 376
Gath, A.   88
Gavranidou, M.   109, 111, 113
Gelles, R.   194
George, C.   242, 243, 347
Gersten, J. C.   299
Gilbert, R.   267, 269
Gilutz, G.   334
Given, K.   196, 201
Gjerde, T. F.   300
Glen, N.   195
Goldberg, S.   119
Goldberg, W. A.   83, 84, 85, 86, 91, 92, 104, 105, 106, 107, 122, 124, 125
Goldricks, W.   196
Goldsmith, H. H.   69, 73
Goldstein, S.   121, 200
Goldwyn, R.   243, 256
Gossett, J.   18
Goth-Owens, T. L.   104, 105, 107
Gottesman, I. I.   293
Gottman, J.   83, 183, 273, 334
Gottman, J. G.   89, 90
Gottman, J. M.   225, 302, 316, 356
Graziano, W.   200
Greenberg, M. J.   121, 200, 332
Greenberg, M. T.   70
Grossmann, K.   32, 33, 76, 77, 241, 242, 251, 252, 256, 257, 346, 371, 380–2
Grossmann, K. E.   242, 251, 256, 346
Grotevant, H.   12–14, 18, 369
Gruendel, J.   28
Gruneboum, M.   203
Grusec. J. E .   144
Guttmann, D.   239
Guy, L.   121, 200

Hagan, M. S.   316
Hahlweg, K.   109
Hales, R. E.   359
Haley, J.   263, 280

Hall, F.   219
Hampel, R.   108, 124, 132
Harlow, H.   296
Harmon, R. J.   88
Harns, T. O.   86, 286, 333
Harter, S.   29, 333
Hartner, M. S. S.   109
Hartup, W. W.   336
Harvey, O. J.   334
Haviland, J.   198
Hay, D.   335
Hazzard, A.   276, 277
Heard, D. H.   333
Heinicke, C. M.   104, 105, 196, 201
Heinig, L.   109, 111
Heiss, J.   195, 227
Held, T.   219
Heming, G.   202
Henderson, S.   342
Hengeller, S. W.   334
Herjanc, B. L.   296
Herrenkohl, E. C.   121, 194
Herrenkohl, R. C.   121, 194
Herrmann, J.   368
Hess, R. D.   241
Hesse, E.   29
Hetherington, E. M.   85, 87, 207, 311, 312,
   313–15, 316, 318, 320, 322, 329, 332,
   371–3, 379, 382
Hinde, R. A.   2, 3, 27, 48, 52, 61, 63, 65, 68,
   71, 72, 122, 145, 178, 206, 283, 292, 303,
   305, 306, 333, 361, 366, 368, 369, 372, 373,
   374, 377, 378, 382
Hodges, J.   381
Hodges, K.   59
Hoffman, L.   263, 279
Hogan, R.   132
Hok, C.   202
Hollier, A.   312
Hollingshead, A. B.   286
Holmes, T. H.   299
Honig, P.   279
Hood, W. R.   334
Hops, H.   286, 303
Horowitz, M.   360
Howe, N.   173
Howes, P. W.   104, 116
Huesmann, L. R.   220, 293, 295
Hunter, R.   194
Huston, A.   72
Huston, T. L.   104
Huyck, M.   202
Hwang, C.-P.   92

Iannotti, R.   98
Isabella, R.   10–12, 143, 168, 181

Izard, C. E.   92, 138, 198

Jacklin, C. N.   72
Jacob, T.   89
Jacobson, J. L.   346
Jacobson, N.   304
Jacobson, N. S.   302
Jacobson, S.   202, 203
Jacobvitz, D.   28, 29, 38, 44, 121, 194, 207,
   209
Jaspers, J. M. F.   375
Johnson, S. M.   89, 99
Jones, L.   315
Jones-Leonard, D.   99
Jöreskog, K. G.   294
Justkowski, R.   202

Kagan, J.   72, 99, 335
Kahn, M.   312, 322
Kalmuss, D.   194, 196
Kaltreider, W.   360
Kantor, D.   17, 143
Kaplan, N.   72, 86, 121, 133, 144, 198, 220,
   242, 243, 254, 255, 342, 354
Karagozian, A.   267
Kaufman, J.   194
Kaye, K.   357
Kelly, J. B.   317, 322
Kelly, E. L.   116
Kelvin, P.   334
Kendrick, C.   143, 170, 172, 173, 176, 183,
   176, 181, 334
Kessen, W.   48
Ketten, E. S.   230
Kidd, K. K.   375
Kilstrom, W.   294
King, C. E.   280
Klerman, G.   200
Kline, J. S.   59
Knutson, J. F.   296, 297
Kochanska, G.   62, 64
Komarovsky, M.   219
Korbin, F.   195
Korn, S. J.   88
Kotsch, W. E.   92
Kramer, K.   195
Kreppner, K.   144, 148, 149, 365, 366, 368,
   369, 377, 379
Kropp, J.   200
Krupnick, J.   62, 360
Kuczynski, L.   64, 285, 302, 347
Kulka, R.   195

Lachman, M. E.   88

Lahey, B. 200
Lake, B. 333
Lamb, M. 92, 104, 106, 143, 168, 335
Langner, T. S. 299
La Rossa, M. M. 143
LaRossa, R. 143
Larsen, A. 17, 143, 147
Lautenschlanger, G. 200
Lebovici, S. 361
Lee, L. C. 122, 134, 335
Lefkowitz, M. N. 220, 293, 295
Lehr, W. 17, 143
Leibman, R. 279
Leiderman, P. H. 88
Leifer, A. D. 88
Lerner, R. M. 145
Levenson, R. W. 302, 356
Levi, L. 17
Levine, L. 201
Levitt, M. J. 121
Lewis, J. 18
Lewis, J. M. 104, 105, 196, 200
Lewis, M. 143, 198
Liddell, C. 334
Liker, J. K. 116, 226, 227
Lirson, N. 230
Lobdell, J. 203
Lobitz, G. K. 89, 99, 266
Lohmöller, J.-B. 109, 112, 126
Longfellow, C. 200
Looney, J. 18
Lorenz, K. 241
Luborsky, L. 359, 360
Lund, M. 368
Lutkenhaus, P. 346
Lyons-Ruth, K. 203

McCall, R. B. 68
McCarthy, J. 200
McCartney, K. 231–2
Maccoby, E. E. 49, 72, 73, 143
McCluskey, K. 340
McCord, J. 87
McCord, W.. 87
McCrae, R. 199, 202, 203
McCubbin, H. 17, 143, 147
McDevitt, S. C. 70
McDonald, D. W. 302
McEnroe, M. 18
Macfarlane, J. W. 218
McHale, S. M. 104
McKinnon, C. 173
McNew, D. 59
McLellan, A. T. 359, 360
Madge, N. 120, 220
Magnusson, D. 371

Main, M. 27, 71, 72, 86, 121, 133, 144, 198,
    220, 242, 243, 254, 255, 256, 342, 347, 354
Malatesta, C. 198, 199
Mangelsdorf, S. 28, 38, 44, 121
Margolin, G. 16, 88, 263, 265, 267, 269,
    270, 276, 277
Markman, H. J. 104, 116, 273
Marmar, C. 360
Martin, B. 89
Martin, J. A. 49, 143
Marvin, R. S. 70
Maslin, C. A. 122
Matas, L. 28, 60
Mayfield, A. 62
Mehm, J. G. 296, 297
Meller, R. 182
Mednick, S. 293
Messe, L. A. 104, 105, 107
Meyer, H.-J. 120, 372
Michaels, G. Y. 104, 106
Michalson, L. 198
Milofsky, E. 204
Minde, K. 196
Minuchin, P. 8, 21, 77, 96, 143, 365, 366,
    371, 379
Minuchin, S. 17, 18, 21, 27, 84, 85, 264,
    280, 378
Mischel, W. 199
Miyake, K. 359
Monroe, S. 299
Moos, R. H. 285
Moore, S. 195
Morris, D. 195
Morrison, A. 85, 87, 95, 97
Mott, F. 195
Motti, F. 34
Mueller, C. 120, 195, 207, 227
Mueller, D. 195
Munn, P. 15–17, 175, 181
Muxen, M. J. 17, 143, 147

Naiman, S. 97
Nash, S. C. 84
Nelson, K. 28
Newcomb, N. 202
Newson E. 169
Newson, J. 169
Nixon, S. 144
Notarius, C. I. 116, 273
Nottelmann, E. 51, 52, 59, 63, 64

Oates, D. S. 104, 105
O'Brien, C. P. 359, 360
O'Brien, E. 199
Oh, W. 201
O'Leary, K. D. 87, 88

Oliveri, M. 18
Olson, D. 17, 18, 20,143, 147
Oltmanns, T. F. 88
Olweus, D. 32, 228
O'Shea, G. 219
Osofsky, H. J. 143, 357, 358
Osofsky, J. D. 143, 357, 358
Osteen, V. 286
Owen, M. T. 104, 105, 196, 200

Pagelow, M. 194
Pancake, V. R. 31, 32
Pankey, W. B. 70
Parke, R. D. 83, 143, 183, 194, 334, 335
Papatola, K. 194
Parmlee, A. H. 50
Parsons, T. 219
Pasahow, R. J. 99
Pastor, D. 33
Patterson, G. R. 75, 76, 85, 89, 135, 228,
    283, 284, 285, 286, 291, 294, 298, 299, 302,
    303, 304, 305, 372, 378, 380, 382
Paulsen, S. 144, 148
Pawl, J. H. 88
Pawlby, S. 219
Paykel, E. 200
Pedersen, F. 83, 84, 85, 89, 200
Pellegrini, A. D. 83, 84
Pellegrini, D. S. 116, 336
Peplau, A. 203
Pepler, D. J. 143, 181
Perlmann, D. 203
Perry, B. A. 265
Peshkess, I. 104, 105, 107
Petarsky, J. H. 88
Peterson, J. L. 294, 311
Phillips, V. 18
Pickford, J. 202
Platt, J. R. 357
Plomin, R. 69, 72, 73, 124, 125, 174, 193,
    204, 361, 375
Pollock, V. 293
Pope, H. 195, 120, 207, 227
Porter, B. 87
Power, M. J. 87
Power, T. 83, 183, 334
Provence, S. 354

Quinlan, D. M. 202, 203
Quinton, D. 205–7, 220, 296, 329, 332, 337,
    342, 382

Radke-Yarrow, M. 51, 52, 59, 63, 64, 73,
    197–8, 285, 302, 347, 365–8, 370–3, 379

Rahe, R. H. 299
Ramsey-Klee, D. 196, 201
Ragozin, A. S. 121, 332
Raskin, A. 203
Rausch, H. 196
Reatig, N. 203
Reid, J. B. 283, 284, 285, 291, 294, 299
Reiss, D. 18, 143, 147
Rempel, H. 202
Resnick, G. 85, 87
Revenson, T. 298
Reznick, J. S. 72, 99
Richters, J. 365
Ricks, M. 195, 220, 241, 256, 257, 342
Riedel, C. 104, 105, 196, 200
Rizley, R. 233
Robins, L. N. 292, 296, 302
Robinson, N. M. 121, 332
Rohner, R. P. C. 332
Roscoe, B. 194
Rose, R. J. 72
Rosenberg, D. M. 31
Rosman, B. 18, 84, 85, 264, 280, 378
Ross, A. O. 87
Rothbart, M. K. 72, 92
Rotter, J. 28
Routh, D. K. 104
Rovine, M. 88
Rowe, D. C. 193, 375
Roy, P. 344, 345, 347
Rubenstein, C. 203
Rudolph, J. 243, 244
Ruehlman, L. S. 99
Rushton, J. P. 382
Russell, C. 18
Russell, R. J. H. 382
Rutter, M. 63, 68, 69, 85, 87, 120, 195, 198,
    205, 206, 207, 210, 220, 296, 329, 332, 335,
    336, 340, 342, 346, 348, 349, 372, 375, 376,
    378, 379, 382
Ryder, R. 196

Saltar, K. 267
Sandberg, D. 121, 200
Sandberg, S. 348
Saunders, E. 200
Savard, R. 17
Santrock, J. W. 311, 313
Scalf-McIver, L. 104, 105, 196, 200
Scarr, S. 231–2, 286, 375
Schachter, F. 14
Schachter, F. F. 334
Schaffer, H. 72
Schaffer, H. R. 122, 126, 334
Scheffe, H. 270
Schoenberg, E. 87

Schulterbrandt, J. 203
Schultze, Y. 144, 148
Schwan, A. 256
Seashore, M. J. 88
Secord, P. F. 237
Segal, J. 50
Selg, H. 108, 124, 132
Severance, G. 267
Shapiro, V. 241, 255, 361
Shaver, P. 203
Shore, E. 334
Shouldice, A. E. 70
Shelton, R. A. 195
Sherman, T. 64
Sherif, C. W. 334
Sherif, M. 334
Shipman, V. C. 241
Shore, E. 334
Sigel, I. V. 83, 84
Signori, E. 202
Simcha-Fagan, O. 299
Simpson, A. E. 58, 72, 373, 382
Sirignano, S. W. 88
Skinner, M. 298, 299, 304
Skolnick, A. 202
Skuse, D. 68, 206
Slaby, R. G. 335
Smith, R. S. 332
Snidman, N. 72
Snyder, D. 196, 237
Solnot, A. J. and Provence, S. 354
Sörborn, D. 294
Spangler, G. 151, 242, 332
Sorey, E. C. 87
Spanier, G. B. 88, 91, 228, 302, 315
Sprenkle, D. 87
Sroufe, L. A. 27, 28, 29, 31, 32, 33, 38, 44,
    60, 70, 71, 76, 99, 121, 168, 195, 198, 207,
    208, 209, 303, 347, 348, 365, 366, 372, 380,
    381
Stayton, D. J. 132, 255, 303
Steinmetz, S. 194
Stern, D. N. 357, 361
Stevenson-Hinde, J. 2, 48, 52, 54, 58, 61, 63,
    65, 68, 70, 72, 74, 283, 292, 303, 305, 306,
    365, 366, 372, 373, 374, 378, 379, 381, 382
Stierlin, H. 17
Stocker, C. 173
Stollak, G. E. 104, 105, 107
Stoneman, Z. 173
Storaasli, R. D. 104, 116
Straus, M. A. 194
Strodtbeck, F. L. 91
Stroebe, M. S. 84
Stroebe, W. 84
Suejda, M. 97
Suess, G. 242, 251

Sullaway, M. 280
Sullivan, H. S. 231
Suomi, S. J. 296
Suster, A. 104, 105, 196, 200
Swalsky, J. 200
Swann, W. B. 237
Sweet, J. 195
Syme, S. L. 339–342

Tamplin, A. 72, 182
Taraldson, B. 134
Tellegan, A. 75, 199, 200
Terman, L. 196, 201, 202
Thomas, A. 69, 73, 74, 122, 230
Thompson, R. A. 144, 335
Thurber, E. 87
Tizard, B. 381
Toedter, L. J. 194
Tomkins, S. 198
Tracy, R. L. 255
Trevarthen, C. 357
Troutman, B. R. 122, 133
Troye, M. 29, 32, 33
Turner, R. H. 227

Uddenberg, N. 219
Unzner, L. 242, 251
Ursano, R. J. 359

Vaillant, C. D. 204
Vaillant, G. E. 204
Van Nguyen, T. 291, 300
Vaughn, B. E. 122, 134
Vega-Lahr, N. 121, 200
Veit, B. 243, 244
Veit, C. 200
Viken, R. 299
Vincent, J. P. 302
Vogel, E. F. 264
Voss, H.-G. 120

Wachtel, P. L. 231, 232
Waite, L. 195
Wakefield, J. 106
Walder, L. 220, 293, 295
Waldron, H. 104
Wall, S. 31, 70, 71, 121, 359, 369, 380
Wallace, J. R. 88
Waller, W. 226
Wallenstein, R. 360
Wallerstein, J. S. 311–13, 317, 322, 332
Ward, M. J. 28, 38, 44, 121, 168
Ware, J. 200

Warshak, R. A.   313
Wartner, U.   257
Waters, E.   28, 74, 332, 333, 335, 336, 341, 346
Watson, D.   199, 201
Watts, P.   104, 105, 107
Watzlawick, P.   17
Weber, R. A.   121
Wein, S. J.   202, 203
Weingarten, N.   195
Weiss, R.   302, 317, 318
Weiss, R. L.   265, 303
Weissman, M.   200
Wells, P. A.   382
Welsh, J. D.   64
Wente, A. S.   92
Werner, E. E.   332
West, P. A.   296
West, S. G.   99
Weston, D.   27, 71
Wheller, K.   194
White, B. J.   334
White, S. W.   84
Whiting, B.   42
Whiting, J.   42
Whittock, F.   203
Wille, D. E.   346

Wills, T. A.   340
Wold, H.   109, 112, 126
Wilner, W.   360
Wilson, A.   198, 199
Wilson, M.   17, 143, 147
Wolfe, D. A.   99
Wolkind, S.   219, 340
Woodward, K.   312
Woody, G. E.   359, 360
Worthington, E. L.   104

Yahraes, J.   50
Yang, R.   200
Yarrow, M. R.   230
Youngblade, L.   194, 197

Zahn-Waxler, C.   62, 197, 198
Zaleski, Z.   202, 216
Zaslow, M.   200
Zelkowitz, P.   200
Zeren, A. S.   88
Zigler, E.   194
Zill, Z.   311
Zoll, D.   203

Subject index

adolescence 12–14, 204–5, 313, 345
adult attachment interview 243–58
affect expression and regulation 43–4, 52–65, 72–3, 83, 89–100, 263–80, 302–3, 377–80; *see also* conflict; fear; irritability; shyness
anger, *see* affect; irritability
anti-social trait 284–306
anxiety, *see* negative emotionality
arousal 356
attachment
  behaviour 28–38, 242
  representations 244–58
  sequelae 31–8, 64, 70–4, 86–7, 244–58, 332–3, 335, 340–1, 342–8, 358, 380–1
attribution 335

behaviour system 69–70
birth, effect on family 10–12
boundaries,
  between generations 16, 28, 263–4, 277–80
  between subsystems 15, 44–5
buffering effects 87, 340, 376

case history studies 64
chaos, in families 21–2, 50, 56–7, 60–1, 228–38; *see also* family distress
child characteristics and parenting 133–6
child–parent relationships: long-term influences 10–12, 38–41, 119, 121, 127–30, 132–3, 194–210, 220–38, 250–58
child–teacher relationships 34–8
child maltreatment 194–6
child problem behaviour 277–8
circularity, in families 8
coherence and continuity in relationships 28–30, 38–40, 144–5, 161–4
communication, within family 15, 160–1, 264–80
compensatory hypothesis 106, 110–11, 114–16
competition 377
conflict 15–16, 22, 28, 32–3, 55–6, 58–9, 75, 92–6, 109–16, 169–79, 197, 264–80
continuity 59–61

cross-generational transmission, *see* intergenerational transmission
cultural differences 42–3
cumulative continuity 232

deidentification 14
depression 59, 64, 200–3, 206, 285–7, 339, 302; *see also* negative emotionality
deutero-learning 162–3
developmental changes 14–16, 23, 86, 99, 115–16, 143–65, 313, 374
direction of effects 71–3, 84, 114–16, 122–32, 169, 176, 338
discontinuity 206–8, 235–7, 256–7, 337–48, 354, 357–62, 382
divorce
  and parent–child relationship 316–29
  and remarriage 194–6, 311–28

emotional disturbance affecting relationships 169–70
emotional need 171–2
emotion and personality 198
extreme groups 99, 348, 355–6, 370

family
  alliances 263–5, 278–80
  cohesion 18, 21, 272–80, 366–7
  concepts 8–10, 17–18
  decision making 18
  distress 265–80
  flexibility 18
  functions 41–5
  rules 15
  stability *see* chaos
  style 17–20, 366
  systems 7–26, 29–30, 77, 85, 143–65, 333
  techniques for study 18–19, 143–65
  world view 17–20, 366
family therapy 361–2
fear of the unfamiliar 69–75
focused hostility 172–3

generalizing across relationships 178

gender differences 36–8, 39–41, 57–9, 72–3, 87, 219–20, 232–3, 316–29, 373–4, 376, 382
genetic transmission 292–3, 295, 343, 375

heritability 292–3
homeostatis and change 9, 22–4, 379

identity exploration 12–14
incest 39–41
individual vs relationship characteristics 68–78
infant psychiatry 360–1
inhibition 69–75
interactional continuity 232
interactional style 76, 231–38, 294–5, 380
interactions
    between subsystems 9
    coding of, 13–14
    within families 11, 13
    within relationships 1, 11, 169
interdependence within families 8, 13–14, 38–41, 143–65
inter-generational transmission 120–1, 126–7, 194–209, 218–38, 283–306
internal working model 28–9, 31, 33, 72, 147, 160–2, 198, 323, 336, 347, 366
internalization of relationships 28, 245–9, 254–8
irritability, parental 121, 283–306

jealousy 173–4, 186–8, 321, 334, 377

leadership 334
level of analysis 365–8
limitations on generalizations 372–5
LISREL 126–33
levels of social complexity 2, 365–7

marital instability 194–7
marital relationship
    and affect 89–100
    effect of baby birth 10–12, 84
    influenced by child characteristics 87–9, 220–38
    and family organization 16, 264–80
    and parenting 83–100, 104–16, 119–36, 204–7, 220–38, 263–81, 320–40, 332, 337–42
mate selection 30, 233–6, 292–3, 337–42, 382
meaning 51–62, 334, 354–7, 358, 368

model, see internal working model
modelling 76, 265, 296, 378–9
monitoring of mother and sibling 174–6
mother–child relationship and sibling relationship 168–79, 181–9, 322–8
multimethod approaches 366

negative emotionality 121, 223–36, 380
negativity, see affect
neuroticism, see personality
non-shared family environment 361

observational learning 197
observational methodology 182–9, 368–9
organization of families 8, 42–5, 272–80, 366–7

parent–child seductiveness, sensuality 28, 38–9, 44–5
parental control 56–7, 85, 92, 95–6, 111–12, 114–16, 284–306, 317–29
parental illness 18–24
parental monitoring 317, 376
path analysis 112, 126–33, 223–6, 294–7
peer relationships 31–8, 60, 344–7
peer–teacher relationships 31–8
perceived child difficultness 108–9, 125
perceptual bias screen 99
personality 69–76, 198–200, 222–3
    and developmental history 132–3, 202–10, 222–38
    and emotion 198
    and relationships 3–5, 107–16, 198–210, 222–38, 284–306, 312–29, 334, 336
projective approaches 62
psychotherapy 359–60

rare events 357
relationship
    characteristics of 1–2, 27–9, 374
    defined 1, 27–9
    and individual characteristics 2–3, 63–5, 68–78
    multidimensionality of 367–8
    network 1–2
    representation 355
    study in psychology 48–50
relationship representation 355
reputation, effects of 334
retrospective evidence 10–11, 244–58, 296–7, 372
roles, family 2, 219–20, 241, 334–5
role reversal 38–44

sample size 370–1
self perception 378
self-report data 12
sensitive periods 336
separation experiences 219–20, 296, 337–48
shyness 58–9, 64–5, 69–75
sibling relationship 14–16, 168–79, 181–9, 275–6, 312, 322–9, 334, 377
social class (disadvantage) effects 55–7, 286–8, 339, 356
social learning 85, 265, 335–6, 378–9
socio-cultural structure 2, 4
spill-over hypothesis 105, 110
spouse abuse 194–6
spouse choice, see mate selection
stepfathers 317–29
stonewalling 356
strange situation classification 31–2, 242–58, 358–9

stress-amplification 297–302
support (emotional, etc.) 206–9, 257, 332, 337–42, 348, 355, 357–62, 376
systems, see family systems; behaviour systems

temperament 69–75, 92–7, 177, 335, 379
transitions, in families 22, 86, 104–16, 145–65
triadic interactions 181–9

values, social 2, 72–3, 372–3

wholeness
    in relationship systems 29–30
    of families 8